Contents

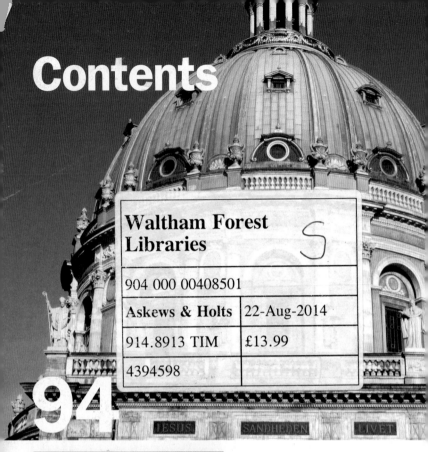

94

171

219

166

108

Time Out Copenhagen

Editorial
Editor Anna Norman
Copy Editors Dominic Earle, Cath Phillips, Ros Sales
Listings Checkers Emma Beaumont, Grace Clarke
Proofreader John Shandy Watson
Indexer Rebecca Knott

Editorial Director Sarah Guy
Management Accountant Margaret Wright

Design
Senior Designer Kei Ishimaru
Designer Thomas Havell
Group Commercial Senior Designer Jason Tansley

Picture Desk
Picture Editor Jael Marschner
Deputy Picture Editor Ben Rowe
Freelance Picture Researcher Lizzy Owen

Advertising
Advertising (Copenhagen) Jinga Media Ltd
(www.jingamedia.com)

Marketing
Senior Publishing Brand Manager Luthfa Begum
Head of Circulation Dan Collins

Production
Production Controller Katie Mulhern-Bhudia

Time Out Group
Chairman & Founder Tony Elliott
Chief Executive Officer Tim Arthur
Chief Commercial Officer Kim O'Hara
Publisher Alex Batho
Group IT Director Simon Chappell
Group Marketing Director Carolyn Sims

Contributors
Copenhagen's Top 20 Anna Norman. **Copenhagen Today** Anna Norman. **Itineraries** Anna Norman. **Diary** Anna Norman.
Copenhagen's Best Anna Norman. **Explore** Anna Norman, Nikolaj Steen-Møller, Patrick Welch, Yolanda Zappaterra. **Gay & Lesbian** Daniel Ayala, Anna Norman, Patrick Welch. **Nightlife** Trudy Follwell, Thomas Dalvang-Fleurquin, Anna Norman.
Performing Arts Trudy Follwel, Jane Graham, Anna Norman. **Day Trips** Michael Booth, Anna Norman, Yolanda Zappaterra.
History Michael Booth, Anna Norman. **Design & Architecture** Michael Booth, Anna Norman. **Hotels** Thomas Dalvang-Fleurquin, Jan Graham, Anna Norman. **Essential Information** Cecilie Hahn-Patersen, Anna Norman.

Maps JS Graphics Ltd (john@jsgraphics.co.uk).

Cover and pull-out map photography Chris Hepburn/Getty Images.

Back cover photography Clockwise from top left: copenhagenmediacenter.com; Designmuseum Danmark; Anna Norman; Heloise Bergman; Bjarne Bergius Hermansen.

Photography Pages 2/3 vvoe/Shutterstock.com; 4 (top), 13 (top), 15 (bottom), 29, 31 (second down), 52 (top), 59, 62/63, 64, 65, 69, 74, 76, 77, 82, 94, 102, 106, 120, 124, 125, 128, 132, 136, 139, 141, 142, 144, 146/147, 151, 155, 160, 161, 162, 164, 165, 168, 174, 177, 180 (bottom), 208 Heloise Bergman; 4 (bottom), 171 Costin Radu; 5 (bottom left), 21, 28/29 (top and bottom), 42/43, 70, 71, 84/85, 86, 118/119, 126, 127, 138, 152/153, 166, 169 (bottom) Joe Mortensen; 7, 199 Aleksandar Mijatovic/Shutterstock.com; 10/11, 27, 33, 38 (bottom), 87, 116, 134 (right), 154, 188/189, 210, 242/243 copenhagenmediacenter.com; 10/11, 13 (middle), 15 (top left), 16/17 (bottom), 17 (middle), 20, 22, 28, 31 (top and middle), 34/35, 46/47, 56/57, 84, 132/133, 137, 175 (top right) copenhagenmediacenter.com/ Ty Stange; 12 (second up) copenhagenmediacenter.com/Ireneusz Cyranek; 12 (bottom) Frank Bach/Shutterstock.com; 13 (bottom), 103 copenhagenmediacenter.com/Rasmus Flindt Pedersen; 14 (top) Rogit/Shutterstock.com; 14 (bottom) diak/Shutterstock.com; 15 (top), 18/19, 96, 163 copenhagenmediacenter.com/Christian Alsing; 16 (middle) jps/Shutterstock.com; 16/17, 32, 68 (top) Alan Kraft/Shutterstock.com; 25 Jaroslav Moravcik/Shutterstock.com; 26, 90 copenhagenmediacenter.com/Cees van Roeden; 26/27 (top), 55, 56 copenhagenmediacenter.com/Morten Jerichau; 26/27 (bottom) Nanisimova/Shutterstock.com; 28/29 (middle), 107, 167, 215 Anna Norman; 31 (second up) Kristoffer Juel Poulsen; 31 (bottom) Jose Antonio Sanchez; 32/33 Ramblersen; 36 (bottom), 36/37 Kristoffer Juel Poulsen; 37 (bottom) DFAagaard/Shutterstock.com; 38 (top) copenhagenmediacenter.com/Christian Lindgren; 40/41 (top) Bucchi Francesco/Shutterstock.com; 40/41 (bottom) copenhagenmediacentre.com/Poul Buchard/Broendum & Co; 44/45 anshar/Shutterstock.com; 46 copenhagenmediacenter.com/Per-Anders Jorgensen; 50 Rasmus Hansen; 53 (bottom) Nils Z/Shutterstock.com; 67 (top) Ditte Isager; 72 Sergey Goryachev/Shutterstock.com; 78 Ole Akhøj; 80 Ole Woldbye; 93 Columbus Leth; 94/95 Vlada Z/Shutterstock.com; 100 Imagno/Austrian Archives/Getty images; 104 (top) Pernille Klemp; 108/109 Shutterstock.com; 111, 187 (bottom) Mikhail Markovskiy/Shutterstock.com; 114 Thomas Ibsen; 117 copenhagenmediacenter.com/Morten Bjarnhof; 118 Martin D. Vonka/Shutterstock.com; 130 tomtsya/Shutterstock.com; 134 (left) copenhagenmediacenter.com/Iwan Baan; 140 (top) ARENA Creative/Shutterstock.com; 140 (bottom) Oleksandr Lysenko/Shutterstock.com; 146 Morten Bjarnhof Pht/Wonderful Copenhagen; 148 Roland Halbe; 157, 211 Adam Mørk; 158 ZDF/BBC; 169 (top) Martin Daugaard; 173 Bjarne Bergius Hermansen; 174 Anibal Trejo/Shutterstock; 175 (left) Lars Schmidt; 178/179 Cher_Nika/Shutterstock.com; 180 (top), 182, 183 Louisiana Museum of Modern Art; 184 (top) Thijs Wolzak; 184 (bottom) Luca Santiago Mora; 185 mary416/Shutterstock.com; 186 (top) kimson/Shutterstock.com; 186 (bottom) Antony McAulay/Shutterstock.com; 187 (top) Rolf_52/Shutterstock.com; 190/191, 192, 195, 196, 197 De Agostini/Getty Images; 200 John Phillips/Time Life Pictures/Getty Images; 207 Andreas von Einsiedel / Alamy; 209 Victor Jones.

The following images were supplied by the featured establishments: 5 (top and bottom right), 12 (top two), 14 (middle), 24, 36 (middle), 67 (bottom), 79, 83, 99, 104 (middle and bottom), 108, 129, 204/205, 206, 212/213, 214, 219, 220, 221, 224, 225.

About the Guide

GETTING AROUND

Each sightseeing chapter contains a street map of the area marked with the locations of sights and museums (❶), restaurants (❶), cafés and bars (❶) and shops (❶). There are also street maps of Copenhagen at the back of the book, along with an overview map of the city and a Metro and local trains map. In addition, there is a detachable fold-out street and Metro/train map inside the back cover.

THE ESSENTIALS

For practical information, including visas, disabled access, emergency numbers, lost property, websites and local transport, see the Essential Information section. It begins on page 212.

THE LISTINGS

Addresses, phone numbers, websites, transport information, hours and prices are all included in our listings, as are selected other facilities. All were checked and correct at press time. However, business owners can alter their arrangements at any time, and fluctuating economic conditions can cause prices to change rapidly.

The very best venues in the city, the must-sees and must-dos in every category,

have been marked with a red star (★). In the sightseeing chapters, we've also marked venues with free admission with a FREE symbol.

THE LANGUAGE

Most Copenhageners speak good English, but attempts at basic Danish phrases are always appreciated. You'll find a primer on page 235.

PHONE NUMBERS

All telephone numbers in Copenhagen have eight digits. There are no area codes in the country. From outside Denmark, dial your country's international access code (00 from the UK, 011 from the US) or a plus symbol, followed by the Danish country code (45), dropping the initial zero, and the eight-digit number as listed in the guide. So, to reach the Nationalmuseet, dial +45 33 23 44 11. For more on phones, including details of local mobile phone access, *see pp233-234.*

FEEDBACK

We welcome feedback on this guide, both on the venues we've included and on any other locations that you'd like to see featured in future editions. Please email us at guides@timeout.com.

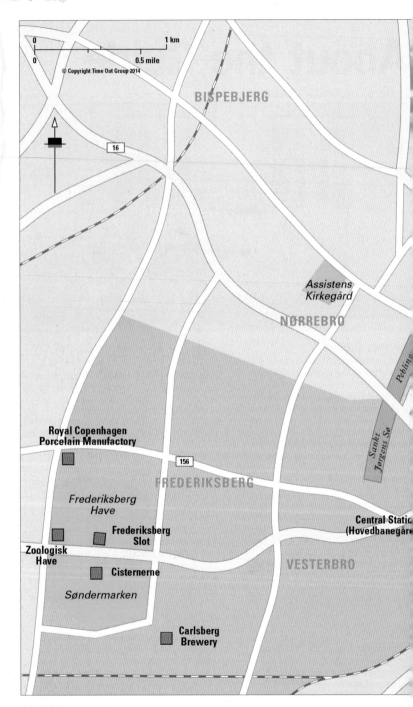

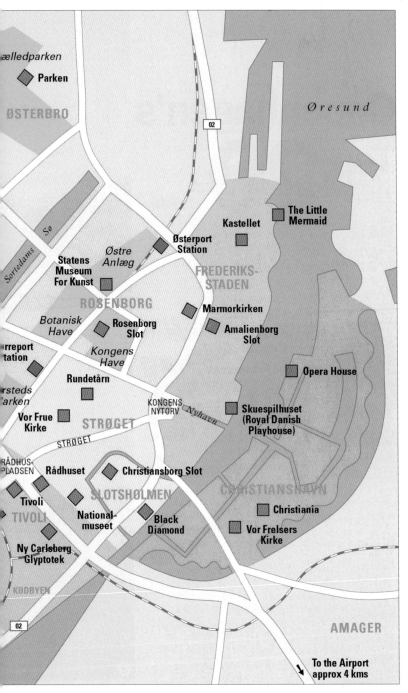

ælledparken

Parken

ØSTERBRO

Øresund

Sortedams Sø

The Little
Mermaid

Kastellet

Østerport
Station

Statens
Museum
For Kunst

Østre
Anlæg

FREDERIKS-
STADEN

ROSENBORG

Marmorkirken

Botanisk
Have

Rosenborg
Slot

Amalienborg
Slot

rreport
tation

Kongens
Have

Opera House

Rundetårn

rsteds
arken

KONGENS
NYTORV

Nyhavn

Skuespilhuset
(Royal Danish
Playhouse)

Vor Frue
Kirke

STRØGET

STRØGET

RÅDHUS-
PLADSEN

Rådhuset

Christiansborg Slot

SLOTSHOLMEN

CHRISTIANSHAVN

Tivoli

TIVOLI

National-
museet

Black
Diamond

Christiania

Vor Frelsers
Kirke

Ny Carlsberg
Glyptotek

KØDBYEN

AMAGER

To the Airport
approx 4 kms

Copenhagen's
Top 20

From city biking to royal palaces, we count down the essentials.

1 Torvehallerne
(page 87)

Copenhagen's covered gourmet food market has been a success since opening in Israels Plads in 2011, on the site of a previous market that closed in the late 1950s. The two purpose-built glass food halls house a huge array of tempting Danish delicacies and international foodstuffs, with highlights including stalls for Coffee Collective, porridge bar Grød, tea specialist Tante T, Danish takeaway spot Cofoco, and Gorm's, for tasty Italian pizza.

2 Louisiana Museum for Moderne Kunst

(page 182)

Founded by industrialist and art collector Knud Jensen in 1958, Louisiana is as much about its blissful setting as the modern artworks it houses. Located in Humlebæk, a 45-minute train ride from Copenhagen, its sculpture-filled grounds cascade down to the shore. As well as its diverse permanent collection – with works by Alexander Calder, Asger Jorn and Francis Bacon – it also houses dynamic temporary exhibitions.

3 Copenhagen's bike lanes

(page 24)

It's no secret that Copenhagen is one of the world's most bike-friendly cities – Amsterdam is the only real rival for the crown – but it's not until you get on your own two wheels that you realise what a joy it is to cycle here. The bike lanes usually have kerbs to separate riders from other road users, making cycling here much safer than in most other cities, and the number of bikes scattered around the city never ceases to amaze first-time visitors. You can hire bikes at many hotels, but for cheaper bike rental, head to Baisikeli (*see p25*).

4 New Nordic cuisine
(page 67)

The food movement known as 'New Nordic' started taking shape a decade or so ago, when Claus Meyer and René Redzepi opened Noma, now Copenhagen's most renowned restaurant. It's only in the past few years, though, that the movement has been catapulted into the culinary mainstream, with New Nordic restaurants – many run by ex-Noma chefs – now dotted all around the city. Most serve tapas-size dishes made with organic produce grown in the Nordic regions and inspired by traditional Scandinavian techniques. Fish, root vegetables, grains, soft cheese, wild berries and herbs feature heavily, as do porridge, pickling and salting. If you can't afford Noma, try Amass (*see p111*).

❹

5 Marmorkirken
(page 105)

❺

The breathtaking 'Marble Church' was designed by Nicolai Eigtved in the 1740s as the focal point of the new quarter of Frederiksstaden – though the building wasn't completed until the late 1800s. Its impressive dome, inspired by St Peter's in Rome, remains one of the largest of its kind in Europe, and offers far-reaching views from the top.

6 Rundetårn
(page 58)

❻

Copenhagen's 17th-century Round Tower is unique in European architecture for its cobbled spiral walkway that winds seven and a half times round its core for 209 metres (686 feet). Peter the Great supposedly rode all the way to the top in 1716, pulling a carriage behind him containing the Tsarina. The top of the tower houses Europe's oldest functioning astronomical observatory, and offers superb views of the city.

7 Christiania
(page 115)

The Freetown of Christiania is now one of Denmark's biggest tourist sells, though it can't be pigeonholed into any of the normal visitor attractions. Home to around 1,000 people, the hippie commune was set up in the 1970s in a former military barracks, and until recently was a community that existed within Copenhagen, but outside its laws and conventions. The place has been 'normalised' somewhat over the past few years, though it's still dominated by the sale of soft drugs (the taking of photos here is strictly prohibited) and by an alternative cultural ideology. The most interesting thing about Christiania, however, is its extraordinary hand-built houses lining the water.

8 Kødbyen
(page 120)

Vesterbro's Meatpacking District is now home to some of Copenhagen's best restaurants and bars, all housed in low-rise former butchers' shops and slaughterhouses. Men in white coats, sometimes carrying carcasses, mill around next to trendy newcomers. Highlights here include Mother, offering delicious sourdough pizzas; Kul, for international dishes from the grill; Fiskebaren, for top-notch seafood and contemporary decor; and Bakken, for late-night drinks and electronic music.

9 Tivoli
(page 48)

The amusement park in the centre of Copenhagen is a blend of escapist, fairytale gaiety and defiant traditionalism, home to a variety of rides (including a 100-year-old rollercoaster), funfair activities, music venues and high-profile restaurants. As Denmark's No.1 tourist attraction, it draws the crowds; but it's much more than an ordinary theme park, being close to the hearts of most Danes. In many ways, it's the definitive Danish experience, and the ultimate expression of the Danish term *hygge*, used to express a desire for close community and contentedness.

10 Designmuseum Danmark
(page 104)

Set around a grand courtyard in the old Frederiks Hospital, Denmark's most high-profile design museum is a lovely space in which to explore the country's prolific furniture-design heritage. The range of mid-century modern items has increased in recent years, with many functionalist pieces – chairs, in particular – by the likes of Finn Juhl and Arne Jacobsen on display. The shop is also a huge highlight for those looking for good books on design or covetable homewares.

11 Nyhavn
(page 96)

This quayside's wonderfully colourful buildings are probably Copenhagen's most photographed spot. The stretch of restaurants and bars attracts tourists in their droves, but it's still a pleasant place in which to sup a beer in

the sunshine (if you're lucky). Hans Christian Andersen lived at three different addresses on Nyhavn, at a time when it was a disreputable place, full of drinkers' bars, knocking shops and tattoo parlours.

12 Jægersborggade
(page 134)

This Nørrebro street, just north of the cemetery, was something of a no-go zone a decade or so ago; now, it's the city's coolest street, lined with an interesting range of fashion and homewares boutiques, ceramics studios, coffee shops and cutting-edge restaurants, including porridge specialist Grød (*see p139*) and the Michelin-starred Relæ (*see p138*).

13 Thorvaldsens Museum
(page 83)

Denmark's oldest art museum displays the works of its greatest sculptor in an inspiring building containing celestial blue ceilings, elegant colonnades and mosaic floors. Bertel Thorvaldsen developed his sculptural style – which was heavily influenced by Greco-Roman mythology – in Rome, where he lived for nearly 40 years, before returning to Denmark in the 1830s.

14 Summer bathing
(page 151)

Copenhagen's possibilities for summer dips have increased dramatically of late, especially since the construction of the Islands Brygge Harbour Baths complex next to the Langebro bridge in 2003. The opening of the baths followed a drive by local authorities to improve the quality of the harbour water, and they've been a huge success. Outdoor swimming fans also have the options of the urban beaches at Amager Strandpark, Kastrup Søbad and Svanemøllestranden.

15 Botanisk Have
(page 91)

A favourite spot for locals at weekends, the centrally located Botanical Garden was laid out in 1871 to designs by HA Flindt, with a lake that was once part of the city moat as its centrepiece. You'll find examples of most of Denmark's flora here, as well as those exotic plants that can be persuaded to grow this far north, inside a complex of historical glasshouses – the most notable of which is the Palm House, built in 1874.

16 Ny Carlsberg Glyptotek
(page 54)

With a breathtaking line-up of ancient sculptures, and an exceptional array of more recent Danish and French paintings and sculpture – including an impressive collection of French Impressionist works – the Ny Carlsberg Glyptotek is a world-class museum. Its Winter Garden palm house and café makes for an inspiring place for a coffee break.

17 Royal Danish Theatre
(page 177)

Originally confined to one building, the Royal Danish Theatre – known locally as Det Kongelige Theater – is now split into three impressive venues. The lavish original building in Kongens Nytorv, built in 1874, is now used principally for ballet, while the purpose-built Skuespilhuset (Royal Danish Playhouse), constructed in 2008, is the city's principal site for theatre. Opposite the Skuespilhuset, across the water, is the Henning Larsen-designed Operaen, the city's modern opera house, which is now one of Copenhagen's landmarks.

18 Amalienborg Slot
(page 102)

Copenhagen's grand Frederiksstaden quarter is home to the Amalienborg Palace, the residence of the Danish royal family since 1794. Composed of four rococo buildings, the palace provides a major photo-op for tourists with its daily changing of the guards ceremony. Nearby is the lovely harbourside park of Amaliehaven.

19 Assistens Kirkegård
(page 135)

Nørrebro's graceful, tree-filled cemetery is the final resting place of many famous Danes, including Hans Christian Andersen and the cemetery's own namesake, philosopher Søren Kirkegaard. But it's also used as a public park by locals still living – who come here for bike rides, pleasant strolls, picnics and sometimes even to sunbathe on the gravestones.

20 Smørrebrod
(pages 92 and 105)

The traditional Danish lunch option of *smørrebrod* has undergone a renaissance in recent times as part of the general revival of Nordic cuisine. *Smørrebrod* is usually translated as 'open sandwich' in English, which overly simplifies the complex layering method involved in the dish. Toppings can vary from highly elaborate gourmet confections featuring caviar, prawns and egg (as at Ida Davidsen and Aamanns) to the more prosaic liver paste and cucumber. Basically, anything goes, as long as it's savoury, but toppings will typically include the likes of boiled egg and dill, prawns, beetroot, herring, or various cold meats.

Copenhagen Today

City of the moment.

Copenhagen is at the very heart of Denmark. Not literally, of course. In fact, it couldn't be further from the centre of the country, lying as it does on the far eastern coast of Sjælland, closer to Sweden than most of Denmark – though once-upon-a-time this was the centre of the Danish empire, which then included southern Sweden, Norway and Iceland. But with over a quarter of the country's population living in the city, Copenhagen can justly lay claim to being, if not the soul, then at least the political, cultural and economic nerve centre of the country.

Although Copenhagen has a total population of 1.7 million when you include all of its 26 communes, only 600,000 live in Indre By, the city centre proper. But its compact size is a large part of the city's appeal. You can amble across the centre in an afternoon; take in most of its main sights in a long weekend; and really get to know your way around in a week. This is an accessible city, in all senses: English is spoken to a high level; the transport system and bike lanes are unsurpassed; there are world-renowned restaurants; and, these days, following a massive hotel boom, there is plenty of good accommodation.

WORLD'S HAPPIEST NATION?

About the only thing that isn't quite so easy to get to know about Copenhagen is its people. The Danes are a close-knit tribe: if strangers meet, within a minute they will be able to find a common acquaintance. And although Danes are notably good-natured, they are neither welcoming nor unwelcoming towards strangers.

This makes it harder to penetrate the oft-reported claim that Danes are the happiest people on earth. Denmark has been the recurring *numero uno* on global 'happiness indexes' since the mid noughties. But how does this translate into day-to-day living? And what do the Danes think about their new-found status as 'world's happiest nation'?

VIKING MINDSET

The people of Denmark have grown used to making headlines around the world in the last decade, what with the outrage provoked by the publication of cartoons of the prophet Mohammed by Danish newspaper *Jyllands-Posten* in 2005, and René Redzepi's Noma being declared the World's Best Restaurant by *Restaurant* magazine for three years in a row (until 2013, when it was knocked off the top spot by Spain's El Celler de Can Roca). Nevertheless, many Danes initially reacted with some bewilderment to the proclamations that they are the happiest people in the world. ('Why did no one tell us?' pondered one columnist back in 2006.)

First-time visitors might also be foxed, as the Danes are not the most obviously joyous

of people – satisfied, perhaps, but gay in the old-fashioned sense of the word? No. True, they have a carnival once a year, and they like a drink, but, at heart, they remain a rather serious Nordic race in the true Viking tradition. Yes, this is the country that gave us Aqua's 'Barbie Girl', but don't forget it is also the birthplace of Existentialism (Søren Kierkegaard was a Copenhagener), as well as Lars von Trier, the film director responsible for some of the most depressing films ever made. What's more, Danes have one of the world's highest uses of anti-depressants, with one in 12 reportedly using them in 2011, according to the Danish Ministry of Health.

SOCIAL TRUST AND COHESION

So why are the Danes, supposedly, so happy? It doesn't hurt that this is a small country with a small capital city, and small countries, particularly small European countries, always do well in life-satisfaction surveys due to their inherent sense of collectivism, which breeds a greater sense of civic pride and social support.

This has also made the Danes a trusting and trustworthy bunch. Though their obsessive obedience to rules can make them seem sheep-like from time to time – you'll notice that locals never cross the road unless the green man tells them to – their general feeling of trust towards strangers and politicians is enviable (*see p121* **A Breath of Fresh Air**), and creates a tangible feeling of cohesion. Danes tend to have faith that their politicians will act in the public interest, and this has helped the country's national and local governments to implement progressive policies that would be far more controversial elsewhere (*see below* **Planet Organic**).

LIFESTYLE, SECURITY AND THAT WARM FEELING

Money probably has something to do with it as well, of course. In the early noughties, the Danish economy boomed, thanks to an unexpected North Sea oil bonanza, and world-class technology and pharmaceutical sectors. Though not quite as wealthy as their neighbours the Norwegians, Denmark has one of the lowest rates of unemployment in Europe and some of the highest wages. It also, crucially, has one of the smallest gaps between rich and poor of any country in the world. Essentially, the Danes are one giant

middle class, with all that implies for the national character (both good and bad).

Social and economic stability ensures Danes are well looked after by the state in terms of healthcare, education, childcare and social benefits. The streets of Copenhagen are clean, safe and buzzing with confidence. Public transport is efficient and reasonably priced, and the popularity of the bike as a form of transport creates a strong sense of community on the city's streets.

But aside from the comfort of hard cash, the Danes seem to have mastered several other fundamental prerequisites of contentment. They work a little less than the rest of us, spend more time with their families, read more, don't complain nearly as much as you might expect about their taxes, and get lots of fresh air, spending most of the summer

---

PLANET ORGANIC

Organic food is becoming the norm.

It's no secret that Copenhagen has led the way when it comes to the 'green cities' movement. More and more hotels in the city are becoming carbon-neutral, the harbour water is now clean enough to swim in, and bike culture goes from strength to strength – facts that led the European Environment Commission to name Copenhagen 'European Green Capital' in 2014.

What's less well known outside Copenhagen is the fact that the authorities have given a big push to the organic sector in the past few years. Not many cities can match Copenhagen when it comes to consumption of organic food. Around ten per cent of food purchases are now organic, and you'll see the word '*økologisk*' and the Ø symbol (the equivalent of the UK's Soil Association stamp) on restaurant menus throughout the city. Many restaurants even state on their menus how organic they are as a percentage, with **Relae** (*see p128*), **Manfreds & Vin** (*see p137*), **Restaurant Radio** (*see p131*) and **Soupanatural** (Sankt Peders Stræde 31, www.soupanatural.dk) nearing 100%.

All this is impressive enough, but what's really astounding is the fact that around

75 per cent of all food consumed through public kitchens – schools, nursery schools and civic institutions – is organic, a figure that the authorities, via the independent foundation **House of Food** (www.kbh madhus.dk), are trying to raise to a whopping 90% by the end of 2015 (without increasing spending). What's more, it seems that this new organic policy has been readily accepted by most Copenhageners – which says much about their general trust that those in power will act in the public interest.

ON THE WATERFRONT

New architecture, Michelin-starred restaurants and cultural gems.

Opera House.

Until around 15 years ago, Copenhagen was in denial of its seaside location. You would hardly have known that the Øresund Sea and harbour bordered half the city. But in recent years the city has embraced its surroundings, with radical new buildings overlooking the water, the ambitious lagoon development on Amager Strand (Amager Beach) and the construction of open-air swimming pools in the harbour itself (*see p151* **Come on In, the Water's Lovely**), the best known of which is at Islands Brygge near Langebro.

In terms of public buildings, you can date the city's harbour renaissance to the 1999 opening of the **Black Diamond** extension to the National Library, by architects Schmidt Hammer Lassen. This dramatic parallelogram, just north of Langebro, is made from Zimbabwean granite and paved the way for several large-scale leviathans overlooking the water, including the Nordea Bank building beside Langebro, the windswept apartment blocks in Tuborg Havn and the gigantic £232-million **Opera House** (*see p172*) by Henning Larsen. The Michelin-starred Scandinavian restaurant **Søren K** (*see p83*) is located in the Black Diamond, with waterside views.

On the other side of the water, in Christianshavn, sits another Michelin-starred restaurant, the world-renowned **Noma** (*see p114*, the New Nordic eaterie

that has spawned a host of imitators. It's housed in the Nordatlantens Brygge (North Atlantic House), which it shares with a popular cultural centre and the Embassy of Iceland.

Newer arrivals include the Norway ferry terminal in Nordhavn by architects 3XN, which resembles a giant lightbox; and the dazzling new stage of the **Royal Danish Theatre** (aka Skuespilhuset, *see p174*) – located at Kvæsthusbroen on the site of the old ferry terminal, opposite the Opera House – which opened in 2008. The latter is also the site of an exciting new waterfront urban space, **Kvæsthus Projektet** (www.kvaesthusprojektet.dk), which should be completed by summer 2015. The pier-like space will be used for outdoor performing arts events, and is another example of how Copenhagen leads the way when it comes to creating urban spaces that engender a sense of community.

In fact, these days virtually every stretch of Copenhagen's waterfront is being developed; Holmen, Amager Strand and Sydhaven (South Harbour) are all erupting with cool, modern apartment blocks. Of particular note is the extraordinary **Gemini Residence**: two massive, converted grain silos by Dutch architects MVRDV, each boasting that all-important sea view – essential to any self-respecting 21st-century Danish yuppie.

outdoors. Above all, they try to keep things *hygglige* – which is the name for their unique brand of amiable cosiness and perhaps one of the key secrets to their happiness.

THE FLIP SIDE

There are downsides to life in Copenhagen, of course. The weather is the most obvious one. Bluntly put, it sucks for much of the year. You may expect this not to bother the stoic locals, but it does, and many enter a kind of hibernation during the winter, emerging for the December Christmas festivities (which Copenhagen does very well, incidentally).

The high cost of living is another potential gripe, with cars costing around three times the price they do in the UK; visitors will wince at 25 per cent VAT and the often exorbitant cost of dining out. The latter means that many Copenhageners still approach eating out as a rare treat, rather than a weekly occurence.

As for temperament and political outlook, to the outside world the Danes are liberal, open-minded and tolerant. They were pornography pioneers in the 1960s; they have a fairly tolerant outlook when it comes to soft drugs; and same-sex marriage was legalised in Denmark in 2012. There has been less tolerance when it comes to other political issues, however…

THE IMMIGRATION ISSUE

The Danes rejected the euro through a referendum in 2000, while subsequent proposed referendums in 2008 and 2012 were cancelled. In fact, 'Europe' seems to have been put on the political back-burner in recent years, with issues such as social welfare and immigration being deemed far more pressing by political leaders.

The latter topic played to the advantage of the odious far-right Dansk Folkepartie (Danish People's Party) in the first decade of the 21st century. The DF, under its sinister 'mother' figure, Pia Kiersgaard, provided parliamentary support for the centre-right governments of Anders Fogh Rasmussen and Lars Løkke Rasmussen during the noughties, which led to Denmark's tightening of its immigration laws – and to allegations that the country's strict rules violated EU norms. Immigration is a divisive issue here; for example, even liberal, well-educated Copenhageners still sometimes talk of 'second-generation

'The expansion of the Metro is one of the most ambitious projects of the moment.'

Danes', referring to people who, though they have been born in Denmark, have lived in Denmark, speak Danish and pay Danish taxes, are still not, well, you know, white.

Some of the country's anti-immigration legislation has, however, been rolled back by the centre-left government of Denmark's first female prime minister, Helle Thorning-Schmidt. The Social Democrat, who came to power in 2011 – and who became an internet sensation in December 2013 for her 'selfie' with Barack Obama at the Nelson Mandela memorial – now leads a coalition of the Social Democrats and the Danish Social Liberal Party (after the Socialist People's Party quit the three-party coalition in early 2014).

BUILDING BOOM

Visitors spending a weekend in Copenhagen won't, of course, pick up on many of the intricacies of Danish society and politics. What they are more likely to notice are the policies implemented in bricks and mortar. A huge number of major construction and urban design projects have been completed in and around Copenhagen in recent years, including the Øresund Bridge from Amager to Malmö in southern Sweden; the ever-expanding Metro; new bicycle 'green routes'; and the various snazzy concrete and glass buildings overlooking the harbour (*see p22* **On the Waterfront**). And the building continues apace – in particular on the island of Amager, where the new town of Ørestad continues to expand (for more on this, *see p211* **Design & Architecture**). The expansion of the Metro is one of the most ambitious projects of the moment, with 17 new stations currently being created as part of the new City Ring extension. All this means that the building works currently cropping up all around the city will continue until 2018.

BIKE COPENHAGEN

Probably the most bike-friendly city in the world.

Scandinavians are famous for using bicycles as everyday transport. And Danes cycle, on average, 600 kilometres (375 miles) per year. But Copenhageners take things a step further: almost everyone – regardless of income or social status – cycles in this city. Some 37 per cent of all commuter trips in Copenhagen are made by bike – a figure that authorities hope will rise to 50 per cent by the end of 2015.

Copenhagen's bike lanes and bike culture have become a model for forward-thinking cities around the globe, to the point where a new verb, 'Copenhagenize', is now used to describe urban planning that emulates the city. And despite, or because of, the international attention, Copenhagen hasn't rested on its laurels: the first city-to-suburb 'bicycle highways' opened at the end of 2011, and 22 new 'green routes' are being built throughout the city.

THE URBAN CYCLING INFRASTRUCTURE

Although Copenhagen's first bike lanes were created around the lakes in 1910, it wasn't until the 1980s that the city's present-day lanes – with their kerbs segregating cyclists from other road users – came into effect. As elsewhere, the 1960s witnessed a decline in cycling culture, with the increasing affordability of cars. But by the '70s, cycling experienced a revival in the city, in line with the growing green movement in Denmark. In the mid 1980s, local planners such as Jan Gehl began to develop the urban infrastructure for a bike- (and pedestrian-) friendly city, which now boasts some 390 kilometres (242 miles) of bike lanes. And from the early 1990s, cycling as a form of transportation has steadily risen year by year.

Of course, the comparatively small size of the capital, and its flat terrain, are particularly conducive to a strong cycling community. But the extensive and well-designed system of bike lanes and cycle paths, along with other measures to encourage cycling – such as being able to easily take your bike on the Metro and local trains – are what has really earned the city the tag of 'most bike-friendly city in the world'.

The busiest cycling street in Copenhagen is Nørrebrogade, and the bicycle rush hour on the connecting Dronning Louises Bridge is a sight to behold; join the throngs, and you'll feel a sense of community and belonging that just isn't possible in a car.

The city's 100 kilometres (62 miles) of new 'green routes' aim to provide especially safe routes in the city, and include the creation of new green spaces. Many have already been completed, including the Nørrebro green route, which runs from Emdrup in the north to Valby in the south. And many city-to-suburb 'bicycle highways', which extend the city's cycling infrastructure to the suburbs and beyond, have been completed in the last few years.

ETIQUETTE AND PRACTICALITIES

There are certain cast-iron rules that visitors should take note of when cycling around the city. For instance, passengers at bus stops (either embarking or disembarking) have right of way: all cyclists must stop and wait until the bus doors have closed. Left-hand turns on main roads are not permitted for cyclists: you must cross the road (with the green light, of course) as a pedestrian

would. As a rule, you should ride on the right-hand side of the cycle path; if someone rings a bell behind you (never more than once, that is considered rude), it is to indicate that you should move over and let them pass on the left. When you want to stop, raise your right hand, in a sort of salute, to signal this to other cyclists. None of these rules apply to cycle couriers, however. They do as they please.

Although Copenhageners are, on the whole, a trustworthy bunch, bicycle theft does still happen (though the thief is more likely to be a drunken chancer coming back from a bar than a member of an organised-crime racket). So remember to lock your bike. Most bikes in Copenhagen have locks built into the back wheel, meaning that locking up is quick and simple. You should also make sure that you use lights at night, lest you get pulled over by local police, who are often only too happy to issue a fine.

It's possible to take bikes on the Metro and on S-trains, local, regional and InterCity trains outside rush hour (so not between 7-9am and 3.30-5.30pm). All trains require a special bike ticket, which can be purchased at the station. Most S-trains have a special area for bikes.

Copenhageners are a hardy bunch, and many cycle all year round – even during January blizzards. Local authorities keep bike lanes well gritted throughout the winter, ensuring that the bike is a viable form of transport even in the coldest months.

BIKE HIRE AND CYCLE TOURS

The public bike rental scheme Bycykler (City Bikes) ended in 2012, but has been replaced with a new bicycle-sharing scheme, called **GoBike** (www.gobike.dk), which launched in summer 2013. The sophisticated bikes have GPS and navigation touchscreens with, for instance, train information, and can be booked online (from 20kr-25kr per hour, plus a one-off fee of 20kr).

A better bet is to rent a bike from a bike shop (see p229). Typical cost is 80kr-100kr per day for a simple three-speeder. Bikes can often be hired from your hotel, but it can be cheaper to go direct to the rental place. **Baisikeli** (Ingerslevsgade 80, 26 70 02 29, www.baisikeli.dk, open 10am-6pm daily) is especially recommended, being a well-priced, friendly and ethical bike-hire organisation set in a large space overlooking Dybbølsbro station.

For boutique bike shops in Copenhagen, see p70 and p127. For information on the city's iconic Christiania bikes, see p116 **Cargo Collective**.

Itineraries

NOON

*Plot out your perfect trip
to Copenhagen with our
step-by-step planners.*

9AM

3PM

Day 1

9AM Copenhagen is small by city standards, and eminently walkable or cyclable, so it's not difficult to pack several key sights into one day. Start the day with an espresso at the Black Diamond's café, **Øieblikket** (p83), taking in the harbourside views, before heading over to neighbouring Slotsholmen, the 'island' where the city was founded. Slotsholmen is home to the **Christiansborg Slot** (p79) and the Daniel Libeskind-designed building for the **Danish Jewish**

Museum (p81). But our favourite museum on the island is the **Thorvaldsens Museum** (p83), displaying the works of Denmark's pre-eminent sculptor.

If you'd prefer a comprehensive overview of the nation's history, however, then head to the nearby **Nationalmuseet** (p82).

NOON Have a wander around the historic streets between Slotsholmen and pedestrianised Strædet. The colourful cobbled streets are Copenhagen at its most quaint, with **Magstraede** especially iconic. Then head

Clockwise from top left: **Black Diamond, Rundetårn, Geist, Nyhavn**.

down **Strædet** itself (like parallel Strøget, this street is actually made up of several streets – Kompagnistræde and Læderstræde form the central part) to find a café for lunch; **Zirup** (p75) is a long-standing favourite. Once you've been fed and watered, take the ten-minute stroll up pedestrianised Købmagergade to the **Rundetårn** (p58), the city's 17th-century observatory tower. From the viewpoint at the top you can gaze down at the lovely old streets of the **Latin Quarter** (p66), and beyond.

3PM Walk through the **Grønnegade** quarter (p58) to get to Kongens Nytorv square, home to the grand **Kongelige Teater** (Royal Danish Theatre; p96), and then along to **Nyhavn** (p96). This stretch of iconic canalside buildings should be instantly recognisable –

they appear on the cover of this guide.

This is a popular, though expensive, spot for a beer if you're tired from the day's activities, If you still have sightseeing energy left, however, then walk down salubrious Bredgade to reach the awe-inspiring **Marble Church** (p105). Fans of Danish furniture design might prioritise **Designmuseum Danmark** (p104), however, a little way along from here.

7PM Copenhageners tend to dine early. If you're staying in Frederiksstaden to eat, then **Geist** (p99) is a good option. Otherwise, head back into the centre and over to the delightful Gråbrødretorv square, which has a popular option for carnivores: **Peder Oxe** (p69). Or, if you're in the mood for something lighter and more modern, try New Nordic spot **Bror** (p68), or **Höst** (p86).

NOON

10AM

2PM

Day 2

10AM This itinerary focuses on Copenhagen's two most-happening 'bridge quarter' neighbourhoods: **Nørrebro** and **Vesterbro**. The city's most interesting independent shops and cafés are located in these residential districts, and both have distinct characters – you can't really understand contemporary Copenhagen until you visit them. Start the day in Nørrebro at café-bakery **Nordisk Brødhus** (p141), where you can pick up excellent own-made Danish pastries and quality coffee. From here it's a 15-minute walk to nearby **Assistens Kirkegård** (p135), the city's

cemetery, and a popular place for a leisurely amble or bike ride – as well as the final resting place of Hans Christian Andersen.

NOON Exit Assistens Kirkegård at the Jagtvej gate, cross the road, and head up **Jægersborggade** (p134). This street has gone from no-go zone (by Copenhagen standards, at least) to arty locale over the past decade, and now has a Berlin-esque vibe and a clutch of good independent shops. It's a great street for browsing – or indeed buying – clothes, jewellery and homewares from independent brands, with **Ladyfingers** and **Tricotage** (both p142)

definite highlights. And if you're ready for lunch, you'll find a host of good options here; we recommend porridge spot **Grød** (p139), or, if you want to splash out, head to **Manfreds & Vin** (p137), owned by Michelin-starred restaurant Relæ, opposite.

2PM Nørrebro's not just about laid-back cafés and cool shops, however. For an insight into the area's multiculturalism, head north-west up Nørrebrogade (a 25-minute walk, or a five-minute cycle) to **Superkilen** (p135). This new urban park and playground celebrates the area's ethnic diversity with landscaping objects brought from around the world – such as swings from Iraq and

Left:
Assistens Kirkegård.
Top to bottom:
Grød, Superkilen, Torvehallern e, Right:
Mother.

benches from Brazil. After a go on the roundabout, head back down Nørrebrogade and explore the area around **Elmegade, Sankt Hans Torv** and **Ravnsborggade**, with more independent shops. Then, if you still have energy left, cross the Dronning Louises bridge and head over to **Torvehallerne** (p87), the city's covered food market, where you can pick yourself up with an afternoon treat.

7PM The south-western neighbourhood of Vesterbro is Copenhagen's other trendy district. It's been transformed over the past 15 years from red-light district to the city's most-popular 'hood for artists and media types. Its meat-packing district, **Kødbyen** – which still retains its original use to some extent – is now also Copenhagen's most happening nightlife spot, home to cutting-edge restaurants and lively bars. Sourdough pizza parlour **Mother** (p124) is one of the best bets for food, but be sure to get here early to get a table. For a post-meal tipple, head west along Sønder Boulevard to **DyrehavHn** (p125).

COPENHAGEN FOR FREE

Not everything costs the earth in this city.

BOTANICAL GARDENS

Copenhagen's historic Botanisk Have was recently renovated and expanded, with new pathways and greenhouses added. A stroll around the lake here on a sunny morning, followed by a wander through the huge, balmy Palm House makes for a reviving start to the day – and entry is free.

MUSEUMS FOR FREE

Several of Copenhagen's key museums offer free entry, including the Nationalmuseet and Statens Museum for Kunst; the lovely Thorvaldsens Museum is free on Wednesdays while the Ny Carlsberg Glyptotek is free on Sundays. Many of the city's churches are also free to enter – including the Marble Church, with its huge dome and eye-wateringly beautiful interior, and the Alexander Nevsky Kirke.

WATERFRONT WALK

The city's waterfront has been the focus of urban regeneration over the past two decades, and the area is now home to impressive modern architecture, including the Black Diamond and the Royal Danish Playhouse, with the latter opposite Henning Larsen's Operaen. Continue north for the lovely Amaliehaven waterfront gardens, Kastellet, the *Little Mermaid* and wide-open views.

COPENHAGEN JAZZ FESTIVAL

One of the biggest annual events in the city's calendar, the Copenhagen Jazz Festival is a dynamic affair, offering up hundreds of gigs and jam sessions in a host of original venues. And you'll be jazzed to hear that lots of the events – especially those held in public parks and squares – are free of charge.

CHRISTIANIA

Now one of Copenhagen's biggest tourist attractions, Christiania is something of an anomaly in a city obsessed with designer homewares and on-trend fashion. Though the commune – which was established on a former military barracks in the 1970s – has now been 'normalised' by the city authorities, it still offers an interesting counter-cultural experience, especially through its fascinating alternative architecture down by the lake.

Copenhagen's historic housing projects

Copenhagen has been at the forefront of housing design in the past decade or so, with contemporary projects on the island of Amager – such as Bjarke Ingles' VM Mountain and 8Tallet, and Lundgaard & Tranberg's Tietgen Students' Residence (for all, see p211) – inspiring architects and urban designers worldwide. However, it's a lesser-known fact that Copenhagen was also a frontrunner for social housing projects during the 18th and 19th centuries – a time when urban expansion was attracting new workers to the city.

You might like to hire a bike for this tour, both for ease of exploration and to get you in the true Copenhagen egalitarian spirit. Start the day at the city's new food market, **Torvehallerne** (p87), where you can pick up a coffee and a *snegle* (a cinnamon pastry in the shape of a snail) to fuel your bike ride or walk.

The next stops on this tour will be at two residential enclaves that were originally built as social housing projects for the city, in response to a cholera epidemic in the 1850s caused by cramped and unhygienic housing conditions of workers. To find out more about this before starting the tour proper, head to the **Arbejdermuseet** (p86), just two minutes' walk from the market. This museum aims to show how Danish workers' lives have changed since the 19th century.

The first historic housing project we're visiting is **Kartoffelraekkerne** – 'potato rows' in English – consisting of a ladder of narrow streets built in very straight rows (hence the name) on the border of Østerbro, between the Lakes and Østre Anlæg park. All of the 480 terraced houses that make up this 19th-century development have front yards, and the area is now one of the most exclusive in the city – which makes the fact that it was

built (by the Workers Construction Society in the 1870s) for the working classes a little ironic. The houses are in demand partly because of the palpable sense of community here – you'll witness picnic tables in the street, and residents conversing.

From here, head north on the lakeside cycle lanes on Øster Søgade to Østerbro proper. Left off Østerbrogade, just before Sankt Jacobs Kirke, is **Brumleby** (p143), another 19th-century residential district built for Copenhagen's working classes – this time by the Danish Medical Association. The

Anti-clockwise from top: **Brumleby**, **Nyboder**, **Christiania**

rows of distinctive yellow-and-white terraced cottages were built between the 1850s and 1870s, making them one of Denmark's oldest social housing projects, and a model for subsequent projects. Like the potato rows, the houses are now among the city's most sought after.

After a spot of lunch – good options round here are **Café Bopa** (p145) and **Dag H** (p145) – head down towards Frederiksstaden, via Østerbrogade and Dag Hammarskjölds Allé, until you reach **Nyboder** (p91), just past Østerport station. These ochre terraced houses, with their charming red roofs, were built for naval staff and their families in the 17th and 18th centuries, and still house some naval personnel today, though the majority are now occupied by civilians since the area was opened up to the general public in 2006. A small on-site museum, **Nyboders Mindestuer** (p91), informs visitors about the district's history and the humble living conditions here in the first few centuries after they were built.

With these historic social housing projects as a context for contemporary residential architecture, you might now like to cycle south along the harbourfront and over the Knippelsbro bridge to **Amager** (p150) to see the contemporary versions in the new district of Ørestad. On the way, however, head over to **Christiania** (p115) to look at some of the equally community-minded homes down by the water, many of which were built by hand.

Diary

*Plan your perfect weekend
with our year-round guide
to the Danish capital.*

Scandinavians aren't exactly renowned for their love of festivals or for public expressions of joy, but Copenhagen nevertheless has a wealth of annual events that hold great appeal for visitors. Summer is an especially exciting time to visit the city; this is when Danes peel back the layers and let loose after months of winter darkness. The Copenhagen Jazz Festival and Copenhagen Cooking are two of the best-known summer festivals, but Kulturhavn and Distortion also make their presence felt at this time of year. In the colder months, cultural and festive events such as CPH:DOX, Fastelavn and Tivoli Christmas Season keep things cosy and interesting.

Tivoli Christmas
Season. See p39.

Spring

Queen's Birthday
Date 16 Apr.
The Danes are united by their fondness for their multi-talented Queen Margrethe II, and her birthday is cause for celebration across the country. The Queen herself makes an appearance on a balcony at Amalienborg Slot at noon, while the Royal Life Guards mark the occasion by parading in their finest ceremonial dress.

★ CPH:PIX
33 45 47 49, www.cphpix.dk. **Date** Apr.
CPH:PIX is the dynamic result of the merging in 2009 of Denmark's two premier film festivals (NatFilm Festivalen and the Copenhagen Film Festival). Day and night for two weeks in mid April, the city's many cinemas showcase more than 200

PUBLIC HOLIDAYS

New Year's Day (Nytårsdag)
1 Jan

Maundy Thursday (Skærtorsdag)
2 Apr 2015, 24 Mar 2016

Good Friday (Langfredag)
3 Apr 2015, 25 Mar 2016

Easter Sunday (Påske)
5 Apr 2015, 27 Mar 2016

Easter Monday (2.Påskedag)
6 Apr 2015, 28 Mar 2016

Common Prayer Day (Stor Bededag)
1 May 2015, 22 Apr 2016

Ascension Day (Kristi Himmelfartsdag)
14 May 2015, 5 May 2016

Whit Sunday (1.Pinsedag)
24 May 2015, 15 May 2016

Whit Monday (2.Pinsedag)
25 May 2015, 16 May 2016

Constitution Day (Grundlovsdag)
5 June, from noon

Christmas (Jule)
24-26 Dec

ALL THAT JAZZ

Think you hate jazz?
Think again.

The **Copenhagen Jazz Festival** (*see p37*) is a huge affair, with 1,000-plus concerts held over two weeks in July at around 100 venues across the city. Lots of the events – which start at around lunchtime each day, and end in the early hours – are free. Best of all, the atmosphere that imbues the city during the festival makes it a fantastic time to visit, even if you're not a jazz aficionado.

Copenhagen's relationship with jazz goes back to the 1960s, when the likes of Dexter Gordon, Stan Getz and Ben Webster based themselves in a city that was seriously jazz-hot. Half a century on, the definition of 'jazz' is thrillingly broad – everything from New Orleans street bands, world music quartets and louche South American duos to the purer jazz sounds of Sonny Rollins, Herbie Hancock and Ornette Coleman (all past headliners), as well as huge vocal acts such as Dianne Reeves and Cassandra Wilson.

Venues vary from poky bars to illustrious classics including **Jazzhouse** (*see p170*), **Jazzhus Montmartre** (Store Regregade 19A, Indre By, www.jazzhusmontmartre.com) and the elegant, upscale **DR Koncerthuset** (*see p172*). The recent opening of jazz bar **The Standard** (*see p170*) in an art deco building means the city now has a seriously stylish new venue to include on the programme.

It all combines to create a festival that's accessible to everyone – thanks to the numerous free concerts. From parks, squares and gardens to waterside platforms and churches, from museums and galleries to cafés and bars, it's hard not to encounter some performance going on somewhere. In the long days of summer, whether picnicking in a park while watching a children's concert, or sitting on the grass outside the Zaha Hadid-designed café of the Ordrupgaard museum, listening to the Jan Harbeck Quartet, every aspect of the festival is a genuine delight.

If you prefer the bluesier, more melancholy sides of the genre, you might prefer **Vinterjazz** (*see p39*), which takes place each February. Either way, you're sure to find something to your taste – even if you don't like jazz.

Top:
Copenhagen Jazz Festival.
Left:
CPH:DOX.
Right:
Marathon.

films, with directors often turning up to talk about their work after the screenings.

May Day
Fælledparken, Østerbro. Bus 1A, 95N.
Map p248 E12. **Date** 1 May.
Head to Østerbro for this trade unions-led festival of the working man, complete with live music and ethnic food.

Ølfestival (Beer Festival)
Tap 1, Ny Carlsbergvej 91, Frederiksberg (www.beerfestival.dk). Train Enghave, or bus 18, 26. **Tickets** 100kr-250kr; available in advance from BilletNet (www.billetnet.dk). **Date** late May.
The growth of microbreweries has finally challenged the stronghold of Carlsberg, and interest in beer has been growing fast in Denmark over the past decade. This is the country's leading beer festival, drawing crowds of over 10,000. Tastings, talks and, of course, monster hangovers are all part of the three-day event.

Copenhagen Marathon
35 26 69 00, www.copenhagenmarathon.dk.
Admission 600kr-650kr; 300kr reductions.
Date 3rd weekend in May.
Professional and amateur runners from around the world pound the cobbles from Vesterbro to Nørrebro, Østerbro and Vester Voldgade.

★ Sankt Hans Aften

Date 23 June.
St Hans Night is one of the biggest celebrations of the festival calendar for Danes, who have marked the longest day of the year since pagan times with bonfires and songs. The major gatherings are usually held on beaches or in parks.

Danish Derby

Klampenborg Galopbane, Klampenborgvej, Klampenborg (39 96 02 13, www.galopbane.dk). Train Klampenborg, or bus 388. **Admission** 100kr; 50kr reductions; free under-18s. **No credit cards. Date** late June.
Denmark's leading equine event takes place at Klampenborg racecourse, to the north of the city.

Roskilde Festival

Roskilde (46 36 66 13, www.roskilde-festival.dk). Train Roskilde. **Tickets** 1,910kr (full festival incl camping); available in advance from BilletNet (www.billetnet.dk). **Date** late June/early July.
Held over eight days, Roskilde is Scandinavia's largest outdoor music event. In 2014, crowds of 80,000 are set to enjoy headline acts including the Rolling Stones, Arctic Monkeys, and Drake. The festival is famous for its relatively crime-free party atmosphere; for many teenage Danes, their first Roskilde Festival is an important coming-of-age milestone. A shuttle bus runs from Roskilde Station to the festival grounds on the outskirts of this ancient town in the centre of Sjælland.

Round Sjælland Yacht Race

Helsingør (www.sjaellandrundt.dk). Train Helsingør. **Date** late June/early July.
Sailors compete in one of Europe's major yacht races over three days.

★ Copenhagen Jazz Festival

33 93 20 13, www.jazz.dk. **Date** 1st Fri-2nd Sun July.
As soon as Roskilde is over, the two-week long Copenhagen Jazz Festival gets under way. The Danes love their jazz, and, thankfully, that passion

Summer

Copenhagen Photo Festival

www.copenhagenphotofestival.com. **Admission** varies. **Date** early June.
This relatively new two-week festival (launched in 2010) showcases contemporary photography from established Danish and international names. Exhibitions and events take place in cultural institutions, galleries, museums and public spaces around the city – and many of them are free.

Distortion

www.cphdistortion.dk. **Tickets** 450kr-550kr. **Date** early June.
Copenhagen's biggest street party takes place over four days in early June, and attracts around 100,000 revellers. As well as the (free) street parties, there are freestyle dance performances and club nights, with electronic music and hip hop dominating the sound systems. Venues include Culture Box, Jazzhouse, Rust and Pumpehuset, and there are also special events in one-off locations such as swimming pools and museums, leading up to a pumping final party on Saturday afternoon/night.

isn't limited to the Dixieland tourist-fodder you'll hear on Nyhavn of a summer's afternoon. The festival is delightfully ad hoc, with impromptu gigs, jam sessions, improvisations, free outdoor concerts and street parades happening all over the city. Naturally, you need to book early for any big names. *See also p36* **All That Jazz**.

★ Shakespeare at Kronborg

Kronborg Slot, Helsingør (49 21 69 79, www. hamletscenen.dk). Train Helsingør. **Tickets** 200kr-500kr. **Date** early Aug.
Productions of *Hamlet* have been staged at Kronborg Castle since 1816, many by British companies. Laurence Olivier and his wife Vivien Leigh played here in 1937, but John Gielgud's 1939 *Hamlet* is generally regarded as the definitive performance. Since then, Richard Burton, Michael Redgrave, Derek Jacobi, Kenneth Branagh and Simon Russell Beale have all played notable Hamlets. It's not just *Hamlet*, though: the ten-day festival includes other Shakespeare plays, plus films and special productions for kids.

Kulturhavn (Culture Harbour)

Islands Brygge, Amager (33 66 38 50, www.kulturhavn.dk). Metro Islands Brygge. **Date** early Aug.
On the first weekend in August, over 80 events – from diving to dance, water polo to dragon boat races, and theatrical performances to fireworks – take place on and around the water beside Islands Brygge and up to Refshaleøen.

Ny Cirkus Festival

33 15 15 64, www.kit.dk. **Date** Aug.
Flagship project of the Copenhagen International Theatre, the Ny Cirkus Festival presents international contemporary circus, theatre and dance acts in streets and venues across the city, over nearly three weeks. The line-ups are impressive and have included Philip Glass.

Copenhagen Pride

Throughout Copenhagen (www.copenhagenpride.dk). **Date** late Aug.
Previously known as Mermaid Pride, this three-day festival is the event of the year for the city's gay and lesbian community, drawing crowds of up to 50,000.

★ Copenhagen Cooking

33 25 74 00, www.copenhagencooking.com. **Date** late Aug.
Now in its tenth year, Copenhagen Cooking has become one of the world's leading food festivals, growing hand in hand with the city's reputation as a gastronomic capital. The ten-day festival focuses on Danish culinary traditions, with key figures on the New Nordic scene – such as Rene Redzepi and Claus Meyer – normally playing a big part. There's also a winter version (*see p39*).

Autumn

Copenhagen Blues Festival

70 15 65 65, www.copenhagenbluesfestival.dk. **Date** late Sept.
The city's leading blues festival features local and international blues musicians in more than 60 concerts over five days. Mojo, Huset and Amager Bio are among the 20 venues that take part.

★ Kulturnatten

33 15 10 10, www.kulturnatten.dk. **Date** mid Oct.
As the trees on Kongens Nytorv change colour, there is no mistaking the hint of foreboding in the air as the long, dark Danish winter approaches. To help stave off the gloom, each year on the first night of autumn half-term, Copenhagen lets rip with one last cultural hurrah. Around 300 venues take part, including churches, galleries and other exhibition spaces; many of the museums and palaces stay open until midnight, and even Parliament and the Supreme Court open their doors. There's usually a craft fair in Rådhuspladsen, performances on Strøget, countless other concerts and performances, and rare displays of historic weaponry at the Tøjhusmuseet. 'Culture Night' brings a singular atmosphere to the venues and the city.

Top:
Copenhagen Cooking.
Bottom:
Wondercool.

Tivoli Halloween Season

Tivoli, Vesterbrogade 3 (tickets 33 15 10 12, www. tivoli.dk). Train København H. **Admission** contact venue. **Map** p250 P12. **Date** mid Oct-early Nov.
Tivoli has opened its doors at Halloween since 2006, with special spooky activities for children and a Halloween market.

MIX Copenhagen (LesbianGayBiTrans Film Festival)

www.mixcopenhagen.dk. **Tickets** *Screenings* 80kr. **Date** late Oct.
Ten days of mainstream and underground gay and lesbian films arranged by the Danske Film Institut, and shown at various cinemas around town.

Winter

★ CPH:DOX

33 93 07 34, www.cphdox.dk. **Date** mid Nov.
Copenhagen's International Documentary Film Festival takes place in cinemas throughout the city over ten days.

★ Tivoli Christmas Season

Tivoli, Vesterbrogade 3 (33 15 10 01, www. tivoli.dk). Train København H. **Admission** 75kr; 125kr Fri after 8pm; free under-7s. **Map** p250 P12. **Date** mid Nov-Christmas.
Tivoli turns into a vast Christmas grotto with a special Christmas market, ice-skating, Yuletide grub and an infestation of *nisser* (Danish Christmas pixies). Expect crowds. *Photo p34.*

Christmas Fairs & Parade

www.visitcopenhagen.dk. **Date** from late Nov.
Like most European cities, Copenhagen is lit up with decorations at this time of year. But, the atmosphere is more authentically 'Christmassy' and less commercial than elsewhere (maybe the sub-zero temperatures have something to do with it). At the end of November, Father Christmas ('Juleman') parades through the city in the Great Christmas Parade. Look out for the Hotel d'Angleterre's spectacular decorations.

Christmas

www.visitcopenhagen.dk. **Date** 24 Dec.
The Danes give a great Christmas, both in the privacy of their own homes, with elaborate rituals, feasting and decorations, and on a more grand public scale. Like all Danes, Copenhageners celebrate on Christmas Eve. Having already gone out into the woods to chop down their own tree, Danes will decorate it the night before Christmas and hang it with real candles. Once these are lit, the family dances around the tree holding hands and singing carols, before settling down to a traditional Christmas dinner of roast duck, potatoes and red cabbage followed by rice pudding with a hidden almond (whoever gets the almond wins a present).

New Year

Date 31 Dec/1 Jan.
Rådhuspladsen is the place where locals gather on New Year's Eve for the traditional celebration. In recent years, the firework displays throughout the city (private and public) have been ever more breathtaking, but be warned: the Danes are not too hot on firework safety.

Copenhagen Cooking

33 25 74 00, www.copenhagencooking.com. **Date** Jan.
Part of Wondercool (*see below*), this is the ten-day winter version of the summer food festival (*see 38*).

Vinterjazz

33 93 20 13, www.jazz.dk. **Tickets** see website for details. **Date** early Feb.
Also part of Wondercool (*see below*), this is the winter version of the famous summer Copenhagen Jazz Festival (*see 37*). It's a smaller, more low-key affair, but still brings around 400 concerts over a two-week period. *See also p36* **All That Jazz**.

Wondercool Copenhagen

www.visitcopenhagen.com. **Date** Feb.
Wondercool is the umbrella name for four winter festivals designed to lure visitors to the city in the dark days of February. Events are based around the Copenhagen Fashion Festival, Copenhagen Cooking, the FROST rock festival and Vinterjazz.

Fastelavn

www.visitcopenhagen.dk. **Date** late Feb/early Mar.
Fastelavn is the Danish version of Carnival, at the start of Lent, though in a way it's more like Halloween. Children dress up in costumes and gather together, wielding sticks with which they beat the hell out of a wooden barrel. This is mild compared with what used to happen, when the barrel, containing a live cat, would be suspended from a tree by a rope so that the youths of a town could gallop past on a horse and wallop it until the bottom fell out. These days, the traumatised feline has been replaced by hundreds of sweets.

Copenhagen's Best

Check off the essentials with our list of hand-picked highlights.

View from the Rundetårn.

Sightseeing

VIEWS
Rundetårn p58
The Round Tower contains Europe's oldest observatory.
Vor Frelsers Kirke p111
Christianshavn's landmark church spire begs to be climbed.
Tivoli p51
You can almost see Sweden from Tivoli's Golden Tower ride.
Alberto K p53
The restaurant in Arne Jacobsen's Radisson Blu hotel has 360-degree views.

ART & DESIGN
Louisiana Museum of Modern Art p183
Modern artworks in an unbeatable natural setting.
Ny Carlsberg Glyptotek p54
A breathtaking collection of ancient sculpture.
Designmuseum Danmark p104
Iconic Danish furniture, plus an inspiring shop.
Thorvaldsens Museum p83
Works by the famous sculptor, in a beautiful building.
Statens Museum for Kunst p92
Key paintings from Denmark's Golden Age.

**Louisiana Museum
of Modern Art.**

Arken p149
Contemporary art in a huge
concrete and glass space.

ARCHITECTURE
Black Diamond p171
Royal Danish Playhouse
p175
Operaen p172
Marmorkirken p105
Dansk Arkitekturcenter p110
Christiania p115
Ørestad p150

HISTORY
Nationalmuseet p82
Ice Age tools, Viking ships
and medieval kings.
Museum of Copenhagen
p121
Tracing the city's path
from fishing village to
cosmopolitan capital.
Rosenborg Slot p91
An insight into the lives
of Renaissance kings.
**Ruinerne under
Christiansborg** p81
The palace foundations
feature excavated stonework
from Absalon's fortress.

OUTDOORS
Assistens Kirkegård p135
This graceful cemetery is the
final resting place for many
famous Danes, and a
popular spot for a picnic.
**Islands Brygge Harbour
Baths** p151
The harbour water is now
clean enough to swim in.
Botanisk Have p91
Take a stroll around the lake
in the lovely botanical garden.
Frederiksberg Have p129
The most romantic park
in Copenhagen.

ICONS
Little Mermaid p103
The statue inspired by
Hans Christian Andersen's
famous mermaid.

Rådhuset p55
The town hall is one of the
city's most recognisable
buildings.
Elephant Gate p120
The old Carlsberg Brewery's
landmark entrance.
Nyhavn p96
Colourful canalside buildings
that demand to be
photographed.

CHILDREN
Tivoli p51
Copenhagen's world-famous
amusement park.
Zoologisk Have p130
Tigers, elephants, camels
and giraffes (minus Marius).
Blå Planet p150
Scandinavia's largest
aquarium.

Eating &
drinking

BLOWOUTS
Noma p114
Do believe the hype.
Geranium p144
For Rasmus Kofoed's
culinary greatness.
Kiin Kiin p137
A Thai restaurant with a
Michelin star.
Era Ora p111
Copenhagen's best Italian
restaurant.
AOC p105
Creative Nordic cooking with
a clean backdrop.
formel B p130
Danish cuisine with a French
influence.

NEW NORDIC
Amass p111
Relæ p138
Bror p68
Kadeau p111
Restaurant Radio p131
Höst p86

Höst.

Stilleben.

BUDGET

Mother p124
Delicious sourdough pizza in the Meatpacking District.
Soupanatural p21
Organic soup and a friendly vibe.
Madklubben p51
A contemporary Danish bistro for the wallet-conscious.
Haché p86
Gourmet burger bar.

VEGETARIAN

42° Raw p62
Never has healthy raw food tasted so good.
Cascabel Madhus p105
Vegetarian meals for under 100kr.

SMØRREBROD

Restaurant Ida Davidsen p105
Aamanns Etablissement p92
Café GL Torv p68
Cap Horn p98
Slotskælderen Hos Gitte p73

BARS

Lidkoeb p126
Vesterbro's (hard-to-find) bar of the moment.

Falernum p126
A cosy wine bar on a lovely street.
Log Lady p70
A central bar with a friendly vibe.
Dyrehaven p126
A modern-age Vesterbro *bodega*, with good Danish grub.
Eiffel Bar p167
For an old-school Christianshavn experience.

COFFEE

Coffee Collective p87
Kaffe & Vinyl p126
Kafferiet p107
Ricco's Coffee Bar p127

Shopping

GIFTS & HOMEWARES

Stilleben p71
Extremely covetable cushions, candleholders, jewellery and more.
Designer Zoo p127
Jewellery, ceramics and homewares from six local artisans.
Dora p127
A treasure trove of covetable and supremely stylish items.

Illums Bolighus p52
Get yourself a Copenhagen-style apartment.
Royal Copenhagen p208
The famous collectible Danish ceramics brand.

LOCAL FASHION

Stig P p131
Own-brand womenswear and other cult labels.
Mads Nørgaard p76
Every Copenhagener owns something by Mads Nørgaard.
Bruuns Bazaar p64
Creative but wearable designs.
Norse Store p66
Men's streetwear brand.
Dico p65
Stylish shoes at affordable prices.
Es p127
Cute Vesterbro boutique for Scandinavian womenswear.

The Standard.

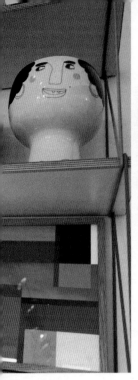

Pluto Børnesko p70
Children's shoes with Scandinavian style.

FOOD & DRINK
Torvehallerne p90
The city's superb gourmet food market.
AC Perchs Thehandel p63
Copenhagen's venerated tea emporium.
Ølbutikken p128
Specialists in microbrewery beer.
Løgismose p107
Frederiksstaden's gourmet supermarket.
Meyer's Deli p131
The best *snegl* (literally, 'snail') pastries in town.

BOOKS & MUSIC
Arnold Busck p70
Politikens Boghallen p55
Danacord p64
Accord p55

ANTIQUES & VINTAGE
Antique Toys p101
… some of which date back to the 17th century.
Time's Up Vintage p71
Fashion-focused vintage clothing.
Green Square Copenhagen p151
An aircraft hangar full of 18th- to 20th-century furniture.

CHILDREN
Lego flagship store p155
The Danish educational bricks are still going strong.
Søstjernen p145
Trendy and cute children's clothing.

Nightlife

JAZZ
The Standard p170
Jazzhouse p170
La Fontaine p170
Drop Inn p74

CLUBS & LIVE MUSIC
Bakken I Kødbyen p181
A hedonistic bar in the trendy Meatpacking District.
Vega p169
International pop and rock musicians, plus DJs.

Rust p169
A longstanding venue for concerts and clubbing.
Global p170
Reggae, fusion and world music.
Loppen p170
Christiania's live-music venue.

Arts

PERFORMING ARTS
DR Koncerthuset p172
Scandinavia's best concert hall for classical music.
Operaen p174
Opera and jazz in a landmark building.
Dansescenen p177
The heart of Copenhagen's dance scene.
Det Kongelige Teater p199
Perfectly suited to traditional ballet performances.

FESTIVALS
Copenhagen Cooking p38
CPH:DOX p39
Copenhagen Jazz Festival p37
Wondercool Copenhagen p39
Tivoli Christmas Season p39
CPH: PIX p35

Tivoli & Rådhuspladsen

In many ways, a visit to Tivoli is the definitive Danish experience. It is the ultimate expression of 'hygge', the unique type of cosiness that the Danes strive to create in all aspects of their lives: there are thrill rides, but none is too extreme (apart from the Demon rollercoaster, perhaps); there are hot dogs and candy floss and beer; and there's a host of family entertainments, from jugglers to parades.

Not far from Tivoli's gates are three of Copenhagen's major landmarks: Arne Jacobsen's world-famous, 22-storey Radisson Blu Royal Hotel – a must for mid-century design enthusiasts; the Ny Carlsberg Glyptotek, with its breathtaking line-up of ancient sculptures; and the iconic Rådhuset, the city's town hall, in Rådhuspladsen (which should already be familiar to fans of *The Killing*).

Alberto K.

Don't Miss

1 Tivoli's rollercoaster This 100-year-old wooden coaster is operated by a brakeman (p50).

2 Alberto K For creative cuisine, Arne Jacobsen furniture and fabulous views (p53).

3 Jens Olsen's World Clock The Rådhuset's horological masterpiece (p55).

4 Ny Carlsberg Glyptotek Ancient sculptures and French Impressionist paintings (p54).

5 Library Bar Top-notch cocktails in a wood-panelled bar (p53).

TIVOLI

Whenever plans are introduced to change Tivoli's appearance, usually to include a fierce new ride, protests erupt. And not just from touchy neighbours who have come to dread half a year of all-day shrieking. The old ladies with season tickets, the visitors from abroad, all the Danes who remember their first visit like it was yesterday – everyone wants the 'Old Garden' to stay more or less the same.

The fact that, year after year, Tivoli attracts major international artists, albeit those with severe MOR tendencies – people such as Tony Bennett, the Beach Boys and Phil Collins – to its open-air stage is testament to its pulling power. Michael Jackson tried to buy the whole place after he played there in the early 1990s, as did Disney a few years back. But the very idea of their beloved Tivoli falling into the hands of Americans, especially Disney, horrified the nation and there was an outcry.

Tivoli's glitzy blend of escapist, fairy-tale gaiety and defiant traditionalism may not be to all tastes, but even the most cynical visitor usually finds themselves won over by its relentless, wide-eyed schmaltz. This is Denmark's No.1 tourist attraction (beating even Legoland on Jutland), and an incredible four million visitors (a figure close to the national population) pass through the gates each year. In all, over 300 million people have visited in over a century.

So what is so special about this relatively small, 82,000-square-metre (20-acre) plot of land, sandwiched between Central Station and Rådhuspladsen? By day, Tivoli is undoubtedly

charming, with its picturesque lake, wide range of rides, overpriced but cosy restaurants and magnificent flowerbeds. It has a particular atmosphere – part traditional beer garden, part Victorian pleasure park, part (whisper it) Disneyland. But it isn't really until night falls, when the 100,000 specially made soft-glow light bulbs and over a million standard bulbs are switched on, and the scenery becomes a kaleidoscope of diffused colour (there is no neon here, and the place is a must-visit for lighting technicians from all over the world) that the magical transformation from amusement park to dreamland takes place.

But Tivoli is expensive, with a steep entrance fee (99kr), and extra (25kr-75kr) for the rides. What's more, Tivoli's many restaurants are among the dearest in the city.

HISTORY

Like most Copenhagen landmarks, Tivoli has royal roots. In 1841, King Christian VIII was vexed by the burgeoning civil unrest in his country and his increasingly untenable position as absolute monarch, and so he allowed the Danish architect Georg Carstensen to build the park as a distraction. 'When people amuse themselves they forget politics,' the king is reputed to have said. Carstensen, a self-made publishing magnate and son of a diplomat, was born in Algiers in 1812. Tivoli grew out of a carnival he arranged for his readers in Kongens Nytorv. Its success is thought to have swayed the king in favour of a permanent site for public pleasure. His new park would blend three main ingredients: light, fairy-tales and music, the king's only condition being that the park would not contain 'anything ignoble and degrading'. The original Tivoli, little changed today, was based on similar gardens then extant in Paris and London, and named after the little Italian town near Rome known for its fountains.

The park opened on 15 August 1843 and welcomed 16,000 visitors on its first day, Hans Christian Andersen among them. However, for Carstensen, the park's success was bittersweet. Buoyed by its popularity, he attempted to repeat the formula abroad, but failed abjectly.

Unlike many other amusement parks, Tivoli is now right in the centre of the city. But it wasn't always so. When it was built, the park stood in the countryside among fields dotted with cattle and crops, on land that was once part of Copenhagen's old fortifications, donated by the government. Today, Tivoli Lake is the model of picturesque charm – with flower borders, weeping willows and, at night, illuminated artificial dragonflies – but it used to be part of the city's defensive moat (the remains of which can be seen in the lakes of Botanisk Have Ørstedsparken and Østre Anlæg park).

IN THE KNOW
GAUGUIN'S DANISH PERIOD

Paul Gauguin lived in Copenhagen for one winter, at Gammel Kongevej 105 (long since demolished) in Frederiksberg. The impoverished artist had met a Danish woman, Mette Sofie Gad, in Paris in 1873; after marrying, they moved to his wife's home. Gauguin never got to grips with the weather, the coldness of the Danes or the suffocating ways of the bourgeoisie, though he did stay long enough to hold his first ever exhibition at the Kunstforeningen (Arts Society). Gauguin fathered five children with Mette during their nine-year marriage (the rest of which they spent in France), and has over 50 descendants living in Denmark. Several of his works are displayed in the **Ny Carlsberg Glyptotek** (see p54).

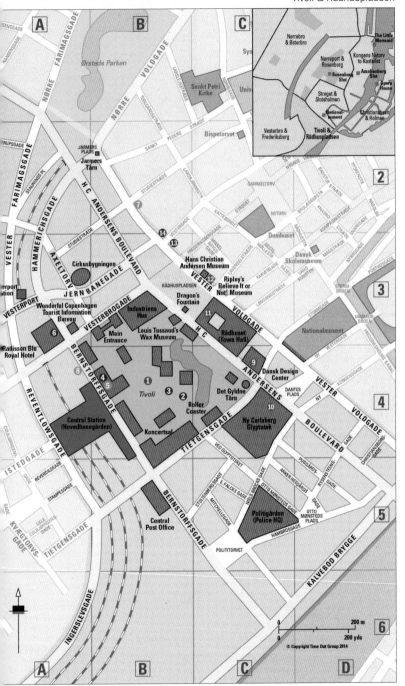

EXPLORE

In 1944, Tivoli's peace was shattered by the occupying forces of Nazi Germany, who were quick to recognise the significance of the park to the Danish people. They used it as a target for retaliatory attacks following the increased activity of the Danish Resistance. The main victim was the original Concert Hall, but within a week the resilient Danes had erected a tent in the grounds to replace it. A permanent, new hall (still standing) was built in 1956.

Many of the buildings constructed in Tivoli in the post-war era were seen by Denmark's architects as an opportunity to let their creative hair down, and so the park is packed with boisterous structures. Elsewhere, many might have been outlawed on grounds of taste, but in Tivoli they somehow seem appropriate.

A TOUR OF TIVOLI

There are three entrances to Tivoli: one is located opposite the main entrance to Hovedbanegården (Central Station); another lies across the road from the Ny Carlsberg Glyptotek; but by far the grandest is the main gate (on Vesterbrogade), a Renaissance-inspired confection decorated with Corinthian columns and a dome, dating from 1889.

On the right as you enter the main gate is a statue to the garden's architect, Georg Carstensen. In front, beside the extraordinary Moorish façade of Nimb Brasserie (breathtaking at night), is a Perspex fountain, with bubbling tubes, like a gigantic lava lamp. It was designed by the Nobel Prize-winning Danish physicist Niels Bohr. On your left is the Peacock Theatre; before you is Plænen (the Lawn), the open-air concert venue; beyond that is the 1956 Tivolis Koncertsal, a camp orgy of pastel colours.

There are over 30 rides to choose from in Tivoli, from tame roundabouts decorated with winsome HC Andersen characters, to the newer Star Flyer carousel and the mad exhilaration of Det Gyldne Tårn (The Golden Tower), a vertical drop built in 1999. The tower was likened by one sniffy critic to a high-tension pylon, but few rides unleash the butterflies with quite the force of this terrifying 63-metre (207-foot) vertical drop. Predictably, the structure – which, like much of Tivoli, is designed in a faux-Arabian style – has prompted accusations of blatant Disneyfication from the older generation of Tivoleans. They would prefer that time had stood still with the tepid wooden rollercoaster, which turns 100 in 2014, and is one of only seven rollercoasters in the world to still be operated by a brakeman.

All the traditional fun of the fair is here too, including shooting alleys, electronic arcade games, a hall of mirrors, bumper cars, a test-your-strength machine, an execrable chamber of horrors, the unintentionally creepy

Tivoli.

HC Andersen fairy-tale ride, and Det Muntre Køkken (The Crazy Kitchen), where you can vent pent-up frustration by hurling tennis balls at crockery targets. The Ferris wheel with its hot-air balloon seats, dating from 1943, is a traditional focus for courting couples.

Many visitors, particularly the elderly, who flock here in their thousands, come simply to enjoy the flora. Tivoli has 850 trees (lime, chestnut, weeping willow and elm) and many more flowers within its perimeter fence.

PERFORMANCE VENUES

Tivoli is a riotous collage of architectural styles, from Moorish palaces to Chinese towers, with everything in between. The oldest building in the park is the remarkable, outdoor, Chinese-style **Peacock Theatre**, designed by Vilhelm Dahlerup (also responsible for Det Kongelige Teater) in 1874. It stages classical pantomime in the tradition of *commedia dell'arte*. The performances are complex, hard-to-follow shows, starring Pierrot, Harlequin and Columbine, but are worth a look if only to see this extraordinary theatre, operated only by cords and pulleys. The theatre's 'curtain' is a peacock's tail feathers, which fold back to reveal the stage. The oriental theme is echoed in the **Chinese Pagoda** – a legacy of Georg Carstensen's peripatetic childhood, which fuelled a love of exotic cultures.

Plænen (*see left*) is Tivoli's largest venue (capacity 50,000). Most spectators stand in the open air before the circus-like stage. This is where returning Danish heroes (rare, but it does happen occasionally), such as the Olsen Brothers, are feted by the crowds, and where big events are celebrated. Performances –

EXPLORE

musical and otherwise (international acrobats are a speciality) – take place twice nightly. A popular innovation has been the Friday Rock Concerts; Danish bands usually headline, but each year an international star or two is booked as a treat, free of charge.

Every Saturday evening, there's a fireworks display, and throughout the summer, you can also catch parades and performances by the Tivoli Garden Guard, a children's marching band, founded in 1844, and made up of 100 or so local boys aged nine to 16. The Guard is on holiday for two weeks in mid July.

The renowned **Tivolis Koncertsal** (*see p177*), which seats 1,900, is home to the Sjælland Symphony Orchestra; visiting orchestras, ballet companies, ensembles and soloists of world repute also play here. You'll recognise the hall by the row of Danish flags along its roof.

Sights & Museums

Tivoli
Vesterbrogade 3 (33 15 10 01, ticket centre 33 15 10 12, www.tivoli.dk). Train København H. **Open** *Mid June-mid Aug* 11am-midnight Mon-Thur, Sun; 11am-1am Fri, Sat. *Mid Apr-mid June, mid Aug-mid Sept* 11am-11pm Mon-Thur, Sun; 11am-midnight Fri, Sat. *Halloween* varies. *Christmas Market* (late Nov-30 Dec) 11am-10pm Mon-Thur, Sun; 11am-midnight Fri, Sat. Closed 24 & 25 Dec. *Ticket centre* 11am-8pm daily. **Admission** 99kr; free under-7s. Multi-ride tickets & packages are also available. **Map** p49 B4 ❶

Restaurants

Kähler i Tivoli
Tivoli, Vesterbrogade 3 (53 73 84 84, www.kahler-i-tivoli.com). Train København H. **Open** 11am-10pm Mon-Thur, Sun; 11am-12.30am Fri; 11am-midnight Sat during Tivoli season. **Set meal** 399kr 3 courses, 599kr 5 courses. **Map** p49 B4 ❷ **Danish**
Danish food meets Danish design in this new concept café-restaurant, which serves innovative sandwiches and three- or five-course dinner menus that offer the likes of roast cod or pork with crackling. Kähler is one of Denmark's best-established ceramics brands, and its pottery and candle-holders can be bought from the restaurant, while Danish design classics, such as Finn Juhl chairs, feature as part of the interior design.

★ Madklubben Grill Royal
Tivoli, Vesterbrogade 3 (33 75 07 55, www.madklubben.dk/grill-royal-tivoli). Train København H. **Main courses** 100kr-250kr. **Open** noon-10pm daily during Tivoli season. **Map** p49 B4 ❸ **Modern Danish**

A contemporary Danish bistro for the wallet-conscious isn't something you come across too often in Copenhagen, especially once you throw in drinks, so Madklubben is a welcome addition to the scene. The conservatory dining room is typically Danish, in that it's smart yet casual, furnished with canteen-style tables sympathetically lit to define spaces, and with wood panelling softening the effect. It's boisterous enough for a large group, yet fun enough for a date and, most importantly, the food is good. The menu changes monthly, but usually features classics such as steak on jerusalem artichoke purée, and catch of the day with roasted fennel. Small plates and children's portions are available, and *smørrebrod* features on the lunch menu.
Other locations Pilestræde 23, Indre By (33 13 33 34); Kongens Nytorv 26, Indre By (38 41 41 64); Admiralgade 25, Indre By (33 13 33 77); Store Kongensgade 66, Frederiksstaden (33 32 32 34); Vesterbrogade 62, Vesterbro (38 41 41 43).

Nimb Brasserie
Nimb Hotel, Bernstorffsgade 5 (88 70 00 10, www.nimb.dk). Train København H. **Open** 7am-11am, noon-3.30pm, 5-10pm daily. **Main courses** 175kr-235kr. **Set meal** 360kr 3 courses. **Map** p49 B4 ❹ **European**
Previously run by Thomas Herman, this restaurant at the chic boutique hotel Nimb (*see p217*) was refurbished in 2012, turning it from a New Nordic special-occasion resturant into a more relaxed space serving European – and especially French – brasserie classics for breakfast, lunch and dinner. Main courses from the lunch and dinner menus include the likes of grilled rib-eye steak with sauce bordelaise, guinea fowl with asparagus, peas and sauce blanquette, and baked cod with artichokes, broccoli and sauce beurre blanc.

Cafés & Bars

For a decent pint at Tivoli, head to the **Bryggeriet Apollo** (Vesterbrogade 3, 33 12 33 13, www.bryggeriet.dk), Copenhagen's first microbrewery, situated next to the main Tivoli entrance. The food is fairly standard tourist fodder.

Andersen Bakery & Café Nimb Tivoli
Bernstorffsgade 5 (33 75 07 35, www.andersen-danmark.dk). Train København H. **Open** *Bakery* 6.30am-7pm Mon-Fri; 7.30am-7pm Sat, Sun. *Café* 10am-6.30pm daily. *Hot dogs* 11am-6.30pm daily. **Map** p49 B4 ❺
Started by Japanese baker Shunsake Takaki in Hiroshima in 1967, the Andersen Bakery mini-chain – now run by his children – returned to Takaki's original place of inspiration in the 1980s, and is now something of a Copenhagen landmark. As well as the traditional Danish breads, cakes and pastries, the place is also known for its gourmet hot

EXPLORE

dogs – own-made sausages wrapped in brioche-style bread and served with remoulade – and its extensive brunch menu.

Other locations Østerbrogade 103, Østerbro (39 29 12 65); Gammel Kongevej 148, Frederiksberg (33 22 44 34).

Shops & Services

Tivoli's **Christmas Market** has been a fixture since 1994, with stalls selling *glögg* (mulled red wine), traditional Scandinavian decorations and candles, chocolates and festive foodstuffs, and craft-style gifts, from late November to 30 December. If you think Tivoli is saccharine in summer, wait till you get a load of this.

Tivoli also has a branch of **Illums Bolighus** (Vesterbrogade 3, 33 91 18 45; *see p76*), selling homewares and gifts from Danish and Scandinavian brands, such as Royal Copenhagen, Georg Jensen and Design House Stockholm.

AROUND VESTERPORT & CENTRAL STATION

From Tivoli's main gates (and, in fact, from just about anywhere in Copenhagen), you can see Arne Jacobsen's 22-storey **Radisson Blu Royal Hotel** (*see p217*). It dates from 1960, and with his customary all-encompassing attention to detail, Jacobsen designed not only

EXPLORE

COPENHAGEN'S SAUSAGE WAGONS

The city's ubiquitous 'pølsevogne' are a Danish institution.

Cute, caravan-like mobile or stationary stalls, with their fold-out windows and counters, have dotted Copenhagen since the 1920s, and their bright red *pølser* (sausages), served in a fluffy white bun, are still a popular snack for locals. The long, thin hot dogs are available in a variety of guises – poking out of a hollowed-out roll, or laid on a long roll sliced lengthways in half, or from a paper plate with bread on the side – and always with plenty of condiments, such as the Danish version of remoulade, as well as mustard, ketchup, pickles and onions.

Some 70 *pølsevogne* are dotted around the city's streets and squares, and you'll come across one without difficulty in the centre. Yet the wagons have undergone a sharp decline in the past decade (they numbered around 500 from the 1950s to the 1990s) due to increased competition from international chains and more 'exotic' takeaway options, as well as increasing health concerns on the part of the Danish public; made of processed and dyed meat, with a sky-high fat and salt content, the humble *pølse* can hardly be held up as a health food. Yet many Danes still flock to the remaining hot-dog wagons.

One of the city's most famous and traditional hot-dog stands is **Harry's Place** (Nordre Fasanvej 269, 35 81 26 69), in the outskirts of Nørrebro. In business for over

half a century, and with two Danish prime ministers on its customer roll call of honour, this is as good a place as any to sample the national snack, with the traditional accompaniment, cold chocolate milk. The seriously hungry should opt for Harry's famously huge 'Børge' sausage.

If you'd like to try the local fast food without the excess cholesterol, there is an alternative. The popular **DØP** (Den Økologiske Pølsemand – 'organic sausage man') *pølsevogne* can be found beside the Round Tower and near the Church of the Holy Spirit on Strøget, and sells a new, higher-quality breed of *pølse* in line with more health-conscious times. DØP's hot dogs are 100 per cent organic, its buns made of sourdough bread with rye and linseeds – bringing the traditional *pølsevogn* into a brave new era.

the exterior, but the interior too – right down to the cutlery still used in the restaurant.

Across the road from the hotel, you'll find the **Visit Copenhagen Tourist Information Bureau** (see p234). A little further down the street stands **Hovedbanegården** (Central Station), from where you can catch trains to the airport, the rest of the country and beyond. The station, which dates from 1911, has a well-equipped centre for InterRailers, complete with showers and lockers, not to mention several food outlets, a bank, a police station and a bookshop.

Close by is the **Copenhagen Plaza** hotel (see p224) with its wood-panelled **Library Bar** (see right), redolent of an English gentlemen's club (this being Denmark, women are admitted).

Immediately north of the main entrance to Tivoli is Copenhagen's cinema district. Here you'll find several cinemas, all within a few minutes' walk (see p161).

Restaurants

★ Alberto K

Radisson Blu Royal Hotel, Hammerichsgade 1 (33 42 61 61, www.alberto-k.com). Train København H. **Open** 6pm-midnight Mon-Sat. **Set meal** 750kr-1,900kr. **Map** p49 A3 ❻

Italian/Danish

Named after the first general manager of the Arne Jacobsen-designed SAS Royal Hotel, this magnificent modern Italian/Danish restaurant ranks among the best of the city's upscale eateries. One of the highlights of eating here is, of course, being surrounded by Jacobsen's famous Swan and Egg chairs, but the food's pretty good too, featuring dishes such as jerusalem artichokes, ham and truffles, or halibut with leek, parsley and mussel sauce, prepared by Bocuse d'Or silver medallist Jeppe Foldager. The 360-degree view of the city from the 20th-floor windows helps too. Prices are relatively high, but portions are large, and the food and service are exceptional.

Cafés & Bars

Bjørgs

Vester Voldgade 19 (33 14 53 20, www.cafebjorgs.dk). Train Vesterport. **Open** 9am-midnight Mon-Wed; 9am-1am Thur; 9am-2am Fri; 10am-2am Sat; 10am-midnight Sun. **Map** p49 B2 ❼

This L-shaped café-bar does a passable impression of an Edward Hopper painting, with its large windows, red sofas and mirrored walls. Although it's from the same stable as Sommersko (see p62) and Dan Turèll (see p63), Bjørgs is less pretentious, and serves as both a local bar and a trendy Saturday-night stop-off.

★ Library Bar

Copenhagen Plaza, Bernstorffsgade 4 (33 14 92 62, www.librarybar.dk). Train København H. **Open** 4pm-midnight Mon-Thur; 4pm-1.30am Fri, Sat. **Map** p49 A4 ❽

Though members of some of the more salubrious gentlemen's clubs in London's St James's will be underwhelmed by the scale of this quiet and faux-exclusive bar within the Copenhagen Plaza hotel, most visitors are taken by its characterful wood panelling, crystal chandeliers, book-lined walls and chesterfield-style sofas. It was once voted one of the finest gentlemen's bars in the world by *Forbes* magazine. Cocktails start at 80kr. If you've any money left over, you may care to nibble on sybaritic snacks such as oysters and parma ham.

RÅDHUSPLADSEN & NY CARLSBERG GLYPTOTEK

Tivoli's neighbour to the east is the usually frenetic **Rådhuspladsen** (Town Hall Square). Though the square is less architecturally appealing than Kongens Nytorv at the other end of Strøget, Denmark's answer to Times Square and Piccadilly Circus is more friendly to pedestrians and, at night, when the neon adverts on the surrounding offices are lit up, quite spectacular. This square, stretching out from the Rådhuset (Town Hall), bustles constantly with a mixture of commuters (the city's bus terminus is here), shoppers, sightseers, *pølse* (Danish hot dog) sellers and, at weekends and holidays, street performers, gatherings and protests. The square is an important focal point for Copenhageners and Danes as a whole (Denmark's football matches are shown here on a big screen during World Cups, for instance). It is also the prime gathering point for New Year's Eve celebrations. A gigantic Christmas tree is lit up in the square on the first Sunday of Advent.

Rådhuspladsen was originally a hay market located outside the medieval city walls, and is also where the last western city gate stood until the middle of the 19th century. All that remains of the medieval fortifications today is **Jarmers Tårn**, a small ruin located on a roundabout in Jarmers Plads (at the north end of Vester Voldgade). In 1888, the square hosted a million visitors at a huge exhibition of industry, agriculture and art. At the time, the 'square' was in fact a shell shape, like the famous main piazza in Siena, but the pressures of the internal combustion engine soon saw its corners squared off.

There's lots to see in and around this area. On HC Andersens Boulevard is a large statue of, guess who? In front of that stands the striking **Dragon Fountain**, by Joachim Skovgaard. Nearby is a small carved stone

EXPLORE

pillar that marks the centre or 'zero point' of Copenhagen. And high on the corner of the Unibank building on HC Andersens Boulevard and Vesterbrogade is one of the city's quirkiest talking points: a barometer erected in 1936 and designed by Danish artist E Utzon-Frank, featuring a girl on a bicycle (if it's fair) or under an umbrella (if it's not).

Towering over the opposite side of Rådhuset is a pillar crowned by a bronze statue of two Vikings blowing *lurs* (S-shaped bronze horns). These are similar to the ones you can see in the Nationalmuseet. The statue, by Siegfried Wagner, was erected in 1914. Next to the pillar is the elegant façade of the Anton Rosen-designed **Palace Hotel** (*see p217*).

Next door is **Ripley's Believe It or Not! Museum**, part of a worldwide chain of freak shows based on an idea by the American showman Robert Ripley. Housed (or rather crammed) within the same complex is a pitiful **Hans Christian Andersen** exhibition, cobbled together to coincide with the 200th anniversary of his birth in 2005, and featuring fibreglass reconstructions of 'olde world' Odense streets and a few factoids about the great man's life. And little else. Bearing in mind that Copenhagen was Andersen's home from the age of 14 onwards, it is sad bordering on outrageous that it is the only permanent exhibition about the writer in the city.

Rådhuset, situated on the southern side of Rådhuspladsen, is the city's administrative and political heart, as well as a venue for exhibitions and concerts. Denmark's second-tallest tower (105.6 metres/346 feet; the tallest, is part of Christiansborg Slot), located on its east side, is almost incidental to the decorative splendour of this, the sixth town hall in Copenhagen's history.

To the south-east of Tivoli and Rådhuspladsen is the **Ny Carlsberg Glyptotek**, which houses a breathtaking line-up of ancient sculptures and the largest collection of Etruscan art outside Italy, as well as an exceptional array of more recent Danish and French paintings and sculpture.

A little further up HC Andersens Boulevard is the beautiful, five-storey, 86-million-kroner **Dansk Design Center** (Danish Design Centre).

Sights & Museums

Dansk Design Center

HC Andersens Boulevard 27 (33 69 33 69, www.ddc.dk). Train København H. **Open** 9am-5pm Mon-Fri. **Admission** free. **Map** p49 C4 **❾**

The Danish Design Centre was designed by Henning Larsen (as was the nearby Glyptotek extension), and opened in January 2000. The centre's focus is now on dialogue between industry organisations, such

as Index: Design to Improve Life, and the Danish Fashion Institute (both of which are based in the building) rather than on informing the general public. This has led to the closure of the museum on Danish design icons, but there's still a café, complete with Danish furniture, and a small shop that sells books and Danish design items.

★ Ny Carlsberg Glyptotek

Dantes Plads 7 (33 41 81 41, www.glyptoteket.dk). Train København H. **Open** 11am-5pm Tue-Sun. **Admission** 75kr; free under-18s. Free to all Sun. **Map** p49 C4 **❿**

The original *glyptotek* (sculpture collection) was donated to the city in 1888 by brewer/philanthropist Carl Jacobsen (son of IC Jacobsen, the founder of the Carlsberg brewery) and his wife Ottilia. He intended the museum to have 'a beauty all its own, to which the people of the city would feel themselves irresistibly drawn.' His vision has been financed, run and expanded by the Ny Carlsberg Foundation for more than a century, and is housed in a building rich in architectural delights that was specially designed for the original collection by Vilhelm Dahlerup and Hack Kampmann. A three-year renovation and expansion project was finished in 2006, resulting in better access for disabled visitors; a revamped cellar level; and the whole collection being displayed in brighter surroundings. The highlight of the old building is the glass-domed Winter Garden – a steamy palm house bursting with monster subtropical plants and graced by Kai Nielsen's beautiful fountain piece, *Water Mother with Children*. The Winter Garden's café is a popular meeting place.

The Glyptotek's thousands of pieces can be roughly divided into two groups: ancient Mediterranean; and 18th- and 19th-century French and Danish. The first four rooms are dedicated to the oldest pieces, some dating back 5,000 years (the Egyptian hippopotamus is a crowd favourite). The exhibits proceed to trace the history of sculpture from the Sumerians, Assyrians, Persians and Phoenicians, through to a collection of ancient Greek pieces (one of the best in Europe) and some highly entertaining, privately commissioned Roman busts. Jacobsen's Etruscan collection – including bronzes, vases, and stone and terracotta sculptures – is another highlight.

The French painting collection is housed in Henning Larsen's intriguing extension. It includes 35 works by the post-Impressionist Paul Gauguin (*see p48* **In the Know**) and one of only three complete sets of Degas bronzes in the world. There are also paintings by the Impressionist movement's leading lights, including Manet, Renoir, Monet and Pissarro, and a remarkable self-portrait by Cézanne. The rest of the post-Impressionist movement is represented by Van Gogh, Toulouse-Lautrec and Bonnard.

Over 30 works by Auguste Rodin dominate the French sculpture rooms. Another surprise awaits in the collection of Danish sculpture: for those who think that Danish sculpture began and ended with

Bertel Thorvaldsen, other leading lights (Dahl, Købke and Eckersberg) are also represented, though the collection of the Danish Golden Age (1815-50) is surpassed by those of Statens Museum for Kunst and Den Hirschsprungske Samling (*see p91*).

Rådhuset

Rådhuspladsen (33 66 25 82/83, www.kk.dk). Train København H. **Open** *9am-4pm Mon-Fri; 9.30am-1pm Sat. Guided tours in English 1pm Mon-Fri; 10am Sat. Rådhuset Tower tour 11am, 2pm Mon-Fri; noon Sat.* **Admission** *Guided tour 30kr. Rådhuset Tower tour 20kr. Jens Olsens Verdensur free.* **Map** p49 C3 ⑪
Completed in 1905, Rådhuset has been the site of numerous elections; home to as many city administrations; endured occupation by the Nazis during World War II; and welcomed the returning football heroes from the 1992 European Championships.

At first glance, the building – inspired, like the square, by its counterpart in Siena – looks imposing, monolithic and a little bit dull, but at close quarters this National Romantic masterpiece by architect Martin Nyrop reveals its witty, sometimes gruesome, but invariably exuberant architectural detail. There's a balcony above the front door, and above that a golden statue *Bishop Absalon* by HW Bissen. Higher up, lining the front of the roof, stand six watchmen, separated by the city flagpole (watch for a swallow-tailed flag on special occasions, such as the Queen's birthday). This rises from the city's coat of arms, presented in 1661 by King Frederik III in thanks for the people's support during a city siege. Across the façade are countless gargoyles, reliefs and individually crafted stone and iron figures.

Ny Carlsberg Glyptotek.

Inside, Rådhuset's endless corridors, halls, council chambers and meeting rooms offer a decorative feast. Highlights include busts of HC Andersen, the physicist Niels Bohr, Professor Nyrop and sculptor Bertel Thorvaldsen; the library; the banqueting hall; and Jens Olsen's World Clock. The last is a horological masterpiece that cost one million kroner to build (and 27 years to make – it was first set in 1955). It's incredibly accurate, losing only milliseconds each century. It displays the local time, sidereal time (gauged by the motion of the earth relative to the fixed background of distant stars, rather than the sun), firmament and celestial pole movement, the movement of the planets, and sunrises and sunsets. The clock is in a room on the right by the main door.

Ripley's Believe It Or Not! Museum

Rådhuspladsen 57 (33 91 89 91, www.ripleys.dk). Train København H. **Open** *Mid June-Aug 10am-10pm daily. Sept-mid June 10am-6pm Mon-Thur, Sun; 10am-8pm Fri, Sat.* **Admission** *85kr; 43kr-68kr reductions; free under-4s.* **Map** p49 C3 ⑫
The grotesque bric-a-brac on display here includes two-headed animals, voodoo dolls and Papua New Guinean penis sheaths. A basic exhibition on Hans Christian Andersen is in the same building.

Restaurants, Cafés & Bars

The area around Rådhuspladsen lacks decent places to eat, with a few fast-food outlets, average sushi joints, and *pølsevogne* (*see p52* **Copenhagen's Sausage Wagons**), but not much else. The café at the **Dansk Design Center** (*see p54*) serves good coffee, while the one at **Ny Carlsberg Glyptotek** (*see p54*) offers brunch dishes, *smørrebrod*, salads and cakes, and is set in the lovely Winter Garden.

Shops & Services

Accord

Vestergade 37 (70 15 16 17, www.accord.dk). Train København H. **Open** *10am-6pm Mon-Thur; 10am-7pm Fri; 10am-4pm Sat; noon-5pm Sun.* **Map** p49 B3 ⑬ **Books & music**
Stacks of old and new vinyl, including a whole floor of 78s, along with hundreds of CDs and DVDs. Techno, house, rock, pop and world music are the main genres. Prices are competitive too.
Other location Nørrebrogade 88-90, Nørrebro (70 15 16 17).

Politikens Boghallen

Rådhuspladsen 37 (30 67 28 06 , www.politikens boghal.dk). Train København H. **Open** *9am-6pm Mon, Tue; 9am-9pm Wed; 9am-7pm Thur, Fri; 10am-4pm Sat.* **Map** p49 B3 ⑭ **Books & music**
Along with Arnold Busck (*see p70*), this is one of the city's biggest bookshops, with a huge range of English-language titles available.

EXPLORE

Strøget & Slotsholmen

Strøget might be the best-known street in Copenhagen, but you won't always find its name on maps. That's because Strøget (meaning 'stripe') is actually made up of five streets – Østergade, Amagertorv, Nygade, Vimmelskaftet and Frederiksberggade – running more than a kilometre from Kongens Nytorv at its eastern end to Rådhuspladsen in the west.

Around the north-eastern side of Strøget lie some of the city's best shopping streets, while excellent restaurants and bars can be found in the Latin Quarter and the vibrant area of Pisserenden, to the north-west. Head south of Strøget for the laid-back parallel street known as Strædet, and further south still for the island of Slotsholmen. The latter is where Bishop Absalon built his fortress in the 12th century, and a city was born.

Gråbrødretorv.

Don't Miss

1 **Rundetårn** The historic Round Tower has great views of the city (p58).

2 **Thorvaldsens Museum** Atmospheric museum for Denmark's most famous sculptor (p83).

3 **Gråbrødretorv** A lively square full of colourful buildings (p66).

4 **Grønnegade district** Scandi fashion and design shops galore (p58).

5 **National Museum** The place to swot up on Danish history (p82).

EXPLORE

EXPLORE

GETTING YOUR BEARINGS

Broadly speaking, Strøget becomes more downmarket as you approach Rådhuspladsen at the western end, with the posh shops, including Gucci and Prada, as well as global chains such as Urban Outfitters and Topshop, clustered at the eastern end towards Kongens Nytorv. The 'posh watershed' is Amagertorv, where you'll find the Royal Copenhagen stores. The middle of Strøget from Amagertorv to Gammeltorv and Nytorv is middlebrow, dotted with the likes of H&M and Zara, while beyond there is a touristy mix of kebab shops and souvenir shops. Keep in mind, though, that 'downmarket' in Copenhagen is still pretty presentable.

Despite its cosmopolitan feel and stylish shopfronts, Strøget's medieval origins have ensured that it has retained an intimate charm. In fact, it makes Oxford Street or the Champs-Elysées look like motorways by comparison. And it helps make Copenhagen one of the most user-friendly shopping cities in the world.

KØBMAGERGADE & THE GRØNNEGADE QUARTER

Starting from Kongens Nytorv, at Strøget's eastern end, the first sight you arrive at is the **Guinness World Records Museum**. Part of a chain, the Guinness attraction lures in the passing crowds. Kids seem to like it, though, and the fact that the **Mystic Exploratorie** (a mix of science and the supernatural) moved here is a bonus.

Head north-west from Østergade to the area that surrounds **Grønnegade**, one of Copenhagen's best shopping districts. The streets situated between Grønnegade and **Købmagergade** (Strøget's pedestrianised tributary) – Pilestræde, Grønnegade, Ny Adelgade and Ny Østergade – are eminently wanderable, and home to lots of excellent independent fashion shops, with Scandinavian brands dominating. **Kronprinsensgade** is home to some particularly good shops and cafés, including Copenhagen's venerated tea emporium and café **AC Perches Thehandel**, which sells lovely tea caddies.

On Købmagergade itself is the **Post & Tele Museum**, a surprisingly well-presented museum dedicated to the 400-year history of

Denmark's communications services. Visit the rooftop café, with views of the old town to rival the Rundetårn's (and here there's a lift). It's open afternoons, and late on Wednesdays, when it has a Danish and international menu.

A little further up is Købmagergade's other main draw: the **Rundetårn** (Round Tower). Completed in 1642 at the behest of Christian IV (it was his last major building project), the red-brick Rundetårn was originally intended as an observatory for the nearby university, and is still the oldest functioning observatory in Europe. Christian is commemorated on the front in a wrought-iron lattice: the letters RFP stand for the famously lecherous king's unlikely motto, *Regna Firmat Pietas* – 'Piety Strengthens the Realm'.

Just beside the tower, at its southern side, is one of the city's most popular *pølsevogne* (hot-dog stands): the **DØP** stall is known for its healthier, organic hot dogs, served in sourdough bread (*see p52*). Behind the tower stands **Trinitatiskirke** (Trinity Church). Opposite the Rundetårn you'll find **Regensen**, built in 1616 as a student hall of residence for the nearby university, and still in use as such today. Around the corner, on Krystalgade, is the city's **Synagoge** (synagogue), dating from 1833.

Sights & Museums

Guinness World Records Museum & Mystic Exploratorie

Østergade 16 (33 32 31 31, www.guinness.dk). Metro Kongens Nytorv. **Open** *Mid June-Aug* 10am-10pm daily. *Sept-mid June* 10am-6pm Mon-Thur, Sun; 10am-8pm Fri, Sat. **Admission** *Museum* 85kr; 43kr-68kr reductions; free under-4s. *Mystic Exploratorie* 67kr; 34kr-54kr reductions; free under-4s. **Map** p60 C5 ❶
This basic museum informs visitors about astounding – as well as sometimes banal – record-breaking facts, such as the number of students to have ever fitted into a phone box. There are interactive exhibits for children.

FREE Post & Tele Museum

Købmagergade 37 (33 41 09 00, www.ptt-museum.dk). Metro/train Nørreport. **Open** 10am-4pm daily. **Admission** free. **Map** p60 C4 ❷
This sweet museum looks at the 400-year old story of Denmark's communications services, exploring how people used to communicate in the era before computers, and how modern technology evolved within the industry. Philatelists will be thrilled to hear about the museum's huge collection of Danish stamps. The rooftop café (open afternoons) offers panoramic views of the surrounding area.

★ Rundetårn

Købmagergade 52A (33 73 03 73, www.rundetaarn.dk). Metro/train Nørreport.

IN THE KNOW INDRE BY

The words 'Indre By' mean Inner City, and this term is used to indicate the central (and most historic) area of Copenhagen, bounded by the Lakes and the Harbour.

Rice Market. *See p62.*

Open *Tower* Late May-late Sept 10am-8pm daily. Late Sept-late May 10am-6pm daily. *Observatory* times vary; see website for details. **Admission** 25kr; 5kr reductions; free under-5s. **Map** p60 C3 ❸

The Round Tower is unique in European architecture for its cobbled spiral walkway that winds seven and a half times round its core for 209 metres (686 feet), almost to the top of the tower, which is 35 metres (114 feet) above the city. There are only a few stairs at the very top, from where the view, as you'd expect, is superb. Peter the Great rode all the way to the top in 1716 (the Tsarina followed in a carriage); while a car is said to have driven up in 1902. Halfway up, an exhibition space (formerly the university library hall) has a changing programme of artistic, scientific and historical displays. The observatory at the top is sometimes open, with an astronomer on hand to explain what you can see through the telescope. The Rundetårn was deemed such a significant building that, in the 18th century, the Royal Danish Academy of Sciences used it as the main reference point for a survey of Denmark.

FREE Trinitatiskirke

Pilestræde 67 (33 37 65 40, www.trinitatiskirke.dk). Metro/train Nørreport. **Open** 9.30am-4.30pm Mon-Sat. *High Mass* 10.30am Sun. **Admission** free. **Map** p60 C3 ❹

Trinity Church was erected in 1637, and features a Baroque altar by Friedrich Ehbisch, as well as a three-faced rococo clock from 1757.

Restaurants

Restaurant L'Alsace

Ny Østergade 9 (33 14 57 43, www.alsace.dk). Metro Kongens Nytorv. **Open** 11.30am-midnight Mon-Sat. **Main courses** 154kr-298kr. **Set menu** 320kr 2 courses, 360kr 3 courses, 410kr 4 courses, 515kr 5 courses. **Map** p60 C5 ❺ **French**

You can hardly move for posh and pricey French restaurants in this part of town, but L'Alsace is more authentic than most, serving such Alsatian delicacies as foie gras, goose and choucroute, along with excellent cheeses and wines. This curious venue combines a whitewashed cellar with a rough and ready conservatory, but it still manages to evoke the crucial *hyggelige* atmosphere so valued by the Danes.

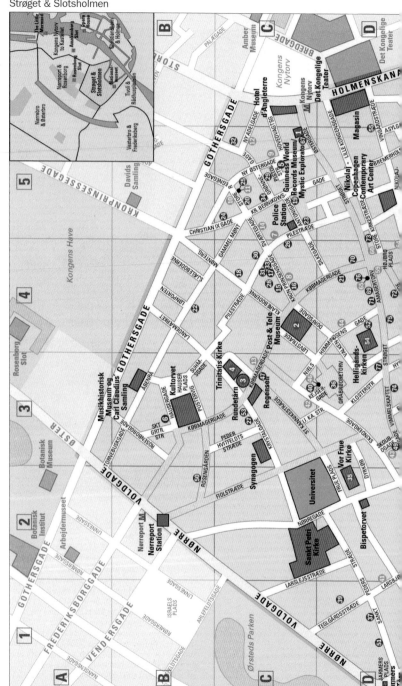

Strøget & Slotsholmen

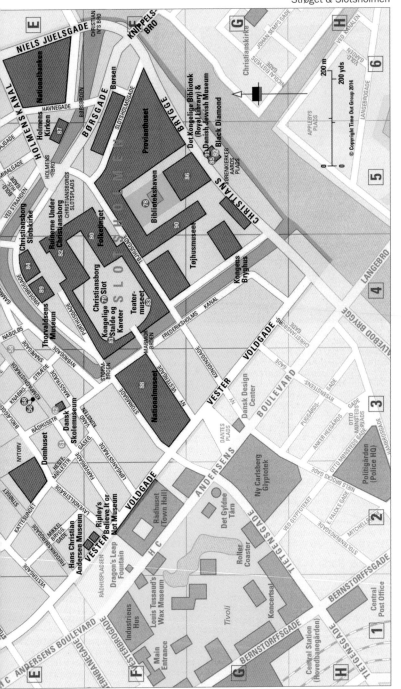

EXPLORE

NIELS JUELSGADE

CHRISTIAN IV'S BRO

KNIPPELS-BRO

Christianskirke

Nationalbanken

HAVNEGADE

Holmens Kirken

HOLMENS BRO

BØRSGADE

Børsen

SLOTSHOLMSGADE

Provianthuset

BRYGGE

CHRISTIANS

Det Kongelige Bibliotek (Royal Library) & Danish Jewish Museum

Black Diamond

SØRENKIERKEG. AARDS PLADS

Ruinerne Under Christiansborg

Christiansborg Slotskirke

CHRISTIANSBORGS SLOTSPLADS

Folketinget

Bibliotekshaven

Tøjhusmuseet

Kongens Bryhus

Thorvaldsens Museum

Christiansborg Slot

Kongelige Stalde og Karater

Teatermuseet

FREDERIKSHOLMS KANAL

Dansk Design Center

LANGEBRO

VESTER VOLDGADE

VESTER BOULEVARD

Nationalmuseet

Domhuset

Dansk Skolemuseum

Ripley's Believe It or Not Museum

HESTE MØLLESTR.

Politigården (Police HQ)

Ny Carlsberg Glyptotek

H C ANDERSENS

VOLDGADE

Hans Christian Andersen Museum

VESTER

Rådhuset (Town Hall)

Det Gyldne Tårn

Industriens Hus

Louis Tussaud's Wax Museum

Dragon's Leap Fountain

RÅDHUSPLADSEN

Roller Coaster

Koncertsal

Tivoli

Main Entrance

Central Station (Hovedbanegården)

BERNSTORFFSGADE

Central Post Office

H C ANDERSENS BOULEVARD

200 m
200 yds

© Copyright Time Out Group 2014

42°Raw.

Rice Market

Hausergade 38 (35 35 75 30, www.ricemarket.dk).
Metro/train Nørreport. **Open** noon-midnight
(kitchen closes 10pm) daily. **Main courses**
75kr-185kr. **Map** p60 B3 ❻ Oriental

This cute little basement restaurant has become a
firm fixture on the city's Asian dining scene, which
is understandable since it comes from the same
hands as Michelin-starred Kiin Kiin (*see p137*).
Consequently, it gets rammed, especially at weekends. Tucked into an L-shaped space, the main dining section is pedestrian, with standard tables and
chairs given a lift by outsize raffia lanterns; the place
to be is in one of the draped-off, private cubicles in
the VIP section. Food consists of crowd-pleasing
classics such as Chinese steamed dumplings; Thai
soups, salads and curries; satay, tempura and stir-
fries. It's all good-quality fare, though ordering
lots of starters and eating your way around Asia,
tapas-style, is the way to go. *Photos p59.*

Cafés & Bars

★ 42°Raw

Pilestræde 32 (32 12 32 10, www.42raw.dk).
Metro Kongens Nytorv. **Open** 10am-8pm Mon-Fri;
10am-6pm Sat; 11am-5pm Sun. **Map** p60 C5 ❼

Devoted to raw cuisine (no food sold here is heated
to more than 42°C – the temperature at which
enzymes are destroyed), 42°Raw is a new and popular concept for Copenhagen. Smoothies and juices,
cookies made with 'raw' chocolate, super-fresh

salads, and dishes such as an unusual but very tasty
version of lasagne, are served in the petite, slick
space. It's also good as a healthy takeaway spot.

Café Sommersko

Kronprinsensgade 6 (33 14 81 89, www.cafe
sommersko.dk). Metro Kongens Nytorv. **Open**
8am-midnight Mon-Thur, Sun; 8am-3am Fri;
8am-2am Sat. **Map** p60 C4 ❽

Sommersko was one of Copenhagen's café pioneers –
it opened in 1976, when a strong café culture hadn't
yet reached the city. Things have moved on since
then, but its wonderfully glamorous kitsch decor
(mirror mosaics, baby grand piano, red vinyl banquettes) is distinctive, which is more than you can
say for many cafés. The menu is predictable (mussels, burgers, salads), however, and service often
leaves plenty to be desired.

Café Victor

Ny Østergade 8 (33 13 36 13, www.cafevictor.dk).
Metro Kongens Nytorv. **Open** *Café* 8am-1am
Mon-Wed; 8am-2am Thur-Sat; 11am-midnight
Sun. *Restaurant* 11.30am-4pm, 6-10.30pm Mon-
Thur; 11.30am-4pm, 6-11pm Fri, Sat; 6-10.30pm
Sun. **Map** p60 C5 ❾

A Copenhagen institution, Café Victor is one of the
city's prime see-and-be-seen venues for celebrities,
football stars, politicians, journalists and the jet set.
At midday, it's packed with lunching ladies, wrapped
in fur or Gucci. The food is ultra-classic French fare
– lobster a l'américaine, sole meunière – of a high

EXPLORE

standard. However, you don't come here just for the food, but to soak up the atmosphere, marvel at the art deco interior and do battle with the supercilious staff. If you don't fancy a full meal, half a dozen oysters at the bar, accompanied by a glass of champagne, will give you a taste of the Victor experience.

Dan Turèll
Store Regnegade 3 (33 14 10 47, www.danturell.dk). Metro Kongens Nytorv. **Open** 8am-midnight Mon-Thur; 8am-2am Fri, Sat; 10am-6pm Sun. **Map** p60 C5 ⑩
One of Copenhagen's most famous cafés, Dan Turèll is named after a well-known 20th-century Danish poet, writer and iconoclast and has been one of *the* places to visit on a Friday or Saturday night for as long as anyone can remember. But the food is middling (salads and sandwiches during the day), the staff can be snobby and the drinks are expensive.

Det Elektriske Hjørne
Store Regnegade 12 (33 13 91 92, www. elhjoernet.dk). Metro Kongens Nytorv. **Open** 11am-midnight Mon; 11am-1am Tue; 11am-2am Wed; 11am-3am Thur; 11am-5am Fri, Sat. *Food served* 11.30am-8pm Mon-Fri. **Map** p60 C5 ⑪
This grand corner café, with an ornate frontage dating from the 1890s, is well located, with dozens of the city's best bars and restaurants nearby. Wisely, the Hjørne doesn't attempt to outdo its neighbours on the food front, but instead trades on its welcome

spaciousness and comfortable sofas. The basement has table football, darts and pool.

★ Palæ Bar
Ny Adelgade 5 (33 12 54 71, www.palaebar.dk). Metro Kongens Nytorv. **Open** 11am-1am Mon-Thur; 11am-3am Fri, Sat; 4pm-1am Sun. **No credit cards. Map** p60 C5 ⑫
This esteemed boho *bodega*, just around the corner from the Hotel d'Angleterre, tends to appeal to more mature drinkers who prefer its unrushed, understated mood and rich, old-fashioned Parisian-style boozer atmosphere. Popular with journalists and writers, Palæ exudes a kind of old-world intellectualism (or so it seems, after a few glasses of wine).

★ Studenterhuset
Copenhagen University, Købmagergade 52 (35 32 38 61, www.studenterhuset.com). Metro/train Nørreport. **Open** 8am-midnight Mon, Tue; 8am-1am Wed, Thur; 8am-3am Fri; 10am-1am Sat; 10am-10pm Sun. **No credit cards. Map** p60 C3 ⑬
This subsidised student drinking den and music venue is a few steps from the Rundetårn. The decor is grotty-chic to match the clientele's dress sense, and prices are set for those on a government-grant budget. There's usually something fun happening of an evening, from boardgame tournaments to swing-dance nights to live music.

Zoo Bar
Sværtegade 6 (33 15 68 69, www.zoobar.dk). Metro Kongens Nytorv. **Open** 5-11pm Tue, Wed; 5pm-2am Thur; 11am-4am Fri, Sat. **Map** p60 C5 ⑭
A favourite hangout for the fashion crowd, this capacious bar has DJs at weekends, decent food (try the Zoo burger) and an excellent cocktail list (Zoo passion-fruit martini, anyone?).

Shops & Services

★ AC Perchs Thehandel
Kronprinsensgade 5 (33 15 35 62, www.perchs.dk). Metro Kongens Nytorv. **Open** *Shop* 9am-5.30pm Mon-Thur; 9am-7pm Fri; 9.30am-4pm Sat. *Café* 11.30am-5.30pm Mon-Fri; 11am-5pm Sat. **Map** p60 C4 ⑮ **Food & drink**
Copenhagen's most venerated and venerable tea emporium dates from 1834 and is currently in the hands of the sixth generation of the Perch family. The glorious, wood-panelled interior is lined with old-fashioned jars of tea leaves (own blends as well as some more exotic brands), and the staff are only too happy to help you choose. The Darjeeling First Flush comes highly recommended.

Bruno & Joel
Kronprinsensgade 2 (33 13 87 78, www. bruno-joel.com). Metro Kongens Nytorv. **Open** 11am-6pm Mon-Fri; 11am-4pm Sat. **Map** p60 C4 ⑯ **Shoes**

EXPLORE

Unbelievably chic, Danish-designed, Italian-made foot candy for quality-shoe junkies (and people with fat wallets). Both women's and men's styles are sold.

Bruuns Bazaar

Kronprinsensgade 8-9 (33 32 19 99, www. bruunsbazaar.com). Metro Kongens Nytorv. **Open** 10am-6pm Mon-Thur; 10am-7pm Fri; 10am-4pm Sat; 10am-5pm 1st & last Sun of mth. **Map** p60 C4 🅱 **Fashion**
Set up by the two brothers Bruun in the mid 1990s, Bruuns Bazaar has since found its way on to catwalks around the world. Its mainstays are creative designs in attractive colours and top-of-the-range fabrics. The women's shop also sells a good range of delicate, colourful footwear.

Butik for Borddækning

Møntergade 6 (33 32 61 01, www.butikfor borddaekning.dk). Metro Kongens Nytorv. **Open** 11am-6pm Mon-Fri; 11am-4pm Sat. **Map** p60 C4 🅱 **Gifts & souvenirs**
Handmade ceramics, from the prosaic to the outlandish, with everything from sleek sushi sets and enigmatic espresso cups to artfully wonky water jugs.

By Malene Birger

Galleri K, Antonigade 10 (35 43 22 33, www.by malenebirger.dk). Metro Kongens Nytorv. **Open** 10am-6pm Mon-Thur; 10am-7pm Fri; 10am-5pm Sat; noon-4pm 1st Sun of mth. **Map** p60 C5 🅱 **Fashion**
Luxurious ready-to-wear clothing is the remit of Malene Birger's elegant flagship store, with glamorous but highly wearable designs in beautiful fabrics that have taken the fashion world by storm.

Casa Shop

Store Regnegade 2 (33 32 70 41, www.casa shop.dk). Metro Kongens Nytorv. **Open** 10am-5.30pm Mon-Thur; 10am-6pm Fri; 10am-3pm Sat. **Map** p60 C5 🅱 **Homewares**
Casa is one of the country's premier retailers of contemporary furniture, but there are plenty of smaller, quirkier pieces too, such as Nemo lamps and Ron Arad's flexible Bookworm bookshelf.

Chapeaux Petitgas

Købmagergade 5 (33 13 62 70). Metro Kongens Nytorv. **Open** 10am-5.30pm Mon-Fri; 10am-1pm Sat. **Map** p60 D4 🅱 **Accessories**
Nothing much has changed at Chapeaux Petitgas over the century and a half that it's been covering the heads of Copenhagen's gentlemen – but that, of course, is all part of its charm.

Danacord

Vognmagergade 9 (33 11 22 51, www. danacord.dk). Metro/train Nørreport. **Open** 10am-6pm Mon-Fri; 10am-2pm Sat. **Map** p60 B4 🅱 **Books & music**
Unpretentious, mildly chaotic but as comprehensive as you'll get, this is supposedly Scandinavia's largest classical-music store. Stock is mainly new CDs, but there's some second-hand vinyl too. The shop underwent a significant facelift a couple of years ago, after being taken over by a Danish record label.

DAY Birger et Mikkelsen

Pilestræde 16 (33 45 88 80, www.day.dk). Metro Kongens Nytorv. **Open** 10am-6pm Mon-Thur; 10am-7pm Fri; 10am-5pm Sat; noon-4pm 1st Sun of mth. **Map** p60 C5 🅱 **Fashion**

Bruno & Joel. *See p63.*

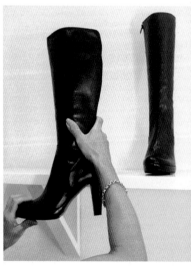

EXPLORE

DAY's flagship store is the only place offering every one of the brand's bohemian glamour lines under one roof, from sophisticated mens- and womenswear to a charming range of cool clothing for kids.

Dico
Christian IX's Gade 2 (33 36 53 90, www. dicocopenhagen.com). Metro Kongens Nytorv. **Open** 10am-5pm Mon-Fri; 11am-3pm Sat. **Map** p60 C5 ㉔ **Shoes**
Women's shoes and boots made with the finest leather, in hip yet solid styles. As well as the own-brand line, the shop also stocks ankle boots by local label AA Copenhagen.

Ganni
Store Regnegade 12 (20 88 53 11, www.ganni.com). Metro Kongens Nytorv. **Open** 10am-5.30pm Mon-Fri; 10am-4pm Sat. **Map** p60 C5 ㉕ **Fashion**
Founded by Frans Truelsen in 2000, Danish womenswear brand Ganni has gone from strength to strength. The clothes, lingerie, shoes and accessories are often more feminine than your typical Danish fashion brand (with delicate patterns and pastel colours), but have the same emphasis on quality fabrics and on-trend cuts. The tights are superb.
Other locations Gammel Kongevej 82, Frederiksberg; Østerbrogade 50, Østerbro.

★ Hay CPH
Pilestræde 29-31 (42 82 08 20, www.hay.dk). Metro Kongens Nytorv. **Open** 10am-6pm Mon-Fri; 10am-5pm Sat. **Map** p60 C4 ㉖ **Homewares**
Walking into Hay's, you might be forgiven for thinking you've stumbled on a chic version of the *Teletubbies* house. Simple, rounded forms and modular, felt-covered chairs in primary colours abound. Tinky Winky is no fool, however, for these Danish designs are supremely comfortable. There's another showroom upstairs and the website gives a good idea of what's in store.

★ Henrik Vibskov
Krystalgade 6 (33 14 61 00, www.henrik vibskov.com). Metro/train Nørreport. **Open** 11am-6pm Mon-Thur; 10am-7pm Fri; 11am-5pm Sat. **Map** p60 C3 ㉗ **Fashion**
Henrik Vibskov's cutting-edge designs – for women and men – are top of every Danish fashion insider's wish list. This flagship store offers the complete Vibskov experience, with the full collection of his coveted, edgy creations on sale.

Le Fix
Kronprinsensgade 9B (88 61 41 01, www.le-fix.com). Metro Kongens Nytorv. **Open** 11am-6pm Mon-Thur; 11am-7pm Fri; 10am-4pm Sat. **Map** p60 C4 ㉘ **Fashion**
Accessed via a passageway off Kronprinsensgade, Le Fix offers streetwear from all the cool heritage

Norse Store. *See p66.*

EXPLORE

brands (Barbour, Baracuta, Grenson) and sports-wear labels (Adidas, Fred Perry, Puma). It also has underground art books and prints for sale, and an on-site tattoo studio.

▶ *Another streetwear shop, Streetmachine (27 89 30 83, www.streetmachine.com), is nearby at Kronprinsensgade 3.*

Munthe plus Simonsen
Grønnegade 10 (33 32 00 12, www.munthe plussimonsen.dk). Metro Kongens Nytorv. **Open** 10am-6pm Mon-Thur; 10am-7pm Fri; 10am-4pm Sat. **Map** p60 C5 ㉙ **Fashion**
Luxurious muted colours abound at this women's clothing shop – reportedly a favourite of supermodel Helena Christensen and Crown Princess Mary.

Naked
Pilestræde 46 (33 15 83 82, www.nakedcph. com). Metro Kongens Nytorv. **Open** 10am-6pm Mon-Fri; 11am-4pm Sat. **Map** p60 C4 ㉚ **Accessories**
Danish women can be somewhat fanatical when it comes to finding cool trainers, and many come here, to this stylish sneaker shop for women, to buy their kicks. Shoes from Adidas, New Balance and Vans are in large supply.
Other location Klosterstræde 10, Indre By (33 15 83 83).

★ Norse Store
Pilestræde 41 (33 93 26 26, www.norsestore. com). Metro Kongens Nytorv. **Open** 10am-6pm Mon-Thur; 10am-7pm Fri; 10am-4pm Sat. **Map** p60 C4 ㉛ **Fashion**
Established in 2004, Norse Projects has become one of the most popular shops in town for style-savvy young men. The clothes combine street fashion, classic workwear and contemporary designs, with a hand-picked selection from its own label and other brands, including Ally Capellino, Folk, Acne, Lee, Levis, Adidas and Penfield. *Photos p65.*

Pure Shop
Grønnegade 36 (33 17 00 70, www.pure shop.dk). Metro Kongens Nytorv. **Open** 10am-6pm Mon-Fri; 10am-4pm Sat. **Map** p60 C5 ㉜ **Health & beauty**
All-natural and hypoallergenic cosmetics, skincare and beauty products from top brands that include Dr Hauschka, Jurlique and Weleda. It also has a make-up department.

★ Summerbird
Kronprinsensgade 11 (33 93 80 40, www. summerbird.dk). Metro Kongens Nytorv. **Open** 10am-6pm Mon-Fri; 10am-4pm Sat. **Map** p60 C4 ㉝ **Food & drink**
This chocolatier specialises in gourmet *flødeboller* – addictive Danish treats consisting of marshmallow and a biscuit base covered in chocolate (a little bit like a Tunnock's teacake). Valrhona chocolate with almonds and marzipan features in several different forms at Summerbird.
Other locations Torvehallerne market, Nørreport; Værnedamsvej 9, Vesterbro (33 25 25 50).

Wood Wood
Grønnegade 1 (35 35 62 64, www.woodwood.dk). Metro Kongens Nytorv. **Open** 10.30am-6pm Mon-Thur; 10.30am-7pm Fri; 10.30am-5pm Sat. **Map** p60 C5 ㉞ **Fashion**
Wood Wood started life as a graphic T-shirt brand, moving on to become one of Copenhagen's most stylish streetwear-influenced labels. A first port-of-call for trendy teens and twentysomethings looking for casual shoes, jackets, T-shirts and more, it now stocks womenswear too.

THE LATIN QUARTER & PISSERENDEN

North of the middle part of Strøget lies what is ambitiously termed Copenhagen's 'Latin Quarter' (on account of its narrow alleyways, cobbled café squares and bustling student life), bordered at its northern end by **Kultorvet**, a large square at the end of Købmagergade that becomes gridlocked in summer with café tables, fruit and veg stalls and beer stands.

At the heart of the Latin Quarter is **Gråbrødretorv**, a delightful restaurant square – like Nyhavn without a canal. It comes alive in summer as tables from its (good but costly) restaurants spill out on to the cobbles. The square was created in 1664 after Corfitz Ulfeldt, the secretary of war, had his mansion torn down as punishment for high treason. After a fire in 1728, many of the houses were rebuilt with triangular gable-ends, typical of the period. Outdoor gigs are often held here during the Copenhagen Jazz Festival.

West, on Nørregade, is Copenhagen's modest cathedral, **Vor Frue Kirke** (Church of Our Lady), where Crown Prince Frederik married his Australian wife, Mary Donaldson.

Next to Vor Frue Kirke is a large cobbled square, **Frue Plads**. The rather grimy building opposite the church is part of Copenhagen University, founded by Christian I in 1479. The building stands on the same site as the original (itself built over the Bishop's Palace), and was designed by Peter Malling and inaugurated by Frederik VI in 1836. The ornate great hall is worth a look and, if you have time, pop into the University Library round the corner in Fiolstræde. Halfway up the stairs is a small glass cabinet containing some fragments of a cannon ball and the book in which they were found embedded after the British bombardment. The title of the book, by Marsilius of Padua, is *Defender of Peace.*

OUT OF NOMA

New Nordic restaurants run by Noma alumni.

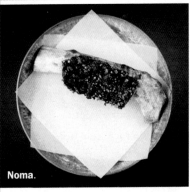

Noma.

The food movement known as 'New Nordic' started taking shape in 2004, when Danish food guru Claus Meyer and his disciple René Redzepi opened **Noma** (*see p114*), and drew up a manifesto for a new type of cuisine and way of eating, with an aim to 'express the purity, freshness, simplicity and ethics' of Scandinavian cooking. Redzepi quickly became one of the most vocal advocates of a cuisine that promoted Nordic produce (especially root veg, grains, fish, soft cheese, wild berries and herbs) and combined Nordic culinary traditions with creative international influences. He began foraging the coast and forests of Denmark and Sweden for wild herbs, plants and funghi that could take the place of basil, mint and coriander, and turned the concept of 'fine dining' upside down with a stripped-back approach to both cooking and decor.

Fast-forward a decade and Noma now has two Michelin stars, and is renowned around the globe, holding the number-one spot on the World's Best Restaurant list for three consecutive years. Which is fabulous, apart from the fact that it means that there has been a three-month waiting list for a table for the past half-decade or so.

However, fortunately for those of us keen to try Noma-style cuisine, but who lack the forethought (or persistency) to plan that far ahead, there are now several other restaurants in the city run by Noma alumni – passionate chefs who have learned the New Nordic ways under Redzepi's tutelage (and who have

attended lectures at his Nordic Food Lab: www.nordicfoodlab.org), and who now want to harness this new-found culinary wisdom in their own establishments.

Christian Puglisi was one of the first to run free. The former Noma sous chef set up **Relae** (*see p138*) with ex-Noma waitress Kim Rossen in Nørrebro in 2011, and has since gone on to establish the more laid-back **Manfreds & Vin** (*see p137*), opposite. Relae now has a Michelin star.

Another former Noma sous chef, Søren Ledet, is behind the incredibly successful (Michelin-starred) **Geranium** (*see p144*), while two others – Samuel Nutter and Victor Wågman – joined forces to set up **Bror** (*see p68*) in spring 2013.

Another good bet is **Restaurant Radio** (*see p131*), opened by New Nordic pioneer Claus Meyer in the old broadcasting house in 2012. Meyer is also behind new jazz bar **The Standard** (*see p170*), which houses two top-notch Scandinavian restaurants (as well as a superb modern Indian one) that adhere to his original manifesto.

Lastly, for a restaurant run by a former Noma head chef, no less, head to the industrial zone north of Christianshavn for **Amass** (*see p108*), where US chef Matt Orlando has, since summer 2013, been doing wonderful things with the produce from his restaurant's Nordic garden.

EXPLORE

Amass.

Vor Frue Kirke.

West of Frue Plads, in an area bordered by Nørregade, Vester Voldgade and Vestergade, lies the liveliest area around Strøget, known as **Pisserenden**. 'Piss' means the same in Danish as it does in English, and this district was so-named due to its notoriety as a malodorous dwelling place for prostitutes and criminals, until it was purged by the first great fire of 1728. Today, Pisserenden is one of the youngest and most vibrant areas of Copenhagen, full of the coolest (but relatively cheap) clothes, skate, book and record shops. Most of the streets (which include Kattesundet, Vestergade, Larsbjørnsstræde and Teglgårdstræde) are also blessed with great restaurants, cafés and bars, and Pisserenden is also Copenhagen's unofficial gay district.

Sights & Museums

FREE Vor Frue Kirke

Nørregade 8 (33 15 10 78, www.koebenhavns domkirke.dk). Metro/train Nørreport. **Open** 8am-5pm daily. **Admission** free. **Map** p60 D2 ⑮
Six churches have stood on this site since 1191, the first five suffering from a variety of misfortunes. The destruction of Vor Frue Kirke's art treasures by the Lutherans during the Reformation in the 16th century stands as one of their more barbaric acts. The current structure, by CF Hansen, was consecrated

in 1829 and replaced the church destroyed by the British bombardment of 1807 (they used its 100m/ 328ft spire as a target). The whitewashed interior is relieved by several figures by sculptor Bertel Thorvaldsen (*see p80* **Denmark's Wandering Hero**), including his famous depiction of Christ. The church often hosts musical events.

Restaurants

Bøf & Ost

Gråbrødretorv 13 (33 11 99 11, www.boef-ost.dk). Metro/train Nørreport, or Metro Kongens Nytorv. **Open** 11am-midnight (kitchen closes 10pm) daily. **Main courses** 189kr-245kr. **Set menu** 345kr-395kr. **Map** p60 D3 ㊱ **Steakhouse**
The rustic wooden tables and stone floor of this cellar restaurant are slightly at odds with the impressive complexity and prices of its food, but the various cuts and preparations of beef (charcoal-grilled is the house speciality) are excellent, as are the game dishes. The restaurant is situated on the southern side of the square in the oldest of the so-called Fire Houses, built after the great fire of 1728 that razed Copenhagen.

★ Bror

Sankt Peders Stræde 24A (32 17 59 99, www. restaurantbror.dk). Metro/train Nørreport, or train Vesterport. **Open** 5.30pm-midnight (kitchen closes 9.30pm) Wed-Sun. **Set menu** 375kr 4 courses. **Map** p60 D1 ㊲ **New Nordic**
Formerly home to Chit Chat Brasserie, this split-level space was taken over by Victor Wågman and Sam Nutter in 2013 to establish Bror ('brother' in Danish). It exemplifies the new breed of New Nordic restaurants, with tapas-sized, experimental dishes made from Nordic ingredients, and a stripped-back wood-heavy interior and laid-back atmosphere. It's a very good bet as an introduction to New Nordic cuisine, and handy for the cool shops and bars of the trendified district of Pisserenden.

Café GL Torv

Gammeltorv 20 (33 12 87 86, www.cafe gammeltorv.dk). Metro/train Nørreport, or bus 11A. **Open** 11.30am-4pm Mon, Tue; 11.30am-10pm Wed-Sat; noon-4pm 1st Sun of mth. **Main courses** 135kr-195kr. **Map** p60 D2 ㊳ **Traditional Danish**
A kind of working man's Ida Davidsen's (*see p105*), this old-style lunch restaurant is frequented by journalists, local businessmen and lawyers from the nearby courthouse. Offering traditional Danish *smørrebrød* in a small, spartan, cellar café with yellowed ceilings and wood-panelled walls, this is an authentic taste of basic Danish cuisine. Owner Peter Damgaard has run the place for over 20 years and is happy to talk you through the menu (English version available), which includes a decent range of typical open-sandwich toppings.

Oliver & the Black Circus

Teglgardsstraede 8A (74 56 88 88, www.
oliverandtheblackcircus.com). Metro/train
Nørreport, or bus 5A, 6A, 11A, 14. **Open**
5.30pm-1am Tue-Sat. **Set menu** 375k 4 courses,
440kr 5 courses, 500kr 6 courses. **Map** p60 D1
⑳ Modern Danish

This modern restaurant and cocktail bar aims to
wow with way-out decor (such as the large gnome
statue giving you the finger), a creative menu and
chatty bar staff. If you're dining in a large group,
and looking for a clubby-type vibe, then you could
do far worse. Cocktails are first-rate, service is good,
dishes (such as tartare of veal, with beetroot and egg
yolk; or scallops with carrots and sea buckthorn) are
innovative and well presented, and the upbeat music
will get you in the mood if you're planning a late one.
The large courtyard out front really comes into its
own in the summer.

★ Peder Oxe

Gråbrødretorv 11 (33 11 00 77, www.peder
oxe.dk). Metro/train Nørreport, or Metro Kongens
Nytorv. **Open** 11.30am-1am daily. **Main courses**
135kr-229kr. **Map** p60 D3 **⑳ Steakhouse**

One of Copenhagen's best-known restaurants, Peder
Oxe is hugely popular with tourists, from home and
abroad. The wide-ranging menu covers all the bases,
from steaks and burgers (made with organic and/or
free-range beef), to light, fresh, Asian-influenced
dishes (such as tuna tartare with avocado and
mango), all of which are well presented and reasonably priced. But Peder Oxe's trump card is its romantic interior, with original wooden floors and exquisite
Portuguese tiling – ample compensation should the
few outside tables be taken.

Cafés & Bars

Atlas Bar

Larsbjørnsstræde 18 (33 15 03 52, www.atlas
bar.dk). Metro/train Nørreport. **Open** noon-
midnight (kitchen closes 10pm) Mon-Sat.
Map p60 D2 **④**

This welcoming cellar bar serves 'food from the
warm countries', which in practice means its influences range from Asia (it does a decent Manila
chicken) to Mexico (humungous burritos). To under-
score the point, the tabletops are decorated with
maps. Well situated in the heart of bustling
Pisserenden, it's also popular with vegetarians.

Flottenheimer

Skindergade 20 (35 38 32 12, www.cafe
flottenheimer.dk). Metro/train Nørreport.
Open 10am-10pm Mon-Thur; 10am-11pm
Fri, Sat; 10am-8pm Sun. **Map** p60 D4 **④**

Based just round the corner from the lovely
Gråbrødretorv square, Flottenheimer is a feminine
space (think fairy lights, vintage tables and a tango
soundtrack), appealing to fashionable ladies who
lunch and discerning tourists. The diverse menu
offers a good range of sandwiches and small bites
(nachos, soup, tzatziki and bread), as well as pasta.

La Glace

Skoubogade 3 (33 14 46 46, www.laglace.com).
Metro/train Nørreport, or bus 11A. **Open**
8.30am-6pm Mon-Fri; 9am-6pm Sat; 10am-6pm
Sun. Closed Sun Apr-Sept. **No credit cards.**
Map p60 C3 **④**

Copenhagen's most vaunted and venerable bakery
and pâtisserie, founded in 1870, is famous for its

EXPLORE

Arnold Busck. *See p70.*

delectable cream cakes, which would tempt even the most fanatical of calorie-counters. The speciality is the Sports Kage (Sport Cake), an over-the-top cream, caramel and nougat mousse confection. Skoubogade is just off the west end of Strøget, which makes La Glace perfect for weary shoppers, but also means that you have to fight your way through a scrum of devoted cocoa-bean groupies most afternoons.

★ Jazzhouse

Niels Hemmingsens Gade 10 (33 15 47 00, www.jazzhouse.dk). Metro Kongens Nytorv. **Open** 6.30pm-5am concert nights. **Map** p60 D3

A stalwart of the Copenhagen nightlife scene, this superb jazz venue (*see p170*) was refurbished in 2012, following flood damage. It has two storeys (with a bar on each), modernised acoustics and a large dancefloor downstairs, and is a dead cert most nights for an excellent atmosphere, interesting clientele and great music. Jazz aficionados head here on Friday and Saturday nights to sample the best concerts in town, but it remains blessedly free of jazz snobs.

★ Log Lady

Studiestræde 27 (50 30 60 85, www.thebloglady cafe.blogspot.co.uk). Metro/train Nørreport, or train Vesterport. **Open** 1-11pm Mon-Fri; 2-11pm Sat. **Map** p60

This *Twin Peaks*-inspired café has suitably mysterious decor (big cacti, brass lamps, neon signs, treestump tables) and a genial, inclusive vibe. It's a good choice for a relaxed drink, even on weekends, thanks to the unobtrusive electronic music, good selection of beers and dark but cosy setting.

Peder Oxe Vinbar

Gråbrødretorv 11 (33 11 00 77, www.peder oxe.dk). Metro/train Nørreport, or Metro Kongens Nytorv. **Open** 11.30am-1am daily. **Map** p60 D3

This stylish, spacious and sociable wine bar near the centre of Strøget opened in 1978 and is located in the vaulted cellars beneath the venerable Peder Oxe restaurant (*see p69*).

Shops & Services

Arnold Busck

Købmagergade 49 (33 73 35 00, www. arnoldbusck.dk). Metro/train Nørreport. **Open** 10am-6pm Mon-Thur; 10am-7pm Fri; 10am-5pm Sat; noon-6pm 1st Sun of mth. **Map** p60 C3 **Books & music**

Busck is one of Denmark's leading bookshops, and this three-storey branch – its biggest – has a large department dedicated to English-language paperbacks and guides. *Photo p69.*

Other location Statens Museum for Kunst, Sølvgade 48-50, Rosenborg (33 74 86 68).

Nordisk Korthandel

Studiestræde 30 (33 38 26 38, www.scanmaps. dk). Metro/train Nørreport. **Open** 10am-6pm Mon-Fri; 9.30am-3pm Sat. **Map** p60 D1 **Books & music**

Nordisk Korthandel is Copenhagen's finest source of maps, travel books and globes, and is staffed by knowledgeable travel enthusiasts.

Peter Beier

Skoubougade 1 (33 93 07 17, www.peterbeier chokolade.dk). Bus 11A, 14. **Open** 10am-6pm Mon-Thur; 10am-7pm Fri; 10am-4pm Sat. **Map** p60 D3 **Food & drink**

The essence of chocolate chic, this modern shop, run by the charming Bagger family, offers premium-quality chocolates, plus dessert and port wines to accompany more refined tasting sessions.

Pluto Børnesko

Rosengården 12 (33 93 20 12). Metro/train Nørreport. **Open** 10am-5.30pm Mon-Fri; 10am-2pm Sat. **No credit cards. Map** p60 B2 **Children**

For nascent foot fetishists everywhere, this children's shoe shop sells trendy footwear for kids whose parents are prepared to pay designer prices.

Sögreni of Copenhagen

Sankt Peders Stræde 30A (33 12 78 79, www.sogrenibikes.com). Metro/train Nørreport, or train Vesterport. **Open** 10am-6pm Mon-Fri; 10am-4pm Sat. **Map** p60 D1 **Bicycles**

EXPLORE

Stilleben.

EXPLORE

This high-end bicycle maker produces a limited quantity of traditional-looking, yet ultra-modern bikes, several of which have been featured in *Wallpaper** magazine and sold at the Conran Shop in London. Bikes cost around 12,000kr.

★ Stilleben
Niels Hemmingsens Gade 3 (33 91 11 31, www.stilleben.dk). Metro/train Nørreport, or Metro Kongens Nytorv. **Open** 10am-6pm Mon-Fri; 10am-4pm Sat. **Map** p60 D4 ❷ **Homewares**
Fans of contemporary Scandi homewares will love this stylish shop, which sells covetable items from artisan designers, including geometric rugs from Tina Ratzer, a large range of handcrafted ceramics and candle holders, and simple gold-plated jewellery. Head upstairs for framed graphics-based prints.

Time's Up Vintage
Krystalgade 4 (33 32 39 30, www.timesupshop. com). Metro/train Nørreport. **Open** 11am-6pm Mon-Fri; 11am-5pm Sat. **Map** p60 C3 ❸ **Fashion**
Located on a lovely street, Time's Up has a well-edited selection of designer vintage clothing, including art deco pieces (with notably good jewellery), and couture from Chanel, Dior and Givenchy. The range of shoes is also strong.

STRØGET & STRÆDET

The eastern end of Strøget, near Kongens Nytorv, is home to lots of designer fashion stores, as well as **Illum**, the city's premier department store, which stretches to the corner of **Købmagergade**. Head south of Illum and you'll come to the historic **Nikolaj Plads**, housing Sankt Nikolaj Kirke. The church dates from the 13th century, but the fire of 1795 destroyed all but the tower; it was rebuilt in 1917. The square is a venue for the Copenhagen Jazz Festival.

Amagertorv (*photo p72*) is the central part of Strøget, an historic part of the street that dates from the 14th century. In the 17th century, a law was passed that meant all the produce grown on Amager island (where Copenhagen Airport is located) had to be sold at the market here, and soon shops grew up around the stalls. This has always been one of Copenhagen's main markets and meeting places, and though the stalls have long gone, the fountain is still much used as a rendezvous. Amagertorv is also the site of **Royal Copenhagen**, the pride of the city's retail portfolio, formed from the amalgamation of three Strøget institutions in 1985. Adjoining Amagertorv, towards Slotsholmen, is another busy square, **Højbro Plads**. Its main feature is a 1902 equestrian statue of **Bishop Absalon**, the founder of Copenhagen, by HW Bissen; it has an inscription that reads: 'He was courageous, wise and far-sighted, a friend of scholarship, in the intensity of his striving a true son of Denmark.'

The next major sight as you continue west along Strøget is **Helligåndskirken** (Church of

Amagertorv. *See p71.*

the Holy Spirit), dating from 1400. West from here, Strøget begins to go downmarket, with various cheap eateries serving pizzas and waffles. The watershed comes at **Gammeltorv** and **Nytorv**, two picturesque cobbled squares, beyond which things start to get very touristy. During the 14th century, Gammeltorv, the oldest square in the city, was the hub of Copenhagen, a busy market, meeting place and (occasional) jousting site for the 5,000 residents of what was then the largest settlement in northern Europe. The two squares became one (though they are bisected by Strøget) after the fire of 1795 destroyed the town hall that separated them.

When visitors arrive in Gammeltorv, one of the first things they notice is the extraordinary **Caritas Springvandet** (Charity Fountain). Dating from 1608, this Renaissance masterpiece, made of copper, depicts a pregnant woman and two children with fishy gargoyles at their feet. On royal birthdays, golden apples dance on the water jets.

Of interest chiefly because of its grand neoclassical façade, featuring six Ionic columns, Copenhagen's imposing and elegant **Domhuset** (Court House) on Nytorv was built in 1805-15 (work was suspended for a while in 1807 due to the bombardment by the British). The dusky pink building was designed by CF Hansen, who was also responsible for Vor Frue Kirke (*see p68*), just a short walk away up Nørregade. Domhuset was built on the site of the former town hall and, until 1905, served as both courthouse and town hall. Today, it houses court rooms, conference rooms and chambers.

The nearby Slutterigade (Prison Street) annexe was built as a jail in 1816 and converted to court rooms and chambers in 1944. It's attached to Domhuset via two recently restored arches, one of which is known as the Bridge of Sighs (as are many such crossings around the world) – prisoners, bemoaning their fate, are led across it when going to and from the court rooms.

In 1848, Nytorv served as the starting point for the relatively peaceful march by 10,000 Copenhageners on Christiansborg Slot, demanding the end of absolute monarchy. Frederik VII had conceded defeat before they even arrived. Søren Kierkegaard (*see p136* **Dead Famous**) lived for a while on Nytorv in a house on a site now occupied by Den Danske Bank. Look out, too, for the outline of Copenhagen's first town hall (before it moved to Rådhuspladsen), traced in the paving of Nytorv beneath the fruit and veg sellers who usually pitch here. Incidentally, Mozart's widow, Constanze, lived with her second husband (Georg Nikolaus Nissen, a Danish diplomat) at Lavendelstræde 1. The street runs from Nytorv's southern corner towards Rådhuspladsen.

The final stretch of Strøget is along **Frederiksberggade**, which opened up between Nytorv and Rådhuspladsen when the 1728 fire razed the buildings here. On the right as you approach Rådhuspladsen is the rough and ready Club Absalon, built on the site of the city's first church, Sankt Clemens Kirke. The church was probably built by Absalon in the 1160s, but was demolished in the early 16th century. Rather ignominiously, some of its foundations can be seen in the bar's toilets. In a city that usually cares for its heritage, this seems something of a dereliction of duty.

South of Strøget is the parallel stretch of **Strædet** (literally 'strait'), which, like Strøget, is actually formed of several streets (Farvergade, Kompagnistræde, Læderstræde, Store Kirkestræde and Lille Kongensgade). These historic streets are lovely to walk around: more laid-back than Strøget, and with a greater number of independent shops and cafés. It's yet another place that the medieval city planners appear to have designed with 21st-century window-shoppers in mind.

South of Stræde, just above the island of Slotsholmen, is **Gammel Strand** (Old Beach), home to some pricey restaurants. In the time of Bishop Absalon, and for centuries afterwards, Gammel Strand was where fish was sold (and it therefore served as the city's commercial centre). It was here that the Øresund herring were landed before they were transported throughout Catholic Europe – fish being vital for a population that often abstained from meat. Gammel Strand remained part of Copenhagen's seafront, which stretched from what is today Fortunstræde, along Gammel Strand to Snaregade, Magstræde and Løngangstræde, until well into the Middle Ages.

By the bridge from Højbro Plads to Slotsholmen is a stout stone statue (dating from 1940) of a foul-mouthed and quarrelsome fishwife grasping a huge flounder by the gills, in memory of a trade that lasted into the 20th century. There's still a fishmonger nearby on Højbro Plads (it does a swift trade in sushi). Cross to the other side of the bridge and look into the water and you'll see the sculpture of the *Merman with his Sons* (it's illuminated at night). All of Gammel Strand, except for no.48, burned to the ground in 1795. In summer, you can take a canal tour or harbour trip to the *Little Mermaid* from Gammel Strand.

Sights & Museums

FREE Helligåndskirken
Nils Hemmingsens Gade 5, Amagertorv (33 15 41 44, www.helligaandskirken.dk). Metro Kongens Nytorv. **Open** noon-4pm Mon-Fri; for services only Sun. **Admission** free. **Map** p60 D4 ⑨
Originally, this was part of the Grey Friars monastery, the oldest religious site in the city, founded in 1238. The early monks were hardy, ascetic souls and their devoted piety earned them much respect, but when they relaxed their standards during the 16th century they were expelled from the city by the Protestant reformers. The current neo-Renaissance structure dates from 1880. In the churchyard is a memorial to the Danish victims of Nazi concentration camps.

Restaurants

Kong Hans Kælder
Vingårdsstræde 6 (33 11 68 68, www.kong hans.dk). Metro Kongens Nytorv. **Open** 6pm-midnight Mon-Sat. **Main courses** 500kr. **Set menu** 1,200kr 8 courses. **Map** p60 D5 ⑮ **French/Danish**
Kong Hans' stylish, whitewashed, vaulted cellar rooms are tucked away down a small side street. Thomas Rode Andersen – one of Denmark's most highly respected chefs, who was due to retire in summer 2014, as this guide went to press – was the restaurant's head chef for 17 years. Mark Lundgård Nielsen is due to take the reins from September 2014, when the restaurant reopens after a summer makeover. Lundgård Nielsen will continue Rode Andersen's work combining the finest regional ingredients with classic French techniques, from an open kitchen. The cellar (*kælder*) space, dating from the 15th century, is said to be the oldest building in the city still in commercial use. At one time, it faced the waterfront and was the site of a vineyard (hence the name Vingårdsstraede, 'vineyard street'). Prices, of course, are set at the sort of high levels you'd expect, which means that the clientele tends to be older and more conservative than the norm.

Riz Raz
Kompagnistræde 20 (33 15 05 75, www. rizraz.dk). Metro Kongens Nytorv, or bus 11A. **Open** 11.30am midnight Mon-Fri; 10am-midnight Sat, Sun. **Main courses** 95kr-125kr. **Buffet** 79kr-99kr. **Map** p61 E3 ⑯ **Mediterranean**
The southern Mediterranean food at this convivial cellar restaurant is a favourite with tourists and Copenhageners, and consistently wins over reviewers from the Danish press. It always seems to be packed with an eclectic mix of diners, in for a quick bite before heading somewhere groovier. The buffet, which in many other places is just an excuse to stuff punters with cheap salads, is, in Riz Raz's case, fresh and tasty, as is their latest innovation of veggie and meat brochettes.
Other location Store Kannikstraæde 19, Indre By (33 32 33 45).

★ Slotskælderen Hos Gitte
Fortunstræde 4 (33 11 15 37, www. slotskaelderen.dk). Metro Kongens Nytorv. **Open** 11am-5pm Tue-Sat. **Main courses** 67kr-125kr. **Map** p60 D5 ⑰ **Traditional Danish**
Everyone who comes to Copenhagen should try authentic, traditional Danish food, at least once. And it doesn't come much more authentic than at Slotskælderen (the castle cellar). This old-school *smørrebrød* restaurant is just across the canal from Christiansborg Slot (home to the Danish parliament), which means the atmospheric, low-lit venue, run by the eponymous Gitte, attracts a decent number of politicians. Simply choose sandwiches, *frikadeller*

EXPLORE

EXPLORE

(meatballs) and *sild* (herring) from the counter, and the attentive staff bring them to your table. Fried plaice and pickled herring are two of the top choices here, classically washed down with a beer and schnapps.

Cafés & Bars

★ Bertels Salon

Kompagnistræde 5 (33 13 00 33, www.bertels kager.dk). Metro Kongens Nytorv. **Open** 11am-8pm daily. **Map** p61 E4 ⑤⑧
This cheesecake café has been a great success since opening in early 2014. American cheesecakes are the speciality, and there are some 20 types on offer; we especially recommend the coconut-pineapple version. Most of the tables are situated upstairs in a charming space. Enjoy your cake with a cup of freshly roasted, top-quality coffee.
Other location Falkoner Allé 54, Frederiksberg (31 16 69 62).

Café Europa

Amagertorv 1 (33 14 28 89, www.europa 1989.dk). Metro Kongens Nytorv. **Open** 7.45am-11pm Mon-Thur; 7.45am-midnight Fri, Sat; 9am-10pm Sun. **Map** p60 D4 ⑤⑨
With a location right in the heart of the shopping district on Amagertorv, Café Europa is one of the city's most popular meeting places. Prices can be high and service frosty, but the food isn't bad and it's a nice place to stop off for a drink during an afternoon's shopping. Sandwiches are reasonable value. There's seating outside in summer.

Café Norden

Østergade 61 (33 11 77 91, www.cafenorden.dk). Metro Kongens Nytorv. **Open** 9am-midnight daily. **Map** p60 D4 ⑥⓪
This grandest and largest (it seats as many as 350 on sunny days) of all Copenhagen's cafés overlooks Amagertorv. Despite its vast, two-storey, Parisian-style interior, complete with chandeliers and wood panelling, it's usually a challenge to find a table. Service is often fairly grouchy (in fact, there's no table service, so you have to order at the bar), but the food (salads, sandwiches, steaks) is adequate, though you will pay around 20% more for everything by virtue of its prime location.

Drop Inn

Kompagnistræde 34 (33 11 24 04, www.drop-inn.dk). Bus 11A, 14. **Open** noon-5am Mon-Sat; 2pm-2am Sun. **Map** p61 E3 ⑥①
With live music every night (jazz, blues and folk), and an open front with pavement seating in summer, Drop Inn is one of those places that never seems to take a rest. Hardly cool or trendy, the place tends instead to attract the more dedicated drinkers, so things can get lively towards the end of the evening.

Galathea Kroen

Rådhusstræde 9 (33 11 66 27, www.galathea kroen.dk). Bus 11A, 14. **Open** 6pm-2am Tue-Thur; 6pm-4am Fri, Sat. *Food served* 6-9pm daily. **Map** p61 E3 ⑥②
Opened in 1953, Galathea is named after a ship that was used as a base for exploring Pacific sea life – and the interior is decorated with mementos from

Café Norden.

the ship's journeys. The moment you enter this charismatic, eclectic mess of a bar, past the totem poles that guard the entrance, you know that it's not one of Copenhagen's more style-conscious places. Maybe it's the jazz on the turntable (this is a strictly vinyl-only joint) or the affable and intriguing clientele, from trendy teens to bohemian oldies; or perhaps it's the engagingly dishevelled decor.

Kafe Kys

Læderstræde 7 (33 93 85 94, www.kafekys.dk).
Metro Kongens Nytorv. **Open** 9.15am-midnight Mon-Thur; 9.15am-2am Fri, Sat; 11am-10pm Sun.
Map p60 D4 ⑬
This enduringly popular bar is unremarkable other than for its pleasant location and its sandwiches, which are slightly more exotic than the usual café fare. That, and the fact that it seems, for some reason, to draw an unusually attractive clientele. Friday night is the hottest of the week for Kys, when it's usually packed with the young and the beautiful bar-hopping their way along Copenhagen's most charming street.

K Cocktail Bar

Ved Stranden 20 (33 91 92 22, www.k-bar.dk).
Metro Kongens Nytorv. **Open** 4pm-2am Mon-Sat.
Map p60 D4 ⑭
This low-slung, flirty cocktail bar is just how you imagine all Scandinavian bars will be: very cool, beautifully designed and with a short but sweet cocktail list featuring tempters such as 'Very Berry Caipirinha' and 'Rude Cosmopolitan'. Bartender Kirsten is a dab hand at martinis – there are 13 to try on the menu. This jewel of a place is tucked away just around the corner from Højbro Plads, a few moments from Strøget.

★ Royal Smushi Café

Amagertorv 6 (33 12 11 22, www.royalsmushi cafe.dk). Metro Kongens Nytorv. **Open** 10am-6pm Mon-Thur; 10am-7pm Fri, Sat; 11am-6pm Sun. **Map** p60 D4 ⑮
Royal Copenhagen's stylish café opened in its (refurbished) flagship store in 2007, and is known for its contemporary, sushi-style, open-faced sandwiches (*smushi*) and classic desserts. The upmarket, feminine space features royal portraits on the walls, and fixtures, fittings and furniture from a range of famous Danish design brands, such as Bang & Olufsen and Fritz Hansen. You might need to wait for a table.

★ Zirup

Læderstræde 32 (33 13 50 60, www.zirup.dk).
Metro Kongens Nytorv. **Open** 10am-11pm Mon-Thur, Sun; 10am-midnight Fri, Sat.
Map p60 D4 ⑯
Zirup is our choice of all the many good cafés on this pretty pedestrian street parallel to Strøget. It has a beautifully lit interior, and a good-value and slightly

adventurous fusion menu (offering everything from stroganoff to curry to Mexican wraps), and there are tables outside when the weather permits. All in all, it's a very pleasant place to pass time. The Sunday morning hangover brunch should be available on prescription.

Shops & Services

Bang & Olufsen

Østergade 18 (33 11 14 15, www.bang-olufsen.com). **Open** 10am-6pm Mon-Thur; 10am-7pm Fri; 10am-4pm Sat. **Map** p60 C5 ㊿ **Electronics**
Danes are justifiably proud of this smart brand of televisions and stereos, the minimalist modern masterpieces of which feature in the world's fashion and design bibles. This store opened in a former Louis Vuitton store in 2012 (replacing the shop previously located in Kongens Nytorv), and has a large selection from the covetable range of electronics.
Other location Falkoner Alle 7, Frederiksberg (38 10 02 00).

Dansk Håndværk

Kompagnistræde 20 (33 11 45 52, www. danskhaandvaerk.dk). Metro Kongens Nytorv. **Open** 11am-5.30pm Mon-Thur; 11am-6.30pm Fri; 11am-3pm Sat. **Map** p61 E3 ㊽ **Children**
Local craftsman Lars Jensen has been producing traditional wooden toys for almost 30 years, and this small cellar shop is full of handcrafted, brightly coloured playthings for under-fives.

Georg Jensen

Amagertorv 4 (33 11 40 80, www.georgjensen. com). Metro Kongens Nytorv. **Open** 10am-7pm Mon-Fri; 10am-6pm Sat; 11am-4pm Sun.
Map p60 D4 ㊾ **Accessories**
The undisputed daddy of Danish silver design, Jensen's showroom has elaborate flower arrangements artfully complementing the ornate jewellery on display. A museum at the back showcases the history of the company.

★ Illum

Østergade 52 (33 14 40 02, www.illum.dk).
Metro Kongens Nytorv. **Open** 10am-6pm Mon-Sat; 11am-6pm Sun. **Map** p60 D4 ㊲
Department store
Illum's interior design and magnificent glass dome make it the more modern of the city's two department stores (the other is Magasin, *see p101*), and it also offers an edgier range of fashion labels. The ground floor has cosmetics and accessories, and a concession for Danish bike brand Velorbis. Womenswear and menswear by Scandinavian designers (including Acne, Bruuns Bazaar, Ganni, WhyRed and Filippa K) and international labels are on the first and second floors, while the basement houses a branch of supermarket Irma and a café.

EXPLORE

★ Illums Bolighus

Amagertorv 10 (33 14 19 41, www.illums bolighus.com). Metro Kongens Nytorv. **Open** 10am-7pm Mon-Fri; 10am-6pm Sat; 11am-5pm Sun. **Map** p60 D4 **71** Homewares

The homewares arm of department store Illum (*see p75*) features a selection of premium brands including Orrefors, Arabia and Alessi, while connecting doors lead into the Royal Copenhagen, Holmegaard and Georg Jensen shops.
Other location Illums Bolighus Tivoli, Vesterbrogade 3 (33 91 18 45).

Kaiku

Kompagnistræde 8 (33 11 19 07, www.kaiku.dk). Metro Kongens Nytorv. **Open** 11am-5.30pm Mon-Thur; 11am-6pm Fri; 10am-4pm Sat. **Map** p60 D4 **72** Homewares

Affordable, design-led homewares and knick-knacks are sold in this friendly, popular shop.

Le Klint

Store Kirkestræde 1 (33 11 66 63, www. leklint.com). Metro Kongens Nytorv. **Open** 10am-6pm Tue-Fri; 10am-4pm Sat. **Map** p60 D5 **73** Homewares

This is the main stockist for Kaare Klint's trademark concertina-style lampshades, including his perennially popular 'Model 1', folded by hand since 1943.

Lego Flagship

Vimmelskaftet 37 (52 15 91 58, www.lego.dk). Metro Kongens Nytorv. **Open** 10am-6pm Mon-Thur; 10am-7pm Fri; 10am-6pm Sat; 11am-5pm Sun. **Map** p60 D3 **74** Children

This impressive Lego flagship store consists of three main areas: a 'Pick-a-Brick' wall showcasing the famous colourful bricks; an interactive play area in the centre of the store; and the 'brand ribbon', which runs the circumference of the store and features displays and presentations of fun facts. Exclusive and hard-to-find sets are for sale, as well as Lego games, Harry Potter-themed sets, the Creator and City lines, Lego Duplo sets for preschool children, and the full selection of classic Lego products and branded merchandise.

★ Mads Nørgaard

Amagertorv 15 (33 32 01 28, www.mads norgaard.dk). Metro Kongens Nytorv. **Open** 10am-6pm Mon-Thur; 10am-7pm Fri; 10am-5pm Sat. **Map** p60 D4 **75** Fashion

A wide range of international labels – Prada, Miu Miu, Dries Van Noten, John Smedley and Carhartt – alongside Mads Nørgaard's own-brand clothing.
Other location Frederiksberggade 24, Strøget (33 12 18 28).

★ Royal Copenhagen

Amagertorv 6 (33 13 71 81, www.royal copenhagen.com). Metro Kongens Nytorv. **Open** 10am-6pm Mon-Thur; 10am-7pm Fri; 10am-5pm Sat; 11am-4pm Sun. **Map** p60 D4 **76** Homewares

With its massive refurbishment in 2007, Royal Shopping spilt into three separate shops, all of which are interconnected: the Royal Copenhagen flagship, housed in a 16th-century building, is the place to head for the famous porcelain, whose designs span the traditional to the modern and include the

Slotsholmen.

Christiansborg Slot. *See p79.*

world-famous 'Flora Danica' collection; Georg Jensen (*see p75*) sells silverware and jewellery; and Illums Bolighus (*see p76*) is for furniture and designer homewares. To complete the royal shopping trip, head to the Royal Smushi Café (*see p75*), in the same building.

Søstrene Grene

Amagertorv 24 (no phone, www.grenes.dk). Metro Kongens Nytorv. **Open** 10am-7pm Mon-Fri; 10am-6pm Sat; 11am-5pm Sun. **Map** p60 D3 **⑰ Gifts & souvenirs**
People either love Søstrene Grene's lucky-dip potential or loathe its often brazenly poor-quality stock, but there's no denying that there are gems aplenty lurking among its collection of oddball crockery, toys, bedding, glassware and miscellaneous gifts.

SLOTSHOLMEN & THE NATIONAL MUSEUM

The island of Slotsholmen, surrounded by harbours and canals, is a more accessible place these days, with its museums, the great Børsen stock exchange and the futuristic Black Diamond royal library. Hang around long enough, and you might even spot a government minister swanning about.

The largest building on Slotsholmen is **Christiansborg Slot** (Christiansborg Castle), the modern-day parliament building that takes up the northern half of the island. For many centuries, the previous castles that stood on this site effectively were Copenhagen, so central were they to the lives and prosperity of the townsfolk and so important were they as a power base for the region.

Christiansborg's development can be divided into three stages: Absalon's fortress dating from 1167; the 17th century; and the current palace. The original building is long gone, but you can still see remnants of its foundations in the enjoyable **Ruinerne under Christiansborg** (Ruins under Christiansborg), a museum dedicated to the 800-year history of the current castle site. The current palace is built directly above and houses the Danish parliament, **Folketinget**, where 179 members sit in a semi-circle in their party groups (of which Denmark has many), facing the Speaker. Government ministers sit on the right-hand side of the chamber, with the Prime Minister closest to the platform.

Close by the Ruinerne museum is the equestrian arena, with entrances to two particularly enchanting royal attractions: the **Kongelige Stalde og Kareter** (Royal Stables and Coaches) and **Teatermuseet** (Theatre Museum). If you can endure the equine odours, the stables, with their vaulted ceilings and marble columns, offer a glimpse into an extravagant royal past. Teatermuseet, which opened in 1922, is housed in the old Royal Court Theatre, designed by the French architect Nicolas Henri Jardin. It dates from 1766 and was modernised in 1842 – HC Andersen once performed in a ballet here in his youth.

Continue across the equestrian arena to the archway beyond and you'll come to Frederiksholms Kanal, which is forded by **Marmorbroen** (Marble Bridge). Quite a fuss is made over this bridge, which was designed by Nicolai Eigtved for Christian IV and completed in 1745, but, frankly, aside from some decorative

EXPLORE

sandstone portraits, it isn't all that special (and it isn't even all marble). A few steps from the bridge is the magnificient **Nationalmuseet**. Housed in a sumptuous former royal palace, boasting some of the finest rooms in the city, and extensively modernised in recent years, Denmark's National Museum is the country's oldest historical collection, with its origins as Frederik II's Royal Cabinet of Curiosities (c1650). It focuses, naturally, on Danish culture and history, but there are also world-class Egyptian, Greek, Roman and ethnographic departments. All exhibits have excellent English captions.

Just north of Christiansborg Slot is the classical stuccoed mausoleum (by Gottlieb Bindesbøll) that houses the definitive collection of works by Denmark's master sculptor, Bertel Thorvaldsen (1768-1844). **Thorvaldsens Museum** is a must, not only for sculpture fans, but for all art-lovers. Immediately behind the museum is **Christiansborg Slotskirke** (Christiansborg Palace Church), one of CF Hansen's neoclassical masterpieces, with a columned façade and a beautiful white stucco interior and dome.

Børsen, on the other side of Christiansborg Slotsplads, is the oldest stock exchange in Europe, built between 1619 and 1640. It still serves as a business centre and Copenhagen's chamber of commerce and, as such, is not open to the public. However, the exterior of this Renaissance wedding cake is a riot of stonework, embellished gables and green copper. Above it towers one of Copenhagen's most recognisable landmarks – a fantastical 54-metre (177-foot) copper spire made of four intertwined dragon tails, built in 1625 to a design by Ludvig Heidtrider. The three gold crowns topping the spire represent the three Nordic nations: Denmark, Sweden and Norway. Børsen (which translates as 'the covered market') was built at the behest of Christian IV, who desperately wanted Copenhagen to become the financial capital of Europe (it didn't).

An unusually ostentatious altarpiece (for a Lutheran church) is the main draw of **Holmens Kirke**, dedicated to sailors. Across the street is a concrete building housing the **Nationalbanken** (National Bank), the work of Arne Jacobsen. Regrettably, its wonderful interior and inner courtyard are not open to the public.

Another treat is the **Tøjhusmuseet** (Royal Arsenal Museum). Comprising an endless vaulted Renaissance cannon hall (the longest in Europe, modelled on the one in Venice), and a mind-boggling array of arms and armour in an upstairs display, this is probably the finest museum of its kind in the world.

Copenhagen's most beautiful 'hidden' garden, **Bibliotekshaven** (Library Garden), lies behind the old ivy-covered **Det Kongelige Bibliotek** (Royal Library), through a gateway on Rigdagsgården, opposite the entrance to Folketinget.

Danish Jewish Museum. *See p81.*

The Danes love nothing more than to juxtapose old and new, but when the designs for the new extension to the Royal Library, by architects Schmidt, Hammer and Lassen, were unveiled, few were prepared for something this radical (despite it having already earned the nickname the **Black Diamond** before it opened in 1999). Perhaps the best way to approach it is by walking through the old library's garden, so that you are suddenly confronted with the vastness of the new structure close up. The Kongelige Bibliotek is also attached to the **Danish Jewish Museum**.

Sights & Museums

Note that a joint ticket is available for the **Christiansborg Slot** (Royal Reception Rooms), the **Ruinerne under Christiansborg** and the **Kongelige Stalde** (Royal Stables). It costs 110kr (55kr-95kr reductions) and is valid for one month.

FREE Bibliotekshaven
Rigsdagsgården (33 92 63 00, www.ses.dk).
Metro Kongens Nytorv. **Open** 6am-10pm daily.
Admission free. **Map** p61 F5 ⓲
Arranged in a square around a fountain and duck pond, the Library Garden blooms beautifully in summer – even the bronze of Søren Kierkegaard looks cheerful. You can see some of the old mooring hoops from Christian IV's time on the surrounding walls.

Christiansborg Slot
Slotsholmen (33 92 63 00, www.christiansborg. dk). Metro Kongens Nytorv. **Open** 10am-5pm daily. *Tours* (in English) 3pm daily. **Tickets** 80kr; 40kr-70kr reductions. **No credit cards.** **Map** p61 F4 ⓲
The warrior-bishop Absalon built a fortress in 1167 on what was then the small islet of Strandholmen. It was ringed by a thick wall of limestone blocks, with its internal buildings made from brick and timber. Bishop Absalon's fortress was badly damaged in 1259 by the avenging Wends and then burned to the ground in 1369 by an alliance of forces led by the Lübeckers against King Valdemar Atterdag. It was replaced by the first Copenhagen Castle. From 1416, when Erik of Pomerania moved in, the castle became the permanent home of the royal family (until they moved to Amalienborg Slot in 1794).

Christian IV had the place demolished in the early 17th century, replacing it with a typically over-the-top Baroque building, with its own chapel and very grand stables. During Frederik II's reign, the castle nearly fell to the Swedes, who, after a two-year siege, in February 1659 advanced towards it across the frozen sea, dressed in white cloaks to camouflage themselves. But the boiling oil, tar and water that the Danes rained down drove them back. Soon after, Frederik III built a new rampart where the Swedes had advanced. This became known as Vestervold (Western Rampart), and between it and Slotsholmen a new quarter, Frederiksholm, grew up.

Frederik IV extensively modernised the castle between 1710 and 1729, but Christian VI tore it down in 1732. The Baroque replacement was one of the biggest palaces in Europe; its foundations alone cost three million *rigsdalers*, then equivalent to the entire value of Sjælland's arable land. On the night of 26 February 1794, the whole lot burned down (bar the stables, which are still in use). The royal family finally gave up on Slotsholmen and bought Amalienborg Slot. Work on the next Christiansborg Slot started in 1803 and the building, a neoclassical masterpiece, was completed in 1828. That too was badly damaged by a fire in 1884.

You would hardly term present-day Christiansborg a castle. Nor is it especially graceful. But it is big. Its neo-Baroque granite and concrete façade was designed by Thorvald Jørgensen and was the first Christiansborg to have been built by the people's representatives. They were apparently still touchy about the monarchy as, during its design, they demanded to have at least the same number of windows overlooking the palace square as the king. Its central tower is the tallest (by 40cm) in Denmark at 106m (347ft). Frederik VIII laid the foundation stone for the current castle in 1907, and the Ruinerne museum displays amazing photographs from that time. *Photo p77.*

FREE Christiansborg Slot: Folketinget
Rigsdagsgården (33 37 55 00, www.ft.dk).
Metro Kongens Nytorv. **Open** *Gallery sittings*

EXPLORE

DENMARK'S WANDERING HERO

Bertel Thorvaldsen is the nation's most famous (and prolific) sculptor.

EXPLORE

Denmark's greatest sculptor was born in Copenhagen on 19 November 1768. He studied at the Academy of Art, where he won the Gold Medal; then, in 1797, a scholarship sent him to Rome, where he lived for nearly 40 years developing a style that was heavily influenced by Greco-Roman mythology and creating works of a wonderfully majestic, classical beauty, frequently on an epic scale. Thorvaldsen's monument to Pope Pius VII is the only work by a non-Italian in Rome's St Peter's Basilica.

His breakthrough, which catapulted him into the highest echelons of the neoclassical sculpture fraternity, came with the piece *Jason and the Golden Fleece*. It was completed in 1803 and is now housed in the **Thorvaldsens Museum** (*see p83*). His figure of Christ, which can be seen in Vor Frue Kirke (*see p68*), became the model for statues of Christ the world over and remains a religious icon to this day.

Thorvaldsen returned to Copenhagen towards the end of his life, and his return helped boost morale and a general artistic revival and contributed to the emergence of a cultural and social essence that is still recognisably Danish today. In 1833, he was appointed director of the Danish Academy of Fine Arts. Before his death in March 1844, Thorvaldsen bequeathed his works (plaster moulds, sketches, finished works in marble) and a collection of ancient Mediterranean art to the city, and the Thorvaldsens Museum. He is buried in the museum's inner courtyard.

The Thorvaldsens Museum, the oldest art gallery in Denmark, is a charming blend of celestial blue ceilings, elegant colonnades and mosaic floors. Although the monumental scale of Thorvaldsen's work and his prolific output are often hard to take in, it is worth persevering. His subjects include not only figures from mythology, epic studies of Christ and numerous self-portraits, but also busts of contemporaries such as Byron, Walter Scott and the Danish poet Adam Oehlenschläger. Also featured are Thorvaldsen's collections of Egyptian and Roman artefacts, contemporary Danish art and personal belongings. Outside, a fresco depicts the return of the sculptor and his works from Rome. Some English information is available.

1st Tue Oct-5 June Tue-Fri. *Guided tours* 1pm on some Sun & bank holidays, and weekdays in parliamentary recess (July-mid Aug); check website for details. **Admission** free. **Map** p61 E4 ⑩

Folketinget is opened annually on the first Tuesday in October, in a ceremony which is attended by members of the royal family. A public gallery is open when parliament is in session, and there are English-language tours during the parliamentary recess in summer. Christiansborg also houses the High Court, several ministries, the prime minister's department, the Royal Reception Chambers (De Kongelige Repræsentationslokaler) and the Queen's Reference Library.

Christiansborg Slot: Kongelige Stalde og Kareter

Christiansborg Ridebane 12 (33 40 26 76, www.christiansborg.dk). Metro Kongens Nytorv. **Open** 1.30-4pm Tue-Sun. **Admission** 40kr; 20kr-30kr reductions. **No credit cards.** **Map** p61 F5 ⑪

The Queen's horses and coaches are still kept in grand style at the royal stables, and are often used for state occasions (as is a rather dusty Bentley convertible from 1969).

Christiansborg Slot: Ruinerne under Christiansborg

Christiansborg Slot, Prins Jørgens Gård 1 (33 92 64 94, www.christiansborg.dk). Metro Kongens Nytorv. **Open** *May-Sept* 10am-5pm daily. *Oct-Apr* 10am-4pm Tue-Sun. **Admission** 40kr; 35kr reductions. **No credit cards.** **Map** p61 F4 ⑫

Housed in three large underground rooms are excavations of the older castles' foundations, including stonework from Absalon's fortress; remnants of Denmark's most famous prison, the Blåtårn (Blue Tower); and what is called Absalon's Well (though it's likely to be from the 19th century). The Blåtårn was used for several centuries to house prisoners of note – most famously, Leonora Christina, daughter of Christian IV. She wrote what was probably the most important piece of 17th-century Danish prose, *Jammersminde*, while held here on suspicion of involvement in her husband's treason plot. Viewing this jumble of ancient masonry is like trying to put together the discarded pieces from several jigsaw puzzles, but the exhibition works hard to help you decipher the rubble (with English captions).

Christiansborg Slot: Teatermuseet

South wing of Christiansborg Slot, Christiansborg Ridebane 18 (33 11 51 76, www.teatermuseet.dk). Metro Kongens Nytorv. **Open** 11am-3pm Tue-Thur; 1-4pm Sat, Sun. **Admission** 40kr; 30kr reductions; free under-18s. **No credit cards.** **Map** p61 F4 ⑬

Exhibits on show at the Theatre Museum include costumes, set designs and artworks. There's also a special cabinet of objects connected with the Royal Ballet choreographer Auguste Bournonville.

FREE Christiansborg Slotskirke

Christiansborg Slotsplads (33 92 63 00, www.christiansborg.dk). Metro Kongens Nytorv. **Open** *Aug-June* noon-4pm Sun. *Easter, July, 1wk mid Aug, 1wk mid Oct* 10am-5pm daily. **Admission** free. **Map** p61 E4 ⑭

This church was completed in 1829 and survived a fire in 1884, but the roof was destroyed by another fire that started during the Whitsun carnival in 1992. It was restored just in time for the 25th anniversary of Queen Margrethe's coronation in 1997.

FREE Det Kongelige Bibliotek

Søren Kierkegaards Plads 1 (33 47 47 47, tours 91 32 48 80, www.kb.dk). Metro Kongens Nytorv. **Open** *Main building* July, Aug 8am-7pm Mon-Sat. Sept-June 8am-10pm Mon-Sat. *Guided tours* 3pm Sat. **Admission** *Main building* free. *Concerts* varies. **Map** p61 G5 ⑮

This malevolent parallelogram, made from glass, black Zimbabwean granite (cut in Portugal and polished in Italy), Portuguese sandstone, silk concrete and Canadian maple, is known as the Black Diamond and abuts the old building with little consideration for the clash of styles that ensues. Its reflective surfaces interact constantly with the sky and water, altering the building's colour by the second. The 500-million-kroner library houses 200,000 books, an exhibition space, a shop, a concert hall, a Michelin-starred restaurant (Søren K; *see p83*) and a café. The basement also holds the National Museum of Photography (40kr), and hosts occasional exhibitions from the Book Museum. The old library, the largest in Scandinavia, with its glorious reading room, is accessed through a glass walkway from the first floor.

Danish Jewish Museum

Kongelige Bibliotek, entrance via garden (33 11 22 18, www.jewmus.dk). Metro Kongens Nytorv. **Open** *June-Aug* 10am-5pm Tue-Sun.

IN THE KNOW
HIDDEN TREASURES

Slotsholmen's museums and sights are generally tucked away behind doors or in unlikely corners, which somehow makes them all the more rewarding when you do manage to track them down – that's a polite way of saying that it's a bit of a labyrinth and its main attractions are, in typical Danish fashion, poorly signposted. It's a good idea to come on a Sunday afternoon when all the attractions are open at the same time.

EXPLORE

Nationalmuseet.

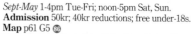

Sept-May 1-4pm Tue-Fri; noon-5pm Sat, Sun.
Admission 50kr; 40kr reductions; free under-18s.
Map p61 G5 ⑯
This striking adaptation of the Royal Boat House
was designed by Daniel Libeskind, responsible also
for the Jewish Museum in Berlin and the new development at Ground Zero in New York. The museum
is inspired by the Hebrew word 'Mitzvah', which
loosely means 'compassion' and refers in part to the
good deeds done by the Danes towards the Jewish
community during World War II. Danish-Jewish art,
history and culture are well represented. *Photos p78.*

FREE Holmens Kirke
*Holmens Kanal (33 13 61 78, www.holmens
kirke.dk). Bus 1A, 26, 66.* **Open** 10am-4pm
Mon, Wed, Fri, Sat; 10am-3.30pm Tue,
Thur; noon-4pm Sun. **Admission** free.
Map p61 E5 ⑰
This church dedicated to sailors is worth visiting to
see Denmark's tallest pulpit (it extends right to the
roof, and has recently been restored). Converted,
aptly, from an anchor smithy in 1619 under the
orders of Christian IV, the church's rather bland
exterior was augmented by the main portal (on the
east side), originally from Roskilde Cathedral.
Holmens Kirke is often used for royal occasions –
Queen Margrethe and Prince Henrik were married
here in 1967. Walk through the side door on the left
of the altar and you'll enter a room dedicated to
Denmark's naval heroes and graced by numerous
ornate sarcophagi.

★ FREE Nationalmuseet
*Ny Vestergade 10 (33 13 44 11, www.
natmus.dk). Bus 1A, 2A, 9A, 11A, 40.*

Open 10am-5pm Tue-Sun. **Admission** free.
Map p61 F3 ⑱
The National Museum's main home is in Prinsens
Palæ (Prince's Palace), and the museum has recently
scrapped all admission fees, so now there's no
excuse not to swot up on your Danish history.
Visitors enter via a large, airy main hall, once a
courtyard, but now enclosed with a glass roof
(it's sometimes used as a concert venue). To the
right, on the ground floor, is the Prehistoric Wing,
showing Danish history from the reindeer hunters
of the Ice Age to the Vikings. Here, you can marvel
at archaeological finds from the Early Bronze Age
unearthed in Denmark's bogs – the most impressive
of which is the collection of large bronze horns, or
lurs (some still playable), played to appease the sun
god. Also on this floor is the Children's Museum
(rooms 51-55), which attempts to condense all the
rest of the museum into an exhibition suitable for
four- to 12-year-olds.

Upstairs, the glorious Medieval and Renaissance
department covers the pre- and post-Reformation
periods, and majors on ecclesiastical and decorative
art. Pieces here come from the era of the great
Renaissance kings: Christian III, Frederik II and
Christian IV. The surviving example of Frederik's
tapestries of kings, made for the Great Hall of
Kronborg Slot, is a marvel.

The Royal Collection of Coins and Medals, though
one of the more specialist sections in the museum, is
intriguing. It is said to be one of the most beautiful
in the city, and has views over Marmorbroen
(Marble Bridge) and Christiansborg Slot. On the top
floor is the museum's Collection of Antiquities, a
mini take on the British Museum, with pieces from
Egypt, Greece and Italy. On the same floor is a

charming toy museum, which begins with a mention of a rattle in Saxo Grammaticus's *Gesta Danorum* and continues through early 16th-century German toys, a spectacular array of doll's houses, Lego (of course) and toy soldiers.

★ Thorvaldsens Museum

Bertel Thorvaldsens Plads 2 (33 32 15 32, www.thorvaldsensmuseum.dk). Bus 1A, 2A, 14, 26, 40, 66. **Admission** 40kr; free under-18s. Free to all Wed. **Map** p61 E4 ⑲
See p80 **Denmark's Wandering Hero**.

FREE Tøjhusmuseet

Tøjhusgade 3 (33 11 60 37, www.thm.dk). Bus 1A, 2A, 14, 26, 40, 66. **Open** noon-4pm Tue-Sun. **Admission** free. **Map** p61 F5 ㉚
The Royal Arsenal Museum is based in what was Christian IV's original arsenal building (1589-1604). On the ground floor, within walls 4m (13ft) thick, are a vast number of gun carriages, cannons, a V-1 flying bomb from World War II and the tiniest tank you ever saw (from 1933). Upstairs, the glass cases, containing everything from 15th-century swords and pikes to modern machine guns, seem to go on forever. Many items, such as the beautiful ivory-inlaid pistols and muskets, are works of art, and the royal suits of armour are stunning. The small-arms section of the museum is housed in Kongens Bryghus (King's Brewery).

Restaurants

Søren K

Det Kongelige Bibliotek, Søren Kierkegaards Plads 1 (33 47 49 49, www.soerenk.dk). Metro Kongens Nytorv. **Open** noon-4pm, 5.30-10pm Mon-Sat. **Main courses** *Lunch* 85kr-180kr. *Dinner* 225kr-250kr. **Set menu** 350kr-500kr. **Map** p61 G5 ㉛ **Contemporary**
This super-cool minimalist Scandinavian restaurant on the ground floor of the Black Diamond is a very popular lunch venue, and dining here is a great way to see the building's interior design. There are probably more atmospheric destinations for a night out, but this is one of the surprisingly few restaurants to take full advantage of Copenhagen's waterside location (but be warned, a stiff sea breeze can blight alfresco dinners even in summer). The food is refreshingly light, imaginatively prepared by head chef Jens Søndergaard, and highly regarded by locals. Style, substance and a view – what more could you ask for?

Cafés & Bars

The small café in the **Thorvaldsens Museum** (*see above*) is delightfully serene, situated as it is in one of the museum's exhibition rooms, with works by the sculptor all around.

Øieblikket

Det Kongelige Bibliotek, Søren Kierkegaards Plads 1 (33 47 49 49). Metro Kongens Nytorv. **Open** 8am-7pm Mon-Fri; 9am-7pm Sat. **Map** p61 G5 ㉜
The Black Diamond's espresso bar is named after the magazine that Søren Kirkegaard used to edit. It's a popular lunch spot, offering decent sandwiches and soups, and good coffee. But the main draw is the view of Copenhagen's waterfront; there are lounge chairs on the terrace during the summer.

Søren K.

Nørreport & Rosenborg

The area around Nørreport station has undergone a renaissance in the past few years, mainly due to the 2011 opening of the covered food market, Torvehallerne, now one of Copenhagen's culinary hotspots. The area between the market and the Lakes is also now home to some arty restaurants and cafés, along with a host of artisan shops, especially on genteel Nansensgade. The area to the north-east, on the other side of Gothersgade, is much greener, dominated by the Botanical Garden, Østre Anlæg park and the 17th-century Rosenborg Slot. Around the palace, you'll find a series of six attractions that make up the so-called 'Parkmuseerne' museum district, including the Hirschsprungske Samling art collection, the Statens Museum for Kunst (National Gallery) and the jewel of the city's cinema scene, the Filmhuset.

EXPLORE

Botanisk Have.

Don't Miss

1 Torvehallerne Gourmet Danish and international foodstuffs and a buzzing vibe (p87).

2 Botanisk Have This lovely botanical garden has recently been expanded (p91).

3 Höst One of the city's most likeable New Nordic restaurants (p86).

4 Rosenborg Slot The city's fairytale palace (p91).

5 Filmhuset The Danish national film theatre is a dynamic institution (p90).

Höst.

NØRREPORT & AROUND

Head north beyond Nørre Voldgade (the northern boundary of the old city ramparts), and you'll arrive at an area dominated by two things: **Nørreport** Metro and S-train station – which has been blighted by construction work for the City Ring Metro development over the past few years – and the city's excellent covered food market, **Torvehallerne**. The latter opened in 2011 in a purpose-built pair of modern food halls in the centre of **Israels Plads**, the public square named in honour of the Danes who helped 7,000 Jews escape during World War II. The gourmet market is now a culinary focus for the city, and has done much to rejuvenate the surrounding area.

Just north of Israels Plads is **Arbejdermuseet** (Workers' Museum). The museum's entrance was once guarded by a statue of Lenin that looks as if it's come straight from a provincial Soviet town square, but the right-wing government of the noughties turned this into a political issue and the statue was moved round to the back of the museum. In fact, the statue is here because the Danish co-operative, the Workers' Fuel Suppliers, helped pay for Lenin's passage from exile in Switzerland home to Russia. Arbejdermuseet was refurbished fairly recently, but remains a rather dry, worthy place and is an unlikely choice for the average tourist.

The area south of Israels Plads is dominated by **Ørstedsparken**, one of a series of parks constructed on the remnants of the old city fortifications, after it was decommissioned in the 1870s. Dominated by a large lake, it's a relaxed spot for a stroll. The north-western side of the park is formed by Nørre Farimagsgade, where you'll find popular New Nordic restaurant **Höst**, one of the latest ventures from excellent local mini-chain Cofoco. Nansensgade, the next street up, is also worth visiting for its genteel atmosphere and traditional artisan shops, many of which are hidden away in unobtrusive basement spaces. On the corner sits **Ibsens Hotel** (*see p221*), its neon-red sign something of a local landmark.

Sights & Museums

Arbejdermuseet
Rømersgade 22 (33 93 25 75, www.arbejdermuseet. dk). Metro/train Nørreport. **Open** 10am-4pm daily. **Admission** 65kr; 55kr reductions; free under-18s. **Map** p88 C4 **❶**
This atmospheric building, formerly the headquarters of the Social Democratic Party, has a wonderful period basement café and *ølhal* (beer hall). While the museum's aim – to show how Danish workers' lives have changed over the past century – is admirable, its political bias gets a little oppressive. The most interesting exhibit is an entire apartment that remained unaltered through the course of the 20th century, and was donated to the museum in 1990. Be warned: the place swarms with school trips on weekdays.

Restaurants

Haché
Rømersgade 20 (33 12 21 16, www.hache.dk). Metro/train Nørreport. **Open** noon-9.30pm Mon-Sat; noon-9pm Sun. **Main courses** 95kr-105kr. **Map** p88 C5 **❷** Burgers
Nothing to do with the UK chain, Haché, next door to the Arbejdermuseet (*see above*) and near the Botanical Garden, is the city's burger bar of choice. The list of 16 burgers includes some original options, such as the Iberico with manchego, chorizo and garlic mayo, and the beef is organic.

★ Höst
Nørre Farimagsgade 41 (89 93 84 09, www. cofoco.dk). Metro/train Nørreport. **Open** 5.30pm-midnight daily. **Main courses** 75kr-215kr. **Set meal** 295kr 3 courses. **Map** p88 C5 **❸** New Nordic

This two-storey restaurant located close to the Lakes is as Nordic as they come, with raw aesthetics – think recycled wood, concrete floors and sheepskin rugs – and dishes made with local produce, such as lobster, beef and Danish cheese. Traditional Nordic recipes are given a modern twist, resulting in combinations such as veal brisket with yellow peas, mustard lettuce, pickled onions and smoked cheese, and smoked lumpfish and lumpfish roe with broccoli and a beer-based foam, which are an easy introduction to New Nordic cuisine. The restaurant is one of the newest offerings from Cofoco (Copenhagen Food Consulting), which is also behind Les Trois Cochons (*see p124*).

Sticks 'n' Sushi

Nansensgade 47 (33 11 14 07, www.sushi.dk). *Metro/train Nørreport.* **Open** 10am-10pm Mon-Thur, Sun; 10am-10.30pm Fri, Sat. **Set menu** 179kr-225kr. **Map** p88 B5 ❹ **Japanese**
If you can forgive the heinous abbreviation in the name, you will find this to be one of Copenhagen's most stylish sushi restaurants (it was also the first), with branches in three of the city's coolest residential streets. The menu varies depending on the fish available, but the quality remains generally high (as do the prices). There is a well-stocked rack of magazines to peruse as you await the arrival of your sashimi. **Other locations** Øster Farimagsgade 16B, Indre By (35 38 34 63); Strandvejen 195, Hellerup (39 40 15 40); Istedgade 62, Vesterbro (33 23 73 04).

Cafés & Bars

Indoor market **Torvehallerne** (*see below* **Market Forces**) is a great spot for a coffee and a good-quality pastry – or even a three-course lunch.

Bankeråt

Ahlefeldtsgade 27-29 (33 93 69 88, www. *bankeraat.dk).* Metro/train Nørreport. **Open** 9.30am-midnight Mon-Fri; 10.30am-midnight Sat, Sun. **No credit cards.** Map p88 B5 ❺

MARKET FORCES

Foodies should make a beeline for Torvehallerne.

Who doesn't love a covered food market? Like a latterday Garden of Eden with no forbidden fruits (or rain), they're a paradise for foodies everywhere. And yet, remarkably, modern Copenhagen didn't have one until 2011, when **Torvehallerne** (*see p90*) opened on Israels Plads.

Made up of two purpose-built glass and steel halls on the former site of, yes, a market that had closed decades earlier, Torvehallerne has, not surprisingly, been a huge success. Seven days a week, the halls, which are home to some 60 stalls, hum with boisterous chatter and teem with activity; the surrounding square is filled with customers' bikes, and both it and the wider area have been rejuvenated.

The emphasis is firmly – but far from exclusively – on Danish food. You could easily work your way from breakfast through to supper, beginning with on-trend porridge from **Grød** (Hall 2, stall A8) and a very superior tea from **Tante T** (Hall 2, stall B2), where the cool mint is a knockout and tea-making accessories will make great gifts. Caffeine-lovers should head for the excellent **Coffee Collective** (Hall 2, stalls C1 & D1), whose coffees change depending on what's in season. For a mid-morning break, **Gorm's** (Hall 1, stalls H1 & G1) does terrific pizzas with both Italian and Danish toppings, while **Smag** (Hall 2, stall B5) offers healthy salads to take away. For heartier meals, fish stall **Fiskerikajen** (Hall 1, stalls H9 & G9) cooks up fish and chips, and there are delicious duck confit sandwiches at **Ma Poule** (Hall 1, stalls F9, E9 & E10), the French-inspired poultry shop imported from London's Borough Market. But it's not all about eating; there are lovely treats to take home too. A wide range of food and drink from the tiny island of Bornholm is on sale at **Spis Bornholmsk** (Hall 1, stall F6), but for the real wow effect, visit the **Summerbird Chocolaterie** stand (Hall 2, stalls A3 & B3) to pick up some Flødeboller – a chocolate-covered marshmallow sweet loved by Danes, and probably by your loved ones at home too.

EXPLORE

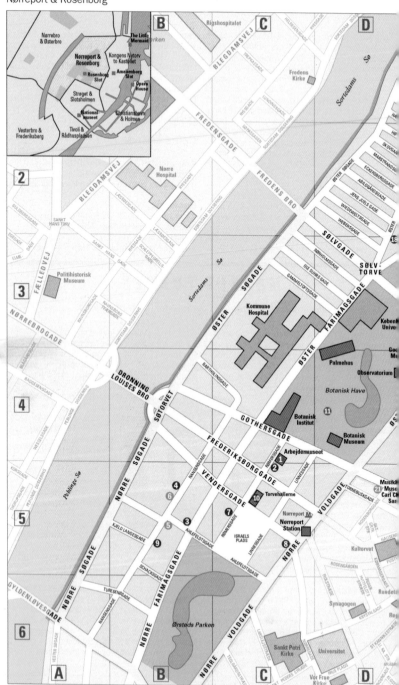

EXPLORE

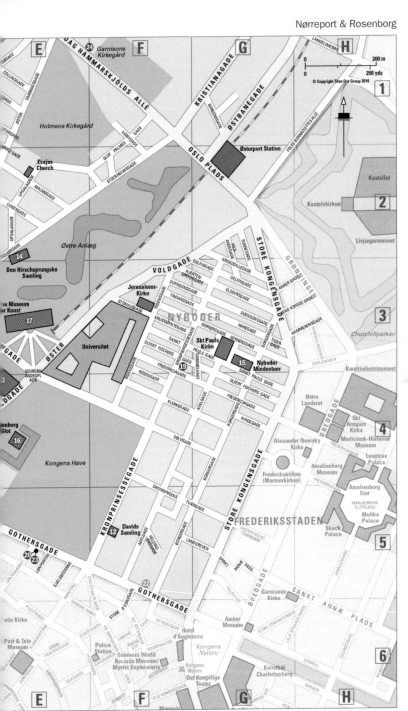

Monster brunches, great tortillas and pasta dishes, plus the quirkiest decor of all Copenhagen's cafés, set this grungy boho cave apart. Brace yourself for a sobering encounter when you descend to the basement loos, as you're confronted by a ghoulish assortment of Gothic taxidermy tableaux – animals standing upright wearing long leather coats are a favourite. And parents, beware, porn awaits. A weird and wonderful place.

Vincaféen Bibendum
Nansensgade 45 (33 33 07 74, www.bibendum.dk). Metro/train Nørreport. **Open** 4pm-midnight Mon-Sat. **Map** p88 B5 ⑥
With a big role in the gentrification of Nansensgade, this cosy, sexy wine bar complements its more rough and ready neighbour Bankeråt (*see p87*) with an extensive range of wines by the glass (unusual in beer-minded Copenhagen) and a flirty cellar ambience. The tapas plates are excellent and the staff knowledgeable. Argentinian wines are a speciality.

Shops & Services

Décor
Rømersgade 9 (33 14 80 98, www.decorvintage.dk). Metro/train Nørreport. **Open** noon-6pm Tue-Fri; 10am-4pm Sat. **Map** p88 C5 ⑦ **Fashion**
Located next to Torvehallerne market on Israels Plads, this wonderful store offers Copenhagen ladies the chance to unearth quality vintage clothing at bargain prices, while Edith Piaf sets a suitably nostalgic tone on the shop stereo.

Østerlandsk Thehus
Nørre Voldgade 9 (33 13 10 00, www.osterlandsk thehus.dk). Metro/train Nørreport. **Open** 10am-6pm Mon-Thur; 10am-7pm Fri; 10am-4pm Sat; 11am-4pm Sun. **Map** p88 C5 ⑧ **Food & drink**
What Perchs is to tea, Østerlandsk Thehus is to Copenhagen's coffee scene. The interior, originally by the designer behind Tivoli's chinoiserie decor, has recently been restored to its former glory. You'll find the finest coffee beans from around the world, own blends and a dazzling assortment of gleaming coffeemakers and equipment.

★ Piet Breinholm – The Last Bag
Nansensgade 48 (42 32 73 91, www.piet breinholm.dk). Metro/train Nørreport. **Open** 11am-7pm Fri; or by appointment. **Map** p88 B5 ⑨ **Accessories**
Colourful leather satchels inspired by traditional school bags, designed by Copenhagener Piet Breinhol. The shop is located in an atmospheric space on Nansensgade, close to other artisan shops and art dealers.

★ Torvehallerne
Frederiksborggade 21 (70 10 60 70, www. torvehallernekbh.dk). Metro/train Nørreport.

Open 10am-7pm Mon-Thur; 10am-8pm Fri; 10am-6pm Sat; 11am-5pm Sun. **Map** p88 C5 ⑩ **Food & drink**
See p87 **Market Forces**.

ROSENBORG SLOT & AROUND

North of Gothersgade is the **Botanisk Have & Museum** (Botanical Garden & Museum), providing Elysian relief from the city's streets in summer, while its balmy Palmehus (Palm House), modelled after the one at London's Kew Gardens, can provide refuge from the arctic frost of winter. The garden has been extensively renovated in recent years, and looks better than ever. Just to the north is the **Geologisk Museum** (Geological Museum), while further north, the lakes of the **Østre Anlæg** park follow the line of the city's old defensive moat. Within the park are two fine museums: **Statens Museum for Kunst** is Denmark's national gallery and largest art museum, a position that it consolidated in 1998 with the opening of an extension by architect Anna Maria Indrio; **Den Hirschsprungske Samling** (Hirschsprung Collection) contains art from the 19th and early 20th centuries, and is particularly strong on the Danish Golden Age.

Across from Statens Museum is the entrance to the oldest park in Copenhagen, **Kongens Have** (King's Garden), and **Rosenborg Slot** (Rosenborg Palace). A glimpse of this fairy-tale, Dutch Renaissance castle in the heart of Copenhagen never fails to surprise, and more pleasures await inside, not least the crown jewels.

On Gothersgade is **Filmhuset** (Film House; *see p161*), the Danish Film Institute's (DFI) world-class complex devoted to Danish and international cinema, and on Kronprinsessegade

Kongens Have.

is yet another treasure house of a museum, **Davids Samling**, a gorgeous collection of Danish, Islamic and European art.

At the north end of Store Kongensgade is **Nyboder**. While Kastellet was for centuries home to the army, the royal navy lived in the Lilliputian, ochre terraces of Nyboder, built during Christian IV's time, to house over 2,200 naval staff (a purpose it still serves). There's a small museum, **Nyboders Mindestuer** (Nyboder Memorial Rooms).

Sights & Museums

★ FREE Botanisk Have & Museum

Gothersgade 128 (35 32 22 40, www.botanik. snm.ku.dk). Metro/train Nørreport. **Open** *Garden* May-Sept 8.30am-6pm daily. Oct-Apr 8.30am-4pm Tue-Sun. *Palm house* May-Sept 10am-3pm daily. Oct-Apr 10am-3pm Tue-Sun. *Cacti* 1-2pm Wed, Sat, Sun. *Orchids* 2-3pm Wed, Sat, Sun. *Endangered species* 1-3pm Wed, Sat, Sun. *Alpine plants* May-Sept 11am-2pm Wed. *Museum* open only for exhibitions, check online or phone (35 32 22 00). Sept-May closed. **Admission** free. **Map** p88 D4 ⑪

The Botanical Garden was laid out in 1871 to designs by HA Flindt, with a lake that was once part of the city moat as its centrepiece. You'll find examples of most of Denmark's flora, as well as those exotic plants that could be persuaded to grow this far north. The garden recently underwent a three-year, 17-million kroner renovation, reopening in 2012 with enlarged grounds, new paths, irrigation systems and greenhouses, and a small wooden lakeside wharf area. The delightful shop near the entrance is the place to pick up a botanical poster or bar of fragrant soap.

There's also an on-site natural history museum that is currently being expanded to form the nucleus of the upcoming Natural History Museum of Denmark, a new institution that will unite this venue, the Zoological Museum (*see p143*) and the Geologisk Museum (*see right*) in a variety of new and existing buildings. It's expected to be completed in 2018; visit www.nyt.snm.ku.dk for updates.

FREE Davids Samling

Kronprinsessegade 30 (33 73 49 49, www. davidmus.dk). Metro/train Nørreport. **Open** 10am-5pm Tue, Thur-Sun; 10am-9pm Wed. **Admission** free. **Map** p89 F5 ⑫

This art and antiquities museum is housed in what once was the home of its founder, Christian Ludvig David, as well as in another 19th-century property next door. Both buildings underwent comprehensive renovation between 2005 and 2009. David (who died in 1960) was a prominent lawyer, whose collections spanned European 18th-century art, Danish Early Modern works, and Islamic art and artefacts. The last is the largest and most important of the museum's holdings, and has grown to become one of the ten most important collections of its kind in

the Western world, covering the entire classical Islamic world, from Spain to India, and from the eighth to the 19th centuries. The European items include furniture, porcelain and paintings (with lots of Dutch and French portraits).

Geologisk Museum

Øster Voldgade 5-7 (35 32 23 45, www.geologisk-museum.dk). Metro/train Nørreport. **Open** 10am-1pm Tue-Fri; 1-4pm Sat, Sun. **Admission** 40kr; 25kr reductions. **Map** p89 E4 ⑬

Head here for displays of fossils and dinosaurs, as well as exhibitions on the solar system and the geological evolution of Denmark. The museum – which has been looking a little tired of late – is now part of the Natural History Museum of Denmark, which will eventually become a new multi-venue museum based within the Botanical Garden (*see left*), expected to be completed in 2018.

Den Hirschsprungske Samling

Stockholmsgade 20 (35 42 03 36, www. hirschsprung.dk). Metro/train Nørreport. **Open** 11am-4pm Tue-Sun. **Admission** 75kr; 65kr reductions; free under-18s. Free to all Wed. **Map** p89 E2 ⑭

This art collection from the 19th and early 20th centuries is strong on the Danish Golden Age (1800-50). It was created by tobacco manufacturer Heinrich Hirschsprung (1836-1908), who crammed the paintings and sculptures into his home on Højbro Plads. He donated the works to the Municipality of Copenhagen on condition that they be displayed in similarly intimate surroundings, hence the series of small rooms around three larger halls that make up the building. The museum opened in 1911 and has continued to purchase works ever since.

Nyboders Mindestuer

Sankt Pauls Gade 24 (33 32 10 05, guided tours 33 32 79 13, www.nybodersmindestuer.dk). Train Østerport, or bus 1A, 15, 19. **Open** 11am-2pm Sun. *Guided tours* by appointment. **Admission** 15kr; 10kr reductions. **No credit cards**. **Map** p89 G3 ⑮

This charming little museum is based in the oldest part of Nyboder, the naval social housing complex built in the 17th and 18th centuries and consisting of rows of distinctive ochre-coloured houses. It depicts the living conditions of a Nyboder family at the start of the 20th century.

★ Rosenborg Slot

Øster Voldgade 4A (33 15 32 86, www. rosenborgslot.dk). Metro/train Nørreport. **Open** Nov-Apr 11am-4pm Tue-Sun. *May, Sept, Oct* 10am-4pm daily. *June-Aug* 10am-5pm daily. Closed mid Dec-26 Dec. **Admission** 90kr; 60kr reductions; free under-17s. **Map** p89 E4 ⑯

Though it was built at the same time as Frederiksberg Slot, Rosenborg was Christian IV's favourite residence.

EXPLORE

Towards the end of his life, Christian, aged 70, was taken by sleigh through the snow from Frederiksborg to Rosenborg. He literally pulled up the palace drawbridge to escape the harsh economic realities of Denmark's ruin and to contemplate a bitter death.

The castle started as a small summer house. Christian extended it between 1606 and 1634, finishing with the octagonal staircase tower designed by the fantastically named Hans van Steenwinckel the Younger. Rosenborg is still jammed full of the king's fancies: toys, architectural tricks, inventions, art objects and jewellery, which he gathered from across Europe like a regal Mr Toad. A source of great pride was the basement, where his orchestra would perform, the music travelling up through a complex system of pipes connected to his living quarters. These days, the basement houses the Treasury, the stronghold of the crown jewels – a collection in which quality, not quantity, is the watchword. The star piece is the Golden Crown of the Absolute Monarchy, decorated with sapphires, diamonds and rubies, made by Poul Kurtz in 1670, and used by Denmark's kings for 170 years. Christian IV's gold, pearl and jewel-encrusted saddle and crown (1595) are, as you'd expect, jaw-dropping. Newer rooms in the basement display royal weapons and objets d'art of ivory and amber.

Rosenborg was a royal residence until 1838, when these collections were opened to the public, along with the many rooms that had remained intact from the time of Christian IV (1588-1648) to Frederik IV (1699-1730); later rooms were re-created. The decision to arrange the rooms chronologically was, at the time, radical; consequently, Rosenborg claims to be the first museum of contemporary culture in Europe. The 24 rooms (plus six Treasury rooms) currently on show offer an insight into the lives of Renaissance kings that is perhaps unparalleled in Europe for its atmosphere and intimacy. Christian IV's toilet, covered in beautiful blue Dutch tiles, for example, is as fascinating a treasure as the jewels in the basement.

IN THE KNOW PARKMUSEERNE

Though it's been the unofficial 'museum district' of Copenhagen for quite some time, 2014 saw the launch of an official title for the area north of Gothersgade: **Parkmuseerne**. The district encompasses six of the area's visitor attractions – Statens Museum for Kunst, Davids Samling, Den Hirschsprungske Samling, Rosenborg Slot, the Natural History Museum of Denmark and the Filmhuset – as well as its extensive green spaces. A combined ticket provides admission to all these museums, as well as a free screening at the Filmhuset. The ticket costs 195kr and is sold at all six venues; visit www.parkmuseerne.dk for details.

Statens Museum for Kunst

Sølvgade 48-50 (33 74 84 94, www.smk.dk). Metro/train Nørreport. **Open** 10am-5pm Tue, Thur-Sun; 10am-8pm Wed. **Admission** 110kr; 85kr reductions; free under-18s. **Map** p89 E3 ⓱

The Statens Museum for Kunst was founded in 1824, but its world-class collection has its origins in royal holdings from centuries earlier. During the 19th century, it was based in Christiansborg Slot, until a fire meant it had to move (in 1896) to the current building, purpose-built by Vilhelm Dahlerup. A new wing was added in 1998, which has proved to be a controversial space in which to display Danish and European art from the 20th century onwards. Some say the new gallery fails to provide appropriate rooms in which to exhibit the work; others find its combination of vast glass windows (overlooking Østre Anlæg park) and unrelenting stone offers a pleasing spatial puzzle.

The SMK's focus is, of course, Danish art, and the Danish masters from the Golden Age of the early 19th century figure prominently. Rooms are dedicated to CW Eckersburg and his pupils Christen Købke and Constantin Hansen. The landscapes of JT Lundbye, the stark portraits of Vilhelm Hammershøi, the powerful portraits of LA Ring and the symbolist pieces by PC Skovgaard – as well as their forerunners from the 18th century, such as Nicolai Abildgaard and Jens Juel – are among the best treats in the museum. The Skagen artists (Michael and Anna Ancher, PS Krøyer), who specialised in everyday scenes and light, summery landscapes, and the Fyn painters (Peter Hansen, Frits Syberg), are also well represented. Though the works are sometimes sentimental, no one before or since has quite captured the unmistakeable, crisp Danish light as these artists did, and their paintings often depict brutal, beautiful and compelling stories concerning 'real' people's lives.

In the new wing, 25 paintings by Henri Matisse, as well as works by Braque, Munch and Picasso, are highlights, as is the Danish modernist collection featuring the painters Harald Giersing and Karl Isakson, and sculptors Kai Nielsen and Astrid Noack. In the old wing, the Italians are well represented by Titian, Tintoretto, Filippino Lippi, Mantegna and Guardi; Dutch and Flemish masters from the 15th to 17th centuries include Rubens, Bruegel, Rembrandt, Van Dyck and Van Goyen; while Fragonard, Poussin and Lorrain are among the 18th-century French artists.

There's also a children's art museum, a large bookshop and a café. The museum entrance and garden underwent extensive renovation in 2013-14, creating an entirely new (and more accessible) staircase.

Restaurants

★ Aamanns Etablissement

Øster Farimagsgade 12 (35 55 33 10, www.aamanns.dk). Train Østerport. **Open** 11.30am-4pm Tue; 11.30am-4pm, 6-11pm Wed-Sun. **Set meals** 290kr 3 courses; 395kr 5 courses. **Map** p88 D3 ⓲ Modern Danish

Aamanns Etablissment.

At last, a modern spin on the nation's beloved *smørrebrød*. Visit this elegant, light-filled restaurant of scrubbed wood floors and dove-grey walls to sample Adam Aamann's moreish open-topped sandwiches at lunchtime, or a heartier Modern Danish meal, based on local, seasonal ingredients (poached haddock with local veg, say, or braised pork cheeks with creamy spelt) in the evening. If you're here for the *smørrebrød*, choose from inspired combinations such as home-cured herring on leek salad and parsley cream; thick slices of slow-cooked pork belly topped with zingy cranberry purée; or organic Danish blue cheese with hazelnut butter.

▶ *Next door, at no.12, is Aamanns (33 55 33 44), where you can choose lunchtime smørrebrød to eat-in at the small café table or take away in a beautifully packaged box.*

★ Kokkeriet Spisehus & Catering
Kronprinsessegade 64 (33 15 27 77, www. kokkeriet.dk). Train Østerport. **Open** 6pm-1am Tue-Sat. **Main courses** 375kr. **Set meals** 700kr 4 courses; 1,100kr 8 courses. **Map** p89 F3 ⑲
French/Danish
Tucked away in Nyboder, this small, seductive restaurant is really a multifunctional food space that includes a catering company and, more recently, monthly cooking classes (1,800kr). It won a Michelin star in 2006 and is still going great guns to impress. Loved by locals, Kokkeriet has thrived thanks to its superb kitchen and lively dishes, such as veal with Swedish lumpfish roe and marinated beetroot, and wild boar with apples and celery purée. Exceptional quality, and worth hunting out.

Sult
Filmhuset, Vognmagergade 8B (33 74 34 17, www.sult.dk). Metro/train Nørreport. **Open** 10am-10pm Tue-Sun. **Main courses** 100kr-250kr. **Map** p89 E5 ⑳ **Global**

The Danish Film Institute's magnificent film ce. has another draw. Here, skilful chefs successfully combine southern European food and global influences in handsome, modern, New York-ish surroundings (high ceilings, wooden floors, tall windows). Sult (short for *sulten*, which means 'hungry' in Danish – it's named after Henning Larsen's classic 1966 film of the same name).

Cafés & Bars

★ Café Det Vide Hus
Gothersgade 113 (60 61 20 02). Metro/train Nørreport. **Open** 7.30am-6pm Mon-Fri; 11am-5.30pm Sat, Sun. **Map** p88 D5 ㉑
Located in a little white house close to Kongens Have, Café Det Vide Hus is a popular spot for those who take their coffee seriously, and like a homely space in which to enjoy it. The cosy, two-storey café has comfy sofas, newspapers for browsing, views of Rosenborg Slot and excellent brownies, cakes and fruit smoothies. No wonder Noma founder Rene Redzepi is a regular.

Mo'Joe
Gothersgade 26 (33 32 01 05, www.mojoe.dk). Metro Kongens Nytorv. **Open** 7.30am-11pm Mon-Thur; 7.30am-midnight Fri; 9am-3am Sat; 10am-11pm Sun. **Map** p89 F5 ㉒
This corner café on bustling Gothersgade may have changed its name from Mojo to MJ Coffee and then to Mo'Joe, but, thankfully, the quality of the coffee, the lengthy menu and the wonderful cakes remain the same. It's very popular and a great place in which to ruminate while sipping a coffee and watching the world go by, thanks to the floor-to-ceiling windows. Soups, salads and smoothies are also available.

Shops & Services

Filmhusets Film & Boghandel
Filmhuset, Gothersgade 55 (33 74 34 21, www.dfi.dk). Metro/train Nørreport. **Open** 9.30am-3.30pm Mon; 9.30am-10pm Tue-Fri; noon-10pm Sat; noon-7.30pm Sun. **Map** p89 E5 ㉓
Books & music
There's no safer haven for cinephiles than Filmhuset (*see p161*) – headquarters of the Danish Film Institute – and its bookshop is the best place to pick up that elusive tome on Scandinavian cinema, as well as DVDs, film posters and more.

Samarkand
Dag Hammarskjölds Allé 32 (35 38 14 45, www.samarkand.dk). Train Østerport, or bus 1A, 14, 40. **Open** noon-6pm Mon-Fri; 11am-4pm Sat. **Map** p89 E1 ㉔ **Accessories**
Jane Eberlein makes only 100 luxurious Mongolian-style embroidered silk and fur hats a year, and Queen Silvia of Sweden and Hillary Clinton are among the well-to-do heads she has covered.

EXPLORE

Nytorv to Kastellet

EXPLORE

Windswept Kongens Nytorv (literally 'King's New Square') is one of Copenhagen's grandest squares and home to some of its finest buildings, including the Royal Theatre (Old Stage) and the Thotts Palais. Strøget, canalside Nyhavn, and Bredgade all radiate from it. The latter is Frederiksstaden's main thoroughfare. From here, the architecture changes dramatically, from multicoloured gabled houses, to the straight, wide, French-influenced streets laid out in the 18th century for Copenhagen's nobility. Along the water, new architecture – such as the Royal Danish Playhouse – and museums dominate. The area is also home to Copenhagen's reluctant city symbol, the *Little Mermaid*, sitting slumped on a rock just beyond the Kastellet, the city's historic citadel.

Marmorkirken.

Don't Miss

1 Marmorkirken Marble-domed church with awe-inspiring interior (p105).

2 Designmuseum Danmark The works of the country's celebrated furniture designers (p104).

3 The Standard This jazz club houses three superb restaurants (p98).

4 Nyhavn Colourful canalside strip (p96).

5 Royal Danish Playhouse Contemporary building with a terrace offering waterside views (p102).

Nyhavn.

KONGENS NYTORV & NYHAVN

Kongens Nytorv was built in 1680 on the site of former ramparts that ringed the city in an arc all the way from Rådhuspladsen. It is an excellent starting point for a tour of the city, as **Bredgade**, **Nyhavn** and **Strøget** all start from it, and most of the other main sights are within a few minutes' walk. However, the square has resembled a building site for the past couple of years due to the construction of the City Ring Metro line, which won't be completed until 2018 (though digging in Kongens Nytorv should stop long before then).

The square is dominated to the south-east by **Det Kongelige Teater** (the Royal Theatre, Old Stage; *see p177 and p174* **A Three-Act Structure**). Before the opening of the new opera house, Denmark's national theatre was unusual in that it produced opera, ballet and theatre together in two auditoria – Gamle (old) Scene, and Nye (new) Scene – seating 2,550 people. Since the **Royal Danish Playhouse** (*see p175*) was completed at Kvæsthusbroen – round the corner from Nyhavn – the Gamle Scene has been used almost exclusively for ballet.

The main neo-Renaissance building, by Vilhelm Dahlerup and Ove Petersen, dates from 1872, but the theatre was founded in 1748. The Nye Scene was added in 1931, connected via an archway to the other side of Tordenskjoldsgade. The inscription outside, '*Ei blot til lyst*', is taken from the original building designed by Nicolai Eigtved and translates as 'Not just for pleasure'. This may suggest that productions are worthy affairs, but that doesn't stop most selling out way in advance – hence the theatre's need for other venues.

Working clockwise round the square from the theatre, you come to Denmark's first department store, the grand **Magasin**, which replaced the Hotel du Nord in 1894 and now has a stylish Metro station outside its main entrance; Hviids Vinstue, a venerable drinking den dating from 1723; the eastern end of Strøget; and **Hotel d'Angleterre** (*see p219*).

On a corner of the square opposite the hotel is an ornate kiosk decorated with gold relief

that depicts Denmark's early aviators. At no.4 is another of the square's finest buildings, the Dutch Palladian-style **Thotts Palais** (1685), named after a previous owner, Count Otto Thott. Today, the pink stucco palace houses the French Embassy. On the other side of Bredgade is the **Amber Museum**.

East of Kongens Nytorv is the canal of **Nyhavn**. This was opened by King Christian V in 1670 to allow ships access to central Copenhagen, but these days water traffic consists mostly of canal tour boats and a couple of floating cafés. The real traffic now is found on the sunny canalside pavements, outside the colourful buildings.

After the British bombardment of 1807, Nyhavn's so-called 'Palmy Days' of prosperity were brought to a rude end and the wealthy merchants moved out. By coincidence, **Hans Christian Andersen** moved in shortly after, and subsequently lived at three different addresses on the canal. During this time, Nyhavn's quayside saw service as one of the city's red-light districts, and as recently as the 1950s this was a disreputable place, lined with drinkers' bars, knocking shops and old-school tattoo parlours.

These days, Denmark's greatest writer would hardly recognise the place. If the sun so much as peeps from behind the clouds, hundreds of tables (plus, in autumn, the all-important umbrella heaters) from Nyhavn's ever-popular restaurants and cafés are put out on to the quayside. It has to be said that the restaurants along Nyhavn vary from decent to dreadful and few represent good value (**Cap Horn** at no.21 is an exception),

IN THE KNOW
WEAK AT THE KNEES

In the centre of Kongens Nytorv is a faintly absurd statue (by Abraham-César Lamoureux, dating from 1687) of the square's patron, King Christian V, depicting him as a Roman general astride his horse. The weight of the gilded lead statue finally proved too much for the horse's legs and it had to be recast in bronze in 1946.

EXPLORE

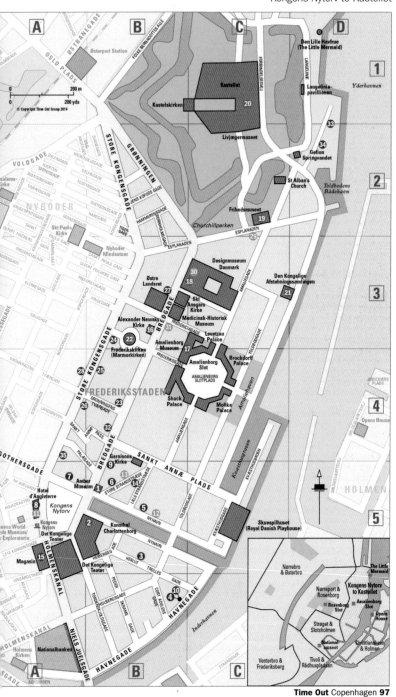

but the quayside is always a great place for a beer or two before heading elsewhere.

Two charming shopping streets lead off the north side of Nyhavn: **Store Strandstræde** and **Lille Strandstræde** are both good for antiques, clothes, art and ceramics. On the quieter south side, the main draw is the 17th-century Dutch baroque palace of **Charlottenborg**, now home to Det Kongelige Kunstakademi (Royal Academy of Fine Arts) since 1754. The former palace offers a changing programme of contemporary art exhibitions in the **Kunsthal Charlottenborg**. Further south-east, on waterside Havnegade, is the **Standard**, a new jazz club (see p170) and gastronomic temple; owned by New Nordic culinary pioneer Claus Meyer and jazz musician Niels Lan Doky, the art deco former hydrofoil terminal (which previously housed Terence Conran's Custom House) is home to three high-profile restaurants and welcomes jazz musicians from Scandinavia and around the world.

Sights & Museums

Amber Museum
Ravhuset, Kongens Nytorv 2 (33 11 67 00, www.houseofamber.com). Metro Kongens Nytorv. **Open** *May-Sept* 10am-6.30pm daily. *Oct-Apr* 10am-5.30pm daily. **Admission** 25kr; 10kr under-12s. **Map** p97 B5 ❶
This small museum, housed in a 17th-century building, has displays of amber antiques and artefacts, with lots of prehistoric entombed insects. If you just want to look at amber, browse in the shop below.

Kunsthal Charlottenborg
Nyhavn 2 (33 74 46 39, www.kunsthal charlottenborg.dk). Metro Kongens Nytorv. **Open** 11am-5pm Tue, Fri-Sun; 11am-8pm Wed. **Admission** 60kr; 40kr reductions. Free after 5pm Wed. **Map** p97 B5 ❷
This huge gallery alternates between Danish and international exhibitions of contemporary art, architecture and decorative arts. The hall was built in 1883 at the request of an influential group of Danish artists and is now run by the Ministry of Culture.

IN THE KNOW KVÆSTHUS

An exciting new waterfront space, **Kvæsthus Projektet** (www.kvaesthus projektet.dk) is currently being built at the end of Sankt Annæ Plads. Expected to be completed by late 2015, the pier-like public square sits next to the Royal Danish Playhouse and will be used for outdoor performing arts events in the summer months.

Restaurants

1.th
Herluf Trollesgade 9 (33 93 57 70, www.1th.dk). Metro Kongens Nytorv. **Open** from 6.30pm Wed-Sat. **Set meal** 1,395kr 8 courses incl wine. **Map** p97 B5 ❸ **Scandinavian**
This unusual and really rather splendid restaurant seems more like a private dinner party (or a piece of performance art) than a commercial catering enterprise. You pay when you book (two to three weeks in advance is advised to be sure of a table) and receive an invitation by return of post. When you arrive ('promptly at seven'), you buzz a discreetly labelled intercom on the door of an ordinary, turn-of-the-19th-century apartment block in the quiet residential area behind the Kongelige Teater, before being shown into a drawing room in which other 'guests' are mingling over aperitifs. After a while, doors are opened with a theatrical flourish to reveal a spacious dining room with an open kitchen. The set menu of contemporary, unfussy Scandinavian fare usually more than lives up to this elaborate preamble, though 1.th will have to work hard to stop the format from becoming tired now that it's been open several years.

★ Almanak at the Standard
Havnegade 44 (72 14 88 08, www.thestandard cph.dk/almanak). Metro Kongens Nytorv, or bus 11A, 66. **Open** 11.30am-2.30pm, 5.30-11pm Tue-Sat; 11.30am-2.30pm, 5.30-9pm Sun. **Main courses** 195kr-225kr. **Set meal** 350kr 3 courses. **Map** p97 B6 ❹ **New Nordic**
The Standard's ground-floor restaurant (on the right-hand side of the building) is a showcase for New Nordic cuisine and style. The kitchen, headed by Denny Vangsted, previously head chef at Nimb, is very focused on the local and the seasonal. This translates as a fairly short menu, but you can always expect to find a good offering of fish and meat paired with local herbs and produce – perhaps juniper-smoked salmon with horseradish and sorrel for lunch, or baked pollock with 'foamy' sauce and endive for dinner. *Smørrebrød* is also offered at lunch, and presented immaculately. Desserts, such as caramelised apple ice-cream and toffee with lemon thyme and crème fraîche, are especially innovative and indulgent. You're unlikely to be disappointed by the flavours, though do be prepared for small plates and occasionally slow service.

★ Cap Horn
Nyhavn 21 (33 12 85 04, www.caphorn.dk). Metro Kongens Nytorv. **Open** 10am-midnight daily. **Main courses** 139kr-199kr. **Map** p97 B5 ❺ **Traditional Danish**
When Danes think of Nyhavn, they usually think of herring and *smørrebrød*, and for that you need a proper Danish *værtshus* (pub). Nowhere along this postcard-perfect but very touristy stretch of canal

EXPLORE

Geist.

does it better than Cap Horn. Situated in one of the beautiful old townhouses built by King Christian IV in the 17th century, the place oozes old world atmosphere and was a popular haunt for sailors and ladies of easy pleasure before reaching its current rather more salubrious state. It's popular for Sunday jazz brunches (125kr), when tourists and locals gather round a log fire, clinking glasses and generally making merry. *Smørrebrød* is good value at 59kr-69kr. There's outdoor seating from April to September.

Els

Store Strandstræde 3 (33 14 13 41, www. restaurant-els.dk). Metro Kongens Nytorv. **Open** 11am-midnight daily. **Main courses** 198kr-295kr. **Set meal** 348kr 3 courses. **Map** p97 B5 ❻ **French**

There is no doubting the pedigree of this posh (and slightly stuffy) restaurant, but people come here largely for a taste of Copenhagen past. Els has been around since Hans Christian Andersen's day (he wrote a poem in appreciation of its hospitality), and the original mid 19th-century interior underscores the mood, which is more 'well-heeled tourist on a

spree' than 'regular local in for a treat'. Expect classical French cuisine: rich, buttery and utterly decadent, with dishes such as lobster soup topped with slivers of smoked butterfish, grilled veal liver with lentils and cheese, and chocolate crème brûlée.

Geist

Kongens Nytorv 8 (33 13 37 13, www.restaurant geist.dk). Metro Kongens Nytorv. **Open** 6pm-1am daily. **Dishes** 65kr-195kr. **Map** p97 A5 ❼ New Nordic

Run by an ex-Noma chef, Geist has been getting largely positive reviews since it opened in 2011 – especially from people who were already New Nordic fans. If small plates and experimental cuisine aren't your thing, however, then this place is unlikely to change your mind, following as it does the classic format of tapas-sized dishes and unusual pairings of ingredients – think scallops with salted turnips, young duck with morels and fried egg, or pot-roasted cauliflower with black truffle. A minimum of three dishes per person is typical, meaning that the experience isn't cheap, though it is flavourful. Other highlights are the stylish contemporary decor with muted lighting and candles;

friendly service; top-notch cocktails; and the now-legendary 'air in air in air tiramisu'.

Marchal

Hotel d'Angleterre, Kongens Nytorv 34 (33 12 00 94, www.marchal.dk). Metro Kongens Nytorv.
Open 7-10.30am, noon-4.30pm, 6-10pm Mon-Thur; 7-10.30am, noon-4.30pm, 6-11pm Fri, Sat.
Main courses 160kr-1,500kr. **Set lunch** 375kr
3 courses. **Map** p97 A5 **❽** **French**
This ornate room in the city's grandest hotel, overlooking Kongens Nytorv, was given a makeover a

few years ago, taking it from the rather nutty inspiration of whimsical Danish artist Bjørn Wiinblad, to an altogether more restrained modern style. This involved a major rebuild of the hotel frontage, while keeping the glamorous gold panelling on the walls, and ankle-deep carpets. It's now an extremely pleasant place to be, the decor perfectly matching a brilliantly executed menu of dishes such as grilled monkfish with potatoes, mussel sauce and mussels; and fried pigeon with sweetbread, truffle purée, beetroot and a 'mystery' sauce. Marchal was awarded a Michelin star in 2014.

THE STORY OF A MAN AND A CITY

Hans Christian Andersen was beguiled by his adopted city.

He may have been born in the Fyn town of Odense, but Denmark's greatest writer, Hans Christian Andersen, couldn't wait to leave and seek his fortune in Copenhagen. Andersen arrived on Monday 6 September 1819 (he had to walk the last few miles into town because he couldn't afford the full fare), a day so momentous that he marked it as his 'second birthday' every year thereafter.

He arrived virtually penniless and alone – but for a few names he thought worth contacting. Yet he possessed an almost supernatural self-confidence. Andersen believed he was something special from an early age and immediately set about making something of his talents at the Royal Theatre. On his first visit, the very night he arrived in the city, he was so naive that he accepted a ticket from a tout as if it were a gift.

Andersen's confidence was shaken by the rejection of his ballet dancing, singing and acting skills, but slowly he built up contacts among Copenhagen's cultured bourgeoisie, who would sponsor his education and finance his early attempts at writing. These were not instantly successful, but his first published piece of any significance, a fantasy based on a walk on New Year's Eve across the city to Amager, was a moderate hit. It was all the encouragement his pathological need for recognition required. Poetry, plays and novels followed, few of

which hold up to scrutiny today. But in 1835, almost as an afterthought, he published a small book of stories that would be the works for which he would be remembered.

Over 150 stories were to follow, many becoming world-famous. Tales such as *The Little Mermaid, The Emperor's New Clothes, The Snow Queen, Thumbelina, The Princess and the Pea, The Red Shoes* and *The Little Match Girl* remain widely read and translated, their messages and morals as universal today as when they were written. Copenhagen features often in these stories, both its places and its people. When Tivoli Gardens opened in 1843, Andersen was among the first through the gates; in fact, it was after one of his frequent later visits that he was inclined to compose his celebrated story, *The Nightingale.*

Andersen travelled more widely in Europe than any other Dane of his time. He also never owned his own house, instead living at various addresses in Copenhagen and, in his later years, at the homes of aristocratic friends. He died, aged 70, in 1875 and is buried in Assistens Kirkegård (*see p135*). There are statues of Andersen in Rådhuspladsen and Kongens Have, and plaques on his old residences in Nyhavn (nos.18, 20 and 67) and Vingårdstræde (no.6). And, of course, the city's symbol, the *Little Mermaid* statue, is inspired by one of his darkest fairy tales.

★ MASH

Bredgade 20 (33 13 93 00, www.mashsteak.dk).
Metro Kongens Nytorv, or bus 1A, 26. **Open**
noon-3pm, 5.30-10pm Mon-Wed, Sun; noon-3pm,
5.30-11pm Thur-Sat. **Main courses** 145kr-495kr.
Map p97 B5 ❾ **Steakhouse**

Another winner from long-time Copenhagen resident
and veteran chef Francis Cardenau (also of Umami,
see p106, and Le Sommelier, *see p106),* MASH is
indeed a 'Modern American Steak House' – and
more. Head down a corridor lined with glass-fronted
fridges stocked with steaks so deeply marbled and
tender-looking you could scoff them raw, and into a
darkly glamorous setting of intimate leather booths,
soft lighting and lots of red. Start with a signature
margarita, followed by Cardenau's extraordinarily
crisp-on-the-outside, gooey-in-the-middle grilled veal
sweetbreads, followed by a dry-aged Danish steak –
hung for 90 days until spoon-tender – with onion
rings, and all-American cheesecake to finish.

★ Verandah at the Standard

Havnegade 44 (72 14 88 08, www.thestandard
cph.dk/verandah). Metro Kongens Nytorv, or
bus 11A, 66. **Open** 5-11pm Tue-Sat. **Set meal**
495kr 5 courses. **Map** p97 B6 ❿ **Indian**

This contemporary pan-Indian restaurant – the
brainchild of celebrated Indian chef Karam Sethi and
pastry chef Rizwana Merchant – focuses on fragrant
dishes that are lighter than those in your average
Scandinavian curry house, but which still have the
requisite spiciness that's so often lacking. The short
menu uses local, seasonal ingredients, blending them
with freshly ground spices to create flavourful
mains, such as Keralan seafood biryani, or
Rajasthani korma with lamb, cashew nuts and car-
damom. The space suits the cooking, being light and
modern – with fabulous harbour views too. If you
just want a bite to eat before a jazz concert, head to
the bar and lounge, which serves Indian tapas and
carefully crafted cocktails.

Cafés & Bars

★ Balthazar Champagne Bar

Hotel d'Angleterre, Kongens Nytorv 34, bar
entrance on Ny Østergade 6 (33 12 12 62,
www.balthazarcph.dk). Metro Kongens Nytorv.
Open 4pm-2am Wed, Thur; 2pm-2am Fri, Sat.
Map p97 A5 ⓫

Contemporary style meets classic institution at
Balthazar. This flash yet relaxed Hotel d'Angleterre
bar, which opened in 2012, is named after the word
for a 12-litre champagne bottle – and if you're
already familiar with that term, this is probably your
sort of place. Offering more than 160 different cham-
pagnes, as well as a menu of champagne cocktails,
it's the spot to head to if you're discerning about fizz
and like to feel grand. Snacks are appropriate, coming in the form of caviar and oysters, and there are
DJ lounge sessions on Friday evenings.

Fisken

Nyhavn 27 (33 11 99 06, www.skipperkroen-
nyhavn.dk). Metro Kongens Nytorv. **Open** 8.30am-
1am Mon-Thur; 8.30am-2am Fri, Sat; 8.30am-
midnight Sun. *Food served* until 10.30pm Mon-
Thur, Sun; until 11pm Fri, Sat. **Map** p97 B5 ⓬

One of Nyhavn's most *hyggelige* (cosy) pubs is in the
cellar underneath Skipperkroen restaurant. The
decor is heavy on maritime references (although it's
hard to tell how authentic any of it really is) and
there's live folky, guitar-based music every evening.

Union

Store Strandstræde 19 (no phone, www.the
unionbar.dk. Metro Kongens Nytorv). **Open**
6pm-late Tue-Sat. **Map** p97 B5 ⓭

This classy cellar bar aims for an exclusive vibe with
its hidden entrance (no sign, but look for a black door
and then ring the gold doorbell), but inside the
atmosphere is friendly and relaxed. Top-notch –
though expensive (around 125kr) – cocktails, made
by experienced bartenders, are the drinks of choice
here, while music tends towards jazz and blues, in
line with the Prohibition feel.

Shops & Services

Antique Toys

Store Strandstræde 20 (33 12 66 32, www.
antique-toys.dk). Metro Kongens Nytorv.
Open 2-5.30pm Tue-Fri; and by appointment.
Map p97 B5 ⓮ **Antiques**

This has to be one of Copenhagen's cutest shops,
selling a huge range of antique toys in all shapes and
sizes (model cars, train sets, doll's houses), some dating from as far back as the 17th century.

Magasin

Kongens Nytorv 13 (33 11 44 33, www.magasin.dk).
Metro Kongens Nytorv. **Open** 10am-8pm daily.
Map p97 A5 ⓯ **Department store**

This was Scandinavia's first department store and
remains its largest, with five floors of fashion, high-
class cosmetics, household goods, books, fine food
and two juice bars. Womenswear is a strong point,
while parents will find a large selection of children's
clothes and toys and a comprehensive childcare area.
Other location Field's Mall, Arne Jacobsens Allé
12, Amager (32 47 06 00).

FREDERIKSSTADEN
& KASTELLET

Frederiksstaden was the vision of Frederik V,
who wished to celebrate the 300th anniversary of
the House of Oldenburg in 1749 with a grand new
building project. The king didn't, however, fancy
paying for it, so, instead, he donated the land on
the condition that members of Copenhagen's
nobility commission rococo architect Nicolai
Eigtved to build a stylistically uniform quarter.

EXPLORE

Today, **Bredgade** is itself packed with treasures, some more obvious than others.

The main auction houses are based here, as are numerous art and antiques dealers from the higher end of the market, which make for good window-shopping. A short way down Bredgade on the right is **Sankt Annæ Plads**, a quiet tree-lined square, with a statue of King Christian X at its head and a dull, red-brick church, **Garnisonskirken**, to the right. Another, far more impressive, church, Frederikskirken, better known as **Marmorkirken** (Marble Church), is a short walk away.

Down Frederiksgade are the four rococo palaces surrounding a grand cobbled square that together make up **Amalienborg Slot** (Amalienborg Palace). Home to the royal family since 1794, the palaces were originally built by four wealthy traders as part of Frederik V's scheme for the area. The royal family commandeered the buildings after a fire destroyed their previous home, Christiansborg. As you enter the square along Frederiksgade from Marmorkirken, the palaces are (clockwise from the left) Levetzau Palace, Brockdorff Palace, Moltke Palace and Schack Palace (originally Løvenskjold Palace).

The current, much-loved *Dronning* (Queen) **Margrethe II** lives in Schack Palace (formerly Christian IX's palace). The Danes' unstinting love for their *Dronning* is one of the great paradoxes of the national psyche. Bearing in mind their determined egalitarianism in other areas of life, including democratic equality, this royalism can seem downright peculiar to foreigners. Every Dane you meet, while perhaps not loving the abstract notion of a monarchy, won't have a bad thing to say about their Queen. And the explanation is simple: Margrethe is a charming, modern, talented, conscientious and hard-working royal. And she smokes, which is always likely to endear her to the Danes.

A major photo op for tourists visiting Amalienborg is the changing of the guards, featuring the ever-present Royal Life Guards, whose duty it is to protect Queen Margrethe in the highly unlikely event of an attack. The guards stand in their blue, red and white uniforms beside their pretty red boxes day and night. The daily ritual actually begins at the barracks beside Rosenborg Slot (*see p91*) at 11.30am, from where the soldiers process through the streets, with the military band playing a few tunes. The route takes them south-west to Kultorvet, down Købmagergade, left on to Østergade (part of Strøget), around Kongens Nytorv and up Bredgade, before taking a right into Frederiksgade and Amalienborg Slotsplads at noon. The Queen's birthday, on 16 April, is the cause for more impressive pageantry and crowds.

The **Amalienborg Museum** (within Levetzau Palace) features several private rooms and studies of the royal Glücksborg family in the late 19th/early 20th centuries. In the middle of the square stands French sculptor Jacques Saly's 12-metre (39-foot) statue of Frederik V, modelled on the equestrian statue of Marcus Aurelius on the Capitoline Hill in Rome. It took 20 years to complete due to a financial wrangle over payment from the backers, the East Asiatic Company, but remains an important piece of European sculpture.

Behind the mighty statue of Frederik V is **Amaliehaven**, a small harbourside park donated by the industrialist AP Møller in 1983. In summer, the walk from the vast cruise ships that dock here, past the Royal Cast Collection, the spectacular, newly restored Gefion Fountain and on to the *Little Mermaid*, is extremely popular among Copenhagen's perambulators, dog walkers and joggers. You may even bump into Queen Margrethe or Prince Henrik, who walk their dachshunds here.

South of Amaliehaven, along the harbourfront, lies a row of classic warehouses facing the Kvæsthusbroen dock. Behind Kvæsthusbroen, by the corner of Nyhavn, is where the new **Royal Danish Playhouse** (*see p175*) has been built jutting halfway into the actual harbour, with walkways above the water that surround the venue.

A short distance north along the waterside from Amaliehaven is **Den Kongelige Afstøbningssamling** (the Royal Cast

Gefionspringvandet.

EXPLORE

Collection), the exterior of which is marked by a bronze replica of Michelangelo's *David*. Inside, 2,000 plaster casts of the world's most famous sculptures span a period of 4,000 years.

A walk along the old harbour brings you to Copenhagen's most eye-catching piece of public statuary, **Gefionspringvandet** (Gefion Fountain). Built in 1908 by sculptor Anders Bundgaard, the statue of the goddess Gefion commanding four ploughing bulls is inspired by the Norse saga of the birth of Sjælland. Gefion was told by the King of Sweden that she could keep as much land as she could plough in a night, and that hard night's labour, with the help of her sons who were transformed into bulls for the purpose, earned her Sjælland.

Finally, after passing the ramparts of **Kastellet** along Langelinie, you arrive at **Den Lille Havfrue** (*Little Mermaid*). Sculptor Edvard Eriksen's statue, inspired by the Andersen story, was erected in 1913 and funded by the brewer Carlsberg. Since 1964 it has been the victim of vandalism on several occasions. She has been painted red twice, had her head hacked off three times, an arm lopped off once and been blown from her rocky perch beside windswept Langelinie harbour by a bomb. The winsome waif was based on the prima ballerina Ellen Price, and (together with the urinating toddler in Brussels) must rank as one of the most overexposed and overrated pieces of sculpture in the world.

Opposite the *Mermaid* is the island of **Holmen**, home to the Danish navy for several hundred years. A good walk further along the harbour takes you to Copenhagen's main cruise-liner port, busy from spring to late summer.

Back on Bredgade, a few hidden treasures await. Just around the corner from Marmorkirken is a smaller, but equally fascinating church, **Alexander Nevsky Kirke**, the only Russian Orthodox church in Denmark. Copenhagen's small but beautiful neo-Romanesque Catholic cathedral, **Sankt Ansgar Kirke**, built in 1841, is next door. Immediately north of the cathedral is the **Designmuseum Danmark**, Copenhagen's excellent design history museum, focusing on industrial design and applied arts, and with a section on 20th-century Danish furniture designers that has expanded hugely over the past decade.

Bredgade ends at a small park, **Churchillparken**, located in front of Kastellet, and named after Britain's wartime leader (there's a small, curmudgeonly bust of him here). Maintaining the British theme, you'll also find **St Alban's Church**, a perfect English Gothic flint church (bizarrely, part of the Anglican Diocese of Gibraltar), which looks like it's been lifted straight from the Sussex Downs. Also here is **Frihedsmuseet** (Museum of Danish Resistance), though it is currently closed

Den Lille Havfrue

following a serious fire in 2013. Most of the museum's contents were saved, but the main part of the building was destroyed; it was completely demolished in January 2014, and rebuilding started a few months later and is expected to take a couple of years.

Frihedsmuseet is overlooked by **Kastellet**. Built by Frederik III in 1662 after the Swedish siege of 1658, this vast, star-shaped fortress with its five bastions was the base for the Danish army for many years. Ironically, it was right in front of Kastellet that the Germans landed many centuries later in 1940. These days, the path around the ramparts makes a good jogging track. From the north-east, you get a good view of the *Little Mermaid* and the Swedish coast.

Sights & Museums

FREE Alexander Nevsky Kirke

Bredgade 53 (33 13 60 46, tours 26 83 51 22, www.ruskirke.dk). Bus 1A, 26. **Open** varies; call for details. **Admission** free. *Tours* 25kr; 20kr reductions; by appointment only. **No credit cards. Map** p97 B3 ⑮

Denmark's only Russian Orthodox church is easily identified by its three incongruous gold onion domes; to step inside is to travel back into pre-Revolutionary Russia. The church was built in 1881-84 at the behest of Princess Dagmar, daughter of Christian IX, who married Grand Duke Alexander, later Emperor Alexander III, and converted to Orthodoxy. Apparently, she needed somewhere to worship when she visited Copenhagen (and the fact that Nevsky, Prince of Novgorod, once famously defeated a Swedish army in the 13th century can only have helped get the project through). On the right-hand side of the church, an icon of the Holy Virgin, painted in a monastery on Mount Athos in Greece in 1912, and mounted on its own stand, is said to weep real tears occasionally in spring. If you doubt it, you can see for yourself where water has run from her eyes and tarnished the paint. The nearby icon of St Nicholas is said to have been the only item to have survived the wreck of a Russian warship.

Amalienborg Museum

Christian VIII's Palace, Amalienborg Plads (33 12 21 86, www.dkks.dk). Bus 1A. **Open** *May-Oct* 10am-4pm daily. *Nov-Apr* 11am-4pm Tue-Sun. Also open some Mon in Feb and Apr; call for details. **Admission** *Mon-Fri, Sun* 70kr; 50kr reductions; free under-17s. *Sat* 90kr; 60kr reductions; free under-17s. *Guided tours* 660kr-880kr plus admission fee. **Map** p97 C4 ⓱

The Amalienborg Museum consists of private rooms and studies of the royal Glücksborg family dating from 1863 to 1947, starting with Christian IX. Note Frederik IX's pipe collection, Queen Louise's rococo drawing room and some abysmal pieces of art created by members of the family over the years (in contrast to the works by the current, more gifted queen).

★ Designmuseum Danmark

Bredgade 68 (33 18 56 56, www.design museum.dk). Bus 1A, 26. **Open** 11am-5pm Tue, Thur-Sun; 11am-9pm Wed. **Admission** 90kr; free under-26s. **Map** p97 C3 ⓲

Denmark's largest and oldest museum of Danish and international design is housed around a grand courtyard in the old Frederiks Hospital, designed by Nicolai Eigtved (and, incidentally, where Søren Kierkegaard died in 1855). The focus is on industrial design and applied arts, with a permanent collection featuring some 300,000 items – chairs dominate, but there are also textiles, carpets, clothing, ceramics, cutlery, silverware, glassware, art and other furniture on display. Objects range from the late Middle Ages to the present day, with particularly extensive sections on 20th-century Danish furniture designers, such as Arne Jacobsen and Finn Juhl, and with English captions throughout. The strength of the museum is its blending of the old with the contemporary in a pleasant, soothing, rococo setting, and the exploratory temporary exhibitions. The shop (which has an excellent range of books on Danish design) and Klint café (*see p107*) are also well worth a visit, and can be entered without buying a ticket for the exhibitions. The courtyard serves as a summer performance space for the Grønnegård Theatre.

Designmuseum Danmark.

Frihedsmuseet

Churchillparken (33 47 39 21, www. frihedsmuseet.dk). Bus 1A. **Open** Closed until 2016 at the earliest. **Map** p97 C2 ⓳

The wooden hall that previously housed the Museum of Danish Resistance was destroyed by fire in 2013 – though most of the museum's contents were saved. A new building is being constructed on the same site, but the museum is unlikely to reopen before 2016. When it does, you'll be able to hear numerous moving testimonies to the endeavours of

the Danish Resistance and the suffering of their country under Nazi occupation.

FREE Kastellet

Langelinie (no phone, www.kastellet.info). Bus 1A. **Open** 6am-10pm daily. **Admission** free. **Map** p97 C1 ❷⓪

Built by Frederik III in 1662 after the Swedish siege of 1658, the Citadel was the base for the Danish army for many years and still houses troops in attractive red terraces inside the ramparts. Note that only the grounds are open to the public, not the buildings.

FREE Den Kongelige Afstøbningssamling

Vestindisk Pakhus, Toldbodgade 40 (33 74 84 94, tours 33 74 84 84, www.smk.dk). Bus 1A. **Open** 10am-4pm Tue; 2-5pm Sun. *Guided tours* 10am-2pm Mon-Fri. **Admission** free. **Map** p97 C3 ❷①

The Statens Museum for Kunst (National Gallery) displays its 2,000-strong collection of plaster casts in this building, a former sugar and rum warehouse. The casts have been taken from statues and reliefs in museums, churches, temples and archaeological sites around the world, and feature pagan gods, characters from Christian stories, and, unsurprisingly, a large number of naked figures. It's a fascinating collection, but note that most factual information is in Danish, and opening hours are limited.

★ FREE Marmorkirken

Frederiksgade 4 (33 15 01 44, www.marmorkirken.dk). Bus 1A. **Open** 10am-5pm Mon, Tue, Thur, Sat; 10am-6.30pm Wed; noon-5pm Fri, Sun. *Dome* 15 June-30 Aug 10am, 3pm daily. Sept-14 June 1pm, 3pm Sat, Sun. **Admission** free. *Dome* 25kr; 10kr under-12s. **No credit cards**. **Map** p97 B3 ❷②

Although today it is one of Copenhagen's most breathtaking sights, the circular, domed Marmorkirken (Marble Church) very nearly didn't get built. Work on the church, designed by Nicolai Eigtved as the focal point of the new quarter, began in 1749 with the laying of the foundation stone by the king, but was halted in 1770 due to its exorbitant cost, when the walls were still only 10-15m (33-50ft) high. It wasn't until the deep-pocketed industrialist CF Tietgen intervened in the late 1800s that the church (by then a grass-covered ruin) was finished – in cheaper Danish Faxe marble, instead of the original Norwegian marble. It was topped with a 46m (150ft) dome by the architect Ferdinand Meldahl; inspired by St Peter's in Rome, the dome is one of the largest of its kind in Europe (from the top you can see Sweden).

Restaurants

★ AOC

Dronningens Tværgade 2 (33 11 11 45, www.restaurantaoc.dk). Metro Kongens Nytorv, or bus 1A, 26. **Open** 6pm-1am Tue-Sat. **Set meals** 650kr-2,695kr. **Map** p97 B4 ❷③ New Nordic

The iceberg-white arches of this unusual-looking cellar restaurant could be chilly, but, in fact, the place oozes a cathedral-like serenity. The school of thought is: the cleaner the backdrop, the more attention you pay to the food, and these dishes certainly make an impact. Although the reference point is clearly Noma (*see p114*), head chef Søren Selin impresses with his precision cooking and generally Nordic flavour combinations – and dishes come out looking like works of colourful contemporary art. The restaurant retained its Michelin star in 2014 for inspired creations such as lamb with fermented parsnips and ceps, and monkfish with juniper.

Cascabel Madhus

Store Kongensgade 80-82 (33 93 77 97). Metro Kongens Nytorv, or bus 1A. **Open** 9.30am-6pm daily. **Main courses** 20kr-50kr. **Map** p97 B3 ❷④ Vegetarian

Notable mainly as one of the few veggie restaurants in a town that favours carnivores, Cascabel may not look much from the outside (or on the inside, for that matter), but it's reliable for fresh, light, vegetarian food. Above all, it's cheap. You can fill up on healthy pastas, salads and muffins for under 100kr – the sundried tomato pasta salad with aubergine, olives, jalapeño peppers and sunflower seeds is a meal in itself. Understandably, Cascabel draws a loyal, local crowd of Danes and expats. Not open for dinner.

Restaurant Ida Davidsen

Store Kongensgade 70 (33 91 36 55, www.idadavidsen.dk). Metro Kongens Nytorv, or bus 1A. **Open** 10.30am-5pm Mon-Fri. **Smørrebrød** 65kr-190kr. **Map** p97 B4 ❷⑤ Traditional Danish

Ida Davidsen is the undisputed queen of *smørrebrød*, and a visit to her warm, cosy little cellar restaurant

---

IN THE KNOW HER MAJESTY

Denmark's queen, Margrethe Alexandrine Thorhildur Ingrid, daughter of King Frederik IX and Queen Ingrid, was born in 1940, during the dark days of Denmark's occupation by Germany. In the 1960s, she studied at Copenhagen, Cambridge, Århus, London and the Sorbonne, her main subject being political science. She also spent time in the Women's Flying Corp and the WAAF in England. In 1967, she married a French diplomat, Henri, Comte de Laborde de Monpezat (now Prince Henrik). They have two sons, Frederik (the crown prince, born in 1968, and wildly popular, as is his Australian wife Mary) and Joachim. Margrethe became queen in 1972 – the Danes had voted in a referendum in 1953 to overturn the laws of succession, to allow a female to take the throne.

EXPLORE

Le Sommelier.

is the perfect introduction to the art of the open sandwich. Ida, who works behind the counter most days, is the fifth generation of her family to run this 100-year-old lunch restaurant, concocting ornate open-topped sandwiches that could rank as works of art in any gourmand's book. Home-made rye bread is piled high with toppings, such as home-cured pickled herring with raw red onion and dill, smoked salmon and caviar, or silky beef tartare with a raw egg yolk plopped into the middle. From the 250 or so sandwiches, the Victor Borge is a monster, featuring salmon, lumpfish roe, shrimps, crayfish and dill mayonnaise, and a favourite with the royals, who pop in from their gaff round the corner.

Restaurant Rebel
Store Kongensgade 52 (33 32 32 09, www. restaurantrebel.dk). Metro Kongens Nytorv, or bus 1A. **Open** 5.30pm-midnight Tue-Sat. **Set meals** 349kr 3 courses; 1,400kr 7 courses (incl wine). **Map** p97 A4 ㉖ **French/New Nordic**
Martin Hylleborg and Lars Pedersen's bistro distinguishes itself from the rest of the contemporary Danish bistro scene by incorporating French flavours and methods into its dishes. Pedersen trained under Rebel's ex-head chef, Rasmus Oubæk, and his influence comes through in dishes such as poussin with mussels and cabbage, and tartare of beef with pickled berries and herb mayo – though the use of local ingredients keeps the overall effect Danish. Impeccable presentation and an elegant yet relaxed interior combine with the cooking to make this one of the most reliable modern restaurants in town.

Le Sommelier
Bredgade 63-65 (33 11 45 15, www.les ommelier.dk). Bus 1A, 26. **Open** noon-2pm, 6-10pm Mon-Thur; noon-2pm, 6-11pm Fri; 6-11pm Sat; 6-10pm Sun. **Main courses** 225kr-275kr. **Set meals** 415kr 3 courses. **Map** p97 B3 ㉗ **French/Danish**

Big, warm and bustling, Le Sommelier is staffed by people who love and know good food and draws customers who know and love good restaurants. It's a very happy marriage. There are three dining rooms: the first surrounds the bar area and has a couple of large, round tables for groups; the second is more intimate and closely packed; and the third is tucked away and discreet, for special-occasion dining. As you might guess from the name, it has one of the finest cellars in Copenhagen, stocked with over 800 bottles (more than 20 reds are sold by the glass) – *Wine Spectator* magazine has given the place an award of excellence. Veteran chef Francis Cardenau continues to deliver ldishes that fuse the best of France and Denmark: bavette of beef with braised salsify; cassoulet with pork shank and foie gras; and a mean zarzuela (fish and seafood stew enriched with saffron). Booking is advised at weekends and for dinner.

★ Umami
Store Kongensgade 59 (33 38 75 00, www. restaurantumami.dk). Metro Kongens Nytorv, or bus 1A. **Open** 6-10pm Mon-Thur; 6-11pm Fri, Sat. **Main courses** 120kr. **Set meal** 650kr 6 courses. **Map** p97 A4 ㉘ **Japanese**
Looking like the backdrop for a *Wallpaper** magazine shoot, this Danish take on Nobu offers an eclectic range of Asian-influenced dishes, from traditional sushi in the large sushi bar on the first floor, to unexpected fusions of classic French and Japanese cuisine (such as seared foie gras with eel, dashi pear, black beans and seaweed salad). Fusion has become something of a dirty word these days, but ask any of the Michelin-starred chefs in the city where they like to eat when off-duty, and this is the place most often mentioned. Everyone in Copenhagen who has anything to do with food has the highest respect for chef Francis Cardenau – also behind Le Sommelier (*see left*) – and several years on, still nothing has trumped it. The interior is seductive, with dark stone walls, walnut flooring and ebony tables, and there's a saké and cocktail bar

on the ground floor, where mixologists come up with some seriously new-wave drinks.

Cafés & Bars

★ Kafferiet

Esplanden 44 (33 93 93 04, www.kafferiet.net). Train Østerport. **Open** 7.30am-6pm Mon-Fri; 10am-6pm Sat, Sun. **Map** p97 C2 ㉙
This tiny café is situated in an elegant 18th-century house with a turquoise and white façade. Inside, things are more arty and kitsch, with fleamarket finds, jars of traditional sweets, beautifully packaged teas and colourful posters. The friendly staff make very good coffee, and there are numerous treats (brownies, cookies) to satisfy a sweet tooth. However, with only a counter by the window to sit at, it's not the best place for groups.

Klint – Designmuseets Café

Designmuseum Danmark, Bredgade 68 (33 18 56 56, www.designmuseum.dk). Bus 1A, 26. **Open** 11am-4.30pm Tue, Thur-Sun; 11am-9pm Wed. **Map** p97 C3 ㉚
Designmuseum Danmark's elegant café is named after Danish furniture designer Kaare Klint. The popular lunch spot serves hearty Danish dishes – with salmon, rye bread, pickled herring, fish cakes and classic dessert *rødgrød* (berry coulis mixed with whipped cream) all appearing on the menu. As you'd hope in a design museum, the space is very stylish, with marble floors and dozens of pendant globe lights. You can visit the café (and adjacent shop) without visiting the rest of the museum, and in summer there are outdoor tables in the lovely courtyard.

Kafferiet.

Oscar Bar & Café

Bredgade 58 (33 12 50 10, www.cafeoscar.dk). Bus 1A, 26. **Open** 10am-10pm Mon-Sat; 10am-9pm Sun. **Map** p97 B3 ㉛
A welcome refreshment stop in what is otherwise a café-starved quarter, this light, spacious and relaxed establishment serves the usual beverages and sandwiches, plus a short menu of crêpes and a more substantial selection of beef, fish and pasta dishes. There are a few outside tables for summer munching. Don't confuse it with Oscar Bar & Café (*see p164*) on Rådhuspladsen.

Shops & Services

The shop at **Designmuseum Danmark** (*see p104*) sells an excellent selection of design books, ceramics, posters, postcards, textiles and jewellery.

Bruun Rasmussen Kunstauktioner

Bredgade 33 (88 18 11 11, www.bruun-rasmussen.dk). Metro Kongens Nytorv, or bus 1A, 26. **Open** 11am-4pm Tue-Thur; 11am-3.30pm Fri. **Map** p97 B4 ㉜ **Antiques**
Denmark's premier auction house also happens to be one of the world's top ten auctioneers, serving the prime end of the antiques and arts market. Rasmussen's sales (usually themed) of art, antiques, furniture, wine and just about anything else take place at least a couple of times each week.

Løgismose

Nordre Toldbod 16 (33 32 93 32, www.loegismose.dk). Train Østerport, or bus 1A. **Open** 10am-7pm Mon-Fri; 10am-5pm Sat. **Map** p97 D1 ㉝ **Food & drink**
What started out as a wine importer attached to the renowned restaurant Kong Hans Kaelder has grown into the best gourmet supermarket in town, with an eclectic mix of items, from Harvey Nichols tins and jars to delicious Valhrona chocolates. The shop also produces its own ready-made meals, and there's an in-house butcher and baker as well.

Monies

Nordre Toldbod 19 (33 91 33 33, www.monies.dk). Train Østerport, or bus 1A. **Open** 10am-5pm Mon-Fri. **Map** p97 D2 ㉞ **Accessories**
Spectacular formal jewellery by designer couple Gerda and Nikolai Monies, who use jade, bone, wood and amber, among other materials, to create truly original sculptural statements.

Susanne Juul

Store Kongensgade 14 (33 32 25 22, www.susannejuul.dk). Metro Kongens Nytorv, or bus 1A, 26. **Open** 11am-5.30pm Tue-Thur; 11am-6pm Fri; 10am-2pm Sat. **Map** p97 A4 ㉟ **Accessories**
Designs by the milliner to Denmark's crown princess Mary range from Tibetan-inspired wool beanies to chic wide-brimmed chapeaux.

EXPLORE

Christianshavn, Holmen & Christiania

Christianshavn is charmingly different from other parts of Copenhagen, with laid-back streets and a canal cutting through the middle. But only a few bridges separate it from the city centre. It's harder to equate nearby Christiania – the self-declared independent state founded by hippies in the 1970s – with mainstream Copenhagen. Here you'll find vegetarian cafés and stalls selling marijuana, though the relaxed atmosphere has been blighted in recent years by a criminal-infused edginess. Holmen, to the north, is different again; the former military zone and dockyard has been on the radar since the opening of the Opera House in 2005 and, more recently, the arrival of New Nordic restaurant Amass. It's now a hub for creatives, with old naval buildings housing studio complexes.

Amass.

Don't Miss

1 **Amass** New Nordic restaurant from Noma's ex-head chef (p111).

2 **Christiania** Alternative architecture (p115).

3 **Vor Frelsers Kirke** Magnificent views from the top of the spire (p111).

4 **Operaen** Henning Larsen's opera house is a city landmark (p110).

5 **Dansk Arkitektur Center** Copenhagen is streets ahead in urban design; find out why here (p110).

THE CANAL DISTRICT

Christianshavn was built to the east of
Slotsholmen in the early 17th century to protect
Christian IV's burgeoning city from attack, and
to ease overcrowding within the city walls. The
king's complex plan, inspired by Amsterdam's
grid of canals, was eventually simplified for
reasons of cost, and the district remains pretty
much intact today following sympathetic
renovation in the 1980s and '90s. Christianshavn's
charming houses and courtyards also escaped
most of the fires that ravaged Copenhagen over
the centuries, though developers are now doing
their utmost to spoil the historic ambience.

Christianshavn's dominant landmark is the
Vor Frelsers Kirke (Church of Our Saviour),
whose fabulous 90-metre (295-foot) spire can be
seen from most parts of the city centre. The
district's other significant church is **Christians
Kirke**, notable for its unusual interior, laid out
in the style of a theatre.

Christianshavn's importance in Denmark's
naval history is attested to in **Orlogsmuseet**
(Royal Danish Naval Museum), which has an
extensive collection of fantastically detailed model
ships. The collection was started by Christian IV
and was originally exhibited in Sankt Nicolaj
Kirke; it moved to its current site of Søkvæsthus,
the old naval hospital, in 1989. Now, instead of
military ships, the focus in Christianshavn is
culinary genius, with several high-profile Michelin-
starred restaurants calling this area home,
including **Noma**, **Kadeau** and **Era Ora**.

On the same waterside street as Noma – historic
Strandgade – is the **Dansk Arkitektur Center**
(Danish Architecture Centre). Exhibitions cover
current Danish projects and international themes
and, though fairly specialised, are worth a look
for those with an interest in architecture. They're
often accompanied by debates and conferences
in the restaurant on the main floor.

One of Christianshavn's easily overlooked
sites is **Lille Mølle** (Little Windmill), a windmill
dating from 1669, situated on the ramparts south-
east of Christiania. It was converted into a private
home in 1916 and the interior has been perfectly
preserved by the Nationalmuseet, which now
owns the site, though currently opening hours
are very limited, with guided tours taking place
only on Culture Night and the fourth Thursday
after Easter (Great Prayer Day). However, next
door is **Bastionen og Løven**, an excellent
café from which you can at least view the
windmill's exterior.

To the north of Christianshavn is **Holmen**,
the old docklands area, which was built on
reclaimed land in the 17th century. Holmen still
has a naval base, but has changed and now
attracts students and arty types on summer
evenings. It's a fascinating place, best explored

by bicycle. The Henning Larsen-designed
Operaen (*see p172*) has put Holmen at the
forefront of Denmark's cultural life, while
New Nordic restaurant **Amass** has made the
area of **Refshaleøen**, just beyond Holmen, a
gastronomic destination. Refshaleøen was also
the site of the Eurovision Song Contest 2014.

To the south of Christianshavn, a short walk
away, you'll come to **Islands Brygge** harbour
baths (*see p151* **Come On In, the Water's
Lovely**), in the shadow of the Langebro bridge
– a popular spot for a dip in summer.

Sights & Museums

FREE Christians Kirke

*Strandgade 1 (32 54 15 76, www.christians
kirke.dk). Metro Christianshavn, or bus 2A, 9A,
40.* **Open** 10am-4pm Tue-Fri; after 10am service
Sun. **Admission** free. **Map** p112 B5/6 1 ❶
This rococo church, with a neoclassical spire, was
designed by Nicolai Eigtved in 1755 for the German
population of Christianshavn. Financed by a lottery,
it was known for a long time as the Lottery Church.

★ Dansk Arkitektur Center

*Strandgade 27B (32 57 19 30, www.dac.dk).
Metro Christianshavn, or bus 2A, 9A, 40.* **Open**
10am-5pm Mon, Tue, Thur-Sun; 10am-9pm Wed.
Admission 40kr; 25kr reductions; free under-15s.
Free to all after 5pm Wed. **Map** p112 C4 ❷
Copenhagen has been a focal point for the worlds of
urban design, city planning and architecture over the
past decade, and the dynamic Danish Architecture
Centre is a gathering point for anyone interested in
these disciplines. With engaging temporary exhibitions, frequent workshops and lectures, guided walking and cycling tours in summer, and an excellent
bookshop stuffed with coffee table-style titles on
architecture, sustainability, landscape design and
cities in general, it's a definite don't-miss for anyone
interested in the built environment.

Orlogsmuseet

*Overgaden Oven Vandet 58 (33 11 60 37, www.
natmus.dk/orlogsmuseet). Metro Christianshavn,
or bus 2A, 9A, 40.* **Open** noon-4pm Tue-Sun.
Admission 60kr; 40kr reductions; free under-17s.
Free to all Wed. **Map** p112 D5 ❸
The oldest model in the Royal Danish Naval
Museum .is of a man-of-war, dating from 1680.
There are countless replicas of more recent ships
(including the interior of a submarine, with sound
effects), as well as a comprehensive history of the
Danish Royal Navy and several historic battle
scenes created in model form. One gallery contains
a splendidly ornate state barge from 1780; another
is dedicated to marine archaeology. Orlogsmuseet
will delight model-making enthusiasts and naval
historians; it's also popular with children, who are
catered for with a well-equipped playroom.

Vor Frelsers Kirke.

World's Best Restaurant list nearly five years before. The two restaurants aren't unrelated – Amass is owned by Californian chef Matthew Orlando, a former Noma head chef who knows a thing or two about unusual flavour pairings (before Noma, he worked at NYC's Per Se and Heston Blumenthal's Fat Duck).

Though Refshaleøen isn't the easiest place to get to (take a taxi), the sense of remoteness adds to the special-occasion feel, which is heightened by the very friendly welcome guests receive. Like Noma, Amass has put together an international and enthusiastic team, who troop out of the kitchen en masse when serving large groups – something of a spectacle. Staff are excellent at explaining each dish on the tasting menu: perhaps razor clams with bone marrow and preserved green tomatoes, or dry-aged beef with carrot and buttermilk. Despite the outlandish-sounding pairings, most dishes work – though you may need extra helpings of the delicious fermented flatbread to feel properly sated. But if you're after experimental plates made by chefs who are passionate about local produce, you're unlikely to be disappointed.

★ Vor Frelsers Kirke

Sankt Annægade 29 (32 57 27 98, www. vorfrelserskirke.dk). Metro Christianshavn, or bus 2A, 9A, 40. **Open** *Church* 11am-3.30pm daily. *Spire* July-mid Sept 11am-7pm daily. Mar-June, mid Sept-mid Nov 10am-4pm daily. Mid Nov-Dec 11am-4pm Sat, Sun. **Admission** *Church* free. *Spire* 35kr; 5kr reductions. **No credit cards**. **Map** p112 D5 ❹

This landmark church was built in 1682 by architect Lambert van Haven for Christian V, in the Palladian Dutch Baroque style, from red brick and sandstone. The extraordinary spire was inspired by the lanterns on the church of Sant'Ivo alla Sapienza in Rome and was completed, in pine with copper cladding and gilt decoration, in 1752. Don't believe stories that the spire's architect, Lauridis de Thurah, threw himself off the top because it wound the wrong way – he actually died in poverty seven years after its completion. On the day of its dedication, King Frederik V climbed to the top to receive a 27-gun salute as crowds cheered below. The spire is open to any visitors who feel they can conquer their vertigo and its 400 or so steps, which spiral ever narrower closer to the summit. The interior of the church is spacious but prosaic, in the typical Lutheran manner, though its immense three-storey organ (completed in 1698) is stupefying.

Restaurants

★ Amass

Refshalevej 153 (43 58 43 30, www.amass restaurant.com). Bus 40, 991, 992. **Open** 6pm-midnight Tue-Thur, Sat. **Set meal** 575kr 6 courses, (950kr incl wine) . **Map** p113 G1 ❺ **New Nordic**

The opening of Amass in the industrial area of Refshaleøen in late 2013 generated the city's biggest culinary buzz since Noma (*see p114*) first topped the

★ Era Ora

Overgaden Neden Vandet 33B (32 54 06 93, www.era-ora.dk). Metro Christianshavn, or bus 2A, 9A, 40. **Open** noon-3pm, 7pm-midnight Mon-Sat. **Set meals** 850kr 4 courses (2,000kr incl wine); 1,150kr 6 courses (2,600kr incl wine). **Map** p112 C5 ❻ **Italian**

This beautifully decorated restaurant, with its gold-leaf lighting, burnt-sienna walls and open courtyard to the rear, serves only set menus, with a choice of fish or meat for the main course. The dedication of the chefs is evident in the complex yet light Umbrian dishes, using ingredients flown in from Italy. The wine list is as impressive (and expensive) as ever, and the service efficient and formal, making it the best Italian in town by a long shot. If your wallet doesn't stretch to these gastronomic heights, there's always its sister bistro L'Altro (Torvegade 62, 32 54 54 06, www.laltro.dk) across the canal.

★ Kadeau

Wildersgade 10 (33 25 22 23, www.kadeau.dk). Metro Christianshavn, or bus 2A, 9A, 40. **Open** 6pm-late Tue, Wed; noon-1.30pm, 6pm-late Thur-Sat. **Set meals** from 625kr 4 courses; from 950kr 6 courses. **Map** p112 C6 ❼ **New Nordic**

Kadeau brings a little slice of Bornholm – a Danish island in the Baltic Sea, known for its culinary offerings – to this airy, smart yet informal space. The Michelin-starred restaurant makes much use of island herbs, meat, cheese, seafood and berries, with recent highlights from the eight-course tasting menu including sirloin with roots, black garlic and black-currant; turbot with mussels, celeriac, whey and hemp; and pear, blue cheese and fermented honey. A meal here doesn't come cheap, so be sure you understand the New Nordic concept (small plates, experimental dishes) before booking a table.

EXPLORE

Christianshavn, Holmen & Christiania

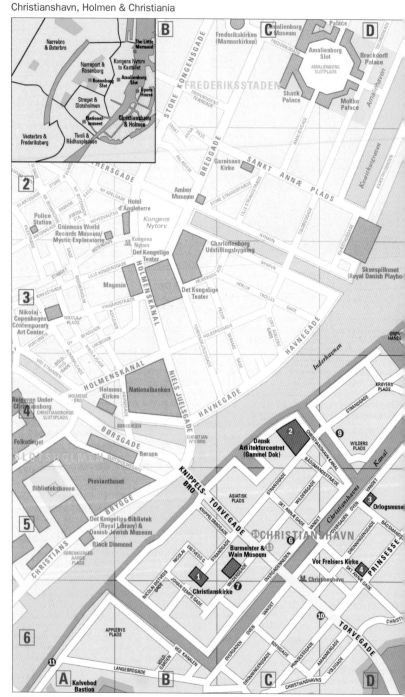

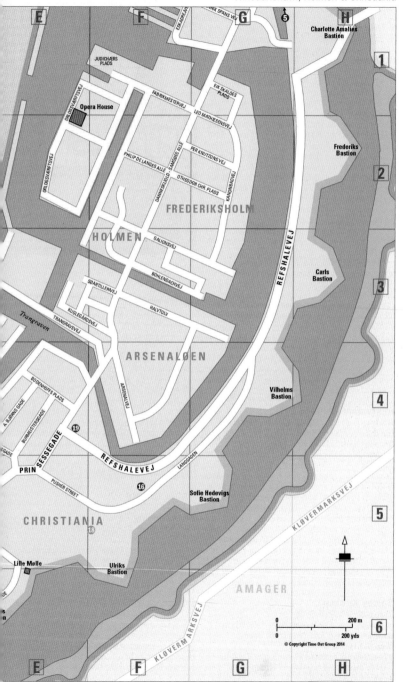

Noma.

★ Noma

Strandgade 93 (32 96 32 97, www.noma.dk). Metro Christianshavn, or bus 2A, 9A, 40. **Open** noon-4pm, 7pm-12.30am Tue-Sat. **Set meal** 1,600kr 20 courses (3,600kr incl wine). **Map** p112 D3 ❽ **New Nordic**

Having worked at legendary Spanish restaurant El Bulli and the French Laundry in California, Denmark's most innovative chef, Rene Redzepi, has tried to focus that kind of out-of-the-box thinking and meticulous attention to detail on Nordic ingredients, with sensational results. Redzepi is a tireless forager, unearthing extraordinary 'substitute' ingredients, such as sea grasses that taste like coriander from beaches in Sweden, truffles from Gotland and herbs from the banks of Christianshavn's ramparts. Recent highlights include dried scallops with grains and watercress; wild duck with pear and kale; a poetic-sounding 'oyster and ocean'; and burnt leek with cod roe. Expect to be amazed, delighted and intrigued, often all at the same time – there's a reason why Noma now has two Michelin stars.

The interior of the converted 18th-century warehouse has a raw, diaphanous quality provided by bleached wooden rafters and large picture windows over the canal, yet the Icelandic sheepskin rugs thrown over chairs, and candles on scrubbed table-tops, add warmth to a dazzlingly Nordic atmosphere. Though far from cheap, it's good value for an experience you'll remember for the rest of your life – if you manage to get a booking in the first place (the waiting list is at least two months, and hard to get on to at all). Note that Noma is upping sticks and moving to Japan for the first two months of 2015.

Restaurant Kanalen

Wilders Plads 2 (32 95 13 30, www.restaurant-kanalen.dk). Metro Christianshavn, or bus 2A, 9A, 40. **Open** 11.30am-midnight Mon-Sat. **Set dinner** 360kr-495kr. **Map** p112 D4 ❾ **Danish**

Tucked away beside the canals in a particularly idyllic corner of Christianshavn, Restaurant Kanalen (which means 'Canal') strikes a happy balance between traditional and modern Danish cooking. You'll find excellent herring and *frikadeller* (meatballs) alongside more intricate dishes that blend the freshest local ingredients with deliciously light sauces and surprise ingredients from around the world, such as pickled mushrooms and *pimientos piquillos* (the sweet little red peppers from Spain). With alfresco dining in summer, sweet service and accessible prices, Kanalen is a great all-rounder.

Spicey Kitchen

Torvegade 56 (32 95 28 29). Metro Christianshavn, or bus 2A, 9A, 40. **Open** 5-11pm daily. **Main courses** Around 70kr. **No credit cards**. **Map** p112 D6 ❿ **Indian**

The number of customers usually found waiting for a table inside this frantic and cramped one-room curry house is testament to its excellent value. The choice of chicken, lamb or fish curries might be a little limited (the chicken and spinach curry is recommended), but that hasn't stopped Spicey Kitchen building a reputation as one of Copenhagen's best cheap and fast eats.

Viva

Langebrogade Kaj 570 (27 25 05 05, www.restaurantviva.dk). Metro Christianshavn, or bus 2A, 5A, 9A, 40. **Open** 5.30-11pm daily (last seating 9.30pm). **Set meal** from 450kr 4 courses. **Map** p112 A6 ⓫ **Global**

Viva is housed aboard a ship moored next to Langebro bridge, across the water from the Black Diamond library. Now in the skilled hands of chef Jonas Petersen, the restaurant offers tapas-sized dishes and is noted for its shellfish. Come summer, the rooftop deck is a great place for a pre-dinner cocktail with views across the harbour.

Cafés & Bars

Bastionen og Løven

Christianshavns Voldgade 50 (32 95 09 40, www.bastionen-loven.dk). Metro Christianshavn, or bus 2A, 9A, 40. **Open** 10am-midnight Mon-Sat; 10am-5pm Sun. **Map** p113 E6 ⓬

This delightful, if rather hard to find, garden café-restaurant is situated in an extension of the Nationalmuseet's Lille Mølle (Little Windmill) on the ramparts of Christianshavn. It's well off the tourist trail and during summer is usually packed with locals, but if you fancy trying one of the city's great culinary institutions – traditional Copenhagen brunch, a simple but satisfying array of cheese, herring, cold meats, bread, fruit and yoghurt – in idyllic surroundings, this is the best place to visit.

EXPLORE

Café Wilder

Wildersgade 56 (32 54 71 83, www.cafe
wilder.dk). Metro Christianshavn, or bus 2A,
9A, 40. **Open** 9am-11pm Mon-Thur; 9am-
midnight Fri, Sat; 10am-10pm Sun. **Map**
p112 C5 ⑬

This lovely café-bar is located just a short walk from
the chaos of Christiania. The food is fresh, cheap and
simple (salads and sandwiches), and the service
charming. This small, L-shaped room is usually
crowded to bursting point with trendy, arty locals
at weekends, so arrive early to be sure of a seat.
Supermodel Helena Christensen lives nearby and is
allegedly a regular when in town. Brunch is 125kr.

★ Sweet Treat

Sankt Annæ Gade 3A (32 95 41 15, www.sweet
treat.dk). Metro Christianshavn, or bus 2A, 9A,
40. **Open** 7.30am-6pm Mon-Fri; 10am-5pm Sat,
Sun. **Map** p112 C5 ⑭

This tiny pit stop is a favourite with smart creatives,
who often stop off en route to work for a cup of their
excellent coffee and a pastry or a boiled egg. But
Sweet Treat is, as its name suggests, also great for
those with a sweeter palate, serving what might be
the best hot chocolate in town. There's also a wide
range of teas, juices and smoothies.

Shops & Services

Nordatlantens Brygge

Strandgade 91 (32 83 37 00, www.nordatlantens.
dk). Metro Christianshavn, or bus 2A, 9A, 40.
Open 10am-5pm Mon-Fri; noon-5pm Sat, Sun.
Map p112 D3/4 15 ⑮ **Gifts & souvenirs**

The best source for Greenlandic handicrafts and
information, this small shop attached to the
Nordatlantens Brygge cultural centre sells books,
jewellery, T-shirts, woollen sweaters (think Sarah
Lund from *The Killing*), CDs, tote bags, exquisitely
forged, hand-ground knives, art and – animal rights
supporters, beware – seal-fur products.

CHRISTIANIA

Christiania, or the Freetown of Christiania to
give it its full title, is a residential area unlike any
other in Denmark. This mess of historic military
buildings, makeshift housing and ramshackle
businesses, which straddles the defensive
moat and 17th-century ramparts to the east
of Christianshavn, is home to approximately
1,000 people (exact figures are difficult to come
by). It attracts around three-quarters of a million
visitors a year, which makes it one of Denmark's
biggest tourist attractions.

Christiania is unique. Until very recently,
it was a community that existed within
Copenhagen, but outside its laws and
conventions. However, recent governments,
and more particularly the rise to power of

right-wing factions within the previous coalition,
put Christiania under threat as never before,
vowing to tear the whole place down, or at least to
close Pusher Street, where soft drugs were being
sold openly from stalls like market produce.

In January 2004, Christiania voted to tear
down the booths selling ready-rolled spliffs,
cannabis resin and other drugs – before the
government ordered the police to do it forcibly,
as they had been threatening. This came
despite the fact that the police felt it would be
counterproductive to send the sale of soft drugs
underground – 'You don't just make a problem
like this go away with a click of the fingers,'
said Copenhagen's drugs tsar at the time.

However, despite violent clashes between
residents and police in 2007, the sale of cannabis
has remained a key feature of Christiania –
though now the trade is mainly in the hands of
(sometimes intimidating) criminals rather than
members of the Christiania community. And
despite a 2011 'normalisation' process, whereby
the state bought up, via a specially created fund,
most of the buildings in Christiania (for 76.2
million kroner), many of its residents remain
committed to their 'alternative' lifestyle.

Until 1971, the 41-hectare (101-acre) site that
Christiania now occupies was an army barracks.
When the army moved out, a group of like-
minded Christianshavn residents decided to
knock down the fence on Prinsessegade and
use the land as a playground and open space.
Meanwhile, an exhibition at Charlottenborg,
Noget for Noget ('Give and Take'), which
examined the hippie movement, and an
alternative lifestyle newspaper, *Hovedbladet*
(*Head Magazine*), galvanised Copenhagen's
experimentalists. The paper ran an article on
the barracks with various proposals for its use,
including as housing for the young. This was all
the encouragement that hundreds of 'drop-
outs' from across Denmark needed, and soon
the site began to fill up. On 13 November 1971,
the new residents founded what they like to call
the Freetown of Christiania, although it was
promptly declared illegal by the authorities.

IN THE KNOW DON'T SHOOT!

You'll notice signs around the Pusher
Street part of Christiania asking you
not to take photos. Take these signs
seriously – locals won't take kindly to you
ignoring them. However, beyond Pusher
Street and its surrounding zone, you can
normally get away with taking pictures of
the fascinating alternative houses that line
the water. Still, it's wise to check first with
a local that it's OK before snapping away.

EXPLORE

However, the number of residents had already grown to the extent that, despite their best and often most violent efforts, the police failed to clear the barricades.

In subsequent years, as the community formed its own system of government, built schools, shops, cafés, restaurants, various co-operatives and music venues, and embarked on recycling programmes and nascent solar- and wind-power projects, the debate about Christiania raged. The bulldozers and batons were never far away. Charity records, concerts, PR stunts and the election to the local council of some of its residents ensured Christiania remained in the headlines and, eventually, in 1991, an uneasy truce was met with the authorities. Christiania agreed to pay rent and cover the cost of water and electricity supplies, as well as to look after the buildings that were of historical importance, while the city council agreed to allow it to continue as a 'social experiment'. In truth, were Christiania to be completely closed down tomorrow, the ensuing housing crisis and crime wave would prove a far greater political hot potato.

Today, with the sale of drugs banished, the community earns money from its restaurants and bars, as well as the sale of its unique Christiania bicycles (see below **Cargo Collective**) and handicrafts. The residents (around 70 per cent of whom receive some kind of government benefit) pay rent, which goes towards the upkeep of buildings, city taxes and services.

A complex system of self-government is headed by the Common Meeting, with power devolved through 15 local Area Meetings. Decisions are arrived at via consensus, as opposed to majority vote, and new arrivals must be approved by the House Meeting. A stunt by a Danish TV show showed how territorial the Freetown is, however, when they turned up and tried to build a house by the lake. Locals tore it down and assaulted the TV crew.

CARGO COLLECTIVE

The Christiania bike is now a Danish design icon.

Almost synonymous with the word 'cargo bike' in Denmark, the **Christiania Bikes** (www.christianiabikes.com) tricycle has been an element of daily life in Copenhagen for over 25 years, becoming one of the city's unofficial emblems. In fact, the bike was awarded the Classics Prize for the Danish Design Centre's (see p54) Danish Design Awards 2010/11, where it was recognised as having 'proven its durability through many years of daily transport of shopping bags and children. The bicycle is a beautiful example of design that springs from a simple, good idea that stays viable due to function and charm.'

Invented in 1984 by Lars Engstrøm, in the car-free commune of Christiania, the bike is essentially a back-to-front tricycle with a plywood box on the front for shopping or kids. The bikes have a fitted rain cover (with window), and Danish children are often carted to and from school in the front box, which comes complete with seats and safety belts; two or three youngsters can often be seen happily snuggled up together in the den-like space.

Copenhagen's flat terrain and safe bike lanes make for ideal conditions for the Christiania (a cargo-bike-based school run in Lisbon or San Francisco, say, would be decidedly more difficult). As well as using the bikes for school runs, locals use them for shopping, taking their dogs to the park, and moving tools, equipment, Christmas trees... whatever large items you might need to transport. Different models have different-sized and -shaped boxes. Postmen even use a specially designed Christiania bike for deliveries, and enterpreneurial types have recently begun using them as mobile drinks and snack stalls. Christiania bikes aren't cheap, costing between 10,300kr and 14,000kr – but you're paying for a high level of craftsmanship and a genuine alternative to the car. What's more, the bike would soon pay for itself when you consider the savings in transport and petrol costs. If you're in Copenhagen with kids, and fancy carting them around in this most convenient and pollution-free way, the bikes can be rented from **Baisikeli** (see p25 **Bike Copenhagen**) or bought from **Christiania Cykler** (see p117).

Christiania.

Christiania is divided by the moat into two distinct areas – the main commercial centre, with its music venues, shops, restaurants and bars; and Dysen, a quiet residential area on the eastern side of the moat. 'Flower power' staggers on here; by way of evidence, no wall is left undaubed with murals, graffiti and, well, daubs, and large, shaggy dogs of indeterminate breed roam unhindered. There are a number of cafés and restaurants: **Spiseloppen** (*spise* means 'eat'; *loppen* means 'the flea') and **Morgenstedet** are the best. In the same building as Spiseloppen is the atmospheric music venue **Loppen** (*see p170*), while **Den Grå Hal**, Christiania's largest music venue (capacity 2,000), has hosted gigs by the likes of Blur and Bob Dylan.

All of Christiania is open to tourists (except the private dwellings, of course). Once you get beyond Pusher Street, with its (now illegal) cannabis stalls and burning oil drums, you can pass a pleasant afternoon in the quieter parts, inspecting the extraordinary variety of housing – from pyramids, railway carriages and tree houses, to sophisticated wooden chalets and the original 17th-century barracks. It's well worth taking the time to explore this remarkable community.

Restaurants

Morgenstedet
Fabriksområdet 134 (no phone, www. morgenstedet.dk). Metro Christianshavn, or bus 9A, 40. **Open** noon-9pm Tue-Sun. **Main courses** 80kr-100kr. **No credit cards.** **Map** p113 F5 ⑯ Vegetarian
This cute clapboard cottage serves organic, vegetarian food at rock-bottom prices. Most of the produce comes from the owner's nearby farm, and the menu changes daily. Depending on the season, expect the likes of wholesome potato gratins, bean stews and mushroom and tofu stir-fries. It's a great place to fill up while on a tour of the old hippie quarter – you can be sure you won't eat quite like this anywhere else in the city.

Spiseloppen
2nd floor, Loppen building, Bådsmandsstræde 43 (32 57 95 58, www.spiseloppen.com). Metro Christianshavn/bus 9A, 40. **Open** 5-10pm Tue-Sat; 5-9pm Sun. **Main courses** 140kr-250kr. **Map** p113 E5 ⑰ Global
What do you get when you cross an Englishman, an Irishman, a Scotsman, a Dane, a Lebanese and an Italian? Spiseloppen's constantly changing rota of international kitchen staff create a different menu every night, but, for once, this isn't a case of 'too many cooks' – the myriad influences at work here rarely fail to conjure something special (the vegetarian dishes are particularly impressive). The entrance to Spiseloppen, through an anonymous door and up some shabby stairs in one of Christiania's warehouses, promises little, but once you enter its low-ceilinged, candlelit dining hall, its true worth becomes clear. Diners tend to be young and arty, not minding the occasional waft of exotic cheroot.

Cafés & Bars

There are a number of cafés and bars within Christiania, some with no obvious name, most with outside benches and tables, and many of which are taken up by local dope smokers, students and teenagers. **Café Nemoland** is one of the friendliest and most established. For music venue **Loppen**, *see p170*.

Café Nemoland
Fabriksområdet 52 (32 95 89 31, www.nemoland. dk). Metro Christianshavn, or bus 2A, 9A, 40. **Open** 11am-midnight Mon-Thur, Sun; 11am-3am Fri. **Map** p113 F5 ⑱
This café and cultural centre sells beer, wine, coffee and snack-style food, such as generous hamburgers. Entertainment is laid on in the form of live music, a pool table and chess sets, and there are plenty of colourful, pub garden-style tables outside. Staff are friendly, and will even let you bring your own beer.

Shops & Services

Christiania Cykler
Refshalevej 2 (32 95 45 20, www.christiania cykler.dk). Metro Christianshavn, or bus 2A, 9A, 40. **Open** 10am-5.30pm Mon, Wed-Fri; noon-5.30pm Tue; 11am-3pm Sat. **No credit cards.** **Map** p113 F5 ⑲ Bicycles
Christiania Cykler's most interesting item is the idiosyncratic Pedersen bike. It's based on an early 20th-century design by Mikael Pedersen, who was tired of getting a sore backside from riding. He devised a swinging hammock-like leather seat, then built a unique pyramid-style frame to support it. Today, the shop builds 40 to 50 specially ordered Pedersen bikes a year, about half of which are shipped abroad. It also sells classic Christiania cargo bikes (*see p116* **Cargo Collective**) and offers a bike rental service.

EXPLORE

Vesterbro & Frederiksberg

Sex and drugs have long been the claim to fame of Vesterbro – the area stretching west from Central Station – but this notoriously sleazy district has been gentrified in recent years. Many of the sex shops are still here, together with exotic food shops and restaurants, but as the trendies have taken over – most notably in Kødbyen, the city's Meatpacking District – hip bars, restaurants and indie design shops have sprung up. And this gentrification is now spreading further south-west, to the border of Valby, where the old Carlsberg brewery sits.

   Quiet and refined Frederiksberg seems worlds away from its blowsy neighbour. Its wide, leafy avenues make this one of the city's most desirable residential areas, and its parks and zoo are popular destinations at weekends.

Elephant Gate.

Don't Miss

1 Kødbyen The city's most vibrant spot to eat out (p120).

2 Istedgade Vesterbro's coolest shopping street (p120).

3 Frederiksberg Have One of the city's most romantic green spaces (p129).

4 Elephant Gate The old Carlsberg brewery's iconic entrance (p120).

5 Værnedamsvej Locals call this street 'Little Paris' (p120).

Museum of Copenhagen.

VESTERBRO

Vesterbro has revelled in its trashy image since the 18th century (when it was the site of numerous music halls and drinking dens), and the second half of the 19th century (when it was filled by an immense block of inhuman corridor flats, to ease overcrowding in the city).

Meat markets, literal and metaphorical, have always been Vesterbro's speciality. Their trade was centred on **Værnedamsvej**, which at one time had Europe's highest concentration of dead flesh. The street, which borders on gentrified Frederiksberg, is now one of the area's nicest, its cute food shops, boutiques and cafés, such as **Falernum** and **Granola**, giving it a Parisian feel. The sex trade is now more centrally located, on the seedier eastern end of **Istedgade**, Vesterbro's artery. For Vesterbro's plethora of fashion and design shops, head to the western, Enghaven (park) end of Istedgade.

Halmtorvet, an oblong square south of Istedgade, is one of the most visible symbols of the area's rejuvenation: it has had the sandblasters and decorators in and the cobbles relaid, and is a popular evening and weekend destination, with several good cafés. The fashionistas, however, flock to **Kødbyen**, just south of here – the new, regenerated Meatpacking District, whose low-rise former butchers' shops and slaughterhouses are now home to cool galleries, restaurants and nightspots (as well as a few remaining butchers), including

late-night bar **Bakken**, pizza parlour **Mother** and new restaurant **Kul**. Many a gallery or magazine launch party takes place around here.

Vesterbro proper has very few traditional tourist attractions, but the **Museum of Copenhagen** gives an excellent overview of the capital's history, while **Tycho Brahe Planetarium**, on Gammel Kongevej, shows a variety of IMAX movies and puts on interplanetary displays. However, in the south-west corner of Vesterbro, where it meets Frederiksberg and Valby, sits the headquarters of what is Copenhagen's, and probably Denmark's, best-known international brand: Carlsberg. The **Carlsberg Visitors Centre & Jacobsen Brewhouse** is a must for beer buffs, while the surrounding area has been ripe for redevelopment since Carlsberg moved its production plant outside Copenhagen in 2006. Renamed Carlsberg City, the district is in the process of transformation; contemporary art galleries have moved in, as well as performing arts spaces such as **Dansescenen** (*see p177*), and an urban masterplan has been drawn up. The plan seeks to make use of the area's vacant old warehouses to create a radical new cultural, residential and commercial quarter over the next decade, featuring green spaces, bike paths, 3,000 low-energy homes, and a range of new shops and cafés. The landmark **Elephant Gate** on Ny Carlsberg Vej – once the entrance to the brewery – is to be preserved as part of the plan.

Sights & Museums

Carlsberg Visitors Centre & Jacobsen Brewhouse

Gamle Carlsberg Vej 11 (33 27 12 82, www.visitcarlsberg.com). Train Enghave, or bus 18, 26. **Open** 10am-5pm Tue-Sun. *Guided tours* (English) 2pm Sat, Sun; (Danish) noon Sun. **Admission** 80kr; 60kr reductions; free under-5s. *Guided tours* 125kr. **Map** p122 C6 ❶

Take a self-guided tour through the various displays on the history of beer and the brewing processes used at Carlsberg. Naturally, visits conclude with a free sample at the bar of the Jacobsen Brewhouse. Guided tours are available at weekends.

Museum of Copenhagen

Vesterbrogade 59 (33 21 07 72, www. copenhagen.dk). Train København H, or bus 6A, 26. **Open** 10am-5pm daily. **Admission** 40kr; 20kr reductions; free under-18s. Free to all Fri. **Map** p123 G4 ❷

This laid-back museum charts the history of Copenhagen from fishing village to cosmopolitan capital, with lots of visual displays depicting how Copenhageners have lived over the last millennium. Its insightful temporary exhibitions have covered topics such as 'Copenhagen Underground' and 'Becoming a Copenhagener'.

Tycho Brahe Planetarium

Gammel Kongevej 10 (33 12 12 24, www.tycho.dk). Train Vesterport, or bus 9A. **Open** noon-7.40pm Mon; 9.30am-7.40pm Tue-Thur; 10.45am-8.50pm Fri, Sat; 10.45am-7.40pm Sun. **Admission** (incl IMAX screening) 144kr; 94kr under-13s. **Map** p123 H4 ❸

The Tycho Brahe Planetarium opened in 1989 in a cylindrical building designed by Knud Munk. It is named after the great Danish astronomer (1546-1601) who painstakingly catalogued the solar system – a crucial contribution to the understanding of the laws of planetary motion. IMAX films are screened during the daytime.

Restaurants

★ Cofoco

Abel Cathrinsgade 7 (33 13 60 60, www.cofoco.dk). Train København H, or bus 10, 14. **Open** 5.30pm-midnight Mon-Sat. **Set meal** 275kr 4 courses. **Map** p123 H4 ❹ **French/Danish**

Such has been the success of the Copenhagen Food Consulting people that their stable has now grown to nine restaurants (see website), all of them top quality. Cofoco and Les Trois Cochons (*see p124*), were among the first restaurants to make eating out fun and affordable in the Danish capital, and they continue to offer some of the most reliable cooking around. The interior at Cofoco is rustic, cosy and casual, with wooden tabletops and a blackboard marked up with the day's specials. The menu offers more than the usual confit and entrecôte, with dishes such as pork braised for 14 hours and served with lemon-scented jerusalem artichoke purée. Hearty portions, easy prices and an atmosphere of bon-homie make it perennially popular with locals.

Fiskebaren

Flæsketorvet 100 (32 15 56 56, www.fiskebaren. dk). Train Dybbølsbro or København H. **Open** 5.30pm-midnight Tue-Thur; 5.30pm-2am Fri, Sat. **Main courses** 105kr-440kr. **Map** p123 H5 ❺ **Fish**

Located in the heart of the ultra-trendy Meatpacking District, Fiskebaren is a shrine to the deliciousness of the deep. The vast, industrial space arranged around a U-shaped bar glows a deep sea blue that seems exactly right for the food: plump, pearl-grey oysters from the icy depths of Limfjorden; Øresund mussels with raspberry and walnut vinaigrette; and white fish from Østersøen and chips from sweet Gotland potatoes with a hearty remoulade.

Kul

Høkerboderne 16B-20 (33 21 00 33, www.restaurantkul.dk). Train Dybbølsbro or København H. **Open** noon-3pm, 6-11pm Mon-Wed, Sun; noon-3pm, 6pm-2am Thur-Sat. **Small plates** 110kr-520kr. **Map** p123 H5 ❻ **International/Grillhouse**

With a menu formed of small plates, Kul – meaning 'coal' in Danish – differentiates itself from other contemporary restaurants in Copenhagen by its focus on the grill. Chef duo Henrik Jyrk and Christian Mortensen create tasty offerings such as grilled shrimp with spicy avocado and coriander, and barbecued ribs with grilled baby gem lettuce – though the size of the plates means you'll need three or four per person to feel sated. The pared-back space includes some seating at the bar, but note that you'll feel the full effect of the grill if you sit there.

IN THE KNOW
A BREATH OF FRESH AIR

Spend a little time in Copenhagen, and you might start to notice a curious Danish custom that often amazes foreigners – the fact that babies are often left in their prams outside cafés while the parent sits inside. The Danes believe strongly in the importance of babies getting lots of fresh air. This, together with their high level of social trust, means that it's common to see prams – which are almost always big, flat vintage-style numbers – lined up outside cafés, with the little ones tucked up under layers of wool blankets.

EXPLORE

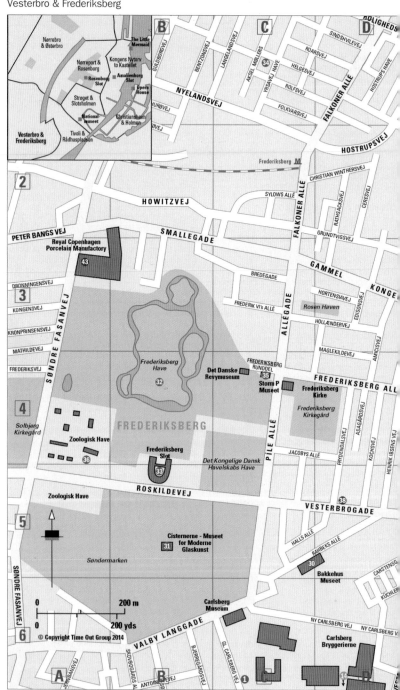

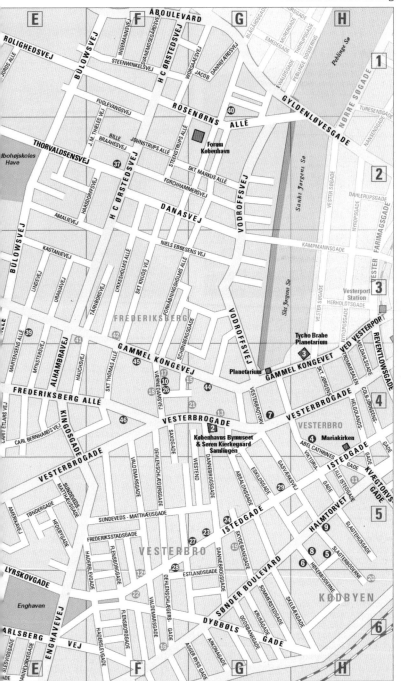

Mother.

Lê Lê

Vesterbrogade 40 (31 31 38 88, www.lele-nhahang.com). Train København H, or bus 6A, 26. **Open** 5-10pm Mon-Thur; 5-10.30pm Fri, Sat. **Main courses** 166kr-220kr. **Set meal** 390kr-640kr. **Map** p123 G4 **Vietnamese**

One of the city's best Asian restaurants, serving authentic, complex Vietnamese dishes – everything from soups and noodles to curries and rice dishes. The venue is cool too, with high ceilings and massive glass windows. It's now so popular that it can be almost impossible to get in at weekends. A takeaway outlet, Lê Lê Street Kitchen (open 11am-9.30pm daily), has opened a few doors away at no.56; it has a handful of tables for eating in, and is a great place for a quick bite, especially if you're dining alone. **Other locations** Lê Lê Street Kitchens: Vesterbrogade 56, Vesterbro (33 22 71 34); Østerbrogade 56, Østerbro (33 22 71 31); HC Andersens Boulevard 8, Indre By (33 22 71 37).

★ Mother

Høkerboderne 9-15 (22 27 58 98, www.mother. dk). Train Dybbølsbro or København H. **Open** 11am-1am Mon-Sat; 11am-11pm Sun. *Café* from 8am Mon-Fri. **Main courses** 75kr-145kr. **Map** p123 H5 ❽ **Pizza**

This trendy pizzeria in the Meatpacking District has been busy since opening a few years ago. The secret lies in the organic sourdough bases, quality toppings and authentic wood-fired oven, which combine to produce simply delicious pizzas. Starters and sides such as bruschetta made from manitoba flour are also excellent. If there's no space when you arrive,

put your name on the list and head to the little bar at the far end, to enjoy a pre-dinner Campari with a largely English-speaking crowd.

PatéPaté

Slagterboderne 1 (39 69 55 57, www.patepate.dk). Train København H. **Open** 9am-midnight Mon-Wed; 9am-1am Thur; 9am-3am Fri; 11am-3am Sat. **Main courses** 85kr-145kr. **Map** p123 H5 ❾ **Mediterranean/Danish**

PatéPaté is a wine bar, restaurant, tapas bar and delicatessen that was opened in summer 2009 by the group that runs Bibendum (*see p90*) and Falernum (*see p126*). The restaurant's name was inspired by the building's previous incarnation as a liver pâté factory. Rustic cuisine is the name of the game, with lots of hearty meat and fish dishes, as well as an excellent wine list. Candlelight and homely decor create a convivial mood.

Les Trois Cochons

Værnedamsvej 10 (33 31 70 55, www.cofoco.dk). Train Vesterport, or bus 6A, 9A. **Open** noon-2.30pm, 5.30pm-midnight Mon-Sat; 5.30pm-midnight Sun. **Set meal** 295kr 3 courses. **Map** p123 F4 ❿ **French/Danish**

Run by the folk behind Cofoco (*see p121*), Les Trois Cochons produces similarly priced, good-value three-course French meals with locally sourced ingredients and an enjoyable lack of formality. Decor is a bit more luxe than at the sister restaurant, with chandeliers and generous armchairs that invite lingering. Dishes are a cut above the usual bistro offerings too, featuring the likes of rabbit cooked in smoked bacon, salsify and wine, or saffron-scented fish. Puddings are equally good and satisfying – think retro rhubarb crumble and ice-cream.

Cafés & Bars

Apropos

Halmtorvet 12 (33 23 12 21, www.cafeapropos. dk). Train København H, or bus 10, 14. **Open** 9am-midnight Mon-Thur, Sun; 9am-1am Fri, Sat. **Map** p123 H5 ⑪
Probably the best of the trendy café-restaurants to have opened on the rejuvenated Halmtorvet in the last few years, Apropos offers mid-priced, southern European café food (the 139kr tapas plate, for example), more substantial French à la carte dishes, brunch menus, and a limited drinks menu. What makes Apropos and its neighbours particularly popular is their great location, with plenty of outdoor seating in summer.

Bang og Jensen

Istedgade 130 (33 25 53 18, www.bangog jensen.dk). Bus 10, 14. **Open** 7.30am-2am Mon-Fri; 10am-2am Sat; 10am-midnight Sun. **No credit cards. Map** p123 F6 ⑫
This café has been a mainstay of Vesterbro's nightlife scene for years, and the area's plentiful fashion victims can usually be relied upon to provide a bit of life most nights. Though the food is the usual Copenhagen café fare, it doesn't detract from Bang og Jensen's appeal as an alluring place to while away an evening (slumped, if you're lucky, in one of its great squashy sofas). Breakfast, with a fine disregard for the dictates of the clock, is served until 4pm daily. The laptop brigade are in abundance during the daytime – it's the classic popular spot for office-less freelancers and bloggers.

Café André Citroën

Vesterbrogade 58 (33 23 62 82, www.andre citroen.dk). Train København H, or bus 6A, 26. **Open** 10am-11pm Mon, Sun; 10am-midnight Tue-Thur; 10am-2am Fri, Sat. *Food served* 10am-10pm Mon-Thur; 10am-10.30pm Fri, Sat; 10am-9pm Sun. **Map** p123 G4 ⑬
With its mirrors, red banquettes and classic brasserie menu, this is like a little bit of Paris transplanted on to busy Vesterbrogade. The food, service and people-watching are all top-notch. Like so many places in town, it serves a traditional Danish lunch and a more mixed bag of French, Italian and Mexican fare in the evening.

Café Elefanten

Pasteursvej 20 (88 81 08 11, www.elefanten net.dk). Train Enghave, or bus 3A. **Open** 8.30am-10pm Mon-Wed; 8.30am-11pm Thur, Fri; 10am-11pm Sat; 10am-5pm Sun. **Map** p122 D6 ⑭
This friendly café and tapas spot is located on the ground floor of an old Carlsberg brewery warehouse,

on the border of Frederiksberg. Upstairs is the rehearsal space for contemporary dance company Dansescenen (*see p177*), so expect to see lots of lithe-looking figures in sweatpants and leg-warmers, as well as plenty of arts and media types. Top-quality sandwiches are the name of the game, as well as posh burgers, very fresh salads, Mediterranean small plates and decent coffee.

Central Hotel & Café

Tullinsgade 1 (33 21 00 95, www.centralhotelog cafe.dk). Bus 9A. **Open** 8am-6pm Mon-Fri; 10am-5pm Sat; 10am-4pm Sun. **Map** p123 G4 ⑮
Situated on the border of eastern Frederiksberg, in a former shoe-repair shop, Central Hotel & Café is a one-room hotel with a cute coffee place below. The café feels like it's been around for decades, being a favourite spot for locals to grab an espresso on the way to work; in fact, it opened only in 2013, the latest venture from local legend Leif Thingtved, who also owns Granola (*see p126*). As well as quality coffee (from Risteriet), there are teas, milkshakes and juices on offer, and sandwiches, pastries and ice-cream if you're feeling peckish.

★ Dyrehaven

Sønder Boulevard 72 (33 21 60 24, www. dyrehavenkbh.dk). Train Dybbølsbro, or bus 10, 14. **Open** 9am-2am Mon-Fri; 10am-2am Sat; 10am-6pm Sun. *Food served* 10am-9pm Mon-Wed; 10am-10pm Thur-Sat. **Map** p123 F6 ⑯
Owned by three young locals, this is an atmospheric spot that attracts small groups of sociable twenty-and thirtysomethings. The appeal is good design, a relaxed vibe, hearty food – classic dishes, such as

Dyrehaven.

smørrebrød and coq au vin – and well-priced drinks. The wood-panelled walls and bar, mounted deer heads, vintage pictures and separate dining cubicles give the bar a distinct 1970s feel. It's as popular for weekend brunch as it is for evening drinks.

★ Falernum

Værnedamsvej 16 (33 22 30 89, www.falernum.dk). Train Vesterport, or bus 6A, 9A. **Open** noon-midnight Mon-Thur, Sun; noon-2am Fri, Sat. **Map** p123 F4 ⓱

Located on one of the neighbourhood's nicest streets, this popular, cosy wine bar/café has plenty of character, thanks to its old wooden tables, candles and agreeable, loyal punters. The wine list is extensive and well thought out, and tapas plates are served in the evening. It's also a good spot for a light breakfast.

▶ *Falernum is part of a successful mini-chain that includes Pánzon, Vincaféen Bibendum and PatéPaté.*

Granola

Værnedamsvej 5 (33 25 00 80). Train Vesterport, or bus 6A, 9A. **Open** 9am-5.30pm Mon-Fri; 9am-4pm Sat. **Map** p123 F4 ⓲

This small café has a strong following. The space evokes the 1930s with its retro decor, and it's one of the few places where you can order the Danish fruit dessert *rødgrød med fløde* (stewed red fruit, usually strawberries, with cream). It also serves classic milkshakes and delicious ice-cream, and stocks an excellent range of top-quality tea and coffee. It's a popular spot for brunch.

Kaffe & Vinyl

Skydebanegade 4 (61 70 33 49, www.sortkaffe vinyl.dk). Train København H, or bus 10, 14. **Open** 8am-7pm Mon-Fri; 9am-7pm Sat, Sun. **Map** p123 G5 ⓳

Serving some of the best coffee in town (from local brand Risteriet), this friendly place draws in a cool bunch of caffeine and vinyl addicts, many of whom get here early in the day for a pre-work boost. The varied collection of records runs the gamut from electronica to rock.

Karriere

Flæsketorvet 57-67 (33 21 55 09, www.karriere bar.com). Train Dybbølsbro or København H. **Open** *Cocktail bar* 4pm-midnight Thur; 4pm-4am Fri, Sat. *Restaurant* 6-10pm Thur-Sat. **Map** p123 H6 ⓴

This ambitious art gallery/cocktail bar/restaurant opened in a former slaughterhouse in 2007, the brainchild of artist Jeppe Hein and his sister Lærke. The interior is designed by renowned contemporary artists (Ulrik Weck, for instance, created lampshades for the bar made of pots, pans and bowls turned upside down), who also supply works for the permanent and temporary exhibitions. Concerts, gigs, lectures and cultural events are also held here.

★ Lidkoeb

Vesterbrogade 72B (33 11 20 10, www.lidkoeb.dk). Train København H, or bus 6A, 26. **Open** 4pm-2am Mon-Sat; 8pm-1am Sun. **Map** p123 G4 ㉑

Lidkoeb.

EXPLORE

Follow a discreet passageway that leads off Vesterbrogade to reach one of Copenhagen's bars of the moment. Housed in a three-storey 18th-century building, Lidkoeb is renowned for quality cocktails (around 110kr each) and a cosy vibe. Choose from the ground-floor long wooden bar with fireplace and piano; the assembly room with smoking balcony; or, at the top, a whiskey lounge with a late-night feel.

Ricco's Coffee Bar
Istedgade 119 (33 31 04 40, www.riccos.dk). Bus 10, 14. **Open** 8am-11pm Mon-Fri; 9am-11pm Sat, Sun. **Map** p123 F6
This tiny, narrow coffee bar and boutique, owned by Ricco Sørensen, has a devoted following among Vesterbro's coffee addicts. Ricco's takes its coffee very seriously, selling a wide range of beans, syrups and paraphernalia. The comfortable room out back has long sofas and vinyl-only sounds.
Other locations throughout the city.

Shops & Services

Cykelfabrikken
Istedgade 92 (27 12 32 32, www.cykelfabrikken.dk). Train København H, or bus 10, 14. **Open** 1-6pm Tue-Fri; 11am-3pm Sat. **Map** p123 G5 **Bike shop**
These well-designed, simple bikes are a perfect blend of track and Scandinavian upright frames. The stylish shop opened in 2009, and fits in perfectly on independents-heavy Istedgade.

Dansk Made for Rooms
Istedgade 80 (32 18 02 55, www.danskmadefor rooms.dk). Train København H, or bus 10, 14. **Open** 11am-6pm Mon-Fri; 11am-4pm Sat. **Map** p123 G5 **Homewares/Accessories**
This light-filled design and homewares shop sells a choice selection of cushions, lamps, minimalist pots and trays, trendy headphones and graphics-led stationery and posters. The fashion branch is situated a few doors down, selling youthful womenswear characterised by bright colours, original patterns and Scandinavian cuts.
Other location Istedgade 64, Vesterbro (32 13 02 55, www.danskshop.dk).

★ Designer Zoo
Vesterbrogade 137 (33 24 94 93, www.dzoo.dk). Bus 6A. **Open** 10am-5.30pm Mon-Thur; 10am-7pm Fri; 10am-3pm Sat. **Map** p123 E5 **Homewares/Accessories**
The brainchild of six young artisans, who work in full view of ogling visitors (hence the name). Furniture, glassware, handmade clothes, jewellery and ceramics, created by the founders and by invited temporary designers, are among the items on sale in the spacious two-storey shop, .

★ Dora
Værnedamsvej 6 (32 21 33 57, www.shopdora.dk). Bus 6A, 9A. **Open** 10am-6pm Mon-Fri; 10am-3pm Sat. **Map** p123 F4 **Homewares/Accessories**
In line with the majority of homewares shops in Copenhagen, Dora has a distinct design focus, stocking a range of highly covetable candles, lamps, cushions, gadgets, storage and other homewares, plus stationery from brands such as Flos, Georg Jensen and Made a Mano. Simple but fashion-forward jewellery is also for sale, alongside sunglasses from Han Kjøbenhavn.
▶ *Dora sits next to the Playtype Concept Store – a cute design boutique that celebrates typography.*

★ Es
Istedgade 108 (33 22 48 28, www.es-es.dk). Bus 10, 14. **Open** 11am-6pm Mon-Fri; 11am-4pm Sat. **Map** p123 G5 **Fashion**
This womenswear boutique opened in 2012, and offers a well-edited selection of stylish Scandinavian and other European brands. Clothes tend towards an aesthetic that could be described as 'thirtysomething cool', with labels such as Hope, Bruuns Bazaar and Gat Rimon on the rails.
▶ *Next door, at no.110, is the Es Leisure shop, which focuses on cult toiletries.*

Kyoto
Istedgade 95 (33 31 66 36, www.kyoto.dk). Train København H, or bus 10, 14. **Open** 11am-6pm Mon-Fri; 10am-5pm Sat. **Map** p123 F5 **Fashion**

EXPLORE

Kyoto was one of the pioneers of trendy new Vesterbro, selling street-influenced menswear from its Istedgade outfit since 2001. The shop moved to a bigger space across the road in 2008, and now sells both mens and women's clothing and accessories from its spacious showroom.

Ølbutikken

Istedgade 44 (33 22 03 04, www.olbutikken.dk). Train København H, or bus 6A. **Open** 1-7pm Tue-Fri; 11am-4pm Sat. **Map** p123 G5 **㊙**

Food & drink

The microbrewery movement exploded in Copenhagen a few years back, and this beer shop rose to the challenge magnificently, selling a selection of Danish craft beers and international alternatives.

Frederiksberg Have.

FREDERIKSBERG

Frederiksberg's appealing character may be partially the result of its distinct political status: like Christiania, Frederiksberg is a separate town within the city of Copenhagen (and a stark contrast to the alternative Freetown). An independent municipality of just over 90,000 people, it has its own mayor, town hall and administration. Apartments tend to be larger and more expensive than elsewhere in the city, especially those along **Frederiksberg Allé**, a long, tree-lined boulevard that could have been lifted straight from an affluent *arrondissement* of Paris. Until the 19th century, Frederiksberg lay well outside Copenhagen, with views from its hill ('berg' means 'hill') over the fields – now Vesterbro – to the city beyond.

The area now officially runs up to the lakes, however. Its most central area, around the concert hall and conference center **Forum Copenhagen** (www.forumcopenhagen.dk) has undergone some rejuvenation in recent years. Rosenørns Allé, in particular, has become more lively since the relocation here of the **Royal Danish Academy of Music** (*see p172*), which has been based in the former DR Radiohusets building since 2009, and which will be joined in September 2014 by a rejuvenated **Musikmuseet** (Rosenørns Allé 22, www.natmus.dk) – the Danish Music Museum, which used to be housed in Rosenborg.

However, most of Frederiksberg still has a unique sense of separateness from Copenhagen: true, the district's conservative character doesn't make for giddy nightlife, but it does have a few sights that are worth the short bus or Metro ride from the centre of town.

The heart of the quarter is **Frederiksberg Have**, a rambling park that was laid out in the formal French style in the 18th century, before being given a more informal English revamp at the turn of the 19th century. In the south-east corner is **Det Kongelige Danske Haveselskabs Have** (Royal Danish Horticultural Garden), a formal, oriental-style water garden, created in 1884.

On the south side of Frederiksberg Have lies **Frederiksberg Slot** (Frederiksberg Palace), a royal summer residence used between the early 18th and mid 19th centuries. Beside Frederiksberg Slot is the **Zoologisk Have** (Zoological Garden), Denmark's national zoo. Founded in 1859, it's one of the oldest in the world, and has a good reputation for its breeding programme.

Across Roskildevej, you'll find more greenery in the form of **Søndermarken**, a more informal but equally picturesque park, which also features one of Copenhagen's most unusual museums. Entrance to **Cisternerne – Museet For Moderne Glaskunst** (Cisterns – Museum of Modern Glass Art) is gained via a Louvre-style

Frederiksberg Svømmehal

glass pyramid in the park, opposite the rear of Frederiksberg Slot.

To the north-east of Frederiksberg Have is the **Royal Copenhagen Factory Outlet**. Moving on from here in a clockwise direction around the park brings you to a small museum that offers a unique insight into the Danish sense of humour: the **Storm P Museet**, showcasing the work of cartoonist Robert Storm Petersen. Opposite is the small, octagonal **Frederiksberg Kirke**, dating from 1734. This pretty Dutch Renaissance church holds regular concerts, and has an altarpiece depicting the Eucharist, painted by CW Eckersberg, while in its cemetery is the grave of 19th-century poet Adam Oehlenschläger.

Moving south from here, and to the east of Søndermarken, is the **Bakkehus Museet**, a converted 17th-century house containing souvenirs of Denmark's early 19th-century Golden Age. It lies literally in the shadow of the old Carlsberg brewery (*see p121*), which is officially just over the border in Vesterbro.

Sights & Museums

Bakkehus Museet
Rahbeks Allé 23 (33 31 43 62, www.bakkehus museet.dk). Train Enghave, or bus 6A, 18, 26. **Open** 11am-4pm Tue-Sun. **Admission** 40kr; free under-17s. **No credit cards. Map** p122 C5 ⑩
This small, eclectic collection is housed in the former home of Knud Lyhne Rahbek, a literature professor and publisher in the early 19th century. The display includes everything from death masks to poet Adam Oehlenschläger's dressing gown.

Cisternerne – Museet For Moderne Glaskunst
Søndermarken (33 21 93 10, www.cisternerne.dk). Bus 4A, 6A, 18, 26. **Open** *Feb-Nov* 11am-5pm Tue-Sun. **Admission** 50kr; 40kr reductions; free under-18s. **No credit cards. Map** p122 B5 ㉛

These former underground water tanks now house an extraordinary museum of glass sculpture, featuring modern and classical stained glass and 3D works. But the amazing, vaulted subterranean rooms leave an equally lasting impression, still dank and wet underfoot, with stalactites and stalagmites surviving as evidence of their former function. This is supposedly the only art museum in Europe to do without natural light, but it manages superbly thanks to the work of theatrical effects expert John Aage Sørensen.

★ FREE Frederiksberg Have
Main entrance: Frederiksberg Runddel (no phone, www.ses.dk). Bus 18, 26. **Open** 6am-sunset daily. **Admission** free. **Map** p122 B4 ㉜
With its tree-lined paths, canals and lake, this is one of the city's most romantic spaces, particularly in spring. In its grounds are a Chinese pavilion, numerous statues and an impressive avenue of stately linden trees, dating from the 1730s. The Royal Danish Horticultural Garden (Det Kongelige Danske Haveselskabs Have, open 10am-sunset daily), located in the south-east corner of the park, features an oriental water garden, and is well worth a visit for horticultural inspiration; it's also one of the outdoor venues for the Copenhagen Jazz Festival.

Frederiksberg Slot
Roskildevej 28A (36 13 26 11, www.frederiksberg slot-frbslot.dk). Bus 6A, 26. **Open** *Guided tours* Jan-May, Aug-Nov 11am, 1pm last Sat of mth. **Guided tours** 50kr; under-14s free. **No credit cards. Map** p122 B5 ㉝
Frederik IV was so taken by the villas he saw while on a visit to Frascati that, between 1699 and 1703, he instructed architect Ernst Brandenburger to build a palace in the Italian style. The two side wings, designed by Laurids de Thurah, were added in 1733-38, on the instruction of Christian VI. Today, the palace is home to the Danish Military Academy and, as such, is not open to the public other than for the occasional guided tour.

Frederiksberg Svømmehal
Helgesvej 29 (38 14 04 00, www.frederiksberg svoemmehal.dk). Metro Frederiksberg. **Open** *Swimming pool* 7am-9pm Mon-Fri; 7am-4pm Sat; 9am-4pm Sun. *Luxury area* 9am-9pm Mon-Fri; 9am-4pm Sat, Sun. *Spa* 11am-8.30pm Mon-Fri; 9am-3.30pm Sat, Sun. **Admission** *Swimming pool* 40kr; under-15s 20kr. *Luxury area* 52kr. *Spa* 160kr. **Map** p122 C1 ㉞
This local institution was built in the 1930s, making it one of Denmark's oldest swimming pools. The walls of the main pool area are decorated with colourful mosaics. There's a heated baby pool, and a 'luxury' area, with steam baths, saunas and cold plunge pools, plus a modern spa section with a large saltwater pool (Saltbassinet), electric massage chairs, a Jacuzzi and a massage parlour. The place remains a popular spot for socialising and relaxing.

EXPLORE

Zoologisk Have.

Storm P Museet

Frederiksberg Runddel (38 86 05 00,
www.stormp.dk). Bus 18, 26. **Open** 10am-4pm
Tue-Sun. **Admission** 45kr; 40kr reductions;
free under-18s. **Map** p122 C4
Danes seem to be divided as to the merits of the
Frederiksberg-born artist and cartoonist Robert
Storm Petersen (1882-1949), better known as Storm P.
For older Danes, he typifies a traditional, aphoristic
strain of Danish humour; for the younger generation,
he is a dusty relic of a bygone era, and about as
funny as a hospital visit. At Storm P Museet, you
can judge for yourself whether his social-critical cartoons display any comedic merit, and whether his
symbolist-influenced paintings hold any profound
philosophical meaning. The museum – housed in
what was Frederiksberg's first police station – was
renovated in 2011-12. There are English captions on
the exhibits.

Zoologisk Have

Roskildevej 32 (72 20 02 00, 72 20 02 80,
www.zoo.dk). Bus 4A, 6A, 26. **Open** *July, Aug*
10am-8pm daily. *June* 10am-6pm daily. *Apr,*
May, Sept 10am-5pm Mon-Fri; 10am-6pm Sat,
Sun. *Oct* 10am-5pm daily. *Mar* 10am-4pm Mon-
Fri; 10am-5pm Sat, Sun. *Jan, Feb, Nov, Dec* 10am-
4pm daily. **Admission** 160kr; 95kr 3-11s; free
under-3s. **Map** p122 A4
Copenhagen Zoo is modest by international standards, but nevertheless has an interesting selection
of exotica, including polar bears, tigers, lions,
giraffes and apes, plus an elephant house designed
by Lord Norman Foster, and a savannah for African
species. An impressive indoor section houses butterflies, crocodiles and tropical birds. The children's zoo
is also a major attraction, its main landmark being
a 40m (131ft) tower, built in 1905, which, on a clear
day, offers spectacular views as far as the Swedish
coast. The Zoo was the subject of international

controversy in February 2014 when it euthanised a
healthy young giraffe that it had no space for; the
dead giraffe – referred to as Marius – was dissected
in front of a large crowd that included many children, and then fed to the lions.

Restaurants

Chai Wong

Thorvaldsensvej 2 (27 52 35 65, www.chai
wong.dk). Metro Forum. **Open** 5pm-midnight
Mon-Sat. **Main courses** 125kr-185kr. **Set meal**
275kr 3 courses. **Map** p123 F2 **Pan-Asian**
This 2011 opening from the owners of Michelin-
starred Kiin Kiin (*see p137*) is more relaxed – and
more affordable – than its cousin, with black bistro-
style tables, sofas to lounge on, dimmed lighting and
a menu inspired by Asian street food. The delicious
dishes might include fricassée of scallops with
spring onions and lemongrass, braised beef curry
with steamed pak choi, or Indonesian fried noodles.
There are also sharing plates and a takeaway menu.

★ formel B

Vesterbrogade 182 (33 25 10 66, www.formel-b.
dk). Bus 6A. **Open** 5.30pm-midnight Mon-Thur;
5.30pm-1am Fri, Sat. **Main courses** 130kr.
Map p122 D5 **French/Danish**
Several of Denmark's best-known chefs have passed
through the kitchen of this small, marble-lined cellar
restaurant at the western end of Vesterbrogade, and
it's held a Michelin star since 2004. Like so many
other places in the city, the concept is a riff on French
and Danish classics, but they do it so well, taking
the notion of modernism in cooking to a whole new
level. It's not, strictly speaking, a fish restaurant, but
that is where it shines. Try a dollop of caviar on a
scoop of jerusalem artichoke ice-cream, then go on
to more robust dishes, such as shellfish salad with
rouille, skate wing with tarragon foam and pickled

potatoes, or west coast turbot with braised veal tails. It draws the city's young and beautiful, so dress up and make a night of it.

Mêlée

Martensens Allé 16 (35 13 11 34, www.melee.dk). Bus 9A. **Open** 5.30pm-midnight Tue-Sat. **Main courses** 105kr-195kr. **Set meal** 395kr 5 courses. **Map** p122 E3 ❸ **Modern Danish Bistro**
This is a *hygge* little spot on a chichi residential street. In summer, there are a couple of tables outside, but it's best to be in the warm dining room to soak up the celebratory atmosphere. The wine list is carefully put together to match the hearty menu. Slabs of home-baked bread and butter accompany cod with pears and caper butter; lusty stews served straight from the pot come with mash.

★ Restaurant Radio

Julius Thomsens Gade 12 (25 10 27 33, www.restaurantradio.dk). Metro Forum. **Open** 5.30pm-midnight Tue-Thur; noon-3pm, 5.30pm-midnight Fri, Sat. **Main courses** *Lunch* from 100kr. **Set meal** 300kr 3 courses, 400kr 5 courses. **Map** p123 G1 ❹ **New Nordic**
The epitome of New Nordic, both in terms of decor and food, this is the latest offering from celebrity chef Claus Meyer, owner of Meyer's Deli (*see below*) and co-founder of Noma (*see p114*). The small plates are conceptual offerings – think scallops with endive and seaweed – but most have flavours that are rich enough to satisfy unexperimental palates. Most of the produce used is organic. It's housed in the old Radio House, over the road from the Forum.

Cafés & Bars

★ Meyers Deli

Gammel Kongevej 107 (33 25 45 95, www.meyersdeli.dk). Bus 9A. **Open** 8am-10pm daily. **Map** p123 E3 ❹
Claus Meyer is one of the leading foodie figures in Denmark. Entrepreneur, TV personality and restaurateur (he's the co-founder of Noma), Meyer opened this magnificent deli-café in the heart of bourgeois Frederiksberg back in 2005. His healthy, innovative eat/heat/cook takeaways have proved popular with time-poor yuppie locals. There's also a branch in the Magasin department store (*see p101*).
Other locations Meyer's Bakery, Jægersborggade 9, Nørrebro; Godthåbsvej 10, Frederiksberg.

Vinstue 90

Gammel Kongevej 90 (33 31 84 90, www.vinstue90.dk). Bus 9A. **Open** 11am-1am Mon-Wed, Sun; 11am-2am Thur-Sat. **Map** p123 F3 ❹
Something of a local legend, this small bar, founded in 1916, is famous for its 'slow beer'; it takes 15-20 minutes to pour a glass, so customers often order a 'normal' beer while they wait. It's all about the

pouring: standard Carlsberg pilsner is on tap, but by pouring very slowly from unpressurised kegs, a smoother taste is produced. They don't serve food, but the friendly owners will happily order *smørrebrød* (or anything else) for you if you call in advance. They'll even provide plates and cutlery. A gem.

Shops & Services

Royal Copenhagen Factory Outlet

Søndre Fasanvej 9 (38 34 10 04, www.royalcopenhagen.com). Metro Fasanvej, or bus 4A, 9A. **Open** 10am-6pm Mon-Fri; 10am-3pm Sat. **Map** p122 A3 ❹ **Homewares**
Cash-strapped fans of Denmark's most famous porcelain brand should head to its factory shop. You can buy discounted dinnerware and figurines that don't quite pass muster for the central Amagertorv shop, as well as discontinued items.

Soulland

Gammel Kongevej 37 (no phone, www.soulland.com). Train Vesterport, or bus 9A. **Open** 11am-6pm Wed-Fri; 11am-4pm Sat. **Map** p123 G4 ❹ **Fashion**
Previously called US Import, this gallery-like shop had a makeover in 2013 when it became the flagship of Soulland, the trend-led menswear label of owner Silas Adler. As well as Soulland's streetwear-inspired garments, shoes and accessories, the shop stocks selected pieces from Acne Jeans, A Kind of Guise and Dana Lee. A range of independent fashion magazines are also on sale, artfully arranged around the counter.

★ Stig P

Gammel Kongevej 91C (72 14 83 14, www.stigp.dk). Train København H, or bus 9A. **Open** 11am-6pm Mon-Thur; 11am-6.30pm Fri; 10am-4pm Sat. **Map** p123 F4 ❹ **Fashion**
Although it was founded back in 1969 (by Stig Petersen), this remains one of Denmark's most on-trend fashion boutiques. As well as wearable and relaxed T-shirts, tops, dresses and knitwear from the eponymous label, all Stig P branches stock clothing and accessories from cult brands such as Kokoon, Vanessa Bruno Athé, Sonia Rykiel, Rag & Bone and Sessùn. The Nørrebro branch also has menswear.
Other locations Kronprinsensgade 14, Indre By (33 14 42 16); Ravnsborggade 18, Nørrebro (35 35 75 00).

Tom Rossau Showroom

Frederiksberg Allé 5 (51 92 47 17, www.tomrossau.dk). Train København H, or bus 6A, 26. **Open** 11am-6pm Tue-Fri; 10.30am-2pm Sat. **Map** p123 F4 ❹ **Homewares**
Self-taught Danish designer Tom Rossau creates retro-inspired lamps from sustainable wood veneers. This flagship store showcases the full range (floor, pendant and table), as well as new shelving units and the TTO1 Convertible coffee-cum-dining table.

EXPLORE

Nørrebro
& Østerbro

Nørrebro and Østerbro, along with Vesterbro, are often referred to as the *Brokvartererne* (literally, the Bridge Quarters). These are the main residential areas outside the city's ramparts and, individual as they are, all have a flavour of 'real' Copenhagen about them that can be lacking in the city centre. Nørrebro can get a bit too real at times, hosting the odd riot, but it remains a pulsating and attractive neighbourhood, home to some of the coolest bars, restaurants and shops in town. Its cemetery, Assistens Kirkegård, is the final resting place for many famous Danes, as well as a popular sunbathing spot for locals still living. Østerbro is more sedate and well heeled, full of boutiques, stylish cafés and smartly dressed couples pushing prams containing equally well-dressed children.

Assistens Kirkegård.

Don't Miss

1 Jægersborggade Street of artisan shops and cool cafés (p134).

2 Kiin Kiin The first Asian restaurant in Denmark to win a Michelin star (p137).

3 Assistens Kirkegård Here lie Søren Kierkegaard and Hans Christian Andersen (p135).

4 Geranium Rasmus Kofoed's culinary skills have earned his restaurant two Michelin stars (p144).

5 Normann Copenhagen Stylish homewares store (p145).

uh___ªla

Superkilen.

EXPLORE

NØRREBRO

Along with Vesterbro (*see pp120-127*), Nørrebro is one of the hippest areas of the city, thanks to its trendy clothes shops, vibrant cafés and burgeoning nightlife. Its epicentre is on **Sankt Hans Torv**, with its two great cafés, **Sebastopol Café** and **Pussy Galore's Flying Circus**, and the boutiques and cafés on pedestrianised **Blågårdsgade**. But **Elmegade** and, in particular, **Jægersborggade** have spread the trendification further. These streets are both lined with innovative boutiques and cool cafés, and the latter – a 'no-go' zone only a decade or so ago – is now also home to destination New Nordic restaurant **Relæ** and its sister spot, **Manfreds & Vin**, as well as to popular porridge café **Grød**.

As with Vesterbro, many younger Copenhageners have found that Nørrebro's ethnic mix is a major element of its appeal as an up-and-coming residential area. But unlike Vesterbro's so-called second-generation Danes, who are more established, Nørrebro's ethnic inhabitants seem less integrated into the community and are generally less prosperous. As a result, the area has suffered from that most un-Danish phenomenon, social unrest, and has even experienced some shocking violent crime, the odd riot on the occasion of a deportation, and some heavy-handed policing. With its dark streets and tightly packed housing, the district is probably central Copenhagen's least safe (as opposed to 'most dangerous') neighbourhood at night – though that statement should be qualified by saying that it is still a relatively secure night-time destination, particularly compared to many other European capitals.

It is ironic, then, that Nørrebro's only museum is the **Politihistorisk Museum** (Police History Museum). This well-presented museum would potentially be of interest to foreign visitors but for the lack of any significant information in English.

Nørrebro also has two historic cemeteries. The Jewish cemetery, **Mosaisk Kirkegård**, on Peter Fabers Gade, is surrounded by a high wall and gates, and is open only for private visits arranged through the local Jewish community. **Assistens Kirkegård**, on the other hand, is open year-round and, for a place of eternal rest, is fairly lively; it's used by many as a local park and picnic place (rehearsing musicians are a common sight).

A much newer Nørrebro public space, completed in 2012, is **Superkilen**, an urban park and playground designed by artists' group Superflex in collaboration with BIG architects. The park is a celebration of the neighbourhood's ethnic diversity, using objects from around the world – including swings from Iraq and benches from Brazil.

As well as fashionable clothing and accessories boutiques, Nørrebro is also known for its antiques shops. The trade is centred on **Ravnsborggade** (just south-east of Sankt Hans Torv) and its extension **Ryesgade**, where just about every store has a selection of old clothes, furniture, porcelain, art, glassware, silverware, gold or bric-a-brac.

Sights & Museums

★ FREE Assistens Kirkegård
Entrances on Jagtvej & Nørrebrogade (35 37 19 17, www.assistens.dk). Bus 5A. **Open** *Apr-Sept* 7am-10pm daily. *Oct-Mar* 7am-7pm daily. **Admission** free. **Map** p135 B2 ❶
Buried among the hundreds of varieties of trees in this graceful cemetery is just about everyone of any note in Danish history over the last two centuries, including old rivals Hans Christian Andersen and Søren Kierkegaard; Niels Bohr; Carlsberg patriarch JC Jacobsen; and the artists Christen Købke, CW Eckersberg, Jens Juel, HW Bissen and Peter Skovgaard. The cemetery's museum, Kulturcentret Assistens (10am-4pm Mon-Fri, admission 20kr), is located within the cemetery grounds in a red-brick building, and provides an overview of the cultural and social history of the cemetery and the stories of many of the Danes contained within it. The centre also provides guided tours, bookable by phone. The cemetery is transformed into an unlikely picnic spot in the summer, and it's always a pleasant place to cycle or stroll through. Locals have even been known to sunbathe on the gravestones. For information on the cemetery's most famous graves, *see p136* **Dead Famous**.

Politihistorisk Museum
Fælledvej 20 (35 36 88 88, www.politimuseum.dk). Bus 5A, 350S. **Open** 11am-4pm Tue, Thur, Sun. **Admission** 40kr; free under-18s. **No credit cards**. **Map** p135 D2 ❷
As well as covering the history of the police force, with old uniforms, equipment and ephemera, the building also houses the Museum of Crime, which documents Copenhagen's nefarious residents (including various infamous murderers) from past centuries. Temporary exhibitions also take place here; a recent one covered the Nørrebro riots of 18 May 1993.

FREE Superkilen
Nørrebrogade 208 (no phone, www.superflex. net/superkilen). Bus 5A. **Open** 24hrs daily. **Admission** free. **Map** p135 B1 ❸
Stretching 750 metres (about half a mile), from Nørrebrogade to Tagensvej, Superkilen is Nørrebro's new urban park. Designed by artists' group Superflex, in collaboration with high-profile architects Birke Ingels Group (BIG), the park is a collection of global influences, to reflect the fact that the local neighbourhood is now home to people from some 50 countries. It's divided into three main areas: the Red Square, for music and sports; the Black Market, with fountains and benches; and the Green Park, for picnics, leisure and dog-walking. Local residents were asked to

EXPLORE

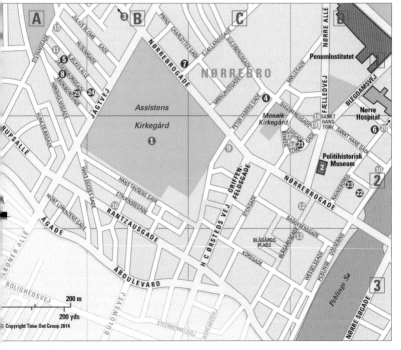

DEAD FAMOUS

Assistens Kirkegård is the final resting place of many a great Dane.

EXPLORE

HANS CHRISTIAN ANDERSEN
Plot no: P1
Assistens' most famous lodger by far, Andersen is probably *the* most famous Dane – period. Born in Odense in 1805, he moved to Copenhagen at the age of 14. He was a playwright, a poet and an excellent origami artist, but became world-famous first and foremost for fairytales such as *The Emperor's New Clothes* and *The Nightingale*. He died in 1875. *See also p100* **The Story of a Man and a City**.

SØREN KIERKEGAARD
Plot no: A17
Born in Copenhagen in 1813, Kierkegaard had a life as plagued by doubt as his existentialist philosophy. Inspired by his strongly religious father, he became a pastor, but after a troubled youth and a broken engagement to the love of his life, Regine, he turned to writing philosophical masterpieces such as *Either/Or* and *The Sickness unto Death*. He died a bitter 42-year-old in 1855.

NIELS BOHR
Plot no: Q4
The 1922 Nobel Prize winner for physics was born in Copenhagen in 1885. Living proof that footballers aren't all dim, Bohr was a fine league player at Akademisk Boldklub. He chose to pursue physics, however, and went on to formulate the principle of atomic fission. Bohr, like thousands of Danish Jews, fled the Nazi occupation in 1943 and wound up in the US, working on the atomic bomb – though he was later to campaign against its use. He died in 1962.

MARTIN ANDERSEN NEXØ
Plot no: H2
A writer of socially minded works about the hardships of common folk around the turn of the 20th century, Nexø was born in 1869 in Copenhagen's early industrial slums. *Pelle the Conqueror* remains his best known work, not least because it was turned into an Oscar-winning movie by director Bille August. A communist, he fled occupied Denmark in 1941 and died in Dresden in 1954.

DAN TURÈLL
Plot no: B13
In his short time on earth (he died from lung cancer in 1993 at the age of 47), Turèll was the prime chronicler of Copenhagen life, ascending from a cult figure to a widely loved literary hero. His breakthrough was the 1974 *Karma Cowboy* – a collection of poems influenced by Zen Buddhism and *Lucky Luke* comics. Over the next 20 years, Turèll wrote weekly columns in the *Politiken* newspaper, as well as numerous volumes of poetry and a series of 12 noir crime novels. He lived in Vesterbro and Frederiksberg.

MICHAEL STRUNGE
Plot no: V15
Alongside Turèll, Strunge was one of Copenhagen's most notable post-war writers. He was a post-punk poet who committed suicide in 1986 in central Copenhagen, diving from a fourth-floor window at the age of just 28. Twenty years later, his romantically bleak Cold War poems of alienation still attract new readers.

nominate objects for the park, resulting in a fountain from Morocco, benches from Brazil, swings from Iraq and a neon sign from a Russian hotel.

Restaurants

★ Kiin Kiin

Guldbergsgade 21 (33 35 75 55, www.kiin.dk). Bus 5A. **Open** 5.30pm-1am (last seating 9pm) Mon-Sat. **Set meal** 495kr 5 courses (early evening only), 825kr 11 courses. **Map** p135 C1 ❹ **Modern Thai**
Chef Henrik Yde Andersen has put five years spent living in Thailand to good effect in this new three-storey restaurant, close to Sankt Hans Torv. Weary of being served the same five dishes in the city's Thai restaurants, Andersen's mission has been to get Danes eating new and interesting Thai food; vegetables and shellfish feature strongly in dishes such as orchid-lemongrass salad, and scallops with young ginger. The menu changes daily and there's a well-chosen wine menu for 775kr. Kiin Kiin is one of the few Thai restaurants in Europe to boast a Michelin star.

Manfreds & Vin

Jægersborggade 40 (36 96 65 93, www. manfreds.dk). Bus 18. **Open** noon-3.30pm, 5.30-10pm daily. **Small plates** 75kr-140kr. **Set meal** 250kr 7 courses. **Map** p135 A1 ❺ **New Nordic**
Manfreds is more intimate and laid-back than its sister restaurant opposite, Relæ (*see p138*), though equally as scrupulous when it comes to sourcing ingredients. Most of the produce is organic and local, with biodynamic vegetables from Kiselgården, roots from Lammefjorden, pork from Grambogaard, herbs from local forests, and wine – a big focus here– from organic and biodynamic vineyards. The emphasis is on sharing, with the menu consisting of small dishes – tartare of beef with cress and rye bread, say, or charred onions with elderflower and havgus cheese.

Nørrebro Bryghus

Ryesgade 3 (35 30 05 30, www.noerrebro bryghus.dk). Bus 5A. **Open** 11am- 3pm, 5-10pm Mon-Sat. **Main courses** 160kr-250kr. **Set meal** 350kr-400kr 3 courses incl drinks (before 7.30pm), 500kr-600kr 5 courses incl drinks. **Map** p135 D2 ❻ **Gastropub**
This split-level modern Scandinavian take on a micro-brewery serves not just great home-brewed beers and ales, but also some good gastropub-style food. The monthly changing menu typically includes plenty of fresh fish, such as fried pepper mackerel with summer cabbage, plus a choice of roast meats. All washed down, of course, with some of the best beers in town.
▶ *Other good microbreweries include Mikkeller & Friends (see p141), Bryggeriet Apollo (Vesterbrogade 3, 33 12 33 13, www.bryggeriet.dk) and Vesterbro Bryghus (Vesterbrogade 2B, 33 11 17 05, www.vesterbrobryghus.dk).*

Oysters & Grill

Sjællandsgade 1B (70 20 61 71, www.cofoco.dk). Bus 5A. **Open** 5.30-9.30pm Mon-Thur; 5.30-10pm Fri, Sat; 5.30-9.15pm Sun. **Main courses** 155kr-195kr. **Map** p135 B1 ❼ **Seafood**

EXPLORE

Jægersborggade. *See p134.*

Grød.

Taking its inspiration from Spanish seafood eateries, Oysters & Grill – one of the latest offerings from local gourmet mini-chain Cofoco – is a relaxed affair. The food, though fine, doesn't compete with some of Cofoco's other establishments, such as Höst (*see p86*) and Les Trois Cochons (*see p124*), but the concept makes for a convivial atmosphere, with lots of dishes to share, and waiters dressed as sailors. Choose from a selection of super-fresh oysters and shellfish (razor clams, scallops, grilled lobster, wild shrimp) and main courses from the grill, such as entrecôte or whole dorade. Desserts include sorbet, and pancakes with ice-cream and chocolate sauce.

★ Relæ

Jægersborggade 41 (36 96 66 09, www. restaurant-relae.dk). Bus 18. **Open** 5.30pm-midnight Wed-Fri; noon-3pm, 5.30pm-midnight Sat. **Set meal** 385kr 4 courses, 675kr 7 courses (after 8pm). **Map** p135 A1 ❽ **New Nordic**

Not many restaurants would have the balls to serve you a raw, pickled carrot with a glass of champagne and call it an amuse-bouche. Then again, Relæ is no ordinary restaurant. Founded by Christian Puglisi (chef) and Kim Rossen (front-of-house), both previously at Noma (*see p114*), it looks all quietly cool with an open kitchen and wrap-around bar, yet rocks to an eclectic sound track: a welcome antidote to more po-faced 'serious' restaurants. Relæ – which now has a Michelin star – serves one meat and one vegetarian menu, both adventurous but accessible, featuring Nordic dazzlers such as barley porridge

with cauliflower 'crumbs' and wild mushrooms, and silky slow-cooked veal heart with jerusalem artichoke purée.

Cafés & Bars

★ Bodega

Kapelvej 1, off Nørrebrogade (35 39 07 07, www.bodega.dk). Bus 5A. **Open** 8am-midnight Mon-Thur; 10am-3am Fri, Sat; 10am-9pm Sun. **Map** p135 C2 ❾

Bodega's food is contemporary southern European fare, the coffee excellent and the interior effortlessly hip, with low ceilings, white walls, expensive leather chairs and a striking wooden bar and tables. DJs play soul, funk and R&B at weekends, and in summer there is limited seating outside, across the road from Assistens Kirkegård (*see p135*).

Café 22

Sortedam Dossering 21 (35 37 38 27, www.cafe 22.dk). Bus 5A. **Open** 9am-midnight Mon-Wed, Sun; 9am-2am Thur-Sat. **Map** p135 D2 ❿

It remains something of a mystery why there aren't more cafés and bars located beside Copenhagen's elegant man-made lakes to the west of the city centre, since it seems such an obviously picturesque spot in which to dine and drink. Perhaps the reason lies hidden in the long cold of Copenhagen's winter, which can whip across the open water here. But we should be grateful for Café 22, an appealing cellar café/bar (with outdoor tables in summer), serving

EXPLORE

excellent sandwiches, pasta dishes, tapas, burgers and tasty desserts.

★ Grød

Jægersborggade 50 (50 58 55 79, www.groed.com).
Bus 18. **Open** 7.30am-9pm Mon-Fri; 10am-9pm
Sat, Sun. **Map** p135 A1
This healthy porridge café is more exciting than it
might sound, seeking as it does to redefine the concept of porridge via exciting recipes and the use of
different grains. The menu changes regularly, but
always includes oat-based breakfast-style porridge
(maybe with blackcurrant sugar, fresh blood orange
and walnuts). There's also rye, kamut or barley-
based versions, and more savoury types of porridge
suited to lunch or dinner – perhaps risotto with beetroot, parmesan, cream cheese and thyme, or 'barley
otto' with celeriac, cheese, croûtons and lovage.
Dishes are well thought out and most of them really
do work – so much so that the café now has a cook-
book for sale.
Other locations Torvehallerne (hall 2, stall A8),
Nørreport (50 59 82 15).

Harbo Bar

Blågårdsgade 2D (no phone). Bus 5A. **Open**
8.30am-midnight Mon-Thur; 8.30am-2am Fri;
9.30am-2am Sat; 9.30am-11pm Sun. **Map**
p135 D2
Designed with a relaxed 'living room' concept in
mind, Harbo Bar reflects the fact that multicultural
Nørrebro is now home to the city's hipster community. Retro fittings, a plethora of laptops (the place
is buzzing with freelancers in the daytime), grazing-
oriented food and decent beer create a vibe more
readily associated with Berlin than Copenhagen.
The place is also known for its organic walnut
brandy. A cornerstone of the 'hood.
▶ *Pedestrianised Blågårdsgade is home to several*
good independent shops and cafés.

Kaffesalonen

Pebling Dossering 6 (35 35 12 19, www.kaffe
salonen.com). Bus 5A. **Open** 8am-midnight Mon-
Fri; 10am-midnight Sat, Sun. **Map** p135 D3
Salonen is blessed with an ideal location close to the
lakes, which allows it to expand on to a large floating
deck during summer. It's the perfect place for a long,
leisurely sundowner, followed by a selection from
the accomplished French-Danish menu.

Laundromat Café

Elmegade 15 (35 35 26 72, www.thelaundromat
cafe.com). Bus 3A, 5A. **Open** 8am-midnight
Mon-Fri; 10am-midnight Sat, Sun. **Map** p135 D2
Combining a coffee shop with a launderette, this has
been a big local hit since opening a decade ago. Stick
your laundry in the washing machine, then take a
seat in the stylish space (think wood-panelled walls
and designer lampshades) to enjoy a grilled sandwich, salad or sweet snack while your clothes are

Laundromat Café.

SKATE COPENHAGEN

The city is now a destination for skaters worldwide.

Despite being burdened with snow and ice for several months of the year, Copenhagen has an active, friendly skateboarding scene that gets plenty of international interest. In fact, its annual **Copenhagen Pro** event (www.cphpro.dk), held in June/July, has grown into Europe's largest professional skateboarding contest since it launched in 2006, attracting some of the world's best skaters, including, of course, local legend Rune Glifberg, who makes the pilgrimage from his home in sunny southern California.

For years, the scene centred around the indoor **Copenhagen Skatepark** in Vesterbro (Enghavevej 78, 33 21 28 28, www. copenhagenskatepark.dk), especially when the weather made skating outdoors difficult. But since 2011, thanks to the refurbishment of Østerbro's **Fælledparken**, skaters have a new 4,000-square-metre outdoor skatepark. Free to use, it was designed by Grindline, which has built parks all over the world that are the antithesis of run-down, under-used local council skateparks. The new park has three areas: a plaza-style street section, containing steps, handrails, flatbars and ledges; a large half-pipe; and a third mixed-terrain space, with bowls, quarter-pipes and ledges, which will also be used for competitions.

Other skateparks include Nørrebro's recently renovated indoor X-hall, with three bowls, and a (slightly more intimidating) indoor bowl in Christiania. For the low-down on the plethora of street spots, head to skate shops **Circus Circus** in Nørrebro (Guldsbergsgade 16, 26 79 62 84, www.circuscircus.dk), **Street Machine** in the centre (Kronprinsensgade 3, 33 33 95 11, www.streetmachine.com) or **Sidewalk** in Vesterbro (Enghave Plads 10, 33 31 32 34, www.sidewalkshop.dk), where staff will be happy to let you know where's currently good to go.

being washed. There's a good range of coffees and a plentiful supply of reading material. It's also a nice spot for weekend brunch. Other branches have opened in recent years; they're similarly stylish but lack the washing machines.
Other locations Århusgade 38, Østerbro (35 55 60 20); Gammel Kongevej 96, Frederiksberg (55 56 55 50).

Mikkeller & Friends

Stefansgade 35 (33 31 04 15, www.mikkeller.dk). Bus 18. **Open** 2pm-midnight Mon-Wed, Sun; 2pm-2am Thur, Fri; noon-2am Sat. **Map** p135 A1 ⑮
The second Copenhagen bar from this popular micro-brewery opened in 2013, just round the corner from Jægersborggade. With shiny turquoise floors, and custom-made benches and tables in unstained wood, the spacious bar is a calming space in which to sink some draught beer. Formed in 2010 by two students and their physics teacher, Mikkeller & Friends now brews some 40 different craft beers, all available on tap here. Cider, Mikkeller spirits and Three Floyds draught beer from the USA are also on offer, while food comes in the form of gourmet sausages and cheese.
Other locations Viktoriagade 8B/C, Vesterbro (33 31 04 15).

★ Nordisk Brødhus

Rantzausgade 58B (31 45 02 24, www.nordisk brodhus.dk). Bus 12, 18, 66. **Open** 8am-10pm Tue-Sun. **No credit cards**. **Map** p135 B2 ⑯
This laid-back bakery/café is run by a friendly couple with a passion for proper bread. Loaves are made from organic grains (ground with an old-fashioned stone grinder to preserve the flavour), without artificial leavening agents – this is a sourdough-only bakery. The on-site wood-fired brick oven produces strong flavoured loaves with a good crust. Pastries and coffee are also available, and the place has recently started offering well-priced (80kr) evening dishes – perhaps own-made pizza, a hearty stew, or a potato dish with goat's cheese, rosemary and bacon. Highly recommended.

Oak Room

Birkegade 10 (38 60 38 60, www.oakroom.dk). Bus 3A, 5A. **Open** 7pm-1am Wed; 7pm-2am Thur; 4pm-4am Fri; 6pm-4am Sat. **No credit cards**. **Map** p135 C2 ⑰
This cramped venue just off trendy Elmegade is always packed and sweaty, with crowds spilling on to the pavement at weekends. It's popular with pre-clubbers on their way to Rust nearby, or moviegoers emerging from the Empire Cinema round the corner. Happy hour lasts until 9pm.

Pussy Galore's Flying Circus

Sankt Hans Torv 30 (35 37 68 00, www.pussy galore.dk). Bus 3A, 5A. **Open** 8am-11pm Mon-Wed; 8am-4am Thur; 8am-2am Fri; 9am-2am Sat; 9am-11pm Sun. **Map** p135 D2 ⑱

Located at the heart of one of the hippest parts of Copenhagen (around Sankt Hans Torv), this archetypal modern Copenhagen café kick-started Nørrebro's popularity. The busy L-shaped bar and dining area, decorated in requisite 1990s minimalist style (including Arne Jacobsen chairs), is the trendy counterpart to the more conventional French food offered by Sebastopol next door (*see below*). The menu is fusion-heavy, with salads and hearty burgers, but quality is variable. As with Sebastopol, Pussy Galore's tables move on to the square in spring. Cocktails are reasonably priced compared to bars in the centre of town.

Sebastopol Café

Sankt Hans Torv 32 (35 36 30 02, www. sebastopol.dk). Bus 3A, 5A. **Open** 8am-midnight Mon-Thur; 8am-1am Fri; 9am-1am Sat; 9am-10pm Sun. **Map** p135 D2 ⑲
Sebastopol's French staples provide tempting, good-value competition to the more erratic offerings of Pussy Galore's (*see left*) next door. The young and hip clientele (musicians, journalists, advertising types and the like) from this ultra-cool part of town provides constant visual entertainment. Sebastopol gets very crowded on summer weekends when, like Pussy's, it bursts exuberantly on to the square.

Pussy Galore's Flying Circus.

Fælledparken.

Underwood Ink

Ryesgade 30A (35 35 55 53, www.underwood-ink.dk). Bus 5A, 6A. **Open** 4pm-2am Wed-Sat. **Map** p135 D2

Saved from closure by new investment, Underwood Ink is a characterful, bohemian spot. Literature lovers should feel right at home: the shelves are stacked with books (mostly English-language) by novelists of the Bukowski ilk, and there's also a range of international magazines. It's a cool yet cosy spot in which to hang out, quietly chat or get into that holiday novel with the help of a warming coffee.

Shops & Services

Acne Archive

Elmegade 21 (33 14 00 28, www.acnestudios.com). Bus 3A, 5A. **Open** 11am-6.30pm Mon-Fri; 10am-5pm Sat. **Map** p135 D2 **Fashion**

Fans of the Swedish high-fashion label will be pleased to hear that this spacious shop sells clothing and accessories from previous seasons at a discount – though that still requires a fairly fat wallet.

Antikhallen

Sortedams Dossering 7C (35 35 04 20). Bus 5A. **Open** 2-6pm Mon-Fri; 11am-3pm Sat. **No credit cards.** **Map** p135 D2 **Antiques**

An unpretentious treasure trove of second-hand and antique furniture, this shop is bursting with eye-catching curiosities, from 19th-century mahogany tables to 1970s moulded orange plastic chairs.

Kim Anton & Co Antiques

Ravnsborggade 14 (35 37 06 24, www.antons.dk). Bus 5A. **Open** 9.30am-5.30pm Mon-Fri; 11am-2pm Sat. **Map** p135 D2 **Antiques**

A two-floor emporium full of ornate 18th- and 19th-century European furniture, plus a selection of fine fabrics from Bevilacqua, and older items related to the royal houses of Europe, such as coats of arms, photographs, medals and porcelain.

★ Ladyfingers

Jægersborggade 4 (no phone, www.lady-fingers.dk). Bus 18. **Open** 11am-5pm Tue-Fri; 11am-3pm Sun. **Map** p135 B1 **Accessories**

This jewellery collective and workshop sells the works of a handful of contemporary designers, all of whom go for handcrafted simplicity over bling. You'll find oxidised silver, battered bronze and gold-plated rings, and a range of bangles, necklaces and earring studs dominated by geometric and experimental shapes. The pieces by Malene Glintborg, in particular, are highly original and covetable.

Tricotage

Jægersborggade 15 (60 67 59 14, www.tricotage.dk). Bus 18. **Open** 11am-5.30pm Mon-Fri; 11am-3pm Sat. **Map** p135 A1 **Fashion**

This lovely womenswear label – founded by Karin Bjørneboe and Ida Anesdatter Schmidt in 2010 – is all about easy-to-wear basics and sustainable materials; think delicately patterned T-shirts, loose trousers and smock dresses in soft organic cotton. There's also underwear in the softest of materials, plus vintage-inspired jewellery from Erica Weiner New York, and stylish sunglasses from Han Kjøbenhavn. **Other locations** Gammel Mønt 25, Indre By (60 67 59 14).

ØSTERBRO

Østerbro, which runs from the eastern side of Nørrebro across to the docks on the coast, is »dominated by Denmark's national stadium, **Parken**, home of **FC København**, the country's top football team, in Fælledparken. Bordered by

Nørre Allé, Blegdamsvej, Østerbrogade and Jagtvej, **Fælledparken** is a large municipal park with a small lake, which underwent massive redevelopment between 2009 and 2013, sparked by its centenary. Its impressive skatepark (*see p140* **Skate Copenhagen**) opened in summer 2011 and is one of the biggest in Europe. Other new initiatives include illuminated exercise paths, playgrounds and sports areas and tree planting, and there's now a café (open April-Oct) in the central pavilion. A more practical open space than Copenhagen's other more historic or ornamental gardens, this is where locals come for a game of football or hockey, to play tennis, cycle, rollerskate, jog or skateboard. During the summer, there are often free concerts here: larger-scale pop and rock concerts by big-name bands and artists take place in the large concrete stadium. To the west of Parken, across Nørre Allé, is the **Zoologisk Museum** (Zoological Museum); while to the east is **Geranium**, one of Copenhagen's best restaurants.

Østerbro itself is a prosperous residential area containing century-old apartment buildings and newer high-rise blocks. A good mix of shops, cafés and restaurants stretches along **Østerbrogade**, and the shops on **Nordre Frihavnsgade** and the bars on **Bopa Plads**

and **Rosenvængets Allé** show clear signs of trendification. The last is home to gourmet organic butcher/café **Gourmandiet**, a popular brunch spot for well-to-do locals. Also just off Østerbrogade is the 19th-century terraced housing development **Brumleby**, once a model for successful social housing, and now one of the most desirable places to live in the city.

At the eastern end of Østerbro is a large dock area that has seen considerable development in recent years. Further north in Nordhavn, the docks become more industrial, though this is also where you'll find the cavernous modern furniture store **Paustian** and a couple of stylish restaurants, as well as Copenhagen's yacht basins. Also nearby is **Svanemøllestranden**, a man-made beach that's much used in summer. In terms of innovative architecture, this is one of the most stimulating parts of the city – but bring a bike, the area is too big to cover on foot.

Sights & Museums

Zoologisk Museum
Universitetsparken 15 (35 32 10 01, www.zoologi. snm.ku.dk). Bus 18, 42, 94N, 150S, 184, 185. **Open** 10am-5pm Tue-Sun. **Admission** 75kr; 15kr-40kr reductions.

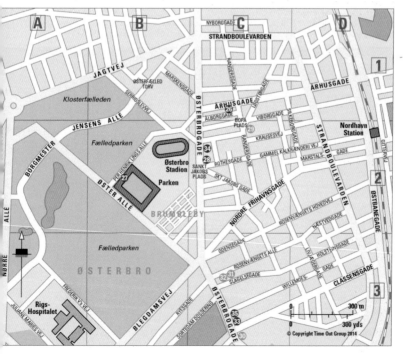

EXPLORE

Though it's a little fusty – the mammals and birds from around the world that are displayed here are all stuffed – the city's natural history museum is still a good place to take children if the weather is bad.

Restaurants

Davids Bistro

Århusgade 22 (46 32 13 21, www.davids bistro.dk). Bus 1A, 3A, 18, 40. **Open** noon-3pm, 5.30pm-midnight Mon-Sat. **Main courses** 195kr-245kr. **Set meal** 350kr 3 courses. **Map** p143 C1 ㉖ **French/Danish**

Chef-patron David de Silva came from a fine-dining kitchen at Kong Hans Kælder, but opted for a more down-to-earth atmosphere when he reopened his own bistro in 2010. There's no standing on ceremony by staff, no lengthy menu descriptions. The bar is built from salvaged doors, none of the chairs match, and the plates are a hotchpotch of antique Danish china. It's a place to have fun and make merry over magnificent food: no-nonsense French bistro classics with a sprinkling of Danish magic. Try lightly salted salmon with liquorice, or chicken liver terrine with home-made pickles and chutneys, followed by a robust pot of boeuf bourguignon.

★ Geranium

Per Henrik Lings Allé 4, 8 (69 96 00 20, www. geranium.dk). Bus 1A, 14. **Open** noon-3.30pm (last seating 1pm), 6.30pm-1am (last seating 9pm)

Mon-Sat. **Set meal** *Lunch* 950kr-1,250kr. *Dinner* 1,500kr. **Map** p143 B2 ㉗ **New Nordic**

In 2011, chef Rasmus Kofoed earned himself the Bocuse d'Or award for culinary greatness, and in so doing firmly established Copenhagen's position as one of the most exciting places in the world to eat. Geranium is one of two restaurants in the city to have two Michelin stars (the other being Noma, *see p114*, of course). Kofoed – like every leading chef in Denmark these days – has if not an entire crusade, than at least a manifesto to shake things up a bit – in his case, a predilection for food that is 'light', 'lucid' and provides 'enriching challenges'. Geranium moved in 2010 from Kongens Have gardens to the more immense parkland of Faelledparken, getting you closer to 'nature' and, if anything, an even finer plate of food. Dishes veer towards molecular gastronomy, but remain recognisable and change with the seasons. Expect sybaritic intrigue along the lines of smoked potatoes, dried peas and lovage, and roast monkfish with 'elements of the sea and ocean'. It doesn't come cheap, though: if you decide to go for the wine pairing, you're looking at spending around 3,000kr per head for dinner.

Le Saint-Jacques

Sankt Jakobs Plads 1 (35 42 77 07, www.lesaint jacques.dk). Bus 1A, 14. **Open** noon-3pm, 6-10pm Mon-Fri; noon-4pm, 6-10pm Sat; 5-10pm Sun. **Main courses** 145kr-195kr. **Set meal** (Sun) 200kr 3 courses. **Map** p143 C2 ㉘ **French**

Zoologisk Museum. *See p143.*

This pricey but inviting French restaurant is set across the street from the national stadium, Parken, in a quiet square just off busy Østerbrogade. Impeccable service, crisp white linen tablecloths, and candlelight that flickers across the glittering gold of the religious icons on the walls ensure that this is a place that locals return to again and again for special treats or a well-earned blow-out. Home-smoked salmon is a speciality.

Cafés & Bars

Café Bopa
Løgstørgade 8 (35 43 05 66, www.cafebopa.dk). Bus 1A, 3A, 18, 40. **Open** 9am-midnight Mon-Wed, Sun; 9am-2am Thur; 9am-5am Fri, Sat. **Map** p143 C2 ㉙
Dark and arty by day, pulsating by night, Bopa is at the heart of this leafy square's young scene. At the weekends, DJs ensure the place is packed and sweaty. Unusually late opening hours are another plus, as are cheap cocktails.

Dag H
Dag Hammarskjölds Allé 36-40 (35 27 63 00, www.dagh.dk). Bus 1A, 14, 15. **Open** 8am-11pm Mon-Thur; 8am-midnight Fri; 10am-midnight Sat; 10am-10pm Sun.* **Map** p143 C3 ㉚
Formerly the coffee cathedral Amokka, this mainstay of Østerbro's café life on Lille Trianglen (Little Triangle, just along from the US Embassy) reopened a few years back with more emphasis on the kitchen. The coffee is still great, but not the centre of attraction as it once was. The excellent food includes fancy burgers and Modern European dishes, as well as quality cakes and generous weekend brunch platters.

Gourmandiet
Rosenvængets Allé 7 (39 27 10 00, www.gourmandiet.dk). Bus 1A, 3A, 14. **Open** 11am-3pm, 5.30pm-midnight Thur, Fri; 10am-2pm Sat, 5.30pm-midnight Sat. **Map** p143 C3 ㉛
This upmarket organic butcher/café has been a big hit with the gentrified neighbourhood's residents, who come here for top-quality steaks and biodynamic wine. The walls are adorned with murals of pastoral scenes, while nicely arranged displays showcase the shop's tempting array of products, including organic charcuterie. It's popular for Saturday brunch, and Gourmandiet also opens for dinner from Thursday to Saturday (the kitchen closes at 10pm).

★ Panzón
Rosenvængets Allé 6 (35 38 98 00, www.panzon.dk). Bus 1A, 3A, 14. **Open** 5-11pm Tue; 5pm-midnight Wed, Thur; 4pm-2am Fri; 6pm-1am Sat. **Map** p143 C3 ㉜
Similar in atmosphere to siblings Falernum (*see p126*) in Frederiksberg and Bibendum near

Nørreport, this is a nice cosy bar in which to enjoy quality wine and a plate of charcuterie or a bowl of smoked almonds. Heartier dishes include meatballs or grilled tuna with salad and rye bread. Decent beer too.

Shops & Services

Goods
Østerbrogade 44 (35 43 05 05, www.goods cph.com). Train Østerport, or bus 1A, 40. **Open** 11am-6pm Mon-Fri; 11am-3pm Sat. **Map** p143 C3 ㉝ **Fashion**
This cool menswear shop is all about quality craftsmanship and cult brands, with knitwear from Folk and YMC, bags from Filson, jeans from Levi's Vintage, T-shirts from Our Legacy and sunglasses from Han Kjøbenhavn. It's the place to head if you want to look like a trendy local.

★ Normann Copenhagen
Østerbrogade 70 (35 27 05 40, www.normann-copenhagen.com). Bus 1A, 3A, 14. **Open** 10am-6pm Mon-Fri; 10am-4pm Sat. **Map** p143 C2 ㉞
Homewares
Normann Copenhagen's flagship is now one of the most popular stores for style-conscious Copenhageners. Homewares take centre stage in the former theatre building, with a huge range of effortlessly sleek and streamlined domestic designer products, from arty vases to achingly modern salad sets. Lighting is another strong point.

★ Paustian
Kalkbrænderiløbskaj 2 (39 16 65 65, www.paustian.dk). Train Nordhavn, or bus 26. **Open** 10am-6pm Mon-Fri; 10am-3pm Sat. **Homewares**
It's a bit of a trek to get over here, but Paustian's stunning warehouse – designed by Jørn Utzon of Sydney Opera House fame – makes the trip worthwhile. Inside, you'll find furniture by the likes of Aalto, Eames, Starck and Jacobsen. There's also a popular restaurant.

★ Søstjernen
Østerbrogade 50 (35 55 46 90, www.sostjernen.com). Train Østerport, or bus 1A, 40. **Open** 10am-5.30pm Mon-Thur; 10am-6pm Fri; 10am-3pm Sat. **Map** p143 C3 ㉟ **Children/Accessories**
Children's shoe shop Søstjernen – 'starfish' in Danish – is the brainchild of Katrine Leisner. Spend some time in the neighbourhood and you'll realise that her shop's cute sandals, chelsea-style boots and desert boots, from brands such as Angulus, Petit Nord and PéPé, are something of a uniform for the area's trendy toddlers. A similar range of highly covetable styles, in larger sizes, is available round the corner at her women's shoe shop.
Other locations Willemoesgade 2, Østerbro (35 55 46 90).

EXPLORE

Further Afield

Copenhagen's outskirts are made up of largely affluent suburbs. Hellerup, to the north of Østerbro, plays host to large family houses, classy restaurants and the excellent Experimentarium children's science museum. Lyngby is another notable suburb, site of Denmark's largest open-air museum, Frilandsmuseet, containing more than 100 historic buildings from Denmark, southern Sweden and northern Germany. The suburb of Ishøj, meanwhile, is known for the Arken Museum for Moderne Kunst, one of Copenhagen's premier modern-art galleries, which was built to celebrate the city's year as European City of Culture in 1996. Another impressive piece of architecture now sits on the island of Amager: the DR Koncerthuset is the concert hall of Denmark's national broadcasting corporation, located in the new district of Ørestad.

Arken Museum for Moderne Kunst.

Don't Miss

1 Ordrupgaard Matisse, Manet and more, plus a dramatic Zaha Hadid extension (p148).

2 Den Gule Cottage Stunning food in a stunning setting at this 19th-century gem (p148).

3 Arken Museum for Moderne Kunst Modern art ahoy at this controversial maritime-vibe museum (p149).

4 Blå Planet The largest aquarium in northern Europe (p150).

5 Islands Brygge Dive into the harbour at these brilliant baths (p151).

Ordrupgaard.

HELLERUP & CHARLOTTENLUND

The affluent coastal suburb of Hellerup, just north of the city centre via Østerbro, has some good shops and restaurants, but the star of the the show is the superb **Experimentarium** science museum.

Continue northwards for **Charlottenlund Slot** (Charlottenlund Palace), the site of a royal residence since 1690. The current Baroque palace was built for Princess Charlotte Amalie in 1730, but its leafy gardens subsequently found favour among city dwellers as a popular destination for Sunday outings. Various other royals have lived in the palace, but since the 1930s it has been home to the Danish Institute for Fisheries, so only the grounds, not the house, are open to the public.

Charlottenlund Fort is a grassy hillock with a nice campsite, and **Charlottenlund Strand**, although small, is the nearest beach to Copenhagen heading north; though most people continue to Bellevue Beach, the former has a large, landscaped grass area. All are a pleasant forest walk from Charlottenlund station. Nearby is the genteel suburb of **Skovshoved**, home to the lovely eponymous hotel and restaurant (*see p225*). Arne Jacobsen fans might also want to head here to see one of his lesser-known but eminently likeable designs, a modernist petrol station (*see p206*).

Culture vultures should visit nearby **Ordrupgaard**, which displays French Impressionist and Danish art from the 19th and 20th centuries. The museum's lovely grounds also contain the **Finn Juhl Hus**, the building where the Danish furniture designer spent the last few decades of his life.

Sights & Museums

Experimentarium
Tuborg Havnevej 7, Hellerup (39 27 33 33, www.experimentarium.dk). Bus 1A, 14, 21.

Open 9.30am-5pm Mon, Wed-Fri; 9.30am-9pm Tue; 11am-5pm Sat, Sun. **Admission** 160kr; 105kr reductions; free under-2s.
Denmark's inventive science museum is filled with imaginative displays and hands-on experiments. Though aimed at children, it attracts its fair share of adults, who are mesmerised by the technology (you can try a human-size gyroscope or programme robots). The museum renders mundane or esoteric topics – alternative power, genetics – fascinating and accessible. Be warned: the noise can be deafening.

★ Ordrupgaard & Finn Juhl Hus
Vilvordevej 110, Charlottenlund (39 64 11 83, www.ordrupgaard.dk). Train Klampenborg or Lyngby, or bus 388. **Open** 1-5pm Tue, Thur, Fri; 1-7pm Wed; 11am-5pm Sat, Sun. **Admission** 110kr; 100kr reductions; free under-18s.
Zaha Hadid's stunning extension, completed in 2005, doubled the size of the Ordrupgaard art museum, which contains works by Manet, Renoir, Matisse and Gauguin, as well as Danish art from the 19th and 20th centuries. Fans of mid-century modern furniture should be sure to visit Finn Juhl's House, in the grounds of the museum; the Danish furniture designer built the house in the 1940s, furnishing it with many of his own designs. He lived there until his death in 1989.

Restaurants

★ Den Gule Cottage
Staunings Plæne, Strandvejen 506, Klampenborg (39 64 06 91, www.dengulecottage.dk). Train Klampenborg. **Open** *May-mid Nov* noon-midnight daily. *Mid Nov-Apr* noon-4pm, 5.30pm-midnight Thur-Sun. **Set meal** 325kr/3 courses.
With a fairytale location in a thatched, half-timbered, 19th-century cottage, set beneath oak trees on lawns that roll down to Bellevue Beach, this tiny restaurant could probably get away with serving hot dogs (in fact, it used to be an ice-cream kiosk). But this is one of the finest restaurants in the region, awarded a Michelin star in 2012 and 2013, and serving elegant,

EXPLORE

fabulously choreographed modern Danish dishes from the freshest seasonal ingredients. Expect local game, fish and meat, funky foams and extravagant desserts in this definitive *hyggelige* venue.

BISPEBJERG

The most striking landmark in Copenhagen's rather monotonous suburbs is **Grundtvigs Kirke** in Bispebjerg, 15 minutes' drive north-west of the city centre.

Sights & Museums

FREE Grundtvigs Kirke

På Bjerget 14B, Bispebjerg (35 81 54 42, www.grundtvigskirke.dk). Train Emdrup, or bus 10, 16. **Open** *May-Sept* 9am-4pm Mon-Sat; noon-4pm Sun. *Oct-Apr* 9am-4pm Mon-Sat; noon-1pm Sun. **Admission** free.

The church is named after Nicolai Frederik Severin Grundtvig (1783-1872), the Danish priest, writer, composer and educational pioneer. And its construction was a family affair: designed by PV Jensen-Klint, it was completed after his death by his son, the designer Kaare Klint. The massive yellow-brick building took almost 20 years to construct (it was finished in 1940), and possesses a stark beauty.

LYNGBY

One of Copenhagen's greener, more attractive suburbs is Lyngby, eight kilometres (five miles) north of the centre and home to Denmark's largest open-air museum, **Frilandsmuseet**. Not to be confused with Frihedsmuseet (the museum of Denmark's Resistance movement), Frilandsmuseet covers 35 hectares (86 acres) and is home to 110 buildings from Denmark, southern Sweden and northern Germany.

Adjacent to Frilandsmuseet is **Brede Vaerk** (Brede Works), once the Brede cloth mill industrial complex (which closed in 1956), and now preserved as a complete industrial village, with workers' cottages and the owner's country house. It's run by the Nationalmuseet. At one time, this whole region was the centre for Denmark's textile industry and there were many factories and mills, stretching all the way from Lyngby to the coast.

Sights & Museums

FREE Brede Vaerk

IC Modewegs Vej, Lyngby (33 47 38 00, www. natmus.dk/brede-vaerk). Train Jægersborg, then train to Brede or bus 194. **Open** *Easter-Oct* 10am-4pm Tue-Sun. Closed Nov-Easter. **Admission** free. *Guided tours* 50kr; 40kr reductions; free under-18s.

Explore the various factory buildings and workers' yellow-painted houses. There's also Brede Manor,

a neoclassical house with an exquisite Louis XVI interior, built in 1795 for the owner of the mill, Peter van Hemert. The house was intended to be a summer residence for his family, but van Hemert went bankrupt in 1805. Ironically, that bankruptcy, and the detailed inventory of the house that ensued, allowed the Nationalmuseet to restore the interior accurately. The original workers' refectory is now a superb French/Danish restaurant, Brede Spisehus.

FREE Frilandsmuseet

Kongevejen 100, Lyngby (33 13 44 11, www. frilandsmuseet.dk). Train Jægersborg, then train to Brede or bus 194. **Open** *Easter-mid Oct* 10am-5pm Tue-Sun. Closed mid Oct-Easter. **Admission** free.

To see and appreciate all of Frilandsmuseet's 110 buildings, which date from the 17th to the 19th centuries, takes at least a day – but to get a good cross-section of architectural styles, the curators suggest you visit buildings 34, 42 and 60-72. Opened in Copenhagen in 1897, and relocated to its present site in 1901 under the auspices of the Nationalmuseet, the museum features wind- and watermills, farm buildings, fishermen's cottages, peasants' houses, factories, and even a 19th-century fire station, all preserved with period decor. There aren't any information signs to spoil the atmosphere. Other attractions include excellent guided tours, and rare-breed Danish cattle. On the downside, thanks to poor signposting (typical of Denmark), it's difficult to find by car. However, you can take the S-train to Jægersborg and catch the local train, which winds its pretty way to Brede station.

ISHØJ

The fourth of Sjælland's world-class art museums (after Louisiana Museum, Statens Museum for Kunst and Ny Carlsberg Glyptotek) is found in the unprepossessing suburb of Ishøj, 15 minutes by train south along the coast from Copenhagen. **Arken Museum for Moderne Kunst** (Arken Museum of Modern Art) was built to celebrate Copenhagen's year as European City of Culture in 1996 and is almost as famous for its architecture as for its exhibits.

Arken is next to **Ishøj Strand** (Ishøj Beach), an artificial but attractive seven-kilometre (four-mile) stretch of sandy beach.

Sights & Museums

★ Arken Museum for Moderne Kunst

Skovvej 100, Ishøj (43 54 02 22, www.arken.dk). Train Ishøj, then bus 128. **Open** 10am-5pm Tue, Thur-Sun; 10am-9pm Wed. **Admission** 95kr; 75kr reductions; free under-18s.

Arken is housed in an extraordinary concrete, glass and steel building designed by Danish architect Søren Robert Lund. His compelling and perplexing construction, with its echoes of marine architecture

EXPLORE

(both inside and out), won the design competition for the new gallery in 1988, and has divided critics ever since. Some applaud its apt maritime references (the museum is near the beach), which give it the appearance of an abstract shipwreck; others say that an art museum should focus on the art, not its own architecture. Many artists hate it, claiming the exhibition spaces compete with, rather than enhance, their work. But visitors are usually won over by Lund's skewed vision. Two extensions in recent years have provided more exhibition space, improved facilities for visitors and created an impressive new entrance.

Arken's permanent collection of more than 350 pieces covers painting, sculpture, graphic art, media art and installation, with an emphasis on work from after 1990. Many works are by Danes, but numerous foreign artists feature, including Damien Hirst, Olafur Eliasson and Katharina Grosse. One of the most famous pieces is the photograph *Flex Pissing/ Björk er en nar (aka Bringing It All Back Home)* by Claus Carstensen and the art group Superflex (the mildly controversial 'Danish Art Mob'). Arken also hosts superb temporary exhibitions of modern and contemporary Danish and international art, often transferred from other major European galleries. Past shows have included retrospectives of Picasso, Munch, Dalí, Miró, Warhol and Christian Boltanski. There's also a cinema, a concert hall and a café.

AMAGER

Amager is the island immediately to the east of central Copenhagen. If you head south-west from Christianshavn (*see p110*) across the old defensive ramparts, you'll come to **Islands Brygge** (*see p151* **Come On In, the Water's Lovely**), which is enjoying a new lease of life after trendy architects Plot built the city's magnificent, permanent, open-air bathing complex here. It's moored on the waterfront beside Langebro bridge; behind, the lawns are packed with sunbathers, basketball players and picnickers. Various trendy galleries and cafés have sprung up in the area too.

Amager proper is home to the city's international airport, as well as the impressive new concert hall **DR Koncerthuset** (*see p173* **Out of the Blue**), completed in 2009 in the new Ørestad district, near the large, protected green space of **Amagerfælled** in the north-west. This area of mostly flat industrial estates, cheap housing and farmland is now the site of some of the city's most exciting new architecture. It also boasts the nearest (and best) beach to the centre of town, **Amager Strandpark**, which sits next to the impressive modern building that is the new National Aquarium, the **Blå Planet**.

On the south-east coast of Amager, among salt flats and farmland bustling with birdlife, lies **Dragør**, with its maze of cobbled lanes and traditional yellow cottages. Like many coastal

settlements in the area, it was founded upon the humble herring – shipped throughout Europe before the Reformation to provide sustenance for the Catholic faithful abstaining from meat during Lent and on Fridays – and prospered during the 14th century as a fishing port. In the 19th century, it found a new lease of life as a centre for shipping and salvage, trading through the Baltic and as far away as England. That came to an end with the advent of steam ships, and since then little has changed here (which is part of its charm).

However, Dragør's sleepy idyll can be misleading. Property prices are high – the village is popular with affluent young professionals who commute into the city. They ensure that Dragør remains an improbably lively, almost cosmopolitan, village. There are also some smart shops on its short high street, as well as several good restaurants and beer gardens. The town has a marina, a small cinema and an equally small museum (**Dragør Museum**), in the town's oldest fisherman's house (dating from 1682).

Five minutes' drive inland is the charming village of **Store Magleby**, founded by Dutch settlers in the early 1500s. It's home to the **Amagermuseet**, which traces the history of the Dutch immigrants in the area.

Sights & Museums

Amagermuseet
Hovedgade 4 & 12, Store Magleby (32 53 93 07, www.amagermuseet.dk). Bus 32, 35, 350S. **Open** *May-Sept* noon-4pm Tue-Sun. Closed Oct-Apr. **Admission** (incl Dragør Museum) 40kr; free under-18s. **No credit cards.**
An open-air museum consisting of two farms and gardens, in an area previously known as the 'Dutch Village'. Children will enjoy the assorted animals.

★ Blå Planet
Jacob Fortlingsvej 1, Kastrup (44 22 22 44, www.denblaaplanet.dk). Metro Kastrup. **Open** 10am-9pm Mon; 10am-6pm Tue-Sun. **Admission** 410kr; 260kr-330kr reductions.
The Blue Planet, northern Europe's largest aquarium, opened in 2013 in a stunning building designed by 3XN architects. Visitors can learn about sea life, and view hammerhead sharks in the Ocean Tank, colourful fish in the Coral Reef section, and piranhas in the Amazon area. It's exciting stuff, with feedings, storytelling and even shark dissections, but note that the aquarium gets packed at weekends.

Dragør Museum
Havnepladsen, Strandlinien 2 & 4, Dragør (32 53 93 07, www.museumamager.dk). Bus 32, 35, 350S. **Open** *May-Sept* noon-4pm Tue-Sun. Closed Oct-Apr. **Admission** (incl Amager Museet) 40kr; free under-18s. **No credit cards.**

EXPLORE

A sweet museum that traces Dragør's development from medieval fishing village to a significant port in the 18th and 19th centuries.

Cafés & Bars

Café 8tallet
Richard Mortensens Vej 81A, Ørestad (32 62 86 28, www.cafe8tallet.dk). Metro Vestamager.
Open 11am-10pm Mon-Fri; 10am-10pm Sat; 10am-9pm Sun.
Situated in an award-winning building designed by architecture firm BIG, the waterside Café 8tallet offers contemporary design and suberb views of the

Kalvebod Fælled nature reserve. It's a popular spot for brunch, but also serves generous *smørrebrod*, good coffee, tasty burgers and grander dishes.

Shops & Services

Green Square Copenhagen
Strandlodsvej 11B, Amager (32 57 59 59, www.greensquare.dk). Metro Lergravsparken.
Open 10am-5.30pm Mon-Thur; 10am-6pm Fri; 10am-4pm Sat.
Green Square occupies a massive aircraft hangar of a building and claims to be northern Europe's single largest antiques dealer.

COME ON IN, THE WATER'S LOVELY

Harbour and sea spots perfect for a summer plunge.

Copenhagen has developed into a great place for summer bathing in the past few years, following the construction, in 2003, of the open-air **Islands Brygge Harbour Baths**, a hundred metres south of the Langebro bridge. The opening of the baths followed a drive by local authorities to improve the quality of the harbour water, which is now as clean as that in the Øresund (and constantly monitored). Many areas have been awarded a Blue Flag.

Consisting of five pools (two for children) and with room for 600 people, the Islands Brygge baths have been an enormous success. Open from the first week in June to the end of August (7am-7pm Mon-Fri; 11am-7pm Sat, Sun), they mark the official start (and end) of summer for many locals. Plans are also in place to add thermal baths and saunas for the winter months, scheduled to open in 2015.

Islands Brygge was the first element of the Copenhagen Harbour Baths facilities; now, there's also **Copencabana**, with three pools, at Vesterbro's Havneholmen (close to the Fisketorvet shopping mall, just south of Kødbyen); and **Sluseholmen** in the South Harbour, which opened in 2011. All the harbour baths are part of the extensive regeneration of the waterfront, which has also included the opening of several landmark buildings (*see p22* **On the Waterfront**). The harbour pools aren't the only option, though – they're actually a supplement to the handful of beaches around the city.

It's easy to forget that Copenhagen is bordered by coastline, but the seaside is within walking distance from the centre,

Islands Brygge Harbour Baths.

making it a perfect summer city. In 2010, an artificial beach (and pier) opened at Østerbro's **Svanemøllestranden**, and there has been an extensive urban beach east of the city at **Amager Strandpark** since 2005. This consists of 4.6 kilometres (three miles) of white sand: you can swim in the sea, rent kayaks, eat ice-cream, or light a bonfire in one of the allocated spots. Slightly further down the coast, and connected to Amager Strandpark by a long wooden bridge, is **Kastrup Søbad** ('the Snail'), while just north of Copenhagen is Klampenborg's 700-metre (half-mile) **Bellevue Beach**.

EXPLORE

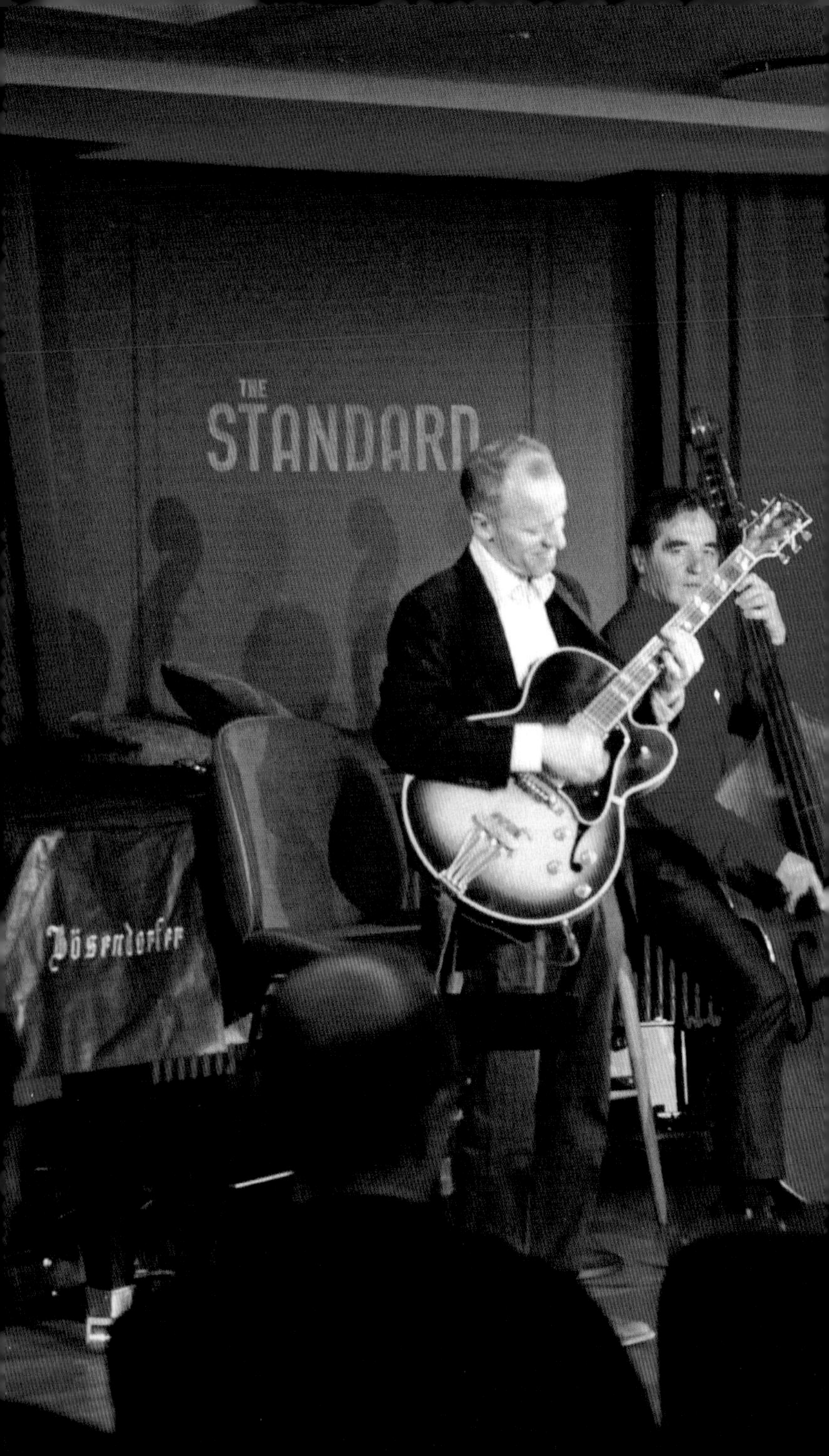
THE
STANDARD
Bösendorfer

Arts & Entertainment

Children

One almost wonders if Copenhagen was created just for children. The city is full of imaginatively designed play parks and fairytale palaces; there are several museums just for kids, and many others have special departments for children; every restaurant has high chairs; every bus can take prams (they favour the Victorian/Mary Poppins-style ones here); the Metro has lifts (are you listening, Paris and London?); and every bicycle seems to have a kid's seat on the back. During the holidays, dozens of performances are laid on for children in theatres and parks. There are nappy-changing facilities in most public buildings, and much of the city centre is pedestrianised. And then, of course, there is Tivoli, the world's cosiest amusement park.

GREAT DAYS OUT

A good way to see Copenhagen with a child is to adopt a geographical approach and base a day's activities around one area of the city.

Tivoli & Rådhuspladsen

A must for every child visiting Copenhagen is **Tivoli** (*see p48*), open throughout the summer, as well as for the month of December and during Halloween. Located right next to Central Station, the historic amusement park can still make every child's heart beat faster. The world's tallest carousel (80 metres/262 feet), the shooting galleries, Valhalla Castle and the Pantomime Theatre are among the attractions that provide action and fun for kids (and many adults), while the flowers and gardens, cafés and restaurants offer parents tranquillity and time to breathe. Food is expensive in Tivoli (take advantage of the plentiful picnic areas) and rides cost extra, but the fireworks on Saturday nights are free, as are many performances on the open-air stage. For children of nappy age, there's a family amenity centre with baby-changing tables, free nappies and microwave ovens for heating baby food.

Across Rådhuspladsen from here is the fun **Ripley's Believe It or Not! Museum** (*see p55*) and the not-so-impressive **Hans Christian Andersen** exhibition (*see p54*).

West of Tivoli is the **Tycho Brahe Planetarium** (*see p121*), with its small exhibition on astronomy and space travel, but the real attraction here is the **IMAX cinema** (*see p161*) which is just as likely to show films about skateboarding or skydiving as the stars. (Ask for headphones with English narration at the ticket office – children must be over three.)

South of Tivoli, older kids will definitely get something from a visit to the renovated **Ny Carlsberg Glyptotek** (*see p54*), especially if they are promised a trip to the popular nearby swimming centre, **Vandkulturhuset** (inside the DGI-Byen sports complex: Tietgensgade 65, 33 29 81 40, www.dgi-byen.dk), which contains a baby pool with fountains, a swimming pool, waterslides, diving boards, climbing walls and a spa where parents can recharge their batteries.

Strøget & Slotsholmen

The long, pedestrianised street **Strøget** can be fun for kids. This is partly because of its shops – there's a toy store, **Fætter BR** (www.br.dk), near the Rådhuspladsen end, as well as the **Lego** flagship (Vimmelskaftet 37, Strøget, 52 15 91 57, www.lego.dk) – but also because of the street performers. Towards the Kongens Nytorv end are the **Guinness World Records Museum & Mystic Exploratorie** (*see p58*), which children seem to enjoy.

Get away from the noise of the street by climbing the 17th-century **Rundetårn** (Round Tower, *see p58*) on Købmagergade. Instead of steps, there is a 209-metre-long (686-foot) ramp, that spirals up inside the tower: a real challenge for buggy-pushers.

Nationalmuseet (National Museum, *see p82*) can be an interesting place to take children (after all, who can resist the Vikings?). There's an excellent hands-on children's museum in the basement, a toy museum on the second floor, and every new exhibition is accompanied by a children's area, with specially designed activities.

For something completely different, hire a kayak from **Kajak-Ole** (www.kajakole.dk) on Gammel Strand (*see p73*). A guide leads the group through the canals, telling anecdotes on the way; a drink at a café in Christianshavn is included in the price. No experience is necessary, as the kayaks are very stable, but children must be 11 or older for a two-person kayak, and at least 15 for a single-person kayak.

South of Gammel Strand on **Slotsholmen**, the double-handed swords, suits of armour and other military paraphernalia at **Tøjhusmuseet** (Royal Arsenal Museum, *see p83*) are usually a hit, especially with boys. Older children might like the spooky atmosphere of the **Ruinerne Under Christiansborg** (Ruins Under Christiansborg, *see p81*), also on Slotsholmen. The excavated ruins of the original castle of Bishop Absalon (the founder of Copenhagen), jumbled together with those of later castles on the site, are situated directly below the current Christiansborg Slot.

Nørreport & Rosenborg

Five minutes' walk north of the east end of Strøget lies **Kongens Have** (*see p90*). This is a really wonderful place to stop for a picnic. The park has a unique wooden playground for one- to four-year-olds, and alongside is one of the most charming of Copenhagen's traditional attractions: the **Marionet Teater** (Marionette Theatre, www.marionetteatret.dk). Performances for children aged two and upwards take place every day in the summer (except Monday) at 2pm and 3pm.

Across the park, **Rosenborg Slot** (Rosenborg Palace, *see p91*) is packed with historical treasures, and is also the place to watch the Queen's Life Guards (who live in

barracks next door) in training. The rooms of special interest to children are the Treasury, the Long Hall and Room 10. The atmospheric Treasury, in the basement, houses the Danish crown jewels, while the impressive Long Hall is decorated in golden stucco and has three silver lions guarding the thrones of the king and queen. Room 10 (on the first floor, in the castle's northern end) features a curious picture by Gaspard Antoine de Bois-Clair in 1692, which shows Frederik IV and his sister Sophie. It's made on a zig-zag folded canvas – when you look at it from the left, you see a girl; from the right, you see a boy.

A couple of minutes' walk north of Rosenborg is the excellent **Statens Museum for Kunst** (National Gallery, *see p92*). It features a children's gallery and a workshop, and offers free guided tours for children aged four to 12 at 1pm on Sundays. These are mainly in Danish, but English-speakers can be accommodated. Young children can also

ARTS & ENTERTAINMENT

Lego

participate in the weekend workshops (45kr per child) that are held between 10.30am and 4.30pm on Saturdays and Sundays, where children can sculpt, draw and paint.

If you need a little downtime from the kids, behind the gallery stretches **Østre Anlæg park**, which contains some of the best playgrounds in Copenhagen.

To the south-west of Rosenborg, between Nørreport and the lakes, is the new covered food market, **Torvehallerne** (*see p87*). Though mainly focused on gourmet food for discerning adults, the sweet cinnamon buns from **Café Rosa** (Hall 1, stall D8), pizza slices from **Gorm's** (Hall 2, stalls G1/H1) and sugar-free ice-cream from **Is á Bella** (Hall 1, stall E8) will go down a treat with most kids.

Christianshavn

Vor Frelsers Kirke (Church of Our Saviour, *see p111*), close to Christianshavns Kanal, has a tower with a spiral staircase twisting around the outside of the spire. It's a fun (if slightly scary) climb up 400 steps, and you're rewarded with a great view. But be warned: when windy, the tower can start to sway a little. Back on terra firma, kids will love a trip to the **Orlogsmuseet** (Royal Danish Naval Museum, *see p110*). While adults may be drawn to the wonderful collection of model ships and maritime art, youngsters might prefer to climb aboard the submarine *Spækhuggeren*, the interior of which has been partially re-created so that visitors can enter the command centre, the radio/radar room and the officers' mess, and even have a peep through the periscope.

From nearby Holmen, you have a lovely view from the Opera House across the water to the royal palace, **Amalienborg Slot** (*see p102*),

which can be reached by hopping on one of the harbour buses. The changing of the guards takes place at Amalienborg every day at noon.

Frederiksberg

At the eastern end of Frederiksberg, close to the lakes and in the same building as the Royal Danish Academy of Music (*see p128 and p172*), is the new space for the **Musikmuseet** (Danish Music Museum; www.natmus.dk), due to reopen in September 2014. This esteemed museum, which first opened in 1898, is known for its collection of old instruments, including Highland pipes from Scotland, launeddas from Greece and hurdy-gurdys from the Czech Republic. The new museum should be able to offer more interplay between the practising musicians from the Academy and the historical exhibits, and there will be on-going projects for children designed to encourage musical exploration.

South-west of here, in Frederiksberg proper, lies **Frederiksberg Have** (*see p129*), a beautiful garden that is perfect for a picnic, with dozens of secluded, leafy corners. To find out more about the royal gardens, take one of the guided boat trips on the lake. The neighbouring **Zoologisk Have** (Zoological Garden, *see p130*) is one of the most attractive in Europe, with plenty of space for its animal residents plus a new elephant house designed by Lord Foster. Attractions include a special petting zoo, pony rides, climbing the zoo tower or just looking at the numerous baby animals. Be warned, though: queues can be long on sunny summer days.

Opposite the rear of Frederiksberg Slot, beneath the lawns of Søndermarken park, is a subterranean glass museum, **Cisternerne – Museet for Moderne Glaskunst** (Cisterns – Museum of Modern Glass Art, *see p129*), housed in former water cisterns. Though not aimed at children, it's dank, spooky and fun.

Kastellet & Around

Just outside the city centre, north along the harbourfront, are the ancient battlements and moat surrounding **Kastellet** (*see p105*), a base for the Danish army for several centuries and still a fun and atmospheric place for kids. Nearby is the much maligned **Den Lille Havfrue** (The Little Mermaid, *see p103*).

Østerbro & Further North

In Østerbro lies the extensive **Fælledparken** (*see p143*), which has several playgrounds, an impressive skate park and an indoor swimming pool. In summer, several festivals, carnivals and play days for children are held here. Another

Blue Planet.

summer attraction in the park is Pavillionen, an outdoor café and restaurant that does very good barbecues. Østerbrogade, Østerbro's main street, is lined with a host of upmarket children's clothes boutiques, including the lovely **Søstjernen** (*see p145*). It's also home to the excellent **Park Bio** cinema (*see p161*), which offers 'Babybio' screenings for parents with small children at 10.30am every Friday (except during July) for 75kr.

Older children might find the stuffed animals a little static, but for younger kids the **Zoologisk Museum** (Zoological Museum, *see p143*), just west of Fælledparken, is a real hoot (especially the full-size replica mammoth). The **Experimentarium** (*see p148*), further north in Hellerup, is one of Copenhagen's great children's attractions. This science centre explores nature, technology, the environment and health issues through more than 300 interactive exhibits. In the kids' pavilion – aimed at children between three and six – are crazy mirrors, water wheels and other delights.

The oldest amusement park in the world, **Bakken** (*see p181*), is located in the forest of **Dyrehaven**, further north of the city at Klampenborg. Open from late spring to early autumn, Bakken has all the usual amusement park attractions, including rollercoasters, shooting galleries and daily shows for children, but note that, although entrance to the park is free, the attractions are not. A pleasant way to see the rest of Dyrehaven (which means 'deer park') is by pony. Little ponies, which can be led by parents, are available at **Fortunens Ponyudlejning** (Ved Fortunen 33, Lyngby, 45 87 60 58, www.fortunensponycenter.dk). Alternatively, take a horse-and-cart ride or simply stroll around the forest. Right next

to Dyrehaven is one of the best beaches in the Copenhagen area – **Bellevue** (*see p151* **Come On In, the Water's Lovely**).

Further north, just a short train journey from the centre of town, the beautifully situated **Louisiana Museum of Moderne Art** (*see p183*) has a children's wing offering daily artistic activities such as drawing and model-making. Louisiana also has a wonderfully designed park, ideal for picnics, and there's a small swimming beach in front of the museum.

Amager

The magnificent open-air **Islands Brygge** (*see p151*) harbour pools near Langebro ('Long Bridge') are open throughout the summer (with winter bathing planned for 2015), and have children's areas. And on the eastern side of Amager, but still just a short Metro ride from the city centre, is the **Amager Strandpark** (*see p151* **Come On In, the Water's Lovely**), a spectacular sandy beach development with gently sloping shallows and plenty of children's entertainment laid on during the summer.

Just south from here is one of Copenhagen's most-hyped children's attractions: the 3XN-designed **Blue Planet** (*see p211*), which opened in 2013 and is northern Europe's largest aquarium. The complex rehoused many creatures from Charlottenlund's now-defunct aquarium. Here, kids can learn about sea life, and also view hammerhead sharks in the Ocean Tank, colourful fish in the Coral Reef section, and piranhas in the Amazon area. It's exciting stuff, with feedings, storytelling and even shark dissections, but note that the aquarium is very crowded at weekends and during school holidays.

Film & TV

The Danes have a prodigious moviemaking history. From the silent era of black and white film with piano accompaniment, through the Dogme collective, to the more recent spate of intelligent feature films and controversial documentaries, Danish filmmakers have had an impact on cinema disproportionate to the country's size and population. This can be credited to the Danes' true love of and devotion to film, as well as government subsidies to create quality products for the international market.

There is also the famous Danish Film School (Den Danske Filmskole) with its steady flow of talented graduates, who have brought Danish cinema several notable triumphs during the last three decades.

ARTS & ENTERTAINMENT

THE DANISH FILM INDUSTRY

Denmark's filmmakers were among the key pioneers in European cinema, and in the decades leading up to World War II had a notable influence on its development. The establishment of the Nordisk Film Kompagni in 1906 galvanised the industry. **Nordisk Film** was the first studio in Europe to focus solely on feature films and it thrived (until the emergence of the American film industry, from around 1913), thanks to its technical superiority and the talent of its directors. As extraordinary as this may sound, in the early days of cinema Denmark was the world's biggest producer of films.

After facing near bankruptcy with the advent of sound, Nordisk Film – whose polar-bear logo is said to have inspired the use of a lion as MGM's symbol – re-established itself in 1929 as a producer of talkies. It remains the oldest working film studio in the world.

Among the most important innovators of early cinema were filmmakers **Benjamin Christensen** and **Carl Theodor Dreyer**. In front of the camera, the world fell in love with **Asta Nielsen**, one of the first great movie stars.

The popularity of cinema – particularly documentary, which is still one of Denmark's strongest genres – exploded in Denmark during the 1930s and, as a result, a film act was passed in 1938, establishing the Film Council, the Film Fund and the National Film Board.

Between World War II and the early 1980s, Danish cinema experienced something of a lull in international terms, with the country's filmmakers focusing their energies on television production. When feature films were made, they were often worthy social dramas or soft pornography (the industry having been de-restricted in 1969). Yet in this period, director **Henning Carlsen** created the masterful *Knud Hamsun's Hunger* (1964), now one of Denmark's film classics.

Government subsidies for film production started in the 1960s, and by the mid '70s most Danish films were made with some element of government aid. By 1989, an even more radical system was introduced, whereby a filmmaker could demand 50 per cent of the film's budget (with no creative strings attached) from the government if the producer could match it with private funding.

INTERNATIONAL SUCCESS

In 1988, *Babette's Feast*, **Gabriel Axel**'s film adaptation of Karen Blixen's short story, won the Oscar for Best Foreign Language Film, which led the way to many more international successes for Danish cinema, including the unprecedented double triumph when **Bille August**'s *Pelle the Conqueror* won in the same category the following year. The film, adapted from Martin Andersen Nexø's novel telling the bleak tale of Swedish immigrants coping with life on 19th-century Bornholm, also won the Palme d'Or at Cannes. The great Swedish actor, Max von Sydow, received an Oscar nomination in the Best Actor category for his role in the film.

ENFANT TERRIBLE

Danish cinema continued to hog the limelight in the 1990s with the international success of director **Lars von Trier**, and the advent of Dogme 95. Von Trier's (the 'von' is an aristocratic affectation) successes over the last couple of decades have earned him a virtually unrivalled reputation for stylistic experimentation and provocative scripts, as well as less than reverential treatment of actors. He established his name on the international arthouse circuit with such films as *The Element of Crime* (1984) and *Europa* (1991), and his spooky 1994 TV series, *The Kingdom*. However, it was his 1996 feature, *Breaking the Waves*, that launched him on the world stage. A torrid and occasionally crudely manipulative film, it set the scene for his future relationship with the world's film critics, who continue to be polarised in their opinions of his work. Von Trier's 1998 Dogme release, *The Idiots*; his bleak 2000 musical *Dancer in the Dark*, which starred Björk; 2009's horror *Antichrist*; and 2013's *Nymphomaniac* have all been hugely controversial for their dark portrayals of violent sex and mental illness.

DOGME STYLE

Von Trier was one of the filmmakers behind the internationally famous Dogme collective, a movement founded in Copenhagen by four Danish directors – von Trier, **Thomas Vinterberg, Søren Kragh-Jacobsen** and **Kristian Levring**. Dogme's mission was to discard the 'trickery' of modern filmmaking to refocus on the characters' emotional journeys.

The Dogme directors declared that Hollywood movies deceived their audience by mythologising the process of filmmaking. But to set themselves aside from all the other bleating, under-funded independent directors, they made it clear that their creed (called the Vow of Chastity) need not preclude Hollywood-sized budgets. As Vinterberg commented: 'The Dogme 95 Manifesto does not concern itself with the economic aspects of filmmaking. A Dogme film could be low-budget or it could have a $100m budget.' The 'Vow' included such draconian commandments as 'Shooting must be on location only', 'The director can receive no credit' and 'Films cannot be of a specific genre'.

No dubbing, tripods, artificial lighting or optical effects were allowed either.

The movement spawned several notable successes, prime among them Vinterberg's second feature film, *Festen* (*The Celebration*, 1998), a disturbing tale of family secrets, set against the backdrop of a 60th birthday party.

However, the movement, which broke up in 2005, also had many critics, who saw it as a pretentious experiment that became as conventional as the genres it criticised.

RECENT PRODUCTIONS

Resonant dramas such as *Facing the Truth* (2002), *Inheritance* (2003), *After the Wedding* (2006) and *In a Better World* (2010) are key examples of the intelligent and high-quality movies made by established directors such as **Nils Malmros, Per Fly, Susanne Bier** – who won the Oscar for Best Foreign Language Film in 2011 for *In a Better World* – and **Anders Thomas Jensen**, who continue to make waves internationally. Meanwhile, a new generation of young filmmakers is redefining genre-oriented films with forceful stories told in highly aesthetic packages, such as **Nikolaj Arcel**'s political thriller *King's Game* (2004), **Nicolas Winding Refn**'s raw and violent drug trilogy, which began with *Pusher* (1996), and **Christoffer Boe**'s modern romances such as *Allegro* (2005), and his thriller *Everything Will Be Fine* (2010). Winding Refn, in particular, has become a name to watch in Hollywood, with *Drive* (2011) and *Only God Forgives* (2013), both starring Ryan Gosling, earning the now US-based director international acclaim. He won Best Director for the former at the Cannes Film Festival in 2011.

DOCUMENTARY

Documentary is also now a major strand of Danish film, partly thanks to Copenhagen's ambitious **CPH:DOX** festival (*see p160 and p33*). This success is also partly down to public funding (administered by the Danish Film Institute) for the development and production of documentary films.

Three seasoned Danish documentary filmmakers – **Jørgen Leth, Jon Bang Carlsen and Anne Wivel** – can be said to have laid the groundwork for many of today's key players, who all play into the brand of Nordic humanism that is so well suited to this genre. Current documentary-makers to note include **Mads Brügger**, whose *Red Chapel* comic documentary on Korea won Best Foreign Documentary at the 2010 Sundance Film Festival; and **Janus Metz**, best known for his controversial *Armadillo* (2010), about Danish soldiers in Afghanistan. US documentary director Joshua Oppenheimer, who directed the powerful and disturbing 2012 Danish-British-

Grand Teatret.

Norwegian film *The Act of Killing*, is also based in Copenhagen, where he works for the documentary production company Final Cut for Real (www.final-cut.dk).

SMALL-SCREEN SUCCESSES

Of course, television drama series have taken on an increasingly important role in Denmark's screen productions over the past decade, with the huge success, at home and abroad, of a number of detective and political thrillers – namely **The Killing** (first series 2007), **Borgen** (first series 2010) and **The Bridge** (first series 2011) – that are responsible for a new 'golden age' for Danish TV. These dramas can also be seen as follow-ups to a TV series from the late 1970s called *Matador*, which provided something of a springboard for drama in Denmark, and which is frequently re-aired on Danish television.

The well-respected national broadcaster **DR** (previously called Danmarks Radio) produced all three of the series mentioned above. The publicly funded organisation gave its production departments a big push in the mid 1990s, sending several of its top dogs to Los Angeles to visit the sets of US dramas such as *24* and *LA Law*. They came back with fresh concepts that were injected into local productions, and the rest is screen history – and DR has a handful of Emmys to prove it. Danish thrillers are now celebrated for their gripping stories and plausible characters, as well as for their strong female leads – reasons why *The Killing* and *The Bridge* have both been remade in the US (and less successfully, at that).

CINEMA-GOING & FESTIVALS

There are plenty of top-quality screens in Copenhagen's city centre, with a choice of multiplexes and arthouses, as well as the dynamic **Filmhuset**. This all points to the locals' insatiable cinemania, which means even the largest cinema in Scandinavia, the **Imperial**, is usually packed to capacity during blockbuster openings. Fortunately for visitors, the vast majority of foreign films are shown in their original language, with Danish subtitles. Tickets usually cost around 80-85kr (60-65kr reductions).

Copenhagen hosts several excellent annual film festivals. **CPH:PIX** (www.cphpix.dk) is the international feature film festival (the result of a merger between NatFilm Festival and Copenhagen International Film Festival). Held in April, the innovative ten-day festival screens some 180 films from around the world.

The International Documentary Film Festival **CPH:DOX** (www.cphdox.dk) has gone from strength to strength since it started in 2003. As the largest documentary film festival in Scandinavia, the ten-day event draws an engaged international crowd to Copenhagen every November, attracted both by the screenings and the professional seminars.

October's Copenhagen Gay & Lesbian Film Festival changed its name to **MIX Copenhagen** (www.mixcopenhagen.dk) in 2011. As one of the longest-running festivals of its type, it attracts gay-centric films from around the world.

★ Filmhuset/Det Danske Filminstitut
Gothersgade 55, Rosenborg & Around (33 74 34 00, www.dfi.dk). Metro/train Nørreport. **Open** *Café* noon-10pm Tue-Sun. *Bookshop* 9.30am-10pm Mon-Fri; noon-10pm Sat; noon-7.30pm Sun. *Documentary archive & library* noon-7pm Tue, Thur; noon-4pm Wed, Fri. **Map** p251 M15.
This world-class film complex is devoted to Danish and international cinema. Among its facilities are a shop selling difficult-to-find film books, posters and DVDs, a restaurant, a documentary archive (open to non-members) and three cinemas.

Multiplexes

CinemaxX
Fisketorvet Shopping Center, Kalvebod Brygge 57, Vesterbro (70 10 12 02, www.cinemaxx.dk/ koebenhavn). Train Dybbølsbro. **Map** p251 Q13.
This multiplex in a shopping mall has Copenhagen's biggest screen. Comfortable but costly.

Dagmar Teatret
Jernbanegade 2, Indre By (70 13 12 11, www. dagmar.dk). Train Vesterport. **Map** p250 O11.
A multiplex devoted to projecting quality films. The main cinema is decent, the smaller screens less so.

Empire Bio
Guldbergsgade 29F, Nørrebro (35 36 00 36, www.empirebio.dk). Bus 5A. **Map** p248 H9.
Nørrebro's local multiplex manages to show both arthouse movies and blockbusters. Comfortable double seats are available in the back row.

★ Imperial
Ved Vesterport 4, Indre By (70 13 12 11, www.kino.dk). Train Vesterport. **Map** p250 O10.
The Imperial is Copenhagen cinema par excellence. A large, old-fashioned auditorium (with just over 1,000 seats), it used to have the biggest screen in

Scandinavia until the CinemaxX giant came to town. Many films première here.

Palads
Axeltorv 9, Indre By (70 13 12 11, www.kino.dk). Train Vesterport. **Map** p250 O11.
Copenhagen's family multiplex is nicknamed 'the birthday cake' for its pink exterior.

Park Bio
Østerbrogade 79, Østerbro (35 38 33 62, www.parkbio-kbh.dk). Train Østerport, or bus 1A, 14. **Map** p248 C13.
A charming neighbourhood cinema showing three different movies a day. There are special baby screenings every Friday at 10.30am (except during July), which are great for parents.

Arthouse Cinemas

Gloria
Rådhuspladsen 59, Indre By (33 12 42 92, www.gloria.dk). Train København H, or bus 11A, 14. **Map** p250 O12.
A small, underground arthouse cinema located in the heart of town.

★ Grand Teatret
Mikkel Bryggers Gade 8, Indre By (33 15 16 11, www.grandteatret.dk). Metro/train Nørreport, or bus 11A, 14. **Map** p250 O12.
This beautiful old building is home to a distinguished cinema (with six screens) showing an impeccable mix of international and arthouse titles.

Posthus Teatret
Rådhusstræde 1, Indre By (33 11 66 11, www. posthusteatret.dk). Metro Kongens Nytorv, or train København H, or bus 11A, 14. **No credit cards**. **Map** p251 O13.
Travel back in time in this tiny (90-seat) cinema, which from the outside could almost be mistaken for a puppet theatre.

★ Vester Vov Vov
Absalonsgade 5, Vesterbro (33 24 42 00, www.vestervovvov.dk). Bus 6A, 26. **Map** p245 Q9.
Vesterbro's charming local cinema has a really cosy feel to it, with comfortable reclining airline seats in its two auditoriums.

IMAX

Tycho Brahe Planetarium Omnimax
Gammel Kongevej 10 (33 12 12 24, www.tycho.dk). Train Vesterport, or bus 9A. **Map** p250 P10.
This city landmark contains an exhibition space and also a spectacular IMAX cinema, showing family-friendly science and nature films.
▶ *The IMAX is housed in the city's planetarium (see p121).*

Palads.

ARTS & ENTERTAINMENT

Gay & Lesbian

Denmark has long been a great place for gays and lesbians. Homosexual sex was legalised way back in 1933, the age of consent equalised in 1977, registered same-sex partnerships were available from 1989, and same-sex marriage was legalised in 2012. This also isn't a nation dragging its heels when it comes to promoting gay culture. In 2009, Denmark hosted the gay and lesbian sporting Outgames; Copenhagen Pride takes place every August; and the annual LGBT film festival, MIX Copenhagen, is held every October. Perhaps, then, with such a so-what attitude to sexuality, it's not surprising that the city's nightlife scene is fairly mixed and its gay scene – concentrated in the Pisserenden part of the centre – small. But what it lacks in size it makes up for with a warmth that few cities can match.

ORGANISATIONS

LGBT Danmark – Landsforeningen for Bøsser, Lesbiske, Biseksuelle og Transpersoner (LGBT)
Nygade 7, Indre By (33 13 19 48, www.lgbt.dk). Bus 11A, 14. **Open** *Phone enquiries 2-5pm Thur.* **Map** p251 N13.
Denmark's national association for gays, lesbians, bisexuals and transgender persons was founded in 1948, and prides itself on being at the vanguard of gay politics.

Stop Aids
Amagertorv 33, Indre By (88 33 56 00, www.stopaids.dk). Bus 11A, 14. **Open** *Phone enquiries 10am-4pm Mon-Thur; 10am-3pm Fri.* **Map** p251 N14.
Stop Aids has been promoting safe sex in Denmark since 1986. Its refreshing approach has included

IN THE KNOW GAY WEBSITES

For an excellent English overview of gay life in Copenhagen, visit www.copenhagen-gay-life.dk or www.out-and-about.dk.

putting up condom-and-lube compartments in cruising parks, offering numerous free workshops and courses, distributing safe-sex kits in gay bars and at larger one-off parties, and providing free massages in exchange for a chat about safe sex.

BARS & CLUBS

Twin Peaks-inspired bar **The Log Lady** (*see p70*) is a lesbian-friendly – in fact, 'everyone-friendly' – bar in Pisserenden.

Admission to the following bars and clubs is free.

BLUS at Huset KBH
Købmagergade 52, Indre By (21 51 21 51, www.blus.dk). Bus 11A, 14. **Open** *Sept-June 7pm-1am Wed.* **Map** p251 M13.
Gay students meet weekly for Wednesday GayDay, although you don't have to be studying to join in with the laid-back poetry readings, political discussions, lectures and music performances. Biannual gay parties pack the place to the rafters.

Café Intime
Allégade 25, Frederiksberg (38 34 19 58, www.cafeintime.dk). Metro Frederiksberg. **Open** *6pm-2am daily.*

This pint-sized but eminently popular piano bar has been around since 1920, and these days draws everyone from older Marlene Dietrich obsessives to younger jazz connoisseurs.

Centralhjørnet
Kattesundet 18, Indre By (33 11 85 49, www.centralhjornet.dk). Bus 11A, 14. **Open** noon-2am Mon-Thur, Sun; noon-3am Fri, Sat. **Map** p250 N12.
Copenhagen's most famous gay bar has been around for more than a century, offering a friendly pub atmosphere that's popular with everyone from the local 'countessa' to gay carpenters downing a pint or three after work. Holidays see the owner's notorious taste for wild decoration come to the fore.

Club Christopher
Knabrostræde 3, Indre By (60 80 71 76). Bus 11A, 14. **Open** 11pm-5am Sat. **Map** p251 N13.
Named after New York's famed homo street, this is a weekly party on the ground floor of what used to be PAN. The club has been known to operate an open bar (drink-as-much-as-you-like) policy for around 200kr, when you can expect messiness.

★ Cosy Bar
Studiestræde 24, Indre By (33 12 74 27, www.cosybar.dk). Train Vesterport, or bus 5A, 6A, 14. **Open** 10pm-6am Mon-Thur, Sun; 10pm-8am Fri, Sat. **Map** p250 N12.
If you're still out and about after a long evening on the town, chances are you'll end up in this dark, boisterous and cruise-oriented bar, where the tiny dancefloor gets ridiculously packed at weekends.

G*A*Y Copenhagen
Vester Voldgade 10, Indre By (33 14 13 30, www.facebook.com/copenhagengay). Train Vesterport. **Open** 4pm-3am Thur; midnight-5am Fri, Sat. **Map** p250 N12.
Located in the building that formerly housed Pony, another popular gay bar, G*A*Y had its grand opening in February 2014. Expect house DJs on Friday and Saturday nights. The bar/club is a mostly smoke-free venue, though there are a couple of tables available for those who can't quite kick the habit.

Jailhouse Copenhagen
Studiestræde 12, Indre By (33 15 22 55, www.jailhousecph.dk). Train Vesterport, or bus 11A, 14. **Open** *Bar* 3pm-2am Mon-Thur, Sun; 3pm-5am Fri, Sat. *Restaurant* 6-9pm Wed-Fri. **Map** p250 N12.
This two-level gay bar and restaurant is decorated with prison bars and jail-related paraphernalia. It's not nearly as hardcore as it sounds: the downstairs bar is noted for being surprisingly relaxed, and staff are friendly and easygoing, despite being dressed in full prison-guard regalia.

★ Masken
Studiestræde 33, Indre By (33 91 09 37, www.maskenbar.dk). Train Vesterport, or bus 5A, 6A, 14. **Open** 2pm-3am Mon-Thur, Sun; 2pm-5am Fri, Sat. **Map** p250 N12.
A giant mural of Scarlett O'Hara and Rhett Butler watches over a diverse, friendly crowd of boys and girls on two floors. As far as the crowd goes, it's a mix of ages and types, though wallet-friendly prices and '80s tunes make it popular with students.

ARTS & ENTERTAINMENT

Copenhagen Pride. *See p164.*

ARTS & ENTERTAINMENT

Men's Bar

*Teglgårdsstræde 3, Indre By (33 12 73 03,
www.mensbar.dk). Metro/train Nørreport,
or bus 1A, 5A, 6A, 14.* **Open** 3pm-2am daily.
Map p250 N12.
The only real men's bar on the scene: jeans, semi-
leather, dimly lit. You know the sort of thing.
Diluting the saucy vibe slightly is the free brunch
from 6pm on the first Sunday of every month.

★ Never Mind

*Nørre Voldgade 2, Indre By (33 11 88 86,
www.nevermindbar.dk). Metro/train Nørreport,
or bus 1A, 5A, 6A, 14.* **Open** 10pm-6am daily.
Map p250 N11.
A lively bar churning out pop and disco hits to a
mainly male crowd, with late-night revellers tending
to bounce between this place and Cosy (*see p163*).
Being situated just across from Copenhagen's cruisi-
est park boosts its appeal dramatically.

Oscar Bar & Café

*Rådhuspladsen 77, Tivoli & Around (33 12 09
99, www.oscarbarcafe.dk). Metro Kongens Nytorv.*
Open 11am-11pm Mon-Thur, Sun; 11am-2am
Fri, Sat. **Map** p250 O12.

Take some sexy bartenders, mix with reliable café
food and garnish with talented DJs spinning some
of the funkiest house and dirtiest disco around, and
you're some way to understanding the popularity of
Oscar. The atmosphere here is trendy but laid-back,
and people-watching is always at the top of the
menu, making this a must for both first-timers and
seasoned pros in Copenhagen.

EVENTS

The two biggest events are the film
festival **MIX Copenhagen** (*see p39*)
and **Copenhagen Pride** (*p38*).

SAUNAS

Amigo Sauna

*Studiestræde 31, Indre By (33 15 20 28, www.
amigo-sauna.dk). Train Vesterport, or bus 5A,
6A, 14.* **Open** noon-7am Mon-Thur, Sun; noon-
8am Fri, Sat. **Admission** 100kr. **Map** p250 N12.
Copenhagen's largest gay sauna is very dark, very
lively and definitely a place for some serious action,
especially at weekends.

HOTELS

Carsten's Guest House

*5th floor, Christians Brygge 28, Indre By
(33 14 91 07). Train København H, or Metro
Christianshavn, or bus 9A.* **Rates** 510kr-585kr
double; 180kr dorm bed; 892kr-1,185kr studio
or apartment. **Map** p251 Q14.
Queens will definitely fall in love with this gay and
lesbian guest house: from the outside, it looks just
like a cake castle; inside, it's a luxurious (but surprisingly affordable) B&B. Past guests have only good
things to say about the amiable proprietors and their
warm, personal service.

Oscar Bar & Café.

Nightlife

For such a small city, Copenhagen's nightlife is surprisingly vibrant. Sure, there isn't the same diverse range of subcultural 'scenes' that flourish in other European capitals – crate-digging audiophiles are largely notable by their absence – but various forms of electronic music are well represented, with top-name international DJs being regularly booked at clubs such as Culture Box, Rust and Vega.

Those looking for the most happening zones should make a beeline for Kødbyen, Copenhagen's regenerated Meatpacking District, and Nørrebro. Kødbyen's low-rise butchers' shops and abattoirs have been transformed into cool bars and clubs over the past decade, while Nørrebro is home to some of the hippest bars in town. For a more old-school vibe, hunt out a so-called *bodega* – a local (often smoke-filled) bar frequented by oldies, students and everyone in between.

THE LOWDOWN

First-time visitors may find Copenhagen's party scene a little elusive. There are a few superb clubs and a multitude of ultra-stylish venues packed with armies of attractive punters, but the best nights are mainly promoter- rather than venue-led, which means it's possible to turn up at even some of the more dedicated clubs – including **Rust** and **Vega** – and find it's an off-night, the place lacking in both atmosphere and people.

As with everywhere else this side of the millennium, Copenhagen is experiencing a blurring of boundaries in terms of pre-clubbing restaurant, café, bar and lounge venues that don't fit into the typical club mould, but which can be equally worthy of a night out in themselves. **Boutique Lize** and **Gefährlich** are two such hybrids, where it's as easy to throw down a few cocktails before heading elsewhere as it is to spend the whole evening partying in the bar, if you don't have the inclination to move on.

The places listed here are the city's main nightlife venues, but clubs come and go and places fall in and out of fashion, so it's also worth checking the local press for updates on regular nights and one-offs. For up-to-date information on forthcoming events, check out the **Copenhagen Post** (www.cphpost.dk), a Danish newspaper in English, available from kiosks and cafés.

For more regular visitors, **Human Office** (www.humanwebsite.com) – a group of organisers, artists and party people – sends out a weekly email that keeps a finger on the pulse of underground art, culture and nightlife events, while Danish website **Hifly** (www.hifly.dk) includes flyers for electronic and house music on its calendar. As always, record stores are a good place to pick up flyers, as are the more streetwear-oriented clothing stores, such as **Le Fix** (*see p65*).

Finally, a word about stimulant use: it may not be as rampant as in other European capital cities, but toilets without lids and one-in-a-cubicle policies demonstrate that it's definitely present. Remember that security do search for drugs and will expel you immediately if they find any.

LOUNGE, COCKTAIL & MUSIC BARS

The following bars don't normally charge admission fees.

★ Bakken i Kødbyen

Flæsketorvet 19-21, Vesterbro (no phone, www.bakkenkbh.dk). Train Dybbølsbro or København H. **Open** 9pm-3am Thur; 11pm-5am Sat.

Currently one of the trendiest nightspots, Bakken is located in the cool Meatpacking District. The area's restaurants and bars, this one included, are all housed in former butchers' shops and slaughter-houses; in fact, some of the district's original tenants remain, so, if you're out until dawn, don't be surprised if you bump into some men in white coats carrying carcasses. Bakken's small, smoky, dark interior is packed with fashion-conscious revellers, who come to socialise, get drunk and move to the dance and indie-rock tunes provided by resident DJs.

Bar Rouge

Hotel Skt Petri, Krystalgade 22, Indre By (33 45 98 22, www.hotelsktpetri.com). Metro/train

Lidkoeb. *See p168.*

Nørreport. **Open** 5pm-midnight Mon, Tue, Sun; 5pm-1am Wed, Thur; 5pm-2am Fri, Sat. **Map** p251 M13.

Hosting everything from the main MTV Music Awards after-party to regular gatherings of top-end model agencies, it's all happening at Hotel Skt Petri, and that's probably thanks to the svelte trappings of Bar Rouge. Hotel guests have priority when it comes to entry, although a timely email can usually secure a much-coveted place on the guestlist, even on a weekend. Music-wise, evenings usually start with a bit of Buddha Bar chill and work their way up to Ibiza-style house.

Boutique Lize

Enghave Plads 6, Vesterbro (33 31 15 60). Bus 3A, 10, 14. **Open** 8pm-3am Thur; 8pm-4.30am Fri, Sat. **Map** p245 S7.

Boutique Lize is one of the best cocktail bars in the city, with queues of people trying to get in from 11pm onwards. It attracts a lot of the area's more mature trendsetters with its hip Vesterbro ambience and reasonably priced cocktails. Happy hour is 8-11.30pm on Thursdays and 8-10pm on Fridays and Saturdays.

Café Bopa

Løgstørgade 8, Østerbro (35 43 05 66, www.cafe bopa.dk). Train Nordhavn, or bus 1A, 18, 40. **Open** 9am-midnight Mon-Wed, Sun; 9am-2am Thur; 9am-5am Fri, Sat. **Map** p248 B14.

A friendly café, bar and restaurant popular with trendy locals. Disco and mainstream dance comprise the tunes, and in summer the café spills out on to Bopa Plads, with deckchairs, rugs and pétanque.

Gefährlich

Fælledvej 7, Nørrebro (35 24 13 24, www. gefährlich.dk). Bus 3A, 5A. **Open** 5pm-midnight Tue, Wed; 5pm-2am Thur; 5pm-4.30am Fri, Sat. **Map** p248 J10.

Gefährlich (German for 'dangerous') claims to be a restaurant, bar, art gallery, coffee shop, record store, cultural centre and nightclub all rolled into one. It may sound a bit over-conceptualised and ambitious, but in reality it's a rather small, low-key affair with an eclectic programme of regular and one-off events, including a rare-soul night on the first Saturday of every month.

LATE-NIGHT LOCALS

Copenhagen's bodegas offer bar-goers a more 'real' experience.

Bored of ubiquitous, clean-lined Scandinavian aesthetics and expensive drinks lists? If you're after a less polished Copenhagen night-time experience, with jukebox tunes, local beers and random conversation, then you'll probably enjoy the atmosphere of a so-called *bodega* – an old-school local bar whose defining characteristics seem to be smoke-stained walls, old men propping up the bar counter, and affordable beer on tap, as well as simple snacks to munch on. The most popular *bodegas* (the meaning of the word is different to both the Spanish and US versions) have a worn-out charm and often a house-party feel after hours, when the old-timers are joined by students, musicians and artists keen to have a sociable (read: inebriated) time.

One of Copenhagen's best-known *bodegas* is **Eiffel Bar** (Wildersgade 58, 32 57 70 92, www.eiffelbar.dk). This Christianshavn institution – once a hangout for drunken sailors – has mirrored walls, well-priced Danish beer and Pernod, a 1950s jukebox and a diverse mix of customers, with a lively vibe on Thursday and Friday evenings. Don't come here if you're allergic to tobacco smoke, however.

Another good late-night bet is **Bo-Bi Bar** (Klareboderne 4, Indre By, 33 12 55 43),

a central spot whose origins also lie in Copenhagen's maritime past – it's said to have been established by an American sailor in 1917, and the red-wallpapered interior has been a second home to artists, journos and office workers ever since. The hard-boiled eggs on the counter help to soak up the beer.

The neighbourhood of Vesterbro is home to several traditional *bodegas*, one of the most popular being **Freddy's** (Gasvaerksvej 28, 33 22 70 95). It's often packed on weekend nights, with revellers rocking out to '80s jukebox tunes. Walk west from here along Halmtorvet and Sønder Boulevard, and within ten minutes you'll come to **Dyrehaven** (*see p125*), the result of a makeover of an old-fashioned bar. This new-school *bodega* appeals to modern sensibilities thanks to its DJ nights, retro ambience and good-quality grub (not to mention smoke-free air), but it retains its *bodega* title through its *smørrebrod* plates, excellent beer and local vibe.

For a more sedate vibe, head to neighbouring Frederiksberg to the eminently likeable **Vinstue 90** (*see p131*). This local legend of a *bodega* opened its doors in 1916, and is now famous for its 'slow beer', poured from unpressurised kegs to produce an exceptionally smooth drink.

Karriere

Flæsketorvet 57-67, Vesterbro (33 21 55 09, www.karrierebar.com). Train Dybbølsbro or København H. **Open** *Cocktail bar* 4pm-midnight Thur; 4pm-4am Fri, Sat. *Restaurant* 6-10pm Thur-Sat. **Map** p250 Q10.

This ambitious art gallery, cocktail bar and restaurant opened in a former slaughterhouse in 2007, the brainchild of artist Jeppe Hein and his sister Lærke. The interior is designed by renowned contemporary artists (Ulrik Weck, for instance, created lampshades for the bar made of pots, pans and bowls turned upside down). The same artists supply works for the permanent and temporary exhibitions. Concerts, gigs, lectures and cultural events are also held here.

★ Lidkoeb

Vesterbrogade 72B, Vesterbro (33 11 20 10, www.lidkoeb.dk). Train København H, or bus 6A, 26. **Open** 4pm-2am Mon-Sat; 8pm-1am Sun. **Map** p245 P8.

Follow a discreet passageway that leads off Vesterbrogade to reach one of Copenhagen's bars of the moment. Housed in a three-storey, 18th-century building, Lidkoeb is renowned for quality cocktails (around 110kr each) and a cosy vibe. Choose from the long, wooden, ground-floor bar with fireplace and piano; the assembly room with balcony for smokers; or, at the top, a whiskey lounge with a late-night feel. *Photo p166.*

Oak Room

Birkegade 10, Nørrebro (38 60 38 60, www. oakroom.dk). Bus 3A, 5A. **Open** 7pm-1am Wed; 7pm-2am Thur; 4pm-4am Fri; 6pm-4am Sat. **Map** p248 J10.

A tiny, stylish lounge bar tucked around the corner from trendy Sankt Hans Torv, the Oak Room is literally that: a single, narrow room dominated by a huge wooden bar. When the place is packed (which it seems to be every weekend), it's very hard to sit in the little wooden booths opposite the bar without getting your drinks knocked over by passers-by; for some, this seems to be a legitimate means of meeting members of the opposite sex. *See also p141.*

Zoo Bar

Sværtegade 6, Indre By (33 15 68 69, www. zoobar.dk). Metro Kongens Nytorv, or bus 11A. **Open** 5pm-11pm Tue, Wed; 5pm-2am Thur; 11am-4am Fri, Sat. **Map** p251 M14.

It may no longer be the most fashionable bar in the city, but Zoo is still a popular central spot in which to meet and warm up with a few drinks before heading out clubbing, and it occasionally throws a decent party in its own right. It's intimate (read: small), and the excellent window seats are perfect for a spot of people-watching on trendy Kronprinsensgade. At weekends, DJs play from 7pm.

Vega.

CLUBS

★ Culture Box

Kronprinsessegade 54A, Indre By (33 32 50 50, www.culture-box.com). Bus 26. **Open** varies; typically midnight-6am Fri, Sat. **Admission** 50kr-90kr. **Map** p247 K15.

Copenhagen's premier techno palace regularly plays host to DJ legends such as Derrick May and Jeff Mills. The sound system has by far the most penetrating bass in town, the VJ shows are superb and the more sedate downstairs dancefloor is perfect for those who don't want to sweat on the main floor. Their pre-clubbing bar next door, Cocktail Box, is open from 8pm.

Jolene

Flaesketorvet 81-85, Vesterbro (20 51 47 64, www.facebook.com/jolenebar). Train Dybbølsbro or København H. **Open** 8pm-4am Thur-Sat. **Admission** varies.

Jolene recently relocated from Sorgenfrigade to this former slaughterhouse in Kødbyen. Of all the bars in the district, it probably is the one that most lives up to its 'meat market' tag – albeit with a studenty fun-packed vibe. A diverse line-up of DJs gets the tightly packed crowds moving.

★ KB3

Kødboderne 3, Vesterbro (33 23 45 97, www. kb3.dk). Train Dybbølsbro or København H. **Open** 11pm-4am Fri, Sat. **Admission** 60kr.

Located in a former meat locker in Kødbyen, KB3 is a huge, 800-capacity nightclub that opened in 2012 with a long bar, an outdoor area, a champagne bar and a programme of high-profile electronic DJs – this is definitely a place you visit to dance. One of its quirkier features is the special 'friend toilet', which has two toilets side by side in one cubicle (it doesn't take too much of a stretch of the imagination to think what it might be popular for).

NASA

Boltens Gård, Indre By (33 93 74 15, www.nasa-cph.dk). Metro Kongens Nytorv. **Open** 11pm-5am Fri, Sat. **Admission** 100kr. **Map** p251 M15.
A long time ago (in a galaxy far, far away), NASA supposedly represented the cream of the cream of Copenhagen clubbing. These days, that accolade seems to refer only to the biomorphic, all-white interior, inspired by the glamour of space travel and Stanley Kubrick's sanitised visions of the future. While it used to be a members-only nightspot with a reputation for being harder to get into than a pair of hotpants, the trendy patina has worn off and it's now a far less discriminatory venue, swearing instead by a policy of 'massclusivity': namely, if you can afford to pay for a table, you're in. Nevertheless, NASA remains one of the most amazing-looking clubs in the world, with some nights – including those hosted by party legend Jean Eric von Baden – that are still good enough to eclipse the air of studied self-consciousness.

Park Café

Østerbrogade 79, Østerbro (35 42 62 48, www.parkcafe.dk). Bus 1A, 3A, 14. **Open** 11pm-5am Fri, Sat. **Admission** 100kr. **Map** p248 B13.
With three dancefloors, a restaurant and a capacity of 2,000, it's not surprising that Park attracts a more mature, dressed-up crowd. On Friday and Saturday (after the restaurant closes), the whole venue turns into a nightclub, featuring mainstream house, pop and R&B.

★ Rust

Guldbergsgade 8, Nørrebro (35 24 52 00, www.rust.dk). Bus 3A, 5A. **Open** 11pm-5am Wed-Sat. **Admission** 40kr Wed, Thur; 60kr Fri, Sat; prices vary according to events. **Map** p246 H10.
Rust is one of the city's best venues for both concerts and clubbing, and an integral part of Copenhagen's nightlife. Its evolution over the years – from political café through to dubious rock club and, finally, the more polished venue seen today – is all the more impressive for its retention of an experimental edge and an ability to roll with the times. The small cocktail bar, Living Room, is a minimalist interpretation of a 1970s lounge, complete with groovy low seating, mellow lighting and a chilled ambience. There's also the sweaty downstairs area, Bassment, living up to its name with plenty of growling beats.

Søpavillonen

Gyldenløvesgade 24 Frederiksberg (33 15 12 24, www.soepavillonen.dk). Metro Forum, or bus 2A, 12, 66, 68. **Open** varies; usually 11pm-5am Fri, Sat. **Admission** 90kr-125kr. **Map** p246 M10.
This beautiful white pavilion on the lake holds one of the meatiest Saturday-night meat markets in town: a seventh heaven for divorced thirtysomethings looking to groove to innocuous pop hits. The building, designed by architect Vilhelm Dahlerup in the 1890s, is spectacular, especially when it's lit up at night.

★ Vega

Enghavevej 40, Vesterbro (33 25 70 11, www.vega.dk). Bus 3A, 10, 14. **Open** *Club* 11pm-5am Fri, Sat. *Concerts* varies. **Admission** *Club* 60kr-150kr. *Concerts* 100kr-400kr. **Map** p245 S7.
Opened in 1996 and housed in a listed landmark building dating from 1956, Vega is the queen of Copenhagen's nightlife. It features a large and small concert hall, Big Vega and Little Vega (1,200 and 550 capacity, respectively), the latter of which doubles up as a nightclub; the Yankee Bar, a lounge and cocktail bar; and the street-level Ideal Bar (*see p170*), a party institution in itself. The list of famous names to have played at Vega in recent years is a testament to its popularity, from secret gigs by Prince and David Bowie to concerts from the likes of Björk. The interior is superb, the service professional and the DJs among the best in town.

The Standard. *See p170.*

LIVE MUSIC VENUES

Nightclubs **Rust** and **Vega** (for both, *see p169*) are also key concert venues, hosting high-profile rock and pop musicians and DJs.

Jazz, blues, folk & world

La Fontaine
Kompagnistræde 11, Indre By (33 11 60 98, www.lafontaine.dk). Metro Kongens Nytorv, or bus 11A. **Open** 7pm-5am daily. **Admission** free Mon-Thur, Sun; 60kr Fri, Sat. **Map** p251 O13.
Though it has a capacity of only 60 people, this cosy, low-key jazz venue is well known for its legendary jam sessions and late, late nights. It attracts music students and other jazz-lovers to its weekend swing and mainstream concerts. It's also one of the few bars to stay open until 5am every night.

Global
Nørre Alle 7, Nørrebro (50 58 08 41, www.global cph.dk). Bus 3A, 5A. **Open** 9pm-1am daily. **Admission** varies. **Map** p246 H10.
This new Nørrebro venue, near Sankt Hans Torv, hosts bands from home and abroad, encompassing nu-folk, jazz, fusion, reggae, blues and more. DJ-led club nights are also on the menu.

★ Jazzhouse
Niels Hemmingsens Gade 10, Indre By (33 15 47 00, www.jazzhouse.dk). Metro Kongens Nytorv. **Open** *Concerts* usually 8pm Mon-Thur, Sun; 9pm, 11pm Fri, Sat. *Club* midnight-5am Thur-Sat. **Admission** *Concerts* varies. *Club* free Thur; 60kr after midnight Fri, Sat. **Map** p251 M13.
The country's premier jazz venue, Jazzhouse reopened in 2012 after extensive refurbishment following flood damage. The spruced-up space has a new concert hall with modern facilities, allowing the well-established club – formerly called Copenhagen Jazzhouse – to continue to build on the legacy of the legendary but long-gone Copenhagen Montmartre jazz club of the 1960s. The venue is subsidised by the government and offers consistently good gigs throughout the year, showcasing both local and international musicians. When weekend concerts finish, the large downstairs dance-floor is filled by an energetic crowd.

IN THE KNOW
COPENHAGEN DISTORTION

Distortion started out by hosting mobile raves in unusual locations (buses and boats, for example), but has since grown into a week-long festival of music and conceptual art every June (*see p37*), with occasional one-off parties throughout the year. Visit www.cphdistortion.dk for details.

Mojo
Løngangstræde 21C, Indre By (33 11 64 53, www.mojo.dk). Bus 11A. **Open** 8pm-5am daily. **Admission** varies. **Map** p251 O13.
A grubby but friendly little blues venue, featuring live entertainment every night.

★ The Standard
Havnegade 44, Indre By (72 14 88 08, www.the standardcph.dk). Metro Kongens Nytorv, or bus 11A, 66. **Open** *Concerts* 6pm, 8.30pm Tue-Sat; 5pm, 8pm Sun. **Admission** 245kr; 149kr reductions. **Map** p252 N17.
Copenhagen's newest jazz bar is a high-profile affair set in an art deco building just round the corner from Nyhavn. Co-founded by Danish jazz pianist Niels Lan Doky and local culinary hero Claus Meyer, it's as much a gastronomic destination (*see p101*) as a musical one, with three top-notch restaurants in the two-storey waterside space. That's not to say that the jazz takes second billing, however; with a programme featuring both emerging local names and well-known international musicians, and an intimate space that makes every performance feel special, the Standard is a first-rate proposition for jazz fans. *Photo p170*.

Rock & pop

Amager Bio
Øresundsvej 6, Amager (tickets Billetnet 70 15 65 65, information 32 86 02 00, www.amagerbio.dk). Metro Lergravsparken, or bus 5A, 12. **Open** varies. **Admission** varies.
One of the largest concert spaces in Copenhagen, with a capacity of 1,000. The programme is strong on old-school rock, blues and country.

Ideal Bar
Vega, Enghavevej 40, Vesterbro (33 25 70 11, www.vega.dk). Bus 3A, 10, 14. **Open** 10pm-4am Wed; 10pm-5am Thur-Sat. **Admission** 60kr-100kr. **Map** p245 S7.
Part of the Vega complex (*see p169*), this intimate, 200-capacity lounge bar hosts regular gigs by established Danish and international musicians, with indie-rock bands often on the rota. The venue also runs club nights and one-off parties.

Loppen
Bådsmandsstræde 43, Christiania (32 57 84 22, www.loppen.dk). Metro Christianshavn, or bus 2A, 9A, 40. **Open** 9pm-2am daily. **Admission** 50kr-200kr. **Map** p252 P18.
Since opening in 1973, Loppen has built an excellent reputation for live music despite its dilapidated surroundings, and its predilection for rock predates the city's rock revival. The booking policy is adventurous, with everything from jazz to rock, but with a strong emphasis on alternative sounds. Loppen is unconcerned with refinement, wallowing in the unique environ-ment of Copenhagen's former hippie enclave.

ARTS & ENTERTAINMENT

Performing Arts

Copenhagen is known for its jazz scene, but it also has much to offer the classical music lover. Not only are there professional outfits such as the Danish National Symphony Orchestra – housed in the new Jean Nouvel-designed DR Koncerthuset – but churches offer regular concerts. The language barrier means some theatre is inaccessible to visitors – aside from a shared awe for the new Royal Danish Playhouse. But as many of the city's directors come from abroad, it is possible for non-Danes to enjoy a night at the theatre. Opera fans, meanwhile, are in for a treat with the impressive Operaen, which has given a new lease of life to the opera scene. Dance has also been reinvigorated, both in terms of small modern dance venues and as a result of the reorganisation of the Royal Danish Theatre.

Classical Music & Opera

ENSEMBLES
Foremost among the professional choirs is **Musica Ficta** (www.ficta.dk), a chamber choir led by composer Bo Holten and performing mostly Renaissance and contemporary music. **Camerata Chamber Choir** (www.camerata.dk) is one of Denmark's oldest choirs; founded in 1965, it has attracted some of the best choral singers in the country, many of them students at the musical department of the University of Copenhagen. For something completely different, try **Concerto Copenhagen** (www.coco.dk), Scandinavia's leading Baroque orchestra and one of Europe's more interesting early music groups.

FESTIVALS
Copenhagen hosts a number of performing arts festivals. In the summer, you can usually find organ festivals, a Baroque festival and Tivoli Koncertsal's season of mini festivals (from April to September). Every other year, national broadcaster **Danmarks Radio** puts on a competition for young ensembles and chamber musicians at DR Koncerthuset, while the **Copenhagen Summer Festival** (www.copenhagensummerfestival.dk) is an annual showcase for both young talent and established names in the classical music world. The festival takes place in late July/early August in the Charlottenborg Festival Hall in Kongens Nytorv, and boasts 12 concerts in 12 days, many with free admission.

Contact the **Wonderful Copenhagen Tourist Information Bureau** (70 22 24 42, www.visitcopenhagen.com) for further details of all of the above, as well as information on its free Wednesday concert series, held at various venues at 5pm throughout the year.

MAJOR VENUES

Black Diamond
Søren Kirkegaards Plads 1, Indre By (33 47 47 47, www.kb.dk). Bus 66. **Box office** 1hr before performances (or from Billetnet, 70 15 65 65, www.billetnet.dk). **Map** p251 P15.
The concert hall – called the Queen's Hall – in the Black Diamond is panelled with Canadian maple and ornamented with black tapestries woven with quotations from Hans Christian Andersen's fairytales. The resident ensemble plays six times a year, with a reper-

toire covering everything from modern classics and newly composed works to experiments in the borderlands between musical styles.

★ DR Koncerthuset

Emil Holms Kanal 20, Ørestad (35 20 30 40, 35 20 62 62, www.dr.dk/koncerthuset). Metro DR Byen. **Box office** noon-5pm Mon-Fri (or from Billetnet, 70 15 65 65, www.billetnet.dk). *See p173* **Out of the Blue.**

★ Operaen

Ekvipagemestervej 10, Holmen (33 69 69 69, www.kglteater.dk). **Box office** 10am-4pm Mon-Sat. **Map** p249 L18.

This Henning Larsen-designed opera house opened in 2005 to widespread praise. Guided tours of the building can be arranged (9.30am, 10am, 4.30pm, 5pm daily) and take 75 minutes. Group tours can be conducted in English, and cost 2,500kr. For a full review of the venue, *see p174* **A Three-Act Structure.**

Royal Danish Academy of Music (Konservatoriets Koncertsal)

Rosenoerns Allé 22, Frederiksberg (72 26 72 26, www.dkdm.dk). Metro Forum, or bus 2A, 68. **Box office** (phone) 9am-3pm Mon-Fri. **Map** p248 M9.

This Functionalist architectural gem, built in 1945 to a design by Vilhelm Lauritzen, housed the Danish Broadcasting Corporation's Radiohusets Koncertsal until the summer of 2008. After renovation work to modernise the building, it's now the venue for the Royal Danish Academy of Music's 200 annual public concerts, many of which are free of charge. The Academy's Concert Hall is also the winter residence of the Copenhagen Philharmonic Orchestra.

▶ *The Musikmuseet (Music Museum; www. natmus.dk) is due to open here in September 2014.*

Tivolis Koncertsal

Tivoli, Vesterbrogade 3 (Tivoli information line 33 15 10 01, ticket centre 33 15 10 12, www.tivoli.dk). Train København H. **Box office** *Mid Apr-mid Sept, mid Nov-23 Dec* 10am-8pm Mon-Thur, Sat, Sun; 10am-11pm Fri. *Mid Sept-mid Nov, 24 Dec-mid Apr* 10am-6pm Mon-Fri. **Map** p250 P12.

Throughout summer (mid April to late September) there is jazz and other popular music in the various little pavilions dotted around the park, while the concerts in the Koncertsal vary from musicals to chamber music. Seasonal times do vary, so visit the website for up-to-date information.

OTHER VENUES

Christianskirke

Strandgade 1, Christianshavn (32 54 15 76, www.christianskirke.dk). Metro Christianshavn, or bus 2A, 40, 66, 350S. **No credit cards.** **Map** p252 P16.

Concerts in this 16th-century church cover the full spectrum of musical genres, from gospel to chamber music, and are held throughout the year. Tickets for many of the concerts here can be bought from Billetet (70 15 65 65, www.billetnet.dk).

Garnisons Kirken

Sankt Annæ Plads 4, Frederiksstaden (33 91 27 06, www.garnisonskirken.dk). Metro Kongens Nytorv, or bus 11A, 29. **No credit cards.** **Map** p252 M16.

The venue itself is unremarkable, but this church hosts a number of enjoyable concerts throughout the year. The gaudy gold and red organ may not be easy on the eye, but it rarely fails to please the ear.

Holmens Kirke

Holmens Kanal, Indre By (33 13 61 78, www.holmenskirke.dk). Metro Kongens Nytorv. **No credit cards.** **Map** p252 O15.

Every Easter and Christmas, Holmens Kirke hosts performances of Bach's sublime Passions – both the *St John* and the *St Matthew* – and Handel's *Messiah*. There's also music throughout the evening on the annual Culture Night in October.

Kastelskirken

Kastellet 15, Frederiksstaden (33 91 27 06, www.kastelskirken.dk). Bus 15, 19. **No credit cards.** **Map** p249 H17.

This beautifully restored, yellow-painted church has unique acoustics and is used for recordings as well as concerts. Sometimes a military brass band performs on the square outside the church, mixing the usual military marches with the occasional ABBA number.

Musikteatret Undergrunden

44 47 49 44, www.undergrunden.com.

Underground Music Theatre is a touring opera company for children founded in 1977 by Niels and Kaja Pihl. It covers everything from avant-garde experiments to repertory works, in a wide range of styles, with puppet operas a regular fixture since 1989.

Theatre

What follows is an overview of the organisations and venues that are most relevant for English-speaking visitors to Copenhagen. More general information can be found at **www.kulturnaut.dk**, **www.aok.dk** and **www.cphpost.dk**.

VENUES

With the opening of the Opera House and Royal Danish Playhouse, the 'Old Stage' of the Royal Danish Theatre on Kongens Nytorv is now mainly used for dance performances – *see p174* **A Three-Act Structure.**

OUT OF THE BLUE

Scandinavia's premier classical concert hall is well worth a visit.

ARTS & ENTERTAINMENT

Selected as the *Wallpaper** 2010 Design Award's Best New Public House, Danmarks Radio's **DR Koncerthuset** (*see p172*) is one of Copenhagen's most exciting architectural projects of the past few years, and a new landmark for the city.

Designed by French architect Jean Nouvel (known for Madrid's Reina Sofía museum extension and London's One New Change shopping centre), the concert hall was inaugurated in early 2009 after six years of construction. The building makes use of its location in Ørestad North: the bright blue of its exterior blends with the waterfront setting, while images are projected on to the surface of the semi-transparent frontage when an event is being held – projections relating to the specific event, as well as reflections from the clouds and the surrounding area. The idea is for the building to appear to be in motion, blending with its environment and changing with the weather and the light. Nouvel proposed that: 'At night the [building] will come alive with images, colours and lights expressing the life going on inside.'

The Koncerthuset has four concert halls; the main auditorium, Studio 1, accommodates an audience of 1,800, and is already renowned for its world-class acoustics (the work of Japan's Yasuhisa Toyota) – as you might well expect for the most expensive concert hall ever built (the project's final figure ran to the tune of some $300 million). As the home of the Danish National Symphony Orchestra (which

provide concerts every Thursday), the building is now the city's – in fact, Scandinavia's – premier venue for classical concerts. As well as symphony concerts, this is the place to head for chamber music and choral performances by all of Denmark's national musical ensembles, as well as numerous concerts by international names. A key aim of the Koncerthuset, however, is for its musical scope to be broad – thus, small-scale jazz concerts are held in the foyer, and rock and pop acts sometimes appear in the three smaller auditoriums.

Even if you don't make it to a concert here, it's worth a trip to DR Byen (*byen* means 'town' in Danish) to see the area, which, since 2007, has also housed the headquarters of Danmarks Radio, the national broadcasting corporation. 'Architecture is like music,' Nouvel stated in reference to the project, 'it is made to move and delight us.' See the building when a big event is on, and you can judge for yourself whether the architect has succeeded.

A THREE-ACT STRUCTURE

The Royal Danish Theatre has expanded to fill three main venues.

Operaen.

Originally confined to one building – Det Kongelige Teater at Kongens Nytorv – the Royal Danish Theatre has been split into three different venues over the past decade. The original building is used principally for ballet these days, and there are two new, spectacular, purpose-built architectural marvels – the Opera House, which opened in 2005, and the Royal Danish Playhouse, completed in 2008 – occupying opposite sides of Copenhagen's waterfront.

Tours can be booked for each venue (contact the individual venue directly for details), and each has excellent restaurants and bars.

Additional Royal Danish Theatre performances take place at the new **DR Koncerthuset** (*see p172*). Productions and information for all the venues can be found at www.kglteater.dk.

OPERAEN (COPENHAGEN OPERA HOUSE)

Opera got a new lease of life in Copenhagen after the inauguration of the marvellous new harbourside Opera House in 2005 – purpose-built for the opera wing of the Royal Danish Theatre. Designed by Henning Larsen, the building is nine storeys high and is home to two stages: the grandiose main stage and

the smaller 'Takkelloftet' (used for more experimental productions and opera for younger audiences). Artistic director Sven Müller continues to strengthen contemporary Danish opera while remaining loyal to the classics, with everything from Tchaikovsky to hip hop fusion on the programme.

Gamle Scene.

Skuespilhuset.

Skuespil huset

The 2014 season includes Mozart's classic *Don Giovanni* and Pietro Mascagni's hot-blooded Sicilian opera *Cavalleria Rusticana*. Plays, ballet and concerts (mainly in Danish) are also performed here.

Against the foyer's red background, the Operaen's chandeliers bear an uncanny resemblance to the flag of Christiania, with its three yellow circles, leading some commentators to look for a hidden meaning.

DET KONGELIGE TEATER, GAMLE SCENE (ROYAL DANISH THEATRE, OLD STAGE)

With the opening of Operaen in 2005, the Royal Theatre shifted for the first time in its history. The opening of the Playhouse three years later was the next development; the original building near Kongens Nytorv – renamed Gamle Scene, 'Old Stage' – is now principally used for ballet (and is the home of the Royal Danish Ballet, *see p177*). It also houses the Royal Danish Theatre's costume department.

The building started life in 1748, but was largely replaced in 1874. The Baroque interior, with crystal chandeliers, red velvet, golden angels and frescoed ceilings, reflects the lavishness of the time. The two bronze statues in front of the building (the exterior was recently given a thorough restoration)

are a tribute to Danish dramatists Adam Oehlenschläger and Ludvig Holberg.

Stærekassen – originally the 'new stage' of the theatre, added as an annexe in 1931 – was so-named because of the way it hangs over Tordenskjoldsgade street (it translates as 'nesting box'). This stage is now owned by the Ministry of Finance, Palaces & Properties Agency, and used for one-off events.

SKUESPILHUSET (ROYAL DANISH PLAYHOUSE)

This stunning – but initially controversial – purpose-built playhouse opened in 2008 on the harbourfront at Kvæsthusgade, round the corner from Nyhavn. Designed by Danish architectural practice Lundgaard & Tranberg, which won a RIBA European Award for the building, its arrival marked the broadening and modernising of the Royal Theatre's role in Danish performing arts. Containing three stages, it's now the principal venue for dramatic theatre in Denmark, but also hosts a small number of music, dance and children's events. Emmet Feigenberg has been artistic director since 2008; he took over from Mikkel Harder Munck-Hansen, who did much to reinvigorate the company.

As this is the national theatre, tickets are subsided by the government. Note, however, that most performances are in Danish.

Folketeatret

Nørregade 39, Nørreport (70 27 22 72,
www.folketeatret.dk). Metro/train Nørreport.
Box office 10am-6pm Mon-Fri; 10am-2pm Sat.
Map p250 M12.
Despite starting out as a down-to-earth competitor
to the Royal Theatre, the 'People's Theatre' – in existence for over 150 years – now offers an eclectic mix
of more modern performances, including musicals,
across three stages.

Grønnegårds Teatret

Bredgade 66, Frederiksstaden (33 16 22 12,
box office 33 32 70 23, www.groennegaard.dk).
Bus 1A. **Box office** *Mid June-Sept* varies.
Map p249 K17.
Grønnegårds Teatret enjoys a unique outdoor loca-
tion, nestling under linden trees in the garden of the
Danish Museum of Art & Design. The season runs
throughout the summer and features a visit by the
Royal Danish Ballet each July, with picnic baskets
available from the museum's restaurant.

Københavns Musikteater

Kronprinsensgade 7, Indre By (33 32 38 30, box
office 33 32 55 56, www.kobenhavnsmusikteater.dk).
Metro/train Nørreport. **Box office** 1-3pm Mon-
Fri & 1hr before performances. **No credit cards.**
Map p251 M14.
This 'music theatre' seems to have gone through an
identity crisis in the past few years: in 2006, it changed
its name from Den Anden Opera to Plex, to reflect a
more international profile; thenn in 2008, it changed
its name again to Københavns Musikteater. It still fills
every floor of its beautiful old Pentecostal church with
installation and sound art, video, dance and experimental music performances. Note that there is an
additional box office in Tivoli (9am-5pm Mon-Fri).

Det Ny Teater

Gammel Kongevej 29, Frederiksberg (box office 33
25 50 75, www.detnyteater.dk). Train København
H. **Box office** noon-6pm Mon, Tue; noon-7.30pm
Wed, Thur; noon-8pm Fri, Sat; noon-3pm Sun.
Map p245 P8.
The misleadingly named New Theatre (it opened in
1908) is best known for staging Danish versions of
money-making international musicals (*Billy Elliot* and
Evita were both on show in spring 2014), but it also
has a restaurant, Teater Kælderen, where actors wait
on tables and perform routines between servings.

★ Skuespilhuset

Sankt Annæ Plads 36, Frederiksstaden (box office
33 69 69 69, www.kgl-teater.dk). Metro Kongens
Nytorv, or bus 11A, 29. **Box office** 2-6pm Mon-
Sat. **Map** p252 N16.
The waterside Skuespilhuset (Royal Danish Playhouse)
opened in 2008, around the corner from Nyhavn,
and has done much to rejuvenate the area. For a full
review, *see p174* **A Three-Act Structure.**

IN THE KNOW CHILD'S PLAY

In addition to an annual festival of youth
theatre (www.aprilfestival.dk), there are
plenty of children's theatre groups in
Denmark. These include **Det Lille Teater**
(The Little Theatre, Lavendelstræde 5-7,
Indre By, 33 12 12 29, www.detlille
teater.dk), Nørreport's **Anemoneteatret**
(Suhmsgade 4, 33 32 22 49, www.
anemoneteatret.dk), Frederiksberg's
Comedievognens Broscene (Lykkeholms
Allé 11, 35 36 61 22, www.comedie
vognen.dk) and the **Marionet Teater i
Kongens Have** (Kronprinsessegade 21,
Indre By, 35 42 64 72, www.marionet
teatret.dk). The last puts on two puppetry
performances daily during summer in the
lovely Kongens Have.

COMPANIES

Copenhagen Internationale Theater (KIT)

33 15 15 64, www.kit.dk.
Since its foundation in 1979, KIT has organised more
than 40 international festivals in Denmark. It's most
visible in summer, when the annual Sommerscene
circus festival showcases some of Europe's best
acrobatic talents, while Hamletsommer brings a production of *Hamlet* to the prince's 'true' home,
Kronborg Castle in Helsingør (Elsinore).

Copenhagen Theatre Circle

www.ctcircle.dk.
The only amateur English-language theatre group
in Denmark, composed of non-professionals working in their spare time and aiming to stage at least
one production per year. Recently performed play-
wrights include Dario Fo and Harold Pinter.

London Toast Theatre

33 22 86 86, www.londontoast.dk.
The enormously successful LTT was established in
1982 by British actress, writer and director Vivienne
McKee and her Danish husband Søren Hall. Its eclectic English-language repertoire spans everything
from the moderns and Shakespeare to stand-up com-
edy and murder mysteries. Its lighthearted
Christmas cabarets have become a fixture of the
Tivoli Christmas season.

Dance

The Royal Danish Theatre's dance monopoly
was broken in 1979 with the foundation of the
Patterson independent dance group. In 1981,
Patterson changed its name to Nyt Dansk Danse

ARTS & ENTERTAINMENT

Teater (New Danish Dance Theatre). A year later, American dancer and choreographer Warren Spears joined the company and began a tradition of inviting choreographers and dancers from abroad, which has since become the lifeblood of contemporary Danish dance. Brit Tim Rushton took over as artistic director in 2001, shortening the company name to **Dansk Danseteater** (Danish Dance Theatre) and helping to popularise contemporary dance with lavish multimedia productions such as *Requiem*.

Dansescenen remains the city's sole venue entirely dedicated to modern dance, while the **Royal Danish Ballet** (based at the Royal Theatre) is recognised as one of the world's top five ballet companies.

VENUES

Bellevue Teatret
Strandvejen 451, Klampenborg (39 63 64 00, www.bellevueteatret.dk). Bus 14, 85N, 185, 388 **Box office** 4-7pm Mon-Fri.
Since 2003, the seafront Bellevue Theatre – designed by Arne Jacobsen – has broadened its appeal by collaborating with Copenhagen International Ballet to produce the famous Summer Ballet under the careful direction of choreographer Alexander Kølpin.

★ Dansescenen
Pasteursvej 20, Vesterbro (33 29 10 10, box office 33 29 10 29, www.dansescenen.dk). Bus 18, 26. **Box Office** 1-3pm daily & 1hr before performances. **Map** p245 S6.
The heart of the city's dance milieu, Dansescenen puts on more than 130 performances a year, including an annual competition for young choreographers, Dansolution, where the audience get to vote for their favourite. Dansescenen also organises

Dansescenen.

development programmes for young artists, and its Junior Company regularly performs at youth festivals. It is now based in the old Carlsberg factory.

★ Det Kongelige Teater, Gamle Scene (Royal Danish Theatre, Old Stage)
Kongens Nytorv, Indre By (box office 33 69 69 69, www.kgl-teater.dk). Metro Kongens Nytorv, or bus 11A, 29. **Box office** 2-6pm Mon-Sat. **Map** p252 N16.
This 1872 neo-Renaissance building for the Royal Danish Theatre was designed by Vilhelm Dahlerup and Ove Petersen, with its 'new stage' – connected via an archway – added in 1931. The building was something of a second home for Hans Christian Andersen. It's now used mainly for traditional ballet performances. For a full review, *see p174* **A Three-Act Structure**.

Tivolis Koncertsal
Tivoli, Vesterbrogade 3 (information 33 15 10 01, www.tivoli.dk). Train København H. **Box office** 9am-5pm daily. **Map** p250 P12.
Tivoli's concert hall (*see also p51*) hosts some of the biggest international dance companies, including the New York City Ballet. The Plænen open-air stage holds many international events, while the Pantomime Theatre is a favourite for kids' shows.

COMPANIES

Åben Dans Productions
35 82 06 10, www.aabendans.dk.
Åben Dans (Open Dance) is one of the most well-toured modern dance companies in Denmark. The majority of performances are accompanied by lectures, workshops and audience debates.

Danish Dance Theatre
35 39 87 87, www.danskdanseteater.dk.
Over the course of its 25-year history, Danish Dance Theatre has redefined modern dance and experimental ballet in Denmark with its high-quality productions. As artistic director, Tim Rushton, continues to take this incredibly prolific company from strength to strength.

Royal Danish Ballet
www.kglteater.dk.
The artistic director of the Royal Danish Ballet is currently Nikolaj Hübbe, previously principal dancer of the New York City Ballet. Most productions are performed at the Old Stage of the Royal Danish Theatre (*see above*).

(Stilleben)
52 41 00 41, www.anderschristiansen.dk.
Anders Christiansen, the artistic director and choreographer of (Stilleben) (Still Life) has achieved cult status in the Copenhagen dance world with his deeply poetic, trance-like performances.

ARTS & ENTERTAINMENT

Escapes & Excursions

Day Trips

Known variously as the 'Danish Riviera' or the 'Beverly Hills' of Copenhagen (this is where most of the showbiz stars reside), the road that leads north along the coast from the capital is flanked by some of the most expensive housing in the country. But there are also several interesting attractions for visitors. Chief among them is the stunning modern art museum, Louisiana Museum for Moderne Kunst. There's also the beautiful home of Karen 'Out of Africa' Blixen and, slightly further north, Hamlet's hometown, Helsingør, with its indomitable castle and new National Maritime Museum. Over to the western part of North Sjælland, in the town of Hillerød, is another of Denmark's important castles: Frederiksborg Slot (not to be confused with Frederiksberg Slot in Copenhagen) is a majestic early 17th-century Dutch Renaissance red-brick castle, with elegant Baroque gardens.

Klampenborg beach.

THE DANISH RIVIERA

The Riviera begins at **Charlottenlund**, with its pleasant beach and camping area. Next is **Klampenborg** with another popular beach, **Bellevue Beach**, as well as the **Bakken** amusement park, which is on the edge of a 1,000-hectare (2,470-acre) former royal hunting ground. Now a rather more serene deer park, **Dyrehaven** dates from 1231 and is to Copenhageners what Richmond Park is to Londoners. The park is closed to traffic; all the better for its large herds of free-roaming deer and the many walkers who come here from the city. Expensive horse-drawn carriage rides are also available. In its grounds is an enigmatic former hunting lodge, Eremitagen, which has wonderful views to the sea (but is not open to the public). Nearby is **Klampenborg Galopbane** (39 96 02 13, www.galopbane.dk), a horse-racing and trotting course.

Dyrehaven, Bakken and Bellevue Beach are within easy walking distance of Klampenborg Station, which is just 18 minutes by train from Copenhagen.

ESCAPES & EXCURSIONS

The next major point of interest along the coast is **Rungstedlund**, the former home of the Danish novelist Karen Blixen, now the site of the **Karen Blixen Museet**. The internationally acclaimed author spent much of her life in Rungstedlund (except for 17 years in Kenya) and is buried in the gardens of the house, at the foot of Ewald's hill, beneath a large beech tree.

The house was also once the residence of another eminent Danish writer, Johannes Ewald (1743-81). He lived here in 1773 and wrote several of his lyric poems and heroic tragedies in verse in the same room in which Blixen also chose to write. Rungstedlund is about ten minutes' walk from the nearest railway station, Rungsted Kyst. Alternatively, catch a train to Klampenborg and take bus 388.

Between Rungstedlund and Helsingør are several more small harbours, but the main attraction is the **Louisiana Museum for Moderne Kunst** (Louisiana Museum of Modern Art). There may be larger modern-art collections in the world, but none is located in more blissful surroundings than Louisiana.

An additional 15 minutes north on the train brings you to **Helsingør** (often written as Elsinore in English-language publications). This port town is a popular day-trip destination

for Swedes, being just a 20-minute ferry ride from Sweden's Helsingborg; many come here for the cheap(er) alcohol, and as such it has a slightly downtrodden atmosphere, with booze shops aplenty, though its half-timbered houses and old cobblestone streets help to redress the balance. Many visitors, however, see little of the town itself, heading straight for **Kronborg Slot** – a 15-minute walk from the station, along the coast – and the new subterranean **Museet for Søfart** (M/S), the National Maritime Museum of Denmark, right in front of it.

Sights & Museums

Bakken

Dyrehavesbakken, Dyrehavevej 62, Klampenborg (39 63 35 44, www.bakken.dk). Train Klampenborg. **Open** *Last Thur in Mar-last Sun in Aug* times

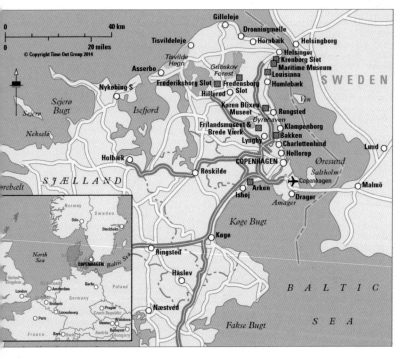

ESCAPES & EXCURSIONS

Louisiana Museum for Moderne Kunst.

vary, but usually noon/2pm-10pm/11pm/midnight daily. **Admission** free. *Rides* (wristband) 249kr; 179kr reductions; reduced prices Wed.

Tivoli may be Denmark's most famous amusement park, but Dyrehavesbakken (known as Bakken for short) is equally popular with Danes. Founded in 1583, it claims to be the oldest amusement park in the world. It's usually regarded as Tivoli's down-market cousin and has more of a funfair/beer-hall atmosphere, but that doesn't mean less enjoyment. There are 100 or so rides (which tend to be cheaper than Tivoli's), as well as 35 cafés and restaurants. Admission to the park is free.

Karen Blixen Museet

*Rungstedlund, Rungsted Strandvej 111, Rungsted (45 57 10 57, www.karen-blixen.dk). Train Rungsted Kyst. **Open** May-Sept 10am-5pm Tue-Sun. Oct-Apr noon-4pm Wed-Fri; 11am-4pm Sat, Sun. **Admission** 60kr; free under-14s.*

This simple, early 19th-century house is set in 16 hectares (40 acres) of gardens that double as a bird sanctuary. The north wing has been preserved as if Blixen had just left, with her furniture, paintings and even her distinctive flower arrangements as they were when she lived here. There's also a gallery of Blixen's drawings and paintings, and a biographical exhibition, library and small cinema upstairs.

Kronborg Slot

*Kronborg 2C, Helsingør (49 21 30 78, www.kronborg.dk). Train Helsingør. **Open** June-Aug 10am-5.30pm daily. Apr, May, Sept, Oct 11am-4pm daily. Nov-Mar 11am-4pm*

Tue-Sun. **Admission** 40kr-80kr; 30kr-35kr 4-17s. Combined ticket with Museet for Søfart 150kr.

Better known as 'Hamlet's Castle' or 'Shakespeare's Castle', this waterside Renaissance fortress – a UNESCO World Heritage Site since 2000 – has, over the centuries, served as a royal residence, a garrison, a tollbooth, a prison and a museum. It was constructed on the orders of Frederik II between 1574 and 1585, though the foundations date from a 1420s fortress built by one Eric of Pomerania. A fire in 1629 destroyed much of the structure, but Christian IV had the exterior reconstructed to the same design (the interior changed radically, with more baroque touches). Shakespeare's famous play, *The Tragedy of Hamlet, Prince of Denmark*, was first performed in Kronborg in 1816 to mark the 200th anniversary of the Bard's death; it has been performed at the castle many times since, with acting legends Laurence Olivier, John Gielgud, Richard Burton and Derek Jacobi all taking to the courtyard stage here, as well as, in 2009, Jude Law.

You can view the (rather plain) Royal Apartments for an insight into Denmark's regal history, though a walk around the (often foggy) grounds is the most atmospheric part of a visit here; better still, try to come in August during the Shakespeare at Kronborg festival (www.hamletscenen.dk).

★ Louisiana Museum for Moderne Kunst

*Gammel Strandvej 13, Humlebæk (49 19 07 19, www.louisiana.dk). Train Humlebæk. **Open** 11am-10pm Tue-Fri; 11am-6pm Sat, Sun. **Admission** 110kr; 95kr reductions; free under-18s.*

Founded in 1958 by the industrialist and art collector Knud Jensen, Louisiana contains more than 3,500 works (mainly painting and sculpture) dating from 1945 to the present. It began life as a purely Scandinavian affair – the first purchases were of works by Danish artists including Asger Jorn, Richard Mortensen and Robert Jacobsen – but the collection soon grew to encompass Auguste Herbin, Josef Albers, Naum Gabo and Alexander Calder; later, works by Dubuffet, Bacon and Rothko were added. Paintings by Picasso from several periods are among the highlights, while the 1960s Pop Art movement is well represented with pieces by Warhol, Lichtenstein, Oldenburg and Rauschenberg. The collection of 1970s German art is also strong. Louisiana is also famed for its dynamic temporary exhibitions and superstar retrospectives (Paul Klee, Ai Weiwei and Olafur Eliasson have all featured in recent years).

The existing 19th-century villa (called Louisiana after the original owner's three wives, who bizarrely were all named Louise) has been added to over the years, and the resulting, much enlarged, complex is characterised by a vaguely Japanese style. The whitewashed rooms with their large windows blur the divide between the indoor galleries and the outdoor sculpture park, creating a harmony between the buildings and their environment that counterbalances the frequently challenging nature of the works on display. And the light is wonderful too.

The south wing was added in 1982, with a corridor (now hung with Mortensen's colourful geometric paintings) connecting it to the old building. A subterranean wing opened in 1991. In the garden, you'll find sculptures by Calder, Henry Moore, Joan Miró,

Max Ernst and Giacometti, among others. Children get their own wing, Bornehuset, with special workshops and activities. Lectures, film screenings and concerts are also held regularly.

After you've had your fill of art, head to the superb café for a *smørrebrod*, beautiful views overlooking the Øresund, a terrace graced by one of Calder's sculptures and a log fire in winter. The large shop sells items from some of Denmark's best designers.

★ Museet for Søfart (National Maritime Museum of Denmark)

Ny Kronborgvej 1, Helsingør (49 21 06 85, www.mfs.dk). Train Helsingør. **Open** *July, Aug* 10am-5pm daily. *Sept-June* 11am-5pm Tue-Sun. **Admission** 110kr; 90kr reductions; free under-18s. Combined ticket with Kronborg Slot 150kr. *See p184* **In Ship Shape**.

Restaurants

Close to Bellevue Beach and Klampenborg Station is the superb, Michelin-starred **Den Gule Cottage** (*see p148*).

Getting There

By train

There are trains at least every 20mins heading north along the coast from Copenhagen Central Station via Nørreport. It takes 18mins to get to Klampenborg, 30mins to Rungsted Kyst, 41mins to Humlebæk and 56mins to Helsingør. For Louisiana, the cheapest option is a combined train/museum ticket for 200kr.

IN SHIP SHAPE

Denmark's boat-shaped maritime museum sits within Helsingør's dry docks.

How do you physically translate the idea of a nation's maritime history and attract visitors to it while remaining invisible? This was the challenge facing renowned architecture practice BIG in building a brand-new **National Maritime Museum of Denmark** (*see p183*) in Helsingør. Because Helsingør is the home of Kronborg Slot (*see p182*) – better known as Hamlet's castle – the new museum had to have a strong physical presence so as to attract visitors, while not obscuring views of this most famous of literary sites.

Taking an innovative approach, BIG – led by the current darling of Danish architecture, Bjarke Ingels – cleverly devised a space built around Helsingør's 60-year-old dock walls, creating an underground ship-shaped museum that is eight metres (26 feet) below sea level but filled with light. Ramped zigzagging bridges and gently sloping floors add a universal aspect of sailing to a dynamic museum whose themes include numerous aspects of life on the rolling seas.

The museum, which opened in autumn 2013, is so absorbing that it will engage most visitors – even those whose interest in maritime history is minimal. From three massive double-level steel bridges that unite the old and new elements of the site to benches based on ship's bollards and a hidden message based on Morse code, it's a site (and sight) that's well worth the

visit, and can also be combined with a trip to the nearby Louisiana Museum of Modern Art (*see p182*).

To come to Denmark and miss out on the country's maritime past, displayed in a continuous motion around the dock and via a mix of exhibits and artefacts, interactive installations and audiovisual material that plays with the fabric of the building, would be a shame. Especially so, as it intertwines big themes such as navigation, war and trade with smaller, more human aspects of maritime life – tattoos and dockers' lives, for example. It all adds up to an absorbing look at man's universal desire for exploration and discovery, and at where it's taken us.

Frederiksborg Slot.

NORTH ZEALAND

If you find yourself in Copenhagen for more than a few days and fancy a breath of old-fashioned seaside air, then a trip to the northern coast of Zealand (called Sjælland, locally) – with its time-warp fishing villages such as Hornbæk, Gilleleje and Tisvildeleje and glorious dune- and forest-backed beaches – could be just the ticket. Many Copenhageners have summer houses in the area, and much of the city decamps to the beach from late June to the end of July, so it can get crowded then, although there are plenty of campsites and holiday homes if you want to stay a night or two.

On your way to the coast – about an hour's drive from Copenhagen, a little longer if you take the train – stop off at one of Denmark's most important castles, **Frederiksborg Slot**.

Sights & Museums

Frederiksborg Slot

Hillerød (48 26 04 39, www.dnm.dk). Train Hillerød. **Open** *Apr-Oct* 10am-5pm daily. *Nov-Mar* 11am-3pm daily. **Admission** 75kr; 20kr-60kr reductions.

This early 17th-century Dutch Renaissance red-brick castle, with ornate spires and sandstone façade, stands on three small islands in Slotsø (Castle Lake), in the middle of the town of Hillerød. The castle is complemented by impressive baroque gardens and an English-style garden with its Bath House. The castle was gutted by fire in 1859 and for a while it looked as if it would remain a ruin. Fortunately, JC Jacobsen volunteered to use some of his considerable Carlsberg Brewery wealth to restore the castle, and

subsequently helped found Det Nationalhistoriske Museum (Museum of National History) within 70 or so of its rooms. Opened in 1882, the museum charts Denmark's history through paintings arranged in chronological order. One of the decorative highlights of Frederiksborg is its chapel, which was used for the coronations of Denmark's monarchs between 1671 and 1840. Since 1693, it's also been the chapel for Danish knights, whose shields hang on the walls; remarkably, it's also the local parish church. The altar and pulpit are the work of the Hamburg goldsmith Jakob Mores, while the priceless Compenius organ, dating from 1610 and boasting 1,000 pipes, is played every Thursday between 1.30pm and 2pm. It's worth timing a visit to hear it.

Restaurants

Restaurant Søstrene Olsen

Øresundvej 10, Hornbæk (49 70 05 50, www. sostreneolsen.dk). **Open** *Mar-Oct* noon-9pm daily. Closed Nov-Feb. **Main courses** 285kr-325kr. **Set meal** 495kr/4 courses.

The setting – a pretty thatched cottage overlooking the beach – couldn't be better, and the Danish food is just as inspiring, with seafood a speciality.

Getting There

By train

To get to Hornbæk and Dronningmølle, catch a train from Copenhagen Central Station and change at Helsingør (about 1hr 30mins in total, 1 train an hour). To reach Gilleleje or Tisvildeleje, take the S-train (S-tog) from Central Station and change at Hillerød (1hr 20mins in total, around 2 trains an hour).

CROSSING THE BRIDGE

It's just a short hop across the sea to Malmö, in Sweden.

Øresund Bridge.

Copenhagen has more than enough sights to occupy you for at least a long weekend, but another city – smaller but equally scintillating – lies just 30 minutes away by train (from Copenhagen Central Station) or car. It happens to be in another country and across a sea, but **Malmö** – Sweden's third-largest city – is worth the short trip via the spectacular Øresund Bridge.

Malmö's unusually cosmopolitan population includes some 15,000 university students, who give the city a vibrant energy. The place is particularly appealing during the summer, when its long sandy beach (a short

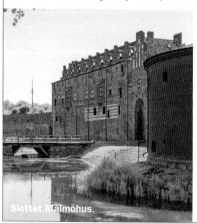

Slottet Malmöhus.

walk west from the city centre) and beautiful parks really come into their own, and when its historic heart, centred around the lovely cobbled square of **Lilla Torg**, comes alive – especially at night. The city has a thriving nightlife scene all year round, however; there are plenty of restaurants and bars on Lilla Torg and on **Södergatan** – the pedestrianised street that connects the Stortorget and Gustav Adolfs Torg squares. But if you want something a bit more memorable, head over to multicultural **Möllevången**, home to two well-established bar-restaurants favoured by the arty set: **Metro** (Ängelholmsgatan 14, 040 23 00 63, www.metropamollan.se), with a fusion menu and DJs on weekends, and **Grand Öl & Mat** (Monbijougatan 17, 040 12 63 13, www.grandolomat.se), a superb lunch and dinner spot with a stylish bar, set in an industrial complex.

Other highlights of Malmö include its atmospheric castle, **Slottet Malmöhus** (Malmöhusvägen, 040 34 44 37, www. malmo.se/museer), which is home to some top-notch museums, including art museum **Malmö Konstmuseum**, and **Stadsmuseet**, the city history museum; its two-kilometre, man-made, sandy beach, Ribersborgsstranden (known as **Ribban**); and some good shops – on Södergatan as well as around **Gamla Väster**, the old town.

If you're heading to the beach, and want an authentically Swedish experience, a visit

to the **Ribersborgs Kallbadhus**
(Ribersborgs Cold Bath House; 040 26 03
66, www.ribersborgskallbadhus.se, 55kr) is
well worth a gamble. This charming wooden
bathhouse, dating from 1898, is at the end
of a short pier on the beach's eastern end
and has segregated open-air deck areas
(men to the left, women to the right) with
modern saunas and bracing sea-water
plunge baths. It goes without saying that
nudity is the norm here. If you like the
retro feel of this, then you'll also like
nearby **Fiskehoddorna**, a row of pretty
wooden huts where local fishermen still
sell their fresh catches every morning
(except Sunday and Monday).

The most recent addition to the city has
been in the Western Harbour area. This was
once one of the most important dockyards
in Europe, but the decline of industry in the
1980s threatened the city's entire economy.
In recent years, however, a radical housing
project, **Bo01**, has sprung up beside the
sea, and won architectural plaudits from
around the globe. The restaurants, harbour
bathing deck, promenades, leisure facilities
and shops here are now a major attraction.
And at the centre of it all is the astonishing
Turning Tower apartment block, designed

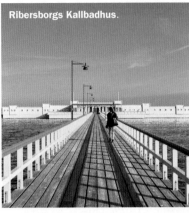

Ribersborgs Kallbadhus.

by Spanish architect Santiago Calatrava.
Completed in 2005, the 54-storey tower is
the tallest building in Sweden and renowned
for its extraordinary external steel 'spine'.

*For more information, contact Malmö Tourist
Office (Börshuset, Skeppsbron 2, 040 34
12 00, www.malmotown.com), located near
Malmö Central Station and the harbour.*

Turning Tower.

ESCAPES & EXCURSIONS

In Context

History

From humble fishing village to 'Barcelona of the north'.

Copenhagen has not always been the capital of Denmark. In fact, it didn't take over as the royal seat until the early 15th century and, up until that point, was a comparatively humble fishing village and place of defence against marauding pirates and Swedes. However, it grew in strength throughout the Middle Ages to become one of the wealthiest cities in northern Europe, a political powerhouse and cultural centre of great importance. At the peak of its glory, Copenhagen was ruled by one of the most fascinating and reckless of Renaissance kings, whose ambition and follies would eventually bring the country to its knees in the 17th century.

But despite being set back by plague, city fires and hardship at various points over the next 200 years, Copenhagen re-emerged in the 19th century as a centre of culture, its 'golden age' producing writers and artists such as Hans Christian Andersen and Bertel Thorvaldsen, who would go on to become world-famous, helping to create a new Danish identity.

Denmark's 'Sun King', Christian IV.

Evidence of human life in Denmark exists from 80,000 years ago in the form of discarded animal bones. But while the rest of Denmark busied itself with reindeer hunting, flint mining, the Bronze Age, the Viking Age, and the repelling of Charlemagne's advance on the southern border of Jylland (c800), Havn (Harbour), as Copenhagen was known, was little more than an insignificant trading centre for the copious quantities of herring that inhabited the Øresund. It was said that this pungent, oily fish – still a staple of the Danish diet – was so common in these waters (which connect the Baltic with the North Sea) that fishermen could scoop them into their boats with their bare hands.

THE VIKINGS

The Vikings, who swept across northern Europe from southern Sweden around 800, established the first Danish state and then rapidly expanded it by invading three of the four Anglo-Saxon kingdoms, as well as Norway. The Vikings (meaning 'sea robbers') even took Seville in 844 and stormed Paris in the 880s. The subsequent retaking by the nascent Danes of Skåne (or Scania, now southern Sweden, directly opposite Copenhagen) was to be the catalyst for

the voracious expansion of Copenhagen 300 years hence, but at the time the villagers probably remained oblivious to their strategic potential. It is likely too that they remained unruffled by the conversion of the unifying Viking king, Harald I, Bluetooth – and eventually the entire country – to Christianity by a German missionary named Poppo around 965. Harald was mysteriously killed while relieving himself in the woods in 987, and many of his successors over the next 170 years met with a similarly murky fate.

GROWING PAINS

In the 12th century, numerous churches blossomed on what was still an unappealing, boggy stretch of coast, among them Vor Frue Kirke (later the site of Copenhagen's current cathedral), and Sankt Petri Kirke (also still a site of worship). In 1238, an abbey of Franciscan Grey Friars was founded; its church (Helligåndskirken) still sits on Strøget, modern-day Copenhagen's main shopping street.

In the late 12th and early 13th centuries, King Valdemar and his sons Knud (Canute) VI and Valdemar II, the Victorious, reigned over a triumphant and expansionist Denmark, which not only conquered the Baltic Wends, but devoured Estonia and Holstein, and

'The Vikings, who swept across northern Europe around 800, established the first Danish state.'

lorded it over Lübeck. This era ended ignominiously with the loss of these Baltic territories in 1227. The second spurt of Copenhagen's growth occurred when Erik VII seized control of the town from the Church in 1417. Not only was the king now in charge, but he had become so fond of Copenhagen that he made it his home. This historic move ended the peripatetic tradition of Denmark's monarchy – wherever it laid its crown was its home.

In 1448, Christian I was crowned King of Denmark, Sweden and Norway in the first royal coronation to be held in Copenhagen. Inevitably, the city now became the economic, political and cultural focus for the nation. By 1500, the town revelled in riches as its guilds dominated those of the Hanseatic League, while the king too grew wealthy from the new tolls demanded of all who sailed from the North Sea through the narrow strait between Helsingør and southern Sweden on their way to the Baltic. There was no doubt that this was now Denmark's capital, and its leading citizens ruled via the Rigsråd (National Assembly), made up of clergy, prominent estate owners and the king. The Machiavellian Christian II, meanwhile, was politically astute enough to marry a sister of Holy Roman Emperor Charles V. However, he had a tendency to recklessness and was replaced, in 1522, by his uncle, who reigned as Frederik I.

CIVIL WAR AND REFORMATION

During Frederik's rule, several popular uprisings – with Copenhagen as a particular hotbed – tried, unsuccessfully, to unseat the monarch and replace him with his exiled nephew, the pro-Lutheran Christian II. When Christian did finally return to Denmark, in 1532, it was as a prisoner to a country ruled entirely by Frederik.

Upon Frederik's death in 1533, the Catholic prelates intervened to postpone the accession of Frederik's son, Christian III, who also had Lutheran tendencies. However, unforeseen by the prelates, the Danish people were as keen on reformation (and the consequent redistribution of clerical property) as the rest of northern Europe, and they wanted Christian II back in power. His supporters in Copenhagen, both peasants and more prosperous townspeople, seized control of the town. Additional support from the German Lübeckers was to provoke one of the most damaging tiffs in Copenhagen's history: the Grevens Fejde (Counts' Feud) of 1534-1536, Denmark's last civil war. The Germans' meddling and the accompanying peasants' revolt so concerned the bishops that they finally relented and allowed Christian III to take the throne and suppress Copenhagen. His coronation charter did, however, include the handing over of power to the aristocracy of the Rigsråd from the Crown. (Christian II, meanwhile, spent the rest of his life imprisoned in Sønderborg Castle, where he died in 1559.)

As things turned out, the bishops were to lose power anyway, as, in order to pay his own German mercenaries (without whom he would never have retaken Copenhagen), Christian III was forced to liquidate many of the Church's assets. As the final stroke of a coup that heralded the Danish Reformation of 1536, Christian III imprisoned the bishops.

In a display of the consensual diplomacy that still typifies Denmark's political machinations, Christian III offered the bishops the 'get-out' of conversion to Lutheranism, with the added sweetener that under the new doctrine they could marry and have children. Nearly all accepted. Lutheranism was now the official state religion of Denmark; Copenhagen celebrated with extravagant festivities. The nobility benefited hugely from the transfer of money from the Church to their all-too-eager hands, not to mention exemption from taxes. Across Denmark, and especially in Copenhagen, this wealth was made manifest in grand Renaissance mansions.

THE SUN KING

Into this brave new world of wealth, expansion and optimism was born one of the great figures of Danish history. Christian IV,

Denmark's 'Sun King', was a man possessed of heroic appetites. He ruled for 60 years (1588-1648), and is probably the nation's best-remembered monarch. He was a complex, highly educated man with interests in music, architecture and foreign affairs. He married Anna Catherine of Brandenburg; after she died in 1612, he went on to father 24 children, half of them out of wedlock by a variety of mistresses.

It's hard to know where to begin in detailing the transformation that Copenhagen underwent during his reign. The city grew in all directions in the grandest of styles, with new buildings; a remodelling of its coastal access; improved defences and housing; the construction of entire new districts, bridges, churches, palaces, towers, observatories and theatres; and all the glittering hallmarks of the Renaissance. Upon his death, however, Copenhagen and Denmark would be a spent force, bankrupt, defeated, humiliated and seemingly doomed to an existence of debt and suppression by its enemies.

The problem was that the many ambitious construction projects undertaken during his rule were becoming a burden on the country's finances. When Christian came to the throne, Copenhagen had little industry to speak of. But, though he tried his best to establish industry in the capital, its wheeler-dealer trading heritage always seemed to undermine the fruitful work ethic that had developed. Copenhagen's products could never match the quality of those made by the best European craftsmen, which was a source of constant frustration and embarrassment to the king.

Christian's first priority was to cement Copenhagen's position as the major harbour of the region and, with this in mind, the channel between Sjælland and the small nearby island of Slotsholmen was straightened, narrowed and reinforced with wharfs. Slotsholmen was extended and, as the 16th century closed, a new armoury (Tøjhuset) and a new supply depot (Provianthuset) were constructed to maintain the fighting readiness of the navy. Further symbols of Christian's reign are found in the expanded palaces, prime among them the Rosenborg Slot (Rosenborg Castle). But the most extraordinary of his creations is the Rundetårn (Round Tower), an observatory graced by a stepless spiral ramp.

Copenhagen-based international trading companies attempted to establish colonies in Africa and Asia, but they were as fleas on the shoulders of comparable Dutch and British enterprises. Instead, to raise money, Christian attempted to turn Copenhagen into the financial capital of Europe by ordering the construction of Børsen (Stock Exchange), but despite the building's unquestionable architectural and decorative splendour that too was a damp squib.

In 1523, Gustavus I of Sweden finally dissolved the Kalmar Union, which had unified the domestic and foreign policies of Denmark, Sweden and Norway (though the union of Denmark and Norway lasted until 1814). During Christian's reign, the increasing strength and confidence of Denmark's northerly neighbour were to threaten the very existence

'Christian IV, Denmark's 'Sun King', was a man possessed of heroic appetites.'

of the Danish state. At stake was control over access to the Baltic, which usually meant control of the region itself. In 1611, in a bid to protect the vital income he received from the Sound tolls (extorted at Helsingør Castle, the model for Shakespeare's Elsinore, north of Copenhagen), and to restore the Kalmar Union, Christian declared war on Sweden. The Kalmar War raged, with Denmark generally dominant, until 1613, when a peace accord brokered by the British concluded with a large ransom being paid by the Swedes to Denmark.

Danish triumphalism was short-lived, however, as Christian and his forces soon became embroiled in the Thirty Years War, in an effort to protect Danish interests on the north coast of Germany from Swedish expansion. The Danes' involvement in the war ended with a devastating defeat by the Swedes at the Battle of Lutter-am-Barenburg in 1626. The Danes got off more lightly than they deserved in the final peace settlement at

Bombardment of Copenhagen. *See p197.*

Lübeck in 1629, in which Christian had to promise to take no further part in the war.

Christian's reign was to be marked by a third fateful conflict, Torstensson's War (1643-1645). It was during this war that the 67-year-old Christian lost his right eye and received 23 shrapnel wounds (his blood-stained clothes are displayed in Rosenborg Slot). A much heftier defeat by united Dutch and Swedish forces ended the war, and a peace treaty signed in 1645 saw Denmark cede large areas of territory (chiefly, central parts of Norway, Halland and the islands of Gotland and Osel) to Sweden, and waive future Sound tolls. This was a dramatic and humiliating moment in Danish history. Thirty years followed in which Denmark barely survived as an independent state.

Christian didn't live to see his nation's darkest moment, however. He'd already been dead ten years when his successor, his second son, Frederik III, Prince Bishop of Bremen (who'd taken the throne after his elder brother drank himself to death), started another Swedish-Danish war in 1658. The Swedes then forced the Danes to accept the humiliating Treaty of Roskilde, by which

Denmark ceded Scania. Not content, King Karl Gustav of Sweden decided he wanted to take the whole of Denmark, and besieged Copenhagen in the winter of 1658-1659. He led his German troops across the frozen sea surrounding Slotsholmen, but, in a last gasp of defiance, Frederik himself is said to have led the fight against Karl Gustav's army. This spirited defence, with cannon shot, bullets, boiling tar and water to melt the ice, gave time for a Dutch army to arrive and save the capital.

The fortuitous sudden death of Karl Gustav at the start of 1660 ended Sweden's ambition to conquer Denmark, but the price of the country's salvation was steep – Frederik was forced to capitulate control of the Sound (and its tolls), as well as all of Denmark's provinces to the east. Europe would never again allow Denmark, now a third of its former size, to hold power in the region.

Once again Copenhagen picked itself up to rebuild and refortify, with the construction of a new rampart to protect Slotsholmen. Out of this came the new quarter of Frederiksholm. The impressive Kongens Nytorv square was laid out in 1670 and was soon surrounded with imposing Baroque houses and abutted by Nyhavn Canal – today one of the city's major tourist draws. An improved water supply, a company of watchmen and new street lighting complemented a fast-growing, modern capital whose population had doubled within 100 years to 60,000 by the early 18th century.

FIRE AND RENEWAL

In 1711, during the reign of Frederik IV, Copenhagen was ravaged by plague in which 23,000 people died. It was also razed by fire twice during the century (in 1728 and 1795). The first fire broke out in a candle-maker's in Nørreport, and strong winds, negligible water supplies and general chaos ensured it travelled swiftly across town, destroying 1,700 houses, the town hall and the university, and leaving 12,000 people homeless. Happily, the building of the new five- and six-storey townhouses, taller than any built before, and the grand public buildings that replaced the combustible low-rise wooden constructions of the 17th

century, were strictly monitored by the building codes of the time, with the result that the capital was reborn more splendidly than ever before. The royal castle was also completely demolished and vast amounts of money were spent replacing it with the Baroque Christiansborg Slot, only for the second fire to return it to the ground.

To celebrate the 300th anniversary of the House of Oldenburg, headed since 1746 by Frederik V, work began in 1749 on a grand new quarter, Frederiksstaden. It was designed by the architect Nicolai Eigtved with wide, straight streets fronted by elegant, light, rococo palaces. At the heart of the new area was Amalienborg Plads, circled by four palaces that were financed by the noblemen of the town. When another fire at Christiansborg levelled a large part of the palace, the royal family found themselves homeless. They commandeered the four Amalienborg palaces, employing CF Harsdorff to connect them with an elegant colonnade, and have lived there ever since.

The Copenhagen Fire, 5 June 1795.

The second, larger fire of the century broke out on Gammelholm in 1795 and was even more destructive than the first, but again this only gave the city's architects and builders the chance to keep up with the fashion for the neoclassical. In 1771, Kongens Have (King's Gardens) opened. This new attraction was a huge success with the flourishing bourgeoisie. One of those less likely to participate fully in the educational revolution was the new king, Christian VII (1766-1808), who managed to rule for 42 years despite frequent and prolonged bouts of insanity.

In 1784, the 16-year-old crown prince Frederik, later Frederik VI, took power and acted as regent until the death of his father (the frequently insane Christian VII) in 1808. By 1801 he probably wished he hadn't, as the first of two bombardments by the British navy took place; Denmark, against its better nature, soon became drawn into the Napoleonic Wars with subsequent losses of territory and power.

During the 18th century, Denmark's neutrality proved increasingly irksome to the British. To protect itself from increased interference by the British navy, the Danes entered into an armed neutrality pact with Russia and its old foe Sweden. As a result, in April 1801, a British fleet under admirals Nelson and Parker sailed into the Øresund and began bombardment of the Danish navy. However, Denmark continued to profit from the trade that had so angered the British, and anti-British fervour swept Copenhagen. That anger would be fuelled six years later when the British, under the Duke of Wellington, returned with a show of force that made the 1801 battle seem a mere fireworks display.

Napoleon was on the move across Europe and, with his fleet already destroyed by Nelson at Trafalgar, there were strong rumours in 1807 that the French were about to commandeer the Danish navy as a replacement. In fact, Frederik was preparing to defend his country from attack by the French in the south when he was visited by a British envoy, who offered him this ultimatum: surrender the Danish fleet to Britain, or the Royal Navy will come and take it. The Danes refused, and so the British sailed again on still-neutral Copenhagen and bombarded it for three days.

Hans Christian Andersen. *See p201.*

Understandably, the Danes then baulked at an alliance with the British, siding instead with Napoleon. It was a decision they were to rue in the painful years ahead when the British blockaded Denmark and Norway. Much of Norway starved, while Denmark fared little better, enduring great hardship until the defeat of Napoleon. The Treaty of Kiel (1814) saw Sweden (now in alliance with Britain) take control of Norway, which had been for 450 years as much a part of Denmark as Sjælland. A period of introspection, from which many say Denmark has never really emerged, followed, typified by the slogan: 'We will gain internally what was lost externally.' In fact, despite a nationwide drive to grow new oak trees with which to rebuild the navy (many of which still flourish in the countryside), Denmark would not officially go to war again until its troops took part in a UN peacekeeping exercise in Bosnia in April 1994.

DANISH IDENTITY TO THE FORE

Fortunately, this was to be a period of cultural growth for a country struggling to come to terms with a new identity based on little more than a shared language and religion. With all hope of playing a role on the international stage gone, and with little financial power to wield either (Denmark as a state was declared bankrupt in 1813 and sold its colonies in Africa and India), the

BLAST FROM THE PAST

Copenhagen's medieval churches, baroque palaces and civic monuments.

BIRTH OF THE CITY 1167-1588

Slotsholmen is where Copenhagen was born. There was said to be a fishing village on the site for hundreds of years before King Valdemar I the Great gave the district to his blood brother **Bishop Absalon**. The ruins of Absalon's 12th-century castle were uncovered beneath the Christiansborg Slot and can be visited in the Ruinerne Under Christiansborg. During the Middle Ages, the town spread out from Slotsholmen towards present-day Rådhuspladsen. The oldest standing building in Copenhagen is **Helligåndskirken** (Church of the Holy Spirit) on Strøget. The city's only surviving medieval building, the church complex includes the remains of a late 13th-century convent and the late Gothic Helligåndhus (House of the Holy Spirit), dating from the 15th century.

CHRISTIAN IV 1588-1648

Christian IV was the first king to play a major role in the planning of Copenhagen. His grand scheme was to double the size of the city. **Rosenborg Slot**, at the northern corner of the old city, and **Kastellet** (Castle, 1662-64), along the coast, would be the two main edifices of this new area. The earliest substantial work of Christian's reign was the transformation (1599-1605) of Slotsholmen: he built a naval yard, supply depot (Provianthuset), and arsenal (Tøjhus). The last still stands and is now the Tøjhusmuseet. To house the new naval yard workers, the king embarked on another major project (starting in 1617): Christianshavn. A number of residences in this Amsterdam-like district survive, notably on **Sankt Annæ Gade** (nos.28, 30 and 32, dating from 1640).

This most ambitious of Denmark's kings was also responsible for several of Copenhagen's most distinctive individual buildings. The long, low **Børsen** (Old Stock Exchange, 1619-24) is one of Copenhagen's most beautiful structures. The king indulged himself most fully in the building of the **Rosenborg Slot** (Rosenborg Palace, 1606-34); with the help of the Dutch architect Hans van Steenwinckel the Younger, he transformed Rosenborg from a small summer house into a lavish palace worthy of Denmark's 'Sun King'. Christian's last project was the extraordinary **Rundetårn** (Round Tower, 1637-42), Europe's oldest functioning observatory, distinguished by its inner spiral ramp, wide enough for a coach and horses to climb.

The disastrous fires of the 18th century meant that little domestic architecture survives from Christian's reign, apart from the modest houses at **Magstræde 17-19**.

BAROQUE AND ROCOCO 1648-1759

Christian IV's successor, Christian V, completed the fortifications at **Kastellet** in 1660. The most striking of the buildings within its five-pronged bastions is the yellow-stuccoed church. He also laid out Kongens Nytorv in the 1680s. **Charlottenborg Slot** (Charlottenborg Palace, 1672-83) faces this most grand square on the corner of Nyhavn; the huge, sober Baroque building marks a decisive break with the previously popular decorated-gable style. An even better example of Danish baroque architecture is **Vor Frelsers Kirke** (Church of Our Saviour, 1682-96) in Christianshavn. It was designed by Lambert van Haven, an expert in European baroque, and has a playful spire (added in 1749) with external staircase.

French rococo ornamentation became popular in the mid 18th century. The aesthetic was used in the most ambitious project of the time: **Christiansborg Slot** (Christiansborg Palace, 1733-45, then burned to the ground in 1794). A combination of pompous Italian baroque buildings with French rococo touches, it came to define Danish rococo style.

Named after King Frederik V (reigned 1746-66), Frederiksstaden was the first major urban building project undertaken

Rosenborg Slot

CIVIC PRIDE AND ART NOUVEAU 1848-1914

Following 1848, the year of continent-wide revolutions, the new king, Frederik VII, accepted the end of absolute monarchy, ushering in a period of major civic building. Among the largest projects were Vilhelm Dahlerup and Ove Petersen's magnificent Italian Renaissance-style **Det Kongelige Theater** (Royal Theatre, 1872-74). Dahlerup was also responsible (along with Georg EV Møller) for the stodgy **Statens Museum For Kunst** (National Gallery, 1889-96) and the richly decorated **Ny Carlsberg Glyptotek** (New Carlsberg Sculpture Museum, 1892-97). Other significant public works built in the red-brick National Romantic style included Martin Nyrop's **Rådhuset** (Town Hall, 1892-1905) and Heinrich Wenck's **Hovedbanegården** (Central Station, 1904-11).

When CF Hansen's **Christiansborg Slot** burned to the ground in 1884, Thorvald Jørgensen designed its replacement, with its neo-rococo façade clad with 750 different types of granite.

NORDIC CLASSICISM 1914-28

Neutral Denmark emerged from World War I in relative prosperity and turned its back on the romantic, nationalistic themes of the previous decades to develop a brutally ascetic version of classicism entirely its own. Public housing projects, such as the massive **Hornebækhus** block by Kay Fisker, show Nordic classicism at its most uncompromising. Belonging to the same period is the sinister-looking **Politigården** (Police Headquarters, 1918-24). Why a social democratic state like Denmark would choose to build such a severe edifice – a chilling precursor of fascist architecture – remains something of a paradox.

For information on Denmark's modern and contemporary architecture, *see p204-211* **Design & Architecture**.

since the time of Christian IV. Court architect Nicolai Eigtved masterminded an ambitious grid-plan quarter, the centrepiece of which were the palaces that today make up **Amalienborg Slot** (Amalienborg Palace, 1750-60), home of the royal family.

CLASSICISM 1759-1848

Christian Frederik Hansen was the central figure in Danish architecture during Denmark's so-called golden age (1800-50), and during his lifetime became an architect of international renown. The destruction caused by the fire of 1795 and the British bombardment of 1807 provided a blank canvas for Hansen's disciplined romantic classicism. Fine examples include **Domhuset** (Court House, 1805-15) on Nytorv and the minimalist **Christiansborg Slotskirke** (Christiansborg Palace Church, 1811-28). In contrast, MGB Bindesbøll's design for **Thorvaldsens Museum** (1839-48) is a late example of neoclassicism.

Carlsberg brewery plant.

country instead began to extend itself in the arts and sciences. The storyteller Hans Christian Andersen (born in Odense, but a longtime Copenhagener), existentialist Søren Kierkegaard (the archetypal Copenhagener) and the theologian Nikolai Frederik Severin Grundtvig each contributed to the emergence of a defined Danish identity during the 19th century.

This was also to be a golden age for Danish art. Many painters learned their craft elsewhere in Europe before returning to Denmark to depict the unique ethereal light and colours of the Danish landscape. Among the most notable were Christen Købke, his mentor and founder of the Danish School of Art, Christoffer Wilhelm Eckersberg, JT Lundbye and Wilhelm Marstrand. Denmark's greatest sculptor, the neoclassicist Bertel Thorvaldsen, also returned to a hero's welcome after 40 years in Rome, while August Bournonville revitalised the Danish ballet at Det Kongelige Teater (Royal Theatre). Denmark also looked to its past to restore its sense of national pride, with the romantic poet Adam Oehlenschläger's mythologising of the country's history in his epic poems, and the historical novels of BS Ingemann. As a counterbalance, the Dagmar Theatre (1883) and Det Ny Teater (1908) became known for their adventurous, modern programming.

In contrast to the aftermath of past wars, Copenhagen rebuilt only modestly following the British attack. The town hall was eventually reconstructed on the eastern side of Nytorv, while Christiansborg and Vor Frue Kirke were also repaired (Thorvaldsen's sculptures gracing the latter's interior). The 'corn boom' of the 1830s revitalised growth and the industrial revolution consolidated the city's revival, with a prosperous shipyard, Burmeister & Wain, starting up on Christianshavn in 1843. Tivoli Gardens opened in the same year. Frederiksberg also became an entertainment centre with its numerous skittle alleys, variety halls and dance venues. To help keep the revellers well oiled, the Carlsberg brewery expanded, moving to the suburb of Valby. Carlsberg's owner, Carl Jacobsen, would later use his profits to create a marvellous art collection, which he opened to the public in 1897 at what is now the Ny Carlsberg Glyptotek.

DEMOCRACY AND GROWTH

With such potent signs of the approaching modern age, Frederik VII knew that the days of absolute power were waning, and when, in March 1848, a demonstration culminated with a loud (but relatively peaceful) protest outside his palace, the king capitulated immediately. Denmark's first written constitution followed in 1849.

Copenhagen's political and artistic life may have been moving with the times during the mid 19th century, but the standard of living for most of its 130,000 inhabitants, crowded tightly in cellars and ever higher tenements, had not kept pace with the higher echelons of society. Housing remained a dire problem, despite the progressive new terraces in Østerbro (see p143), and in 1852 the ban on construction outside the city's defences was lifted. In the latter part of the century a huge building boom saw swathes of land filled with inhospitable blocks of small 'corridor' flats (one-room properties arranged like the rooms of a hotel along one long corridor). Nørrebro and Vesterbro became notorious for the prevalence of such slum housing. Yet as soon as new housing popped up, the population expanded to fill it. By 1900, more than 400,000 people had moved to Copenhagen to escape the grinding poverty of rural areas. The council granted permission for the creation of a new open space, Ørsteds Parken, where the city's levelled ramparts once stood, together with the building of the Botanisk Have (Botanical Gardens), Statens Museum for Kunst (National Gallery) and a brand new observatory. Strøget, the city's main shopping street, flourished with the arrival of the major department stores Illum and Magasin du Nord. Electricity came to the capital in 1892 (electric trams followed in 1897), as did flushing toilets and a vastly improved sewerage system.

In 1913, Copenhagen gained its international emblem, HC Andersen's Den Lille Havfrue (The Little Mermaid), a statue planted on some rocks in Langelinie, south of Frihavn. Ever since, visitors who have flocked to see it have been united in their sense of anti-climax.

OCCUPATION AND FREEDOM

Despite its neutrality, Denmark was in Germany's pocket during World War I. It still, however, made provision for an outright

IN CONTEXT

attack by Germany, calling up 60,000 men to form a defence force, most of whom were stationed on the fortifications of Copenhagen. Fortunately, they weren't needed, and Denmark survived the Great War intact.

Between the wars, the pre-eminent figure to emerge in Danish politics was the Social Democrat Thorvald Stauning, who achieved the feat of transforming his party from near revolutionaries to true social democrats. A champion of inclusive politics and a tactical magician, Stauning appointed the first female government minister and helped revive the shaky Danish economy with the famous Kanslergarde Agreement of 1933, which allowed for the devaluing of the krone against the British pound and the subsequent resuscitation of Danish agriculture.

When World War II broke out in September 1939, Denmark braced itself to hold tight and sit out the conflict in peaceable neutrality, just as it had 25 years earlier. It was soon disabused of that notion, when, at 4am on 9 April 1940, Hitler's troops landed at Kastellet, fired a few shots on Amalienborg Slot (killing 16 Danes) and issued an ultimatum: allow Germany to take control of Denmark's defences or watch Copenhagen be bombed from the sky. After an hour and a half of deliberation, the Danish government and king agreed, and entered into a unique deal whereby the country remained a sovereign state, but Germany gained access to Norway, the Atlantic and Sweden. Denmark's Aryan genes ensured it was welcomed into the bosom of the Third Reich and, as a rich agricultural country, it was spared much of the brutality and suppression endured by neighbouring occupied states.

By the end of the war, the Danish Resistance numbered around 60,000. They were never called upon to fight, however, and documents unearthed after the war revealed that the German army had expected them to be far more troublesome than they were.

POST-WAR DENMARK

After the war, Denmark faced several immediate domestic problems, which the founding of its welfare state would address. Culminating in the Social Security Act of 1976, the provision by the government (an endless series of coalitions dominated by the Social Democrats) of a safety blanket for the

'In 1913, Copenhagen gained its international emblem, HC Andersen's Den Lille Havfrue (The Little Mermaid).'

sick, the unemployed and the elderly has been one of Denmark's most widely admired achievements. Critics, however, point out that it was initially funded by foreign loans and has seen modern Denmark burdened by a vast public-sector workforce and a crippling income tax levied to pay for it.

With its capital more densely crowded than ever, the government sought to decentralise industry and intensify urban planning. An idealistic 'Finger Plan', in which the city's expansion would incorporate open spaces, was drawn up in 1947, but this was soon discarded to make way for more sprawling suburbs. Copenhagen's first tower blocks were built in 1950 at Bellahøj, but a public outcry curbed the extent to which they could be used to solve the perennial housing shortage. Instead, an urban renewal programme saw Adelgade and Borgergade, among other areas, refurbished. Much of Nørrebro and Vesterbro were also developed during the 1960s, and the latter would benefit from a second renewal programme at the end of the 20th century.

The use of cars increased exponentially in Copenhagen during this time and, as a result, Strøget was pedestrianised in 1962. During the 1960s, many citizens of Denmark (along with the rest of the West) embraced the sexual revolution. In June 1967, it became notorious as the first country in the world to legalise pornography. In 1968, Copenhagen's students, like those across the rest of the continent, grew restless. This being Copenhagen, though, their protest was hardly cataclysmic. Aside from storming the office of Copenhagen University's vice-chancellor and smoking all his cigars, the students caused little trouble. Nevertheless, the spineless university still went ahead and abolished professorial powers.

Copenhagen's youth unrest lasted well into the 1970s, and its ultimate trophy still draws tourists from around the world. In 1971, a group of squatters occupied Bådsmandsstræde Barracks, 41 hectares (101 acres) of former military accommodation on the eastern side of Christianshavn. In protest against what they saw as oppressive social norms, the squatters announced the founding of the Free State of Christiania. The police moved in but underestimated the commune, whose numbers had been swollen by many like-minded hippies from across the country. Eventually the government gave in and allowed Christiania to continue as a 'social experiment', and its 1,000 or so inhabitants quickly began creating their own schools, housing, businesses and recycling programmes. The commune became well known across Europe for its tolerance of drugs, but the current government has cracked down heavily on Christiania.

Though Copenhagen's pre-eminence as a port came to an end with the advent of the superships (too big for the Øresund, they made instead for Gothenburg and Hamburg), in the 1970s the city nevertheless enjoyed full employment. That, in turn, led to a shortage of workers, and efforts were made to attract foreigners from southern Europe, Turkey and Pakistan, who tended to settle in Nørrebro and Vesterbro. Like London's docks, Copenhagen's waterside was to be redeveloped with expensive housing, exclusive restaurants and impressive new buildings for the city's cultural institutions (see p22 **On the Waterfront**), such as the Black Diamond national library extension, the Operaen (Opera House) and the new stage of the Royal Danish Playhouse.

EUROPE – TO BE OR NOT TO BE?

In 1973, Denmark joined the European Common Market (as it was then known), mainly to secure its lucrative bacon and butter exports to the UK, but even after 20 years its membership was still the subject of heated national debate. Europe would twice more turn its attention to Denmark, which emerged from the margins of the European Union to stick a spanner in the works of the progression towards federalism. Denmark has never been a wholehearted member of the EU, and 51 per cent of Danish voters went a step further in June 1992, rejecting the pivotal Maastricht Treaty and causing a mighty kerfuffle in the process. There were protests, some violent, on the streets of Copenhagen. In the end, after a re-vote in 1993, the Danes finally ratified the treaty (by a majority in favour of just 51.05 per cent), but only after they had been promised the right to abstain from common defence and currency commitments. A referendum on whether to join the Euro was held in 2000, when the Danes rejected it. The issue has taken more of a back seat in recent times (despite rumours of further referendums), with the issues of immigration and social welfare coming to the fore.

Copenhagen celebrated its tenure as Cultural Capital of Europe in 1996 with several new arts projects, including Arken Museum for Moderne Kunst, and saw major celebrations in 1997 for the 25th anniversary of the reign of Queen Margrethe. In 2000, the eyes of the world were on Copenhagen for the opening of the historic and very expensive Øresund Bridge to Sweden, and again in 2004 for the royal wedding of Crown Prince Frederik to the Australian commoner Mary Donaldson.

Early 2005 saw the re-election of Prime Minister Anders Fogh Rasmussen at the head of a Liberal-Conservative coalition in which the unsavoury power-brokers were the right-wing, anti-immigration Danske Folkepartie (Danish People's Party). Two years later, in 2007, Lars Løkke Rasmussen took over as prime minister, after Anders Fogh Rasmussen stepped down. The political climate has moved further to the left in the past few years, with the election of Social Democrat Helle Thorning-Schmidt in 2011. Denmark's first female prime minister currently leads a two-party coalition of the Social Democrats and the Danish Social Liberal Party, after the Socialist People's Party quit the three-party coalition in early 2014.

In the last few years, Denmark, and Copenhagen in particular, has gained worldwide press more for matters outside the political realm: its New Nordic cuisine – and especially the world-famous restaurant Noma – attracts more and more visitors to the capital, while the city's progressive organic food policies, urban design schemes, innovative architecture and bike culture now make it a model for forward-thinking governments around the globe.

IN CONTEXT

Design & Architecture

*From functionalism
to sustainability.*

Danish design is renowned around the world, beyond all proportion to the size of the nation that fostered it. Collectors and designers flock to Copenhagen to find that original Jacobsen Egg chair or Henningsen lamp in the shops and showrooms of Bredgade and Ravnsborggade, to seek inspiration in the capital's excellent museums, or to clothe themselves in cool Danish threads. But why is Danish design so revered? Why is this the place *Wallpaper** magazine comes to first to furnish its fashion shoots and dip its litmus paper in the test tube of style?

In the first half of the 20th century, a wave of Danish designers and architects emerged on the world stage, influenced in part by the radicalism of the Bauhaus, to change contemporary interiors and buildings forever. They looked anew at the style and function of everyday objects, as well as the materials used to make them, and created icons. Danish design has had a reputation to live up to ever since, and by and large it continues to surpass expectations, not just in furniture, product design and architecture, but also in the fields of industrial design and fashion.

IN CONTEXT

FUNCTIONALISM/INTERNATIONAL MODERNISM 1928-60

Functionalism was first conceptualised by the Swedish architect Gunnar Asplund in an exhibition in Stockholm in 1930, inspiring architects across Scandinavia to adopt the tenets of international modernism. Architect **Kaare Klint** gave a succinct expression of the new Danish design philosophy when he said, 'The form of an object follows its function.' Denmark was a country late to industrialisation, and this, combined with its long heritage of quality craftsmanship, meant that it was in a perfect position to develop an exciting new design industry. The first project to create a major impact in the field of architecture was **Arne Jacobsen**'s **Bellavista** housing development (1934) and accompanying theatre **Bellevue Teatret** (1937). Taking inspiration from the German modernists, Denmark's master builder created in Bellavista an uncompromisingly modern development, with white surfaces and large windows (all apartments have sea views), in a posh coastal suburb north of Copenhagen. Jacobsen's lesser-known **Skovshoved Petrol Station**, situated on the route from Copenhagen to Bellevue, was also built in this era (in 1936).

Throughout the 1930s, Klint (influenced by his father, PV Jensen Klint) wrote again and again in his notes that architecture and interior design should be unified in what he called 'the living life'. Function should be intrinsic to design, and styling should exist only to enhance practicality. Allying this idea with the traditional hallmarks of the best Danish work – industrial quality, outstanding craftsmanship and artistic flair – Klint produced a series of groundbreaking designs, and passed on his theories as a teacher at Copenhagen's Royal Academy of Architecture. Klint's students were advised that if, for example, they were making a chair, then its function (that is, comfort) should be the starting point – studying human proportions and posture, then applying this scientific rationale to the construction of the furniture, should always be the primary objective. **Børge Mogensen**, **Mogens Koch** and **Hans J Wegner** were among his students; their production of simple, practical furniture swept across the country in the 1950s and their designs can be

seen in homes all over Denmark to this day. This was also the era when 'Danish Modern' furniture became known internationally – but mainly through the works of **Finn Juhl** (1912-1989), whose furniture was more sculptural and expressive than the pure functionalists, and almost a protest against their rigidity. The house that Juhl designed in 1942 can be visited at **Ordrupgaard** art museum (*see p148*); the designer lived there for over four decades, and designed most of the furniture and interior details himself.

Arne Jacobsen took the notion of functional and stylistic unity to its extreme when he designed one of Copenhagen's most famous buildings: the **Radisson SAS Royal Hotel** (now Radisson Blu Royal Hotel, *see p217*), completed in 1960. With this still-controversial building (which turned out to be the first and last proper skyscraper to be constructed in the centre of the city), Jacobsen embraced the principle of 'total design' with characteristically obsessive attention to detail, designing not only the building but also its lighting, furnishings and interior, right down to the cutlery in the restaurant (which is awkward to use but looked futuristic enough for Stanley Kubrick to use it in *2001: A Space Odyssey*). Today, everything in the hotel's room 606 (see *p215* **Arne Jacobsen's Room 606**) – the lamps, fabrics, cutlery, glasses, furniture and door

Skovshoved Petrol Station.

handles – is Jacobsen-designed and has been left untouched as a tribute to his genius. Jacobsen's last architectural project was the transatlantic-style 'slab on a podium' **Nationalbanken** (1965-78); it was finished after his death in 1971 by Dissing+Weitling.

EARLY PIONEERS

Denmark is still reaping the benefits of this design explosion. The furniture of that era has been (and still is) hugely influential and remains in great demand, but there were a number of Danish pioneers who influenced concepts of modern functionalism before this.

The silverware created by **Georg Jensen**, for example, was revolutionary in its field. Trained as a sculptor and silversmith, Jensen opened his first silverworks in Copenhagen in 1904. From then until his death in 1935, he constantly challenged the conventions of silver design with creations that were both aesthetically pleasing and user-friendly. The cutlery, bowls and jewellery he created with the painter **Johan Rohde** were then at the vanguard of modern design, and today the Georg Jensen brand is as desirable as ever.

At the same time that Jensen was challenging cutlery conventions, fellow Copenhagener **Poul Henningsen** was innovating in the field of domestic lighting. 'From the top of a tram car, you look into all the homes and you shudder at how dismal they are,' he wrote. 'It doesn't cost money to light a room correctly, but it does require culture. My aim is to beautify the home and those who live there. I am searching for harmony.' So, in 1924, Henningsen designed a multi-shade lamp based on scientific analysis of its function. The size, shape and position of the shade determine the distribution of the light and the amount of glare. The PH lamp, which featured several shades to help correct the colour and shadow effect of the light, won a competition at the Paris World Fair, and Henningsen became a star. His lamps continue to light many Danish households, particularly the classic PH-Contrast (1962).

Other design trailblazers included silversmith **Kay Bojesen**, whose Grand Prix silver service (1938) was the template for aspiring cutlery designers, and the artist **Ebbe Sadolin**, with his plain white tableware, which was considered quite radical at the time.

PH lamp.

PUSHING THE ENVELOPE

Two major talents to emerge in the field of furniture design in the 1950s were **Nanna Ditzel** (who kept working up until her death in 2005) and Jacobsen's contemporary, **Poul Kjærholm** (whose PK22 chair was influenced by Mies van der Rohe's designs). In the 1960s, **Verner Panton**, another of Jacobsen's former colleagues, addressed the frequent criticism levelled at designers – that their work was far too expensive and exclusive – and took on the challenge of pushing the boundaries of design aesthetics even further. Panton trained at the Royal Danish Academy of Fine Arts in Copenhagen, and initially worked in Arne Jacobsen's architectural practice. International attention soon centred on Panton's designs, based on geometric forms, and constructed from cheap, tough plastics that had previously only been used for industrial purposes. Combined with the use of vivid colours and outlandish shapes, Panton's inspirational style helped define the 'pop' aesthetic of the 1960s, with design icons such as the Flowerpot lamp, the Cone chair and the Panton chair. Although some contemporary critics dismissed Panton's work

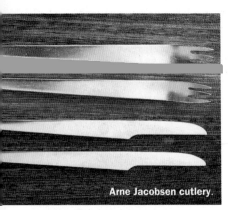

Arne Jacobsen cutlery.

as a fad, before his death in 1998 it was reassessed and a new generation of designers saw it as being way ahead of its time.

SOUND ENGINEERS

While their neighbours to the south in Germany aspire to owning a Mercedes and the Swedes keep up with the Jensens by buying a yacht, the Danes are a more modest bunch, preferring cheap French cars and perhaps a kayak. But there is one luxury status symbol they all yearn for, one treasure every Dane must own before they reach 30: a **Bang & Olufsen** stereo.

The company was founded in Western Jutland in 1925 by two engineers, Peter Bang and Svend Olufsen, in the attic of Olufsen's family manor house. They were the first to produce a radio that plugged directly into the mains instead of using batteries, and by the 1930s they had made a name for themselves with other firsts, including a push-button radio and a radiogram. The Germans destroyed the factory in 1945, but the pair rebuilt the business after the war.

Between launching their first TV in the 1950s and their first fully transistorised radio, the Beomaster 900, in the late 1960s, they made a global name for themselves through their radical yet simple designs – initially heavily influenced by Mies van der Rohe – and superior quality. In the 1970s and '80s, Denmark's furniture took a back seat while Bang & Olufsen and other industrial design brands, such as **Bernadotte & Bjørn** and **Jacob Jensen**, excelled. 'Bang & Olufsen is for those who discuss design and quality

before price,' went the company's advertising campaigns and, accordingly, several B&O products made their way into the Museum of Modern Art in New York.

The Bang and Olufsen families continue to be involved in the running of the company, which, though it now has manufacturing plants all over the world, is still based in their home town of Struer.

PRODUCT PLACEMENT

The best place to see Verner Panton's work is the stylish Panton Lounge in the restaurant (Langelinie 10, 33 12 12 14, www.langelinie.dk), near the Little Mermaid statue. These rooms are upstairs and only open for functions, but if you ask at the bar, someone might show you them. Another café dedicated to the work of a single designer is music café **PH Caféen** (9A Halmtorvet, 33 21 81 80) in Vesterbro, which celebrates the work of lighting designer Poul Henningsen (hence the 'PH'). As well as the Royal Hotel, Arne Jacobsen's pioneering housing complex, **Bellavista**, close to Klampenborg Station, is worth a visit, though the **Jacobsen Restaurant**, which was housed within the complex and was a shrine to his designs, has now closed.

You'll find classic Danish furniture everywhere in Copenhagen, from the chair you sit on in the library, to cool bars and restaurants. For accommodation, the Radisson Blu Royal Hotel is an obvious choice, but best of all for design fans is the **Hotel Alexandra** (*see p217*) on HC Andersens Boulevard. Several of the rooms are furnished with design classics by Jacobsen, Wegner, Ole Wanscher and Finn Juhl.

If you're looking to buy, head for the second-hand and antiques shops on Ravnsborggade in Nørrebro, or the more exclusive dealers on Bredgade in Frederiksstaden. A good one-stop shop for both contemporary and classic Danish design is the design temple **Illums Bolighus** (*see p52*) and the neighbouring **Royal Copenhagen** (*see p208*) stores, selling contemporary and classic porcelain, glassware and silverware. Even if you can't afford a major purchase, it's well worth wandering through the gallery/ museum-style halls to be tempted by a Jensen stainless-steel watch, the perfect

FASHION FORWARD

Danish labels are now stocked in boutiques worldwide.

What do you get if you combine well-funded art colleges with a national history of clothes-making and a talent for innovation? The answer is Denmark, a country that has produced one of Europe's most dynamic fashion industries. Styles and prices vary, but the following designers share an emphasis on quality and originality.

SILAS ADLER

Menswear designer of the moment, Silas Adler is behind local label Soulland. Adler came to fashion via an unconventional route – a keen skateboarder, he started off creating street-style T-shirts, and in so doing found his calling. His designs are clean and simple, with recent collections inspired by American workwear. His Soulland flaghip shop (*see p131*) on Gammel Kongevej opened in late 2013. **www.soulland.eu**

STINE GOYA

Stine Goya has established herself as one of the most interesting female designers in Denmark. With her bold designs, interesting silhouettes and dominant use of colour, she creates collections with a distinct mood. **www.stinegoya.com**

JENS LAUGESEN

London-based and Paris-trained, Jens Laugesen is known for his cerebral yet highly wearable takes on fashion classics. A master of streamlined formal wear in black, white and neutrals, his clothes are sold in Selfridges and Antipodium in London and in countless boutiques across Japan. **www.jenslaugesen.com**

CAMILLA STÆRK

London-based Camilla Stærk's dark, edgy yet eminently feminine womenswear has been featured in *Grazia*, French *Vogue* and UK *Elle*. Her trademark contrast of black and neutrals with delicious splashes of colour has made her work highly coveted in the world's fashion capitals. **www.camillastaerk.co.uk**

HENRIK VIBSKOV

A graduate of London's famed Central Saint Martins art college, Henrik Vibskov is one of Denmark's hottest young designers. His streetwise clothes, recognisable by their distinctive prints, are sold all over the world in ultra-cool shops such as Colette in Paris, Oak in New York and Pineal Eye in London. **www.henrikvibskov.com**

IN CONTEXT

Henrik Vibskov.

porcelain of Bing & Grøndhal, or the crystal creations of contemporary Danish craftsmen such as Michael Bang, Torben Jørgensen and Allan Scharf. Even the area outside the store has designer pedigree: the geometric patterns of the marble-paved fountain square were designed by Bjørn Nørgaard in 1996. Other good shops for new furniture are **Hay** (*see p210*) in the centre, and **Normann Copenhagen** (*see p145*) in Østerbro. For design-led electronics, meanwhile, head to the end of Strøget to Kongens Nytorv for **Bang & Olufsen**'s flagship store (*see p210*).

For those interested in learning more about Danish design, **Designmuseum Danmark** (*see p104*), on Bredgade, is your first port of call. As well as housing an expansive collection of items, it also puts on dynamic temporary exhibitions. The museum had a roof refurbishment in 2013-14, and its beautiful rococo building is now looking better than ever. Its shop is also an excellent place to buy books on Danish design (as well as posters and homewares), and you can sit in the stylish café – called Klint – to read them afterwards.

And since early 2000, Danish design has a purpose-built showcase: Henning Larsen's five-storey **Dansk Design Centre** (*see p54*), opposite Tivoli. The original aim of the centre was for it to act as a 'window to the world' for Danish design. However, the centre's strategy has changed in the past couple of years, with fewer exhibitions for the general public now held, and with a stronger focus on the centre as a meeting place for designers, industry figures and innovators from across the world.

CONTEMPORARY ARCHITECTURE

The designation of Copenhagen as the European City of Culture in 1996 prompted a period of intense development. Two major architectural works to come out of the event were **Henning Larsen**'s Impressionists gallery in the Ny Carlsberg Glyptotek (1996) and **Søren Robert Lund**'s ship-like **Arken Museum for Moderne Kunst** (1994-96). Neither was as spectacular as the **Øresund Fixed Link** tunnel and bridge, however, which joins Copenhagen to Malmö in Sweden, and opened in 2000.

The first decade of the 21st century also witnessed an invasion of global superstar architects working in Copenhagen. **Daniel Libeskind**, architect of the new building for the Twin Towers site in New York and the acclaimed Jewish Museum in Berlin, drew the **Jewish Museum** (2004) – housed in a converted 17th-century royal boathouse beside the National Library; **Jean Nouvel** designed the astonishing, long-delayed blue cube **DR Koncerthuset** (2009) for Danmarks Radio, in central Amager; and even **Lord Foster** has made his mark on the city,

Tietgen Students' Residence.

Blue Planet.

working on, of all things, a new elephant house for **Copenhagen Zoo** (2007).

Projects such as Bjarke Ingels' **Islands Brygge Harbour Baths** (2002; *see p211*), **VM Houses** (2005) and **VM Mountain** (2008); Henning Larsen's **Operaen** (2005); and Lundgaard & Tranberg's circular **Tietgen Students' Residence** (2006), inspired by traditional south-eastern Chinese housing, and 2008 **Skuespilhuset** (Playhouse; *see p176*) have demonstrated that Danish architects still have much to offer. Despite the delay of several schemes following the 2008 international economic crisis – including the Carlsberg City project, which is still in the wings – construction has continued apace. Local commentators are even going so far as to call the current era the new 'golden age' for Danish architecture – with **Bjarke Ingels** emerging as its new golden boy.

The rising global star, who was just 26 when he designed the Harbour Baths, now heads architecture firm **BIG** (Bjarke Ingels Group), which has been behind some of Copenhagen's most talked-about housing projects in the new neighbourhood of Ørestad: VM Houses, mentioned above, was inspired by Le Corbusier's Unité d'Habitation, and led to the now highly coveted apartments

of VM Mountain. This was followed by **8Tallet**, a mixed-use housing development built in the shape of the figure 8, which won the Housing category at the 2011 World Architecture Festival. Ingels is also responsible for the new subterranean **Danish Maritime Museum** (*see p211*), built into a dry dock at nearby Elsinore, with gently sloping floors that resemble a ship.

One other recent building to note is the impressive National Aquarium in Kastrup, the **Blue Planet** (2013; *see p211*), designed by 3XN. With a landmark aluminium exterior, double-glazing units and a seawater cooling system to reduce energy consumption, it's the epitome of a new breed of Danish architecture that celebrates sustainability, water and the merging of Nordic tradition (simple lines, functional design) with the international tendency towards more flamboyant design.

There continues to be a strong focus on design in Denmark too, with the emphasis on sustainability and integration in furniture and industrial design, as well as in architecture. In 2007, the Danish government launched the DesignDenmark initiative, which aims to elicit a new design-focused dialogue and restore Denmark to the international design elite.

Essential Information

Hotels

Copenhagen's hotel landscape has improved dramatically over the past few years. The rates still hurt, but at least you might feel like you're staying in one of Europe's style capitals. Copenhagen can now lay claim to one of the world's most luxurious hotels (the Nimb Hotel, next to Tivoli Gardens), as well as several hotels that celebrate the city's acclaimed design heritage, and to the 'fanciest youth hostel in the world'.

Most low- and mid-range hotels are situated in the trendy Vesterbro neighbourhood, just west of Central Station, where hip designer stores and bars rub shoulders with sex shops. The more prestigious hotels (except for Arne Jacobsen's Radisson Blu Royal Hotel) tend to be found on the other side of the city centre, near Kongens Nytorv and Amalienborg Slot.

PRICES AND INFORMATION

Accommodation in this chapter has been organised by price level, but rates can vary wildly according to season or room category within a single property. As a guide, you can expect to pay around 2,000kr or more per night for a double room in the deluxe category, 1,000kr-2,000kr for expensive hotels, around 700kr-1,000kr for moderate accommodation and less than 700kr for properties listed as budget.

Booking in advance is always a good idea, but if you arrive without a reservation, the **Visit Copenhagen Tourist Information Bureau** (70 22 24 42, www.visitcopenhagen. com) can make same-night reservations for hotels at reduced rates. The service is also available from the tourist information desk situated in Copenhagen Airport's arrivals hall.

STRØGET & AROUND

Deluxe

★ Hotel Skt Petri

Krystalgade 22, 1172 Copenhagen K (33 45 91 00, www.hotelsktpetri.com). Metro/train Nørreport. **Rooms** 268. **Map** p251 M13.

Occupying a former department store in the 'Latin Quarter', this top-notch designer hotel is well located for sights and shopping. Rooms are hugely welcoming, with every feature you'd expect, including large, comfortable beds spread with soft, cool linen, and with a bold, bright (but not overwhelming) use of colour throughout. It's well worth trying to get one of the 55 rooms on the higher floors with a balcony or terrace. The large atrium contains Bar Rouge, a swanky cocktail bar, while the street-level Café Petri is a popular stop for power-shoppers on a break. Central Kitchen is the stylish, relaxed restaurant.

Expensive

Hotel SP34

Sankt Peders Stræde 34, 1453 Copenhagen C (33 13 30 00, www.brochner-hotels.dk). Metro/ train Nørreport. **Rooms** 118. **Map** p250 N12.

The latest in Copenhagen's clutch of design hotels opened in a former townhouse in April 2014. Hotel SP34, owned by the group that was previously behind the now defunct Hotel Fox, is situated in the heart of Copenhagen's 'Latin Quarter'. Highlights include nicely designed rooms with lofty ceilings, an organic breakfast and a rooftop terrace. The suites and penthouse provide lovely views of the old town.

TIVOLI & RÅDHUSPLADSEN

Deluxe

Copenhagen Marriott Hotel

Kalvebod Brygge 5, 1560 Copenhagen V (88 33 99 00, www.marriott.com/cphdk). Train København H. **Rooms** 402. **Map** p251 Q13.

This five-star block of luxury is the place to make for if you want to be pampered in proper American fashion. Standards are high and there are a million extras on offer. But aside from the harbour view, this hotel suffers from a problem that is common in chains: you could be staying in any Marriott hotel anywhere in the world. Be sure to ask for a room on an upper floor on the water side of the building; you could happily sit there all day, sipping champagne and watching the aquatic goings-on below from behind the wall of glass.

Copenhagen Plaza

Bernstorffsgade 4, 1577 Copenhagen V (33 14 92 62, www.profilhotels.com/copenhagen plaza). Train København H. **Rooms** 93. **Map** p250 P11.

The Plaza, which was commissioned by King Frederik VIII in 1913, has been transformed from an old English-style hotel into something a little more 'Scandinavian'. The rooms are airy and pleasant, with big beds. The lobby retains a distinctive early 20th-century atmosphere. The Library Bar (*see p53*) was named 'one of the five best bars in the world' by *Forbes* magazine, and a central pillar in the lounge carries plaques naming the hundreds of famous personalities who have stayed here over the years. The Plaza enjoys a good view over Tivoli across the street, but its location next to Central Station also means windows opening on to heavy traffic or railway noise.

ARNE JACOBSEN'S ROOM 606

The Radisson hotel room that's a must for fans of mid-century modern.

Arne Jacobsen (1902-71) – Denmark's most-famous architect-designer, and one of the pioneers of Functionalism – is probably best known for the hotel now called the **Radisson Blu Royal Hotel** (*see p217*), considered the pinnacle of his career. The world's first design hotel – and Denmark's first skyscraper, at 20 storeys – it was designed by Jacobsen for the Scandinavian Airlines System (SAS), and completed in 1960. Jacobsen designed not only the building itself, but everything inside, from the lighting to the now-iconic chairs that still take pride of place in the lobby, to the ashtrays and the stainless-steel cutlery used in the roof-top restaurant, Alberto K (named after the hotel's first director; *see p53*). The cutlery was futuristic enough for Stanley Kubrick to use it in his film *2001: A Space Odyssey*.

The five-star hotel has undergone several refurbishments over the years, but one guest room has been left untouched for posterity: room 606, whose original 1960s design is as it was when the hotel opened. The room, which can still be booked, contains turquoise

versions of Jacoben's Egg and Swan chairs (as well as the lesser-known, but very cool, Drop chairs), which were designed specially for the hotel, as well as sofas, dark wood-panelled walls, wenge wood sideboards, and desks with built-in make-up mirrors that light up when the desk is opened.

According to the hotel's PR representative, Boline Andersen Karademir, uninformed guests are sometimes intially disappointed by the room, which costs a fair bit more than a standard double, as it's less luxurious than modern-stay standards dictate and the bed is smaller than today's supersize versions. But once guests are told its story, they start to appreciate its singularity. With the huge popularity of TV's *Mad Men*, and the corresponding resurgence of interest in mid-century modern furniture, the Royal is now receiving at least one request a week to view the room.

As most of the rest of the hotel has, sadly, been refurbished with standard furniture and fittings, the hotel is sometimes referred to as Jacobsen's 'Lost Gesamtkunstwerk'.

★ Hotel Alexandra

HC Andersens Boulevard 8, 1553 Copenhagen V (33 74 44 44, www.hotelalexandra.dk). Train København H. **Rooms** 61. **Map** p250 O11.

This 'Danish retro design hotel' is a must for anyone interested in mid-century furniture. Housed in an historic building in an excellent central location, the Alexandra blends classic Danish design with all the facilities you'd expect from a modern hotel. Furniture by the likes of Hans J Wegner and Arne Jacobsen feature in the individually designed rooms. What's more, the hotel has superb green credentials.

Nimb Hotel

Bernstorffsgade 5, 1577 Copenhagen V (88 70 00 00, www.nimb.dk). Train København H. **Rooms** 17. **Map** p250 P11.

The five-star Nimb has featured on several 'world's best hotels' lists since opening its doors in 2008, and is probably the most luxurious place in town to rest your head. Set in a converted 1909 Moorish-inspired building, it has a cosy feel, with each individually decorated and art-filled room containing antique furniture, fireplaces, four-poster beds and top-notch linen. Spacious bathrooms and slick mod cons are further draws, and all the rooms look out over Tivoli Gardens (guests get complimentary entry passes). To top it all off, the hotel also contains a notable restaurant – Nimb Brasserie (*see p51*) – and a first-rate cocktail bar. With just 17 guestrooms (including eight suites) available, you'll need to book well in advance.

Palace Hotel

Rådhuspladsen 57, 1550 Copenhagen V (33 14 40 50, www.palacehotel.dk). Train København H. **Rooms** 169. **Map** p250 O12.

This large luxury hotel stands adjacent to the Rådhuset (Town Hall) and is one of Copenhagen's landmark buildings. It was constructed in 1907-10 to provide prestigious accommodation for visiting officials on business at the then-new Town Hall. It's now run by Scandic and has been upgraded to a five-star hotel. While the reception and bars have kept their old-fashioned looks of wood panelling, and brown and dark red chesterfield chairs, the bedrooms have been smartened up and modernised. The Ambassador Rooms feature private balconies overlooking Rådhuspladsen.

Radisson Blu Royal Hotel

Hammerichsgade 1, 1611 Copenhagen V (33 42 60 00, booking 38 15 65 00, www.radissonblu. com/royalhotel-copenhagen). Train København H. **Rooms** 260. **Map** p250 O11.

For many years, renowned architect-designer Arne Jacobsen's modernist masterpiece was the only designer hotel in Copenhagen, created back in 1960. Although the place has been revamped over the years, just entering the lounge and street-level café, with Jacobsen's Egg and Swan chairs and the Scandinavian Airlines desk, is enough to sweep you into a magical bygone era when airport terminals and avant-garde design were romantic and exclusive. Room 606 has legendary status (*see p215* **Arne Jacobsen's Room 606**). The location is another boon (Central Station and Rådhuspladsen are just across the street), and there are fabulous views of Tivoli from the front-facing rooms – though Copenhagen is so low-rise that any room on the upper floors gives a superb view. For a spot of haute cuisine, visit Alberto K (*see p53*) on the top floor, one of the city's finest restaurants.

Expensive

Imperial Hotel

Vester Farimagsgade 9, 1606 Copenhagen V (33 12 80 00, www.imperialhotel.dk). Train Vesterport. **Rooms** 288. **Map** p250 O10.

This 1956 hotel has been renovated and modernised to good effect, with a major focus given to the indoor 'garden' restaurant and the bedrooms. About half the rooms are decorated in fine Danish contemporary style, and the suites are even better – students at the Danish Design School equip each one as part of their final exam. For those with designer allergy, the rest of the rooms are all far more traditional. The hotel is centrally located near the lakes and the Planetarium, in the middle of the cinema district, and a short stroll from Tivoli.

Kong Frederik

Vester Voldgade 25, 1552 Copenhagen V (33 12 59 02, www.firsthotels.com). Metro/ train Nørreport. **Rooms** 110. **Map** p250 N12.

The Kong Frederik goes full tilt for the traditional English style, with wood panelling, chesterfields and a blazing fireplace. In the lobby hang portraits of all Denmark's (many) King Frederiks, and the restaurant (called, you guessed it, Frederiks) is accessible straight from the street – it's worth visiting both for its decor (imported piece by piece from a London pub) and its haute cuisine. Rooms are comfortable, with appealing, unobtrusive decor, although the bathrooms are a bit small. Guests get free use of the upmarket spa and pool at Kong Frederik's sibling, Hotel Skt Petri (*see p214*).

Moderate

DGI-Byens Hotel

Tietgensgade 65, 1704 Copenhagen V (33 29 80 00, www.dgi-byen.dk). Train København H. **Rooms** 104. **Map** p250 Q11.

Just around the corner from the main railway station and part of the DGI centre, this hotel makes up for its rather desolate location among meat markets and railroad tracks with style, comfort and decent facilities. The ultra-cool Vandkulturhuset (Water Culture House), Copenhagen's state-of-the-art swimming pool and spa, occupies one wing and guests are

admitted free. The spacious rooms are distinguished by minimalist Scandinavian design: lots of light – natural and artificial – and plenty of wood.

Savoy Hotel
Vesterbrogade 34, 1620 Copenhagen V (33 26 75 00, www.savoyhotel.dk). Train København H. **Rooms** 66. **Map** p250 P10.

The Savoy is a recently renovated three-star hotel in a wonderful art nouveau 1906 building designed by Anton Rosen, with a green- and gold-decorated façade; those with a fondness for history will enjoy the original lift (Denmark's first) and staircase. Rooms are large, bright and set back from the street, making them quiet and peaceful. The hotel has its own restaurant with a courtyard terrace.

Square
Rådhuspladsen 14, 1550 Copenhagen V (33 38 12 00, www.thesquarecopenhagen.com). Train Vesterport. **Rooms** 267. **Map** p250 O12.

The Square is a moderately priced temple to elegant, modern Scandinavian decor. The entrance area is impressive, being part-lobby, part light-flooded art installation, and the hotel is located right in the heart of the action on Rådhuspladsen. Ascend the elevators to find uniformly smart and bright rooms, the higher ones (and the sixth-floor breakfast room) commanding great views over the square.

NYHAVN, KONGENS NYTORV & FREDERIKSSTADEN

Deluxe

★ Hotel d'Angleterre
Kongens Nytorv 34, 1050 Copenhagen K (33 12 00 95, www.dangleterre.com). Metro Kongens Nytorv. **Rooms** 90. **Map** p251 M15.

Copenhagen's stand-out five-star Hotel d'Angleterre is traditional to its core, though a huge revamp in 2011-13 has brought it into the 21st century – all rooms have been completely refurbished, and the new Balthazar Champagne Bar is the definition of modern elegance. The massive 18th-century building contains 90 guestrooms, 60 of which are suites. Guests vary from international pop stars to pals of the royal family (Amalienborg Slot, the Queen's residence, is just around the corner). For a cool 22,500kr you too can feel like royalty, with a night in the Presidential Suite. The revamped spa and swimming pool (10m x 12m) are a real treat, while afternoon tea, served at 2.30pm, is a luxurious way to enjoy the art of Danish pastries.

Expensive

★ 71 Nyhavn
Nyhavn 71, 1051 Copenhagen K (33 43 62 00, www.71nyhavnhotel.com). Metro Kongens Nytorv. **Rooms** 126. **Map** p252 N17.

Scandic Front. *See p220.*

Perched at the end of Nyhavn within a splendid early 19th-century warehouse, this relaxed and well-regarded hotel enjoys a prime location. The small, modern bedrooms have managed to keep their character, thanks in part to their wood-beamed ceilings. When you check in, be sure to ask for a view over the water or you could find yourself facing the neighbouring building at the rear. Breakfasts are generally a cut above.

Babette Guldsmeden

Bredgade 78, 1260 Copenhagen K (33 14 15 00, www.guldsmedenhotels.com). Train Østerport. **Rooms** 98. **Map** p249 K17.

The Guldsmeden group's newest hotel opened in early 2014. One of its highlights is the outdoor rooftop Sky Spa, which features a sauna, cold tubs, a steam bath and a relaxation area. The signature design points of the group's other hotels – parquet flooring, Balinese-style four-poster beds and furniture, natural stone sinks in the bathrooms – are all here, and the generous breakfast spread is organic and delicious. As with the other hotels, Babette has impeccable green credentials.

Other locations Axel, Helgolandsgade 7-11, Vesterbro (33 31 32 66); Bertrams (*see p223*); Carlton, Vesterbrogade 66, Vesterbro (33 22 15 00).

Copenhagen Admiral Hotel

Toldbodgade 24-28, 1253 Copenhagen K (33 74 14 14, www.admiralhotel.dk). Metro Kongens Nytorv. **Rooms** 366. **Map** p252 M17.

At the Admiral, you could be forgiven for thinking you're sailing in the hold of some massive wooden galley. The tree-trunk-thick beams criss-crossing the huge lobby area and most of the rooms add to the maritime atmosphere of this waterside hotel, housed in a vast 18th-century warehouse. A 2003 refurbishment created appealing, cosy rooms, well appointed with solid teak furniture. About half the bedrooms have sea views. At Salt, the bar and restaurant downstairs, you can finger the shrapnel scars on the beams from British naval bombardments in the 19th century, or agonise over which of the three different types of salt to pinch over your brasserie-style fare.

Phoenix Copenhagen

Bredgade 37, 1260 Copenhagen K (33 95 95 00, www.phoenixcopenhagen.dk). Metro Kongens Nytorv. **Rooms** 213. **Map** p249 L16.

Housed in a massive building dating from 1780, the Phoenix is one of Copenhagen's most extravagant hotels: the flashy foyer has tall mirrors, a fountain, huge candelabras and paintings. Its chic location, tucked between Kongens Nytorv and Amalienborg Palace, means the hotel is surrounded by some of Copenhagen's hottest art galleries. The elegant bedrooms are decorated in Louis XVI style, and the owner, who is passionate about art, displays only original artworks on the walls.

★ Scandic Front

Sankt Annæ Plads 21, 1250 Copenhagen K (33 13 34 00, www.scandichotels.com/front). Metro Kongens Nytorv. **Rooms** 132. **Map** p252 M17.

While there is now an abundance of chic hotels in Copenhagen, few capture a sense of decadence and

Ibsens Hotel.

fashion as sharply as the Front, which opened in 2006. The owners went for a radical and modern twist with the revamp of the Front: new name, new design, new rooms. There are MP3 players to borrow for the gym, free wireless internet, even personal yoga trainers. The design is all 'hot pink and cosy grey' and the rooms, with the finest designer furniture, combine comfort and extravagance. Ask for a room overlooking the water for the best views from the huge windows. The morning breakfast spread is one of the best in the city. *Photo p219.*

Moderate

Hotel Opera
Tordenskjoldsgade 15, 1055 Copenhagen K (33 47 83 00, www.hotelopera.dk). Metro Kongens Nytorv. **Rooms** 91. **Map** p252 Q16.
A cosy, old-fashioned, three-star hotel with 91 small but very charming rooms. It's named after the old Opera House, not the new one; the hotel is located right next to the Royal Theatre, under the arches. There's a special cheap weekend rate as well as lots of winter offers; check the website for details.

Sømandshjemmet Bethel
Nyhavn 22, 1056 Copenhagen K (33 13 03 70, www.hotel-bethel.dk). Metro Kongens Nytorv. **Rooms** 30. **Map** p252 M16.
The Sømandshjemmet Bethel is perfectly located on Nyhavn and has charming premises in a former seamen's hostel. The bright, pleasant rooms are equipped with bath, telephone and TV. It's worth requesting a quayside view – as long as you're not too sensitive to noise, which can come drifting across from the canal-side bars. Alternatively, you could visit one of them, because alcohol is not sold or allowed inside the hotel.

NØRREPORT & AROUND
Expensive

★ Kong Arthur
Nørre Søgade 11, 1370 Copenhagen K (33 45 77 77, www.arthurhotels.dk). Metro/train Nørreport. **Rooms** 155. **Map** p246 L11.
Given a royal inauguration by King Christian IX in 1882, the Kong Arthur is now a charming, family-run hotel that offers quality accommodation at a competitive price. This beautiful mansion, filled with antique and modern furniture, is conveniently located, sandwiched between the lakes and stylish Nansensgade – home to many independent artisan businesses. Other plus points are its proximity to the city's new food market, Torvehallerne, and the fact that guests have use of the Ni'mat Spa next door. Cosy Hour – when guests are invited to the lobby between 5pm and 6pm for tea/wine and treats – is another nice touch. Kong Arthur is situated just behind its sister hotel, Ibsens (*see below*).

Moderate

★ Ibsens Hotel
Vendersgade 23, 1363 Copenhagen K (33 13 19 13, booking 33 95 77 44, www.ibsenshotel.dk). Metro/train Nørreport. **Rooms** 118. **Map** p246 L11.

ESSENTIAL INFORMATION

Weekend and holidays in Denmark for the whole family

Bring the whole family to one of our 24 Best Western Hotels

Prices from DKK **795,-**

Family room 2 adults and 1 child* incl. breakfast buffet, free internet, double Rewards points** and with you and your family in focus.

LOW R... GUARANT... BESTWESTER...

Best Western Rewards

**Sign up for a membership of Best Western Rewards and earn points for a free night and a lot more!

Stay with people who ca...

 Book your stay today on toll free number **+45 8001 0988** or visit **bestwestern.dk**
f /BestWesternDanmark

This friendly three-star hotel set in a 19th-century building was refurbished in 2011. The bedrooms have been updated from romantic and floral to more design-oriented and cosy, and a new focus on local art has brought works by Nansensgade artists and artisans into the hotel. For instance, Krestin Kjaerholm's textiles decorate the lobby, and Piet Breinholm's (see p90) leather tags are used for the room keys. The location near Nørreport Station is about as central as you can get in Copenhagen, and it's a few minutes on foot to Torvehallerne market at Israels Plads. Guests have complimentary access to the Ni'mat Spa next door.

Budget

Hotel Jørgensen

Rømersgade 11, 1362 Copenhagen K (33 13 81 86, www.hoteljoergensen.dk). Metro/train Nørreport. Rooms 25. Map p246 L12.
This appealing, spotlessly clean budget hotel offers scrubbed wooden floors, a relaxed atmosphere and small, basic rooms with cable TV. For those counting the kroners, it also has dormitory rooms that sleep six to 12 people. It's an easy walk from the city centre, close to Nørreport Station.

VESTERBRO & FREDERIKSBERG

Expensive

Avenue Hotel

Åboulevard 29, 1960 Frederiksberg C (35 37 31 11, www.avenuehotel.dk). Metro Forum. Rooms 68. Map p248 L8.
This three-star hotel is slightly out of town in Frederiksberg, but the location means that handsome neighbourhood and the wilder Nørrebro district are both within easy reach, and the standard is high for the price. The Avenue was completely renovated in 2005, and all rooms now include cable TV, a fridge and free internet access.

★ Bertrams Guldsmeden

Vesterbrogade 107, 1620 Copenhagen V (33 25 04 05, www.guldsmedenhotels.com). Metro Forum. Rooms 46. Map p245 Q7.
This intimate boutique hotel, in a cool part of town, is furnished in Guldsmeden's signature fresh bohemian-Balinese style, with four-poster beds, Persian carpets, feather duvets, organic toiletries and flatscreen TVs. Other pluses are a quiet courtyard garden, a sumptuous breakfast buffet and plenty of green credentials. There are two other branches in Vesterbro (Axel and Carlton) and a newcomer in Frederiksstaden (Babette), all of which share the same high standards.
Other locations Axel, Helgolandsgade 7-11, Vesterbro (33 31 32 66); Babette (see p220); Carlton, Vesterbrogade 66, Vesterbro (33 22 15 00).

Central Hotel & Café

Tullinsgade 1, 1610 Copenhagen V (33 21 00 95, www.centralhotelogcafe.dk). Train Vesterport. Rooms 1. Map p245 P8.
You'll have to book well in advance to stay at this charming spot, which is located above a popular little café just behind Værnedamsvej (dubbed 'Little Paris' by locals). Consisting of just one room, it's an unusual operation, but perfect if you want to get away from chain hotels or the ubiquitous Scandinavian clean-lined design. The design evokes the feeling of a vintage train interior, with lots of wood panelling and retro metal lamps. Lovely touches include postcards (of the hotel, naturally) and stamps for guests to use; an iPhone, complete with downloaded music, for use during your stay; top-quality toiletries; and bikes, which are locked up in the backyard. The only downside is the inability to control the temperature of the room, which can get very hot. *Photos p224.*
▶ *For a review of the café, see p125.*

Moderate

Hotel Tiffany

Halmtorvet 1, 1652 Copenhagen V (33 21 80 50, www.hoteltiffany.dk). Train København H. Rooms 29. Map p250 Q11.
Tiffany bills itself as 'a sweet hotel', and it is. Each spacious, modern bedroom is well equipped with the essentials plus a small kitchen. Add in a friendly atmosphere (fresh rolls are placed outside your door each morning) and it's easy to see why locals often use the hotel to put up overnight guests. It's only a five-minute walk from Central Station, in one of the most attractive squares in Vesterbro.

Budget

Hotel Sct Thomas

Frederiksberg Allé 7, 1621 Copenhagen V (33 21 64 64, www.hotelsctthomas.dk). Bus 6A, 26. Rooms 60. Map p245 P8.
This small hotel is one of our favourites: low rates, a welcoming atmosphere and a great location on Frederiksberg Allé, one of the most sought-after residential areas in town. Although the services offered are limited, the free internet access (in the TV room) and breakfast are much appreciated.

NØRREBRO & ØSTERBRO

Budget

Hotel Nora

Nørrebrogade 18C, 2200 Copenhagen N (35 37 20 21, www.hotelnora.dk). Metro/train Nørreport. Rooms 42. Map p248 J10.
This two-star hotel at the bottom of Nørrebrogade opened around 2002 in an old apartment block and has retained much of the original interior, meaning

ESSENTIAL INFORMATION

Central Hotel & Café. *See p223.*

that the large rooms feel more like those in a flat than a hotel. To find the reception, turn into the courtyard, buzz the door immediately on your left and walk up to the first floor – where the bustle of Nørrebrogade seems hardly noticeable. The design is modern yet unobtrusive, and complimentary welcome drinks can be found in the refrigerators.

FURTHER AFIELD

Deluxe

Bella Sky Comwell

Center Boulevard 5, 2300 Copenhagen S
(32 47 30 00, www.bellaskycomwell.dk).
Metro Bella Center. **Rooms** 812.
Amager's new landmark skyscraper houses this huge hotel – the biggest, in fact, in Scandinavia – aimed at the business traveller. With 23 floors (including 812 guestrooms and 30 conference rooms), this is the place to stay if you want a room with a view, especially as it's situated across the Øresund, facing the city centre. The hotel's much-discussed 'women-only' floor was deemed illegal by the Danish Equality of Treatment Board in 2011, gaining plenty of publicity for the hotel.

Radisson Blu Scandinavia Hotel

Amager Boulevard 70, 2300 Copenhagen S
(33 96 50 00, www.radissonblu.com/scandinavia
hotel-copenhagen). Metro Islands Brygge, or bus 5.
Rooms 544.
The second-biggest hotel in the city houses the Copenhagen Casino, four restaurants, a large lounge bar, a conference centre for 1,200 people and a total of 544 bedrooms. Although it's only a 15-minute walk from Rådhuspladsen, the Scandinavia is not as centrally located as most other Copenhagen hotels – but makes up for it with wonderful views from its 26 floors. There are some 'theme floors' featuring different design styles, such as 'oriental', 'hi-tech' and 'Scandinavian'. Of the restaurants, the flashy 25th-floor Dining Room, which has stunning panoramic views, is well regarded.

Expensive

Crowne Plaza Copenhagen Towers

Ørestads Boulevard 114-118, 2300 Copenhagen S
(88 77 66 55, www.cpcopenhagen.dk). Metro/
train Ørestad. **Rooms** 366.
The four-star Crowne Plaza Copenhagen Towers is one of the city's newest accommodation options, located close to the airport (there's a handy complimentary airport shuttle) in Ørestad. It's also one of the world's greenest hotels. The 25-storey building is carbon-neutral, with solar-powered electricity, a groundwater-based cooling and heating system, low-energy TVs and lighting, and local ingredients in its restaurant dishes. Furnished in a corporate but comfortable modern style, it's a popular pick with

Skovshoved Hotel.

business travellers due to its excellent conference facilities and location.

★ Skovshoved Hotel

Strandvejen 267, 2920 Charlottenlund (39 64 00 28, www.skovshovedhotel.dk). Bus 14. **Rooms** 22.
Among the thatched cottages and grand residences in the charming former fishing village of Skovshoved (about 10km/six miles north of Copenhagen along the Danish Riviera; *see p180*), you'll discover this hotel. It's one of the more romantic places to stay out of town, skilfully blending modernity with tradition, and style with homeliness. It has 22 double rooms (some with sea-facing balconies) and a French gourmet restaurant with a Michelin Bib Gourmand. There are hotel bikes (including electric ones) to borrow, which you could use to cycle to the nearby Ordrupgaard art museum (*see p148*).

HOSTELS

Danhostel Copenhagen Amager

Vejlands Allé 200, 2300 Copenhagen S (32 52 29 08, www.danhostel.dk/en). Metro Bella Center or Sundby, or bus 30. **Rooms** 158.
This modern hostel on the island of Amager, just south-east of the city centre and 15 minutes away by bus, offers private rooms as well as dorms, with or without bathroom. A double room with shower costs 530kr; Breakfast is included in the price and there's an internet café. A Youth Hostel membership card is required to stay here (160kr per annum), but you can buy a temporary card for 35kr per night. The hostel shuts for the last half of December.

★ Danhostel Copenhagen City

HC Andersens Boulevard 50, 1553 Copenhagen V (33 11 85 85, booking 33 18 83 32, www.danhostel copenhagencity.dk). Train København H. **Rooms** 192. **Map** p251 Q14.
Tagged as 'the largest designer hostel in Europe', this five-star establishment opened in 2004 with trendy Scandinavian furniture and a sharp, modern look. Located just five minutes' walk from landmark attractions such as Tivoli and the Royal Library, it also has a fantastic view over Langebro Bridge. It's definitely one of the best ways to stay in Copenhagen on a budget.

APARTMENTS

★ Hay4you

Vimmelskaftet 49, 1161 Copenhagen K (26 28 08 25, www.hay4you.dk).
A good bet if you're staying for three nights or more, Hay4you has an interesting range of nicely furnished, fully-equipped apartments to rent on a temporary basis in central Copenhagen, as well in neighbourhoods such as Vesterbro, Østerbro and Frederiksberg. Service is good, and this is a great way to experience the city from the perspective of a (comfortably-off) local.

Getting Around

ARRIVING & LEAVING

By air

Copenhagen Airport (Københavns Lufthavne, also known as Kastrup) is often voted best in the world by air passengers. It receives direct flights from around 140 cities around the world, and 24.1 million passengers passed through in 2013.

Flight time from London is about 1.5 hours. Direct flights from New York take 7.5 hours, while the fastest direct flight from the west coast is 9.5 hours (from Seattle; coming from LA or San Francisco you'll have to change and journey time is approximately 14 hours). International flights arrive and depart from Terminals 2 and 3. (Terminal 1 is for domestic flights only.) The low-cost airline terminal, CPH Go, opened in 2010, and is currently used by easyJet. The airport is ten kilometres (six miles) south-east of Copenhagen on the island of Amager.

The **Copenhagen Metro** extends as far as the airport, and is the fastest and easiest way to get into central Copenhagen. The Metro runs to and from the airport 24 hours a day, seven days a week, and all trains from the airport go in the same direction (M2 to Vanløse). The station is located in Terminal 3 – just walk straight ahead out of the arrivals hall, and head up the escalator. Metro trains take roughly 14 minutes to reach the centre (Nørreport), and you need a three-zone ticket, which at the time of writing costs 36kr. You can buy tickets from the machines located just before the Metro platform (beyond the airline check-in machines), which take credit/debit cards and coins (no notes). For additional information, call 70 15 16 15 or visit www.m.dk.

Though the Metro is generally the quickest way into town, if you're staying near Copenhagen Central train station (København H), you might find it easier to take the mainline **DSB regional train** from the airport, which also leaves from Terminal 3.

There are plentiful **taxis** at Terminals 1 and 3; the fare to the centre of the city should be around 375kr, depending on traffic. Tips are not expected in Danish taxis.

Local **buses** (5A goes to both Rådhuspladsen and Copenhagen Central Station) run from Terminal 3 every ten to 20 minutes (the night bus is twice an hour), but most visitors take the Metro as the bus fare is only slightly cheaper and the journey longer. For further information on bus services, contact Movia (see p227).

Facilities include restaurants, shops and banks (most open 6am-10pm daily) in the transfer hall and Terminals 2 and 3, as well as cash machines in Terminals 1, 2 and 3 (turn immediately left upon entering the arrivals hall, and there are ATMs on the left-hand side).

There are lockers in Terminals 1 and 2 and left-luggage facilities in Arkaden between Terminals 2 and 3 (see left). Copenhagen is a pedestrian-friendly city, but there are car-hire desks in Arkaden, between Terminals 2 and 3.

A free transit bus runs every ten to 15 minutes between international and domestic terminals.

Copenhagen Airport

Central switchboard 32 31 32 31, flight information 32 47 47 47, www.cph.dk.
The airport website gives live information on arrival and departure times. For more specific flight information, call the relevant handling agent: Air France (82 33 27 01); Alitalia (70 14 24 21); British Airways (70 12 80 22); easyJet (70 12 43 21); Iberia (70 10 01 52); KLM (70 10 07 47); Novia (32 47 47 47); SAS (70 10 20 00); Swiss (70 10 50 64); Turkish Airlines (33 14 40 55).

By rail

DSB (see p227) connects Copenhagen with all of continental Europe's capitals. It also connects to the UK, though you have to change trains in the Netherlands. All international trains arrive and depart from Central Station (København H, or Hovedbanegård).

By road

The Danish capital is 300 kilometres (186 miles) from the German border, and only a half-hour drive to Malmö.
Eurolines runs express coaches to Copenhagen.

Danish Road Directorate

72 44 33 33, Traffic Information Centre 70 10 10 40, www.vej direktoratet.dk. **Open** *Traffic Information Centre 24hrs daily.*
Route, roadworks and traffic info.

Eurolines

Halmtorvet 5, Vesterbro (33 88 70 00, www.eurolines.com). Train København H. **Open** 8am-5pm daily. **Map** p250 P11.
The Eurolines station is located near Central Station.

By sea

There are direct ferries between Copenhagen and Oslo (16 hours) and Swinoujscie in Poland (ten hours). In addition, there's a ferry route from Helsingør (47km/28 miles north of Copenhagen) to Sweden; from Esbjerg (200km/124 miles west) to the UK; from Rødby (150km/93 miles south) to Germany; and from Frederikshavn or Hirtshals (450km/280 miles north-west) to Sweden and Norway.

DFDS Seaways

Copenhagen–Oslo; Esbjerg–Harwich.
Dampfærgevej 30, Østerbro (33 42 30 00, www.dfdsseaways.dk). Phone enquiries 9am-5pm daily.

Scandlines

Helsingør–Helsingborg.
Copenhagen office: Dampfærgevej 10, Østerbro (33 15 15 15, www.scandlines.dk). **Open** *Phone enquiries* 24hrs daily.

PUBLIC TRANSPORT

Trains, Metro & buses

Copenhagen is blessed with an efficient network of local buses (Trafikselskabet Movia), trains (S-tog), run by Danish State Railways (DSB; see p227), and, since 2003, the smart new Metro system, which is in the process of being extended.

The **Metro** has two lines, M1 and M2, both of which run from Vanløse in the north-west to Vestamager and the airport, respectively. Both lines run through Nørreport, Kongens Nytorv and Christianshavn. The driverless, automatic trains run roughly every 4-6 minutes (every 15-20 minutes at night), 24 hours daily. For fares, see p227.

Another big extension of Copenhagen's Metro is currently being constructed. Called the 'City Ring', it will feature 17 stations and link the 'Bridge Quarters' (Vesterbro, Østerbro and Nørrebro) of the city with the centre via an underground tunnel ring. It's due to be completed in 2018. For further information about the Metro, call 33 11 17 00 or visit www.m.dk.

The **S-tog local train** system is made up of seven lines, six of which pass through Central Station (København H).

Handily, the buses, S-tog trains and the Metro all use the same ticket system and zoned fare structure. There's a **map** of the S-tog system and Metro lines on 256 of this guide.

Trains and buses run from 5am Monday to Saturday (from 6am on Sundays) until around half past midnight, although some buses do run through the night.

Movia

Gammel Køge Landevej 3, Valby (36 13 14 15, www.moviatrafik.dk). Train Valby. **Open** *Phone enquiries* 7am-9.30pm daily. **No credit cards. Map** p250 O12.
The Movia office can supply journey plans, timetables, discount cards and lost property information.

Fares & discount cards

The Copenhagen metropolitan area is split into **seven zones**, rings radiating out from the centre of the city. The basic ticket allows passengers to travel within two zones on a variety of transport: buses, trains and the Metro. It costs 24kr (12kr 12-15s; free under-12s when travelling on an adult ticket, though no more than two under-12s can travel on one ticket). As the two central zones include almost every attraction, hotel, restaurant and bar covered in this guide, it's unlikely that visitors will need to buy anything more than this basic ticket (apart from when travelling to and from the airport, when a three-zone ticket is needed).

Such a ticket also allows transfers between buses and trains, providing that the transfer is made within an hour. All tickets are stamped with the date, time and departure zone. Two- and three-zone tickets are valid for a period of one hour from the stamped time; four- to six-zone tickets can be used for 1.5 hours; all-zone tickets are valid for two hours.

Tickets are sold at all railway station ticket offices. They can also be purchased from machines at stations and from bus drivers.

Coloured zone maps can be found at bus stops and in railway stations.

Children

Two children aged under 12 can travel for free when accompanied by an adult. Children aged 12 to 15 pay the child fare or can use a child's discount card. Two 12-15s can travel on one adult ticket or on one clip of an adult's discount card.

Discount cards

Discount 'clip cards' (*klippekort*) are available for ten journeys within zones 1, 2, 3, 4, 5, 6 or all (two-zone cards cost 150kr; 75kr under-16s). When you start your journey, you must 'clip' your card in the yellow machine on the bus or in the station, or your ticket will not be valid and you will very likely be fined.

One clip covers you for travel within the zones printed on the card. If you want to travel beyond those zones, then several simultaneous clips are needed (for example, if you have a two-zone card, two clips allow you to travel within three or four zones, three clips allow five or six zones, and so on). Cards can be bought from stations.

24-hour City Pass

This ticket allows unlimited travel within zones 1, 2, 3 and 4 for 24 hours on Copenhagen's buses and trains. It costs 80kr (40kr 12-16s) and must be clipped in the yellow machines in buses and stations at the start of the journey. Two children under 12 can travel free with an adult holding a 24-hour ticket. The ticket can be bought from manned rail stations. An all-zone 72-hour City Pass costs 200kr (100kr 12-16s).

Copenhagen Card

As well as free admission to 72 museums, galleries and sights, the Copenhagen Card offers unlimited travel by bus and train within Greater Copenhagen. Cards are available in four formats: 24, 48, 72 or 120 hours, costing €48, €65, €78 and €110, respectively (note: euros, not kroner). Children's versions cost around half the price of an adult card. The card can be bought from DSB ticket offices in Rådhuspladsen and Toftegårds Plads. It can also be purchased at main stations, most tourist offices and from many hotels.

National rail system

For mapping out journeys and itineraries, **DSB** (De Danske Statsbaner – Danish State Railways)

has an excellent integrated journey planner on its website (www.dsb.dk) for rail (and bus) journeys within Denmark. The journey planning website **Rejseplanen** (www.rejseplanen.dk) is also useful for finding train departure times. Both websites have English versions.

DSB

Central Station (domestic & international journeys 70 13 14 15, S-tog 33 53 00 33, www.dsb.dk). **Open** *International* 9.30am-6pm daily. *S-tog/domestic* 6am-10.30pm daily. **Map** p250 P11.

Waterbuses

The blue and yellow municipal harbour buses are a cheap alternative to the commercial canal tours that run along the harbourfront, and a useful way of getting from Indre By (the inner city) to Holmen or Amager – though timetables can be fairly limited.

There are four main routes, which all go along or across the harbourfront: routes **901** and **902** stop at Nordre Toldbod, Holmen North, Holmen South/Opera, Nyhavn/Royal Playhouse, Knippelsbro and the Black Diamond (going in opposite directions); route **903** is a shuttle bus between Nyhavn and the Opera House (7am-11pm Mon-Fri; 10am-11pm Sat, Sun); and route **904** stops at Nyhavn/Royal Playhouse, Christian IV Bro/Slotsholmen, Bryggebroen/Islands Brygge, Teglholmen and Sluseholmen.

Harbour buses are operated by **Movia** (*see p227*) and are integrated into the public transport system, so ticket prices are the same as Metro and S-tog train tickets (*see left*).

During the summer, **Strömma** (www.stromma.dk) also runs three hop-on, hop-off waterbus routes around the harbour area. One-day tickets are 75kr (40kr children).

TAXIS

Taxis can be flagged down just about anywhere in Copenhagen. If the yellow 'Taxa' light on the roof of the car is illuminated, the taxi is available for hire. The basic fare is 24kr plus 11.50kr per kilometre (rising to 12.50kr at night and up to 15.80kr at weekends). Fares include a service charge, so there's no need to tip. Most cabs accept credit cards (though, take note: you are supposed to tell the driver at the start if you intend to pay with a card).

DRIVING

When it comes to driving, we have one word of advice: don't. The Danes, or rather their government, detest private cars and do everything to discourage their use.

If you can't do without wheels, here are some tips. The Danes drive on the right. When turning right, drivers give way to cyclists coming up on the inside and to pedestrians crossing on a green light. You must drive with dipped headlights during the day. Drivers have to pay for parking at most places within the city centre from 8am to 8pm Monday to Friday, and from 8am to 2pm on Saturdays.

Car hire

Avis, **Budget Rent a Car** and **EuropCar/Pitzner Auto** all have offices at Copenhagen Airport, Terminal 3 (*see p226*), and in the city centre.

Breakdown services

Falck
Emergency 70 10 20 30, www. falck.com. **Open** 24hrs daily. **Rates** *Non-members* approx 700kr/hr Mon-Fri; 1,300kr/hr Sat, Sun.

CYCLING

Cycling is very popular. In summer you can borrow a **City Bike** (Bycyklen) – now equipped with built-in GPS – from one of the many ranks throughout the city centre for 25kr per hour (*see pp24-25* **Bike Copenhagen**); visit www.bycyklen. dk for more information.

Bike hire

Baisikeli
Ingerslevsgade 80, Vesterbro (26 70 02 29, www.baisikeli.dk). Train Dybbølsbro. **Open** 10am-6pm daily. **Rates** 50kr-110kr/6hrs; 80kr-140kr/24hrs; 270kr-500kr/wk. No deposit. **Map** p250 M11.
This laid-back, ethical bike-hire place has competitive rates. No deposit is required, but customers need to bring a valid passport. Profits go towards financing the collection and shipment of used bicycles to Africa (hence the name: *baisikeli* means bicycle in Swahili). It also has a good bike shop attached, and a nearby café.

Copenhagen Bicycles
Nyhavn 44, Indre By (33 93 04 04, www.copenhagenbicycles.dk). Metro Kongens Nytorv. **Open** 8.30am-5.30pm daily. **Rates** 80kr/6hrs;

110kr/24hrs; 385kr/wk. *Deposit* (cash) 500kr. **Map** p252 N17.

Københavns Cyklebørs
Gothersgade 157, Indre By (33 14 07 17, www.cykelboersen.dk). Metro/ train Nørreport. **Open** 8.30am-5.30pm Mon-Fri; 10am-1.30pm Sat, Sun. **Rates** 75kr-200kr/day; 350kr-1,000kr/wk. *Deposit* 300kr-500kr. **Map** p247 L14.

Organisations

Dansk Cyklist Forbund
Rømersgade 5, Indre By (33 32 31 21, www.cyklistforbundet.dk). Metro/ train Nørreport. **Open** 10am-noon, 1-3pm Mon-Fri. **Map** p246 L12.
The Danish Cyclists Federation has good cycling maps, an excellent website and runs cycling tours.

WALKING

Compact, flat Copenhagen is the ideal walking city. Even the main shopping street, Strøget, is pedestrianised. For organised walking tours, *see right*.

TOURS

By bike

Copenhagen Bicycles (*see left*) runs daily guided tours in Danish and English. The **Danish Architecture Centre** (*see p110*) also offers some city tours by bike, in particular of the new architecture on Amager.

Bike Copenhagen with Mike
Sankt Peders Stræde 30A, Indre By (26 39 56 88, www.bikecopenhagen withmike.dk). Metro/train Nørreport. **Tours** Feb-Dec visit website for times. **Rates** (incl bike rental) 299kr. **No credit cards. Map** p250 N12.
Leaving from bike shop Sögreni (*see p70*), these sociable bike tours take in all the sights, and also get off the beaten track. Booking isn't necessary; just turn up ten minutes before the tour starts. Personalised tours are also available.

Rentyourbikehere
Nørregade 30, Indre By (33 93 62 00, www.rentyourbikehere.dk). Metro/ train Nørreport. **Rates** (incl bike rental) 215kr; 175kr reductions. **Map** p250 M12.
Tours of central Copenhagen and Christianshavn, including Christiania.

By boat

In summer, especially, boat tours are a great way of crossing the city and seeing the sights.

Strömma Canal Tours
32 66 00 00, www.stromma.dk. Departs from Gammel Strand & Nyhavn. **Tours** Late Mar-late Oct half-hourly daily (Gammel Strand). Mid June-late Aug half-hourly daily (Nyhavn). **Duration** 1hr. **Rates** 75kr; 40kr reductions.
Strömma runs guided tours around the harbour, including the Opera House, the *Little Mermaid* and Christianshavn. Dinner tours are available, and there's also a hop-on, hop-off option for those who prefer to tour independently.

Netto-Bådene
32 54 41 02, www.netto-baadene.dk. Departs from Holmens Kirke & Nyhavn. **Tours** all year; times vary. **Duration** 1hr. **Rates** 40kr; 15kr reductions. **No credit cards.**
Harbour and canal tours on the blue Netto boats.

On foot

For details of personal guided tours, visit www.guides.dk. For architectural themed tours, contact the **Danish Architecture Centre** (*see p110*).

Copenhagen Walking Tours
40 81 12 17, www.copenhagen walkingtours.dk. **Tours** Tours can be booked for any day of the week. **Duration** 1.5-2hrs. **Rates** minimum 1,300kr per group (1-13 people). **No credit cards.**
This well-known operator offers private, pre-booked, English-language walking tours on a variety of themes, including Hans Christian Andersen and historic Copenhagen, as well as the city's Jewish heritage. The guides, dressed in red, are hard to lose and they walk all year, in sun or snow.

Ghost Tour
51 92 55 51, www.ghosttour.dk. Departs from Nyhavn 22, next to café ship Liva. **Tours** 8pm Thur-Sat. **Duration** 1.5hrs. **Rates** minimum 2,000kr (up to 17 people). **No credit cards.**
With its old architecture and romantic atmosphere, Copenhagen is ideal for a ghost tour. These guided walks – available in English if arranged in advance – explore some of the spookier sites.

Jazz Guides
26 27 27 49, www.jazzguides.dk. **No credit cards.**
A variety of tours of the city's many jazz venues. Every Thursday, there's an 850kr tour that includes club entrance fees, meal and drinks.

Resources A-Z

ESSENTIAL INFORMATION

AGE RESTRICTIONS

In Denmark, you have to be 18 to drink in a bar, buy cigarettes and drive a car. You can legally have sex at 15.

CUSTOMS

The following can be imported into Denmark without incurring customs duty by non-Danish residents arriving from an EU country with duty-paid goods purchased in an EU country:

● 10 litres of spirits
● 20 litres of fortified wine (under 22 per cent)
● 90 litres of table wine (no more than 60 litres sparkling)
● 800 cigarettes
● 400 cigarillos
● 200 cigars
● 1,000 grams of tobacco
● 110 litres of beer.

Residents of non-EU countries entering from outside the EU with goods purchased in non-EU countries can bring in to Denmark:

● 1 litre of spirits over 22 per cent; or 2 litres of sparkling/fortified wine (maximum 22 per cent)
● 16 litres of beer
● 2 litres of table wine
● 200 cigarettes or 100 cigarillos or 50 cigars or 250 grams of tobacco
● 500 grams of coffee or 200 grams of coffee extracts
● 100 grams of tea or 40 grams of tea extracts
● 50 grams of perfume
● 250 millilitres of eau de toilette
● 10 litres of fuel
● other articles up to a value of 3,250kr if arriving from outside the EU by air; 2,250kr if arriving from outside the EU by car, bus or train.

Only those aged 16 or over can import alcohol and spirits from inside the EU, and you have to be aged 18 or over to import tobacco. From outside the EU you must be 17 or over to use the alcohol and tobacco allowance, including beer: 1,350kr.

It is forbidden to import fresh foods into Denmark unless they are vacuum-packed.

Although duty-free goods within the EU were abolished in 1999 and there is now no legal limit on the quantities of alcohol and tobacco travellers may import into most EU countries (provided they are for personal use), Denmark, Finland and Sweden will continue to impose limits for the foreseeable future. For enquiries about customs regulations, phone 72 22 18 18 or check out the website www.skat.dk.

DISABLED

Facilities for disabled people in Copenhagen are generally excellent, relative to other European capitals. *Access in Denmark – A Travel Guide for the Disabled* is available from the Danish Tourist Board in London at 55 Sloane Street, SW1X 9SY (020 7259 5959).

In addition, much Danish tourist literature, including the Visit Copenhagen website (www.visitcopenhagen.dk), lists places that are wheelchair-accessible plus useful information on specific facilities for the disabled.

Two Danish organisations may be able to offer help:
Dansk Handicap Forbund *Hans Knudsens Plads 1A, 2100 Copenhagen Ø (39 29 35 55, www.danskhandicapforbund.dk).* **Open** *Phone enquiries* 10am-3pm Mon-Thur; 10am-1pm Fri.

Staff members speak English and may be able to help tourists, but members have priority.
Socialstyrelsen *Edisonsvej 18, 1. Sal, 5000 Odense C (72 42 37 00, www.socialstyrelsen.dk).* **Open** *Phone enquiries* 9am-3.30pm Mon-Thur; 9am-3pm Fri. Socialstyrelsen ('Right to Use') can give information about a variety of subjects relating to physical disability in Denmark.

ELECTRICITY

Denmark, in common with most of Europe, has 220-volt AC, 50Hz current and uses two-pin continental plugs. Visitors from the UK will need to buy an adaptor for their appliances, while North Americans won't be able to use their 110/125V appliances without a transformer.

EMBASSIES & CONSULATES

Several embassies – including the American, British and Irish ones – are located in the area around Østerport train station, on the border of Østerbro and the city centre.
American Embassy *Dag Hammarskjöld Allé 24, Østerbro (35 41 71 00, www.denmark.us embassy.gov).* **Open** *Phone enquiries* 8.30am-5pm daily. **Map** p247 G15.
British Embassy *Kastelsvej 36-40, off Classensgade, Østerbro (35 44 52 00, www.britishembassy.dk). Train Østerport.* **Open** 9am-5pm Mon-Fri. *Visa dept (by appt only)* 9am-11am Mon-Fri. **Map** p248 F15.
Canadian Embassy *Kristen Bernikowsgade 1, Indre By (33 48 32 00, www.canadainternational. gc.ca). Metro Kongens Nytorv.* **Open** 8.30am-noon, 1-4.30pm Mon-Fri. **Map** p251 M14.

Irish Embassy *Østbanegade 21, Østerbro (35 47 32 00, www.embassyofireland.dk). Train Østerport.* **Open** 10am-12.30pm Mon-Wed, Fri; 10am-12.30pm, 2.30-4.30pm Thur. **Map** p249 G16.

EMERGENCIES

To contact the police, the ambulance service or the fire service in an emergency, phone **112** (free of charge). For central police stations, *see p233*.

HEALTH

All temporary foreign visitors to Denmark are entitled to free medical and hospital treatment if they are taken ill or have an accident.

Accident & emergency

The following hospitals have 24-hour emergency departments. Note that the largest and most central hospital in the city, the Rigshospital, does not have an accident and emergency department.

Amager Hospital *Italiensvej 1, Amager (32 34 32 34, www.amager hospital.dk). Emergency department: Kastrupvej 63 (32 34 35 00). Bus 2A, 4A.*
Bispebjerg Hospital *Bispebjerg Bakke 23, Bispebjerg (35 31 35 31, www.bispebjerghospital.dk). Bus 6A, 21, 69.*
Frederiksberg Hospital *Nordre Fasanvej 57, Frederiksberg (38 16 38 16, www.frederiksberg hospital.dk). Metro Fasanvej, or bus 29, 831.*

Dentists

Tourist offices (*see p234*) can refer foreign visitors to local dentists.

Dental Emergency Service *Oslo Plads 14 (35 38 02 51, www.tandvagt.dk). Train Østerport.* **Open** 8am-9.30pm Mon-Fri; 10am-noon, 8-9.30pm Sat, Sun. **Map** p247 H15.

Doctors

Lægevagten *70 11 31 31.* **Price** from 400kr per visit. EU citizens are not charged.

Insurance

Citizens of other EU countries are entitled to free medical treatment and essential medication.

The UK has a reciprocal health agreement with Denmark, which means that, in addition to free emergency treatment, UK citizens can usually obtain free medical care from a doctor, and hospital treatment if referred by a doctor.

The European Health Insurance Card (EHIC) has replaced the defunct E111. The free card entitles you to the same state-provided treatment as a resident in European Economic Area countries and is valid for three to five years. For more information, visit www.gov.uk/browse/abroad.

Citizens of non-EU countries should have adequate health insurance before travelling.

Pharmacies

Look for the '*apotek*' sign.

City Helse *Vendersgade 6, Indre By (33 14 08 92, www.cityhelse.dk). Metro/train Norreport.* **Open** 9.30am-5.30pm Mon-Thur; 9.30am-6pm Fri; 9.30am-2pm Sat. **Map** p246 L12.
City Helse stocks a good selection of health food and natural medicine.
Steno Apotek *Vesterbrogade 6, by Central Station, Tivoli & Rådhuspladsen (33 14 82 66).* **Open** 24hrs daily. **Map** p250 P11.

LANGUAGE

See p235 **Vocabulary**. For language classes, *see p233*.

LEFT LUGGAGE

Airport

Copenhagen Airport's left luggage facility is located in Terminal 2 and is open from 6am until 10pm daily, from 5am in the summer months (32 31 23 60). You can store your belongings there for up to four weeks. Charges start from 50kr per piece, per day (odd sizes 70kr per day). Self-service baggage lockers are located in the parking garage, level P4. The charge for a locker is 50kr-75kr per 24 hours, dependent on size. The maximum rental period for the lockers is 72 hours.

Rail station

There are left luggage lockers by the Reventlowsgade entrance of Central Station. Prices are 50kr or 60kr for 24 hours, depending on the size of the locker. Prices for personally supervised storage (available 5.30am-1am Mon-Sat;

6am-1am Sun) depend on the quantity and size of the items and vary from 50kr to 75kr per day.

LIBRARIES

Hovedbiblioteket *Krystalgade 15, Indre By (33 73 60 60, www. bibliotek.kk.dk). Metro/train Nørreport.* **Open** *Apr-Sept* 10am-7pm Mon-Fri; 10am-2pm Sat. *Oct-Mar* 10am-7pm Mon-Fri; 10am-4pm Sat. **Map** p251 M13.
The central library has international newspapers, magazines in English and colour photocopying.
Det Kongelige Bibliotek *Søren Kierkegaards Plads 1, Indre By (33 47 47 47, www.kb.dk). Metro Kongens Nytorv.* **Open** 8am-10pm Mon-Sat. *Study rooms* 9am-9pm Mon-Fri; 9am-5pm Sat. *Exhibitions* 10am-7pm Mon-Sat. All departments close at 7pm during July & Aug. **Admission** *Main building & library* free. *Exhibitions* free-50kr. *Concerts* varies. **Map** p251 P15.
Denmark's national library also serves as a general research centre, a cultural centre and a meeting place.

LOST PROPERTY

The main lost property office is:

Copenhagen Police *Slotsherrensvej 113, Vanløse (38 74 88 22). Train Islev.* **Open** 9am-2pm Mon, Wed, Fri; 9am-5.30pm Tue, Thur. *Phone enquiries* 10am-2pm Mon-Fri.

Airport

If you lose luggage or other possessions on a plane, contact the relevant airline. Any lost possessions at the airport will be registered online at www.cph.dk and kept for 30 days before being moved to the Police lost property office (*see above*).

Buses & trains

If you lose something on a bus, call HUR general information (36 13 14 15; 7am-9.30pm daily). If you lose it on a train or Metro train, phone the relevant terminus or the central S-tog information line (24 68 09 60; 10am-1pm daily).

Taxis

Call the taxi company. After a couple of days, items will be transferred to the central Police lost property office (*see above*).

ESSENTIAL INFORMATION

MEDIA

Newspapers & magazines

Most of the national newspapers in Denmark started out as pamphlets for political parties. Today, they target a wider readership. But with their comparatively small readerships and minuscule pool of journalists (most from the same training course), Danish newspapers struggle to achieve a consistently high standard. Denmark also has its tabloid papers, which can be just as distasteful, sexist and enjoyable as those in the UK.
Berlingske A conservative, right-of-centre broadsheet with decent coverage of Copenhagen. *Berlingske Tidende* is well designed and tries hard, but can be slow with international news.
Børsen *Børsen* keeps tabs on the latest stock-market developments, economic predictions and the major players in the Danish financial world.
BT A tabloid paper that lags a little way behind *Ekstrabladet* in the sleaze and celebrity stakes and so, in recompense, places an emphasis on football and other sports.
Ekstrabladet The most controversial of the Danish tabloids, *Ekstrabladet* relies heavily on celebrity sleaze, opinionated editorials and endless reactionary campaigning. As well known in Denmark as *The Sun* is in the UK.
Information Founded as 'the newspaper of the Danish Resistance' on the night of Denmark's liberation at the end of World War II. Today, the paper has no significant political leaning, its objective being to give its readers important background information on current affairs. Weighty, dry but respected.
Jyllandsposten The most royalist and conservative of the national papers.
Kristeligt Dagblad A Christian publication that focuses on questions concerning ethics, belief and religion.
Politiken Once the paper of the Social-Liberal Party, *Politiken* now focuses on cultural issues. Strong on Copenhagen matters.

English-language press

Copenhagen Post *www.cphpost.dk*
This weekly paper features some Danish news and Copenhagen listings in English.

Radio

Copenhagen's biggest radio stations are all run by the state-owned **DR** (Danish Broadcasting Corporation, formerly called Danmarks Radio), which has a fine tradition of high-quality programming.
P1 *90.8 MHz*
Typical broadcasts include a good range of radio plays, current affairs magazines, documentaries and news.
P2 *88.0 MHz*
P2 is mainly a classical music station, but also plays jazz.
P3 *93.9 MHz*
Targeted mainly at Danish youth, this station features young comedians and DJs who play pop and chart music during the day, with programmes offering more alternative content at night. Broadcasts 24 hours a day.
P4/Københavns Radio *96.5 MHz*
Features pop music, listeners' requests, phone-ins, local news and traffic reports.
POPFM *100.0 MHz*
Plays pop 24 hours a day.
The Voice *104.8 MHz*
A 24-hour chart/dance music station, the Voice is the only commercial station with more than a million listeners a week.

Television

Founded as a public service organisation and funded by individual licence fees, **DR** still dominates the television scene (it actually enjoyed a monopoly on radio and TV broadcasting until 1986).
DR1 The first television channel in Denmark, DR1's strengths include news and current affairs, documentaries, and children's and youth programming.
DR2 The little sister to DR1 and a slightly more alternative watch.
TV2 Despite introducing morning television and *Wheel of Fortune* to the Danes, TV2 pretty much resembles DR1, principally because TV2 is also a licence-financed station, with similar public service obligations.
TV3/TV3+ Targeting young people and families, TV3 is a commercial station that aims to provide quality light entertainment, with Danish soap operas and docu-soaps among the most popular programmes. Its sister channel TV3+ is the leading station for sport.
Kanal 5 Most of the programmes on Kanal 5 (previously known as TVDanmark1) are American sitcoms and soap operas, though it occasionally broadcasts Danish docu-soaps.

MONEY

The Danish *krone* (crown) is divided into 100 *øre*. There are coins in denominations of 25 *øre*, 50 *øre* (both copper), one *krone*, two *kroner*, five *kroner* (all three silver in colour, the latter two with a hole), ten *kroner* and 20 *kroner* (both brass). Notes come in 50, 100, 200, 500 and 1,000 *kroner* denominations. The abbreviation 'kr' is used in this guide, though you may also see 'DKK' or 'KR' before the figure in question.
There is no limit to the amount of foreign or Danish currency you can bring into the country, though you will be required to explain the source of amounts over €10,000 (roughly 75,000kr).

Banks & bureaux de change

Banks in Denmark tend to open from 10am to 4pm on weekdays, with late opening until 5.30pm on Thursday. Some in the centre have longer hours and open on Saturday. Most will change foreign currency, as will bureaux de change.

Tax

Tax on goods (MOMS) in Denmark is levied at 25%. Non-EU residents are entitled to claim back up to 19% of the total price of any item bought in the country (providing that the purchase exceeds 300kr and that Denmark is their final EU destination before returning home). Visitors should ask shops to issue a Blue Tax Free Cheque for each purchase. These can then be stamped and handed in at the Global Blue desk in the Arkaden, between Copenhagen Airport's Terminals 2 and 3 (6am-9pm daily). Alternatively, they can be stamped by Customs (in Terminal 3) before you check in your luggage, and then handed in to Global Blue. For further information, contact Global Blue Danmark (32 52 55 66, www.global-blue.com).

OPENING HOURS

Most shops in Copenhagen open from 10am to 6pm or 7pm on weekdays and from 10am to 2pm or 5pm on Saturday, with only bakers, florists and souvenir shops open on Sunday. Office hours are usually 9am to 4pm Monday to Friday.

POLICE & SECURITY

Copenhagen is generally safe compared with other cities in Europe. There are places where you should exercise caution late at night, however. These include side streets in Vesterbro, and the area around Rådhuspladsen stretching part of the way up Strøget – drunken violence is fairly common here at night. The area behind Central Station stretching up much of Istedgade is a hangout for alcoholics and junkies, but they are peaceable in the main. In the unlikely event that you're a victim of crime, contact the Danish Police immediately. In emergencies, call **112** (free of charge), or dial **114** to be connected to your nearest local station. Open 24 hours, the Police HQ can direct you to your nearest station. These include Central Station (33 15 38 01; map p250 P11); Halmtorvet 20, Vesterbro (33 25 14 48; map p250 Q10) and Store Kongensgade 100 (33 93 14 48; map p249 L16). To connect with any local or sub-station outside of an emergency situation, dial the Police Headquarters switchboard (33 14 88 88) and they will connect you.

Police Headquarters *Politorvet (33 14 14 48).* **Open** 24hrs daily. **Map** p250 Q13.

POSTAL SERVICES

Most post offices open from 10am to 5.30pm Monday to Friday, and from 10am or 11am until noon or 2pm on Saturday. Larger branches have fax facilities. Copenhagen's largest post office is:

Central Station Post Office
Central Station (80 20 70 30, www.postdanmark.dk). **Open** 8am-9pm Mon-Fri; 10am-4pm Sat, Sun. **Map** p250 P11.

Postal rates

In addition to the rates below, express delivery services are also available. Contact any post office for details. Letters up to 50g cost 6.50kr to Denmark, 11.50kr to Europe and 14.50kr to other countries; letters up to 100g cost 14kr to Denmark, 22kr to the rest of Europe and 30kr to other countries.

RELIGION

There are close ties between Church and State in Denmark, and the Constitution declares the Evangelical Lutheran Church to be the national church. The Danish Folkekirken (People's Church) is funded by church members through 'Church Tax', but in spite of the fact that most Danes (82%) are members, a minority of Copenhageners would call themselves religious. Churches are often empty on Sundays, and are mainly used at Christmas, Easter, or for private arrangements such as weddings. The second largest religious community in Denmark is Muslim; the third, Roman Catholic. The following churches hold services in English.

Great Synagogue *Krystalgade 12, Indre By (33 12 88 68).* Metro/train Nørreport. **Services** 6.45am Mon, Thur; 7am Tue, Wed, Fri; 9am Sat; 8am Sun (8.30am in summer). **Map** p251 M13.
Orthodox Judaism.
St Alban's Church *Churchill Parken, Langelinie (www.st-albans.dk). Bus 1A, 15.* **Services** Holy Communion 10.30am Wed; 9am, 10.30am Sun. **Map** p249 J18. Anglican.
Sakrementskirken *Nørrebrogade 27, Nørrebro (35 35 68 25). Bus 5A.* **Services** 5pm Wed (English Mass); 9.30am (Danish); 6pm Sun (English). **Map** p246 J10. Roman Catholic.
Sankt Annæ Kirke *Dronning Elisabeths Allé 3, Amager (32 58 41 02, www.saintanneschurch.dk). Bus 5A.* **Services** 5pm Sat, Sun. Roman Catholic.

SMOKING

Smoking is banned in all indoor public spaces in Denmark, including public transport, cinemas and (most) cafés and restaurants, though some bars still allow smoking.

STUDY

Danish institutions for higher education have a friendly and open-minded policy towards international students. Exchange programmes provide links between Danish universities and their international counterparts, and in recent years exchanges have increasingly been developed through programmes such as Socrates/Erasmus, Lingua and Tempus, which are all supported by the largess of the European Union. Some of the institutions also have summer schools and the largest universities and colleges have their own international offices.

Colleges & universities

Copenhagen's universities and colleges offer a variety of qualifications over a broad spectrum of subjects. The **University of Copenhagen** (35 32 26 26, www.ku.dk) is the city's flagship establishment. Founded in 1479, it is Denmark's oldest educational institution, and, with 35,000 students, can also lay claim to being the largest.

The city has two business schools, **Copenhagen Business School** (38 15 38 15, www.cbs.dk) and **Niels Brock College** (33 41 91 00, www.brock.dk).

Det Kongelige Danske Kunstakademi (33 74 46 00, www.kunstakademiet.dk), the Royal Academy of Fine Arts, offers a variety of fine-art courses and tutoring, as well as incorporating the **School of Architecture** (32 68 60 00, www.karch.dk), the excellent **Danish Film School** (32 68 64 00, www.filmskolen.dk), the **National Drama School** (32 83 61 00, www.teaterskolen.dk) and the **Rhythmic Music Conservatory** (32 68 67 00, www.rmc.dk).

Det Kongelige Danske Musikkonservatorium (72 26 72 26, www.dkdm.dk), the Royal Danish Music Conservatory, offers classical music training.

Language classes

Berlitz *Vimmelskaftet 42A, Strøget, Indre By (70 21 50 10, www.berlitz.com).* **Open** 8am-6pm Mon-Fri. **Map** p251 N13. Courses are taught by native speakers; most are tailored to individual needs.

TELEPHONES

Like most public services in Denmark, the phone system is efficient and simple to use. Danish phone numbers have eight digits and there are no area codes.

Dialling & codes

The international dialling code for Denmark is 45. To dial Copenhagen from outside Denmark, dial 00 45 and then the eight-digit number.

To call abroad from Denmark, dial 00 followed by the country access code, the area code (minus the initial 0, if there is one) and then the local number. The international code for the UK is **44**; **1** for the US/Canada; **353** for Ireland; **61** for Australia.

ESSENTIAL INFORMATION

Mobile phones

Denmark is part of the worldwide GSM network, so compatible mobile phones should work without any problems.

Operator services

For **directory enquiries**, call 118 (domestic) or 113 (international).

TIME

Denmark observes Central European Time, one hour ahead of Greenwich Mean Time, and six hours ahead of Eastern Standard Time. Danes use the 24-hour clock.

TIPPING

Service is often included on hotel and restaurant bills, so any tips should only be given for unusually good service. It's not uncommon, however, to round up a bill.

TOURIST INFORMATION

Danish Tourist Board *32 88 99 00, www.visitdenmark.com.* If you plan to travel beyond the capital, check out the DTB's website – it's very useful for both practical advice and news about forthcoming attractions. The DTB doesn't encourage personal callers.

Visit Copenhagen Tourist Information Bureau
Vesterbrogade 4A, Tivoli & Rådhuspladsen (70 22 24 42, www.visitcopenhagen.dk). **Open** *July, Aug* 9am-7pm daily. *May, June, Sept* 9am-6pm Mon-Sat; 9am-3pm Sun. *Oct-Apr* 9am-4pm Mon-Fri; 9am-2pm Sat. *Phone enquiries* 10am-4pm Mon-Fri, all year round. **Map** p250 O11.

The official Copenhagen tourist office is located opposite the Radisson Blu Royal Hotel, across the road from Tivoli. It has a wealth of information on the city's attractions as well as a small souvenir shop, and offers a free accommodation booking service.

VISAS

Citizens of EU countries (outside Scandinavia) require a national ID card or passport valid for the duration of their stay in order to enter Denmark for tourist visits of up to three months within a period of six months. Tourists (EU citizens) can stay in the country for another three months if they are working or applying for a job.

For stays lasting more than six months, you need a residency visa. US citizens require a passport valid only for the duration of their stay, but citizens of Canada, Australia and New Zealand require passports valid for three months beyond the last day of their visit. South African citizens need to apply for a tourist visa prior to leaving South Africa. For more information, contact the Danish Immigration Service on 35 30 84 90, or visit www.nyi danmark.dk, their multi-language advisory website.

WEIGHTS & MEASURES

Denmark uses the metric system. Decimal points are indicated by commas, while thousands are defined by full stops. In this guide, we have listed all measurements in both metric and imperial.

WHEN TO GO

The climate in Denmark isn't particularly severe. In midsummer it hardly gets dark at all and the evening light can last well past 11pm. However, winter is cold, wet and dark and some tourist attractions are closed. Tivoli, for example, is closed for most of the winter aside from Halloween and Christmas. Spring kicks off in late April, but can take a while to warm up. May and June are usually fresh and bright, with reasonable temperatures. Summer peak season is in July and August, when Copenhagen offers plenty of festivals and open-air events and the weather is probably as good as it ever gets in Scandinavia. Cruise ships bring in plenty of visitors then, but July is also when all of Copenhagen migrates to the seaside for its summer holidays, so the city can seem quieter and many top restaurants and some other businesses are closed.

WOMEN

Denmark is a country famously committed to equal opportunities for all citizens and a lot of effort has been made to achieve equal rights for women.

Female visitors to Denmark are very unlikely to encounter any harrassment problems.

WORK

Even though most people in Denmark speak English, and many companies use English as a

working language, there is still a deeply ingrained prejudice in the workplace against those who are not fluent in Danish. However, the current unemployment rate is very low so there are always some vacancies open to foreigners, particularly in unskilled fields such as cleaning, catering and hotels.

EURES (www.ec.europa.eu/eures) is a database of job vacancies throughout the EU and contains useful information about working conditions throughout Europe.

Det Danske Kulturinstitut
Vartov, Farvergade 27L, 1463 Copenhagen K (33 13 54 48, www.dankultur.dk). Bus 2A, 5A. **Open** 9am-3pm Mon-Fri.
The Institute publishes a range of literature about the country and arranges job exchange programmes for a number of professions.

Work permits

All EU citizens can obtain a work permit in Denmark; non-EU citizens must apply for a work permit abroad and hand in the application to a Danish embassy or consular representation. The rules for obtaining work permits vary for different jobs – contact the Danish Immigration Service:

Udlændingestyrelsen *Ryesgade 53, 2100 Copenhagen Ø (35 36 66 00, www.nyidanmark.dk). Bus 3A, 6A.* **Open** 8am-3pm Mon; 10am-3pm Tue, Sat; noon-5pm Thur; 10am-1pm Fri.

Useful addresses

The EU has a website (www.europa.eu) and helpline (00 800 6789 1011) providing general information on your rights, and useful telephone numbers and addresses in your home country. It also holds specific information on the rules for recognition of diplomas, your rights on access to employment and rights of residence and social security.

For general information about the **Danish tax system**, see the Skatteministeriet (Danish Ministry of Taxation) website (www.skm.dk), or contact SKAT (Customs and tax administration) with more specific questions.

SKAT *Sluseholmen 8B, 2450 Copenhagen SV (72 22 18 18, www.skat.dk).* **Open** *Phone enquiries* 9am-5pm Mon; 9am-4pm Tue-Thur; 9am-2pm Fri.

Vocabulary

If you have a good knowledge of Swedish or Norwegian, you should be able to understand Danish well enough to get by. And if you are fluent in German, you may also recognise a fair percentage of words. For the rest of us, however, Danish is mostly impenetrable.

The problem comes not with the grammar, which is comparatively simple, but with the pronunciation, which is full of its own idiosyncrasies, particularly the seemingly endless glottal stops and swallowing of parts of words. And be warned, Copenhageners are the worst offenders in Denmark – they talk the fastest too. But do not fear, the majority of Danes have excellent English and it's tempting for visitors not to bother to try to learn any Danish at all. But an attempt to learn a few basics is often appreciated.

Here's a brief guide to pronunciation and some useful basic words and phrases.

VOWELS

a – as in 'rather' or as in 'pat'
å, u(n) – as in 'or'
e(g), e(j) – as in 'shy'
e, æ – as in 'set'
i – as in 'be'
ø – a short 'er' sound
o – as in 'rot' or as in 'do'
o(v) – a short 'ow', as in 'cow'
u – as in 'bull' or as in 'do'
y – a long, hybrid of 'ee' and 'oo'

CONSONANTS

sj – as in 'shot'
ch – as in 'shot'
c – as in 'send', but as in 'key' before a, o, u and consonants
(o)d – as the 'th' in 'those'
j – as the 'y' in 'year'
g – as in 'got', when before vowels
h – as in 'heart'
k – as in 'key'
b – as in 'bag'
r – a short guttural 'r' (less guttural after a vowel)
w – a 'v' sound

USEFUL WORDS/ PHRASES

yes *ja, jo* ('yer', 'yo')
no *nej* ('ny')

please *vær så god* ('verser-go'), *vær så venlig* ('verser venlee')
thank you *tak* ('tack')
hello (formal) *goddag* ('godday'); **hello** (informal) *hej* ('hi')
I understand *jeg forstår* ('yie for-stor')
I don't understand *jeg forstår ikke* ('yie for-stor icker')
do you speak English? *taler du engelsk* ('tarler doo engelsk')?
excuse me (sorry) *undskyld* ('unsgull')
go away! *forsvind!* ('for-svin')
entrance *indgang*
exit *udgang*
open *åben*
closed *lukket*
toilets *toiletter* (**men** *herrer*, **women** *damer*)

DAYS/MONTHS

today *i dag*
tonight *i aften/i nat*
tomorrow *i morgen*
yesterday *i går*

Monday *mandag*
Tuesday *tirsdag*
Wednesday *onsdag*
Thursday *torsdag*
Friday *fredag*
Saturday *lørdag*
Sunday *søndag*

January *januar*
February *februar*
March *marts*
April *april*
May *maj*
June *juni*
July *juli*
August *august*
September *september*
October *oktober*
November *november*
December *december*

NUMBERS

0 *nul;* 1 *en;* 2 *to;* 3 *tre;* 4 *fire;* 5 *fem;* 6 *seks;* 7 *syv;* 8 *otte;* 9 *ni;* 10 *ti;* 20 *tyve;* 30 *tredive;* 40 *fyrre;* 50 *halvtreds;* 60 *tres;* 70 *halvfjerds;* 80 *firs;* 90 *halvfems;* 100 *hundrede;* 1,000 *tusind;* 1,000,000 *million*

FOOD & DRINK

apple	*æble*
egg	*æg*
peas	*ærter*
orange	*appelsin*
banana	*banan*
bread	*brød*
beans	*bønner*
mushroom	*champignon*
chocolate	*chokolade*
lemon	*citron*
steamed	*dampet*
vinegar	*eddike*
draught beer	*fadøl*
fish	*fisk*
cream	*fløde*
trout	*forel*
meatballs	*frikadeller*
fresh	*frisk*
fruit	*frugt*
grilled	*grilleret*
stew	*gryderet*
green bean	*grøn bønne*
vegetables	*grøntsager*
carrots	*gulerødder*
tomatoes	*tomater*
garlic	*hvidløg*
ice-cream/ice	*is*
strawberry	*jordbær*
coffee	*kaffe*
cake	*kage*
cabbage	*kål*
potato	*kartoffel*
meat	*kød*
boiled	*kogt*
cold	*kold*
chicken	*kylling*
salmon	*laks*
lamb	*lamme*
onion	*løg*
marinated	*marineret*
milk	*mælk*
nuts	*nødder*
beef	*oksekød*
beer	*øl*
oil	*olie*
cheese	*ost*
roasted	*ovnstegt*
pepper	*peber*
poached	*pocheret*
fries/chips	*pommes frites*
hot dog	*pølse*
rice	*ris*
smoked	*røget*
raw	*rå*
mustard	*sennep*
herring	*sild*
ham	*skinke*
butter	*smør*
fried	*stegt*
sugar	*sukker*
soup	*supper*
pork	*svinekød*
tea	*te*
cod	*torsk*
water	*vand*
warm, hot	*varm*
pastries	*wienerbrød*

ESSENTIAL INFORMATION

Further Reference

ESSENTIAL INFORMATION

BOOKS

Non-fiction

Booth, Michael *The Almost Nearly Perfect People*
A riposte to all the Nordic hype, by a former editor of this guidebook.
Christianson, JR *On Tycho's Island: Tycho Brahe and His Assistants, 1570-1601*
Biography of the famous astronomer.
Dyrbe, Helen, Steven Harris & Thomas Golzen *Xenophobe's Guide to the Danes*
Irreverent dissection of the Danes.
Jones, Gwyn *A History of the Vikings*
A readable account of the not-so-vicious Vikings and their world.
Kingsley, Patrick *How to be Danish: A Journey to the Cultural Heart of Denmark* A *Guardian* correspondent's guide to understanding the Danes.
Levine, Ellen *Darkness over Denmark: The Danish Resistance and the Rescue of the Jews*
The remarkable story of the exodus of Danish Jews to Sweden during World War II.
Monrad, Kasper, Philip Conisbee & Bjarne Jornaes *The Golden Age of Danish Painting*
The works of 17 painters from the first half of the 19th century.
Poole, Roger & Henrik Stangerup *A Kierkegaard Reader*
The leading resource on Denmark's leading philosopher.
Pundik, Herbert *In Denmark It Could Not Happen: The Flight of the Jews to Sweden in 1943*
Another account of the wartime escape of the Jews in Denmark.
Sawyer, Peter (ed) *The Oxford Illustrated History of the Vikings*
An enjoyable survey of the Vikings.
Spangenburg, Ray & Diane K Moser *Niels Bohr: Gentle Genius of Denmark (Makers of Modern Science)*
An accessible analysis of the great Danish nuclear physicist.
Thomas, Alastair H & Stewart P Oakley *Historical Dictionary of Denmark*
An invaluable reference book charting Denmark's cultural history.
Thoren, Victor E *The Lord of Uraniborg*
Detailed biography of 16th-century astronomer Tycho Brahe.

Thurman, Judith *Isak Dinesen The Life of Karen Blixen*
Authoritative biog of one of Denmark's finest prose writers, and most famous daughter.
Wullschlager, Jackie *HC Andersen: The Life of a Storyteller*
Comprehensive biography of Denmark's top tale-teller.

Fiction

Andersen, Hans Christian *The Complete Fairy Tales*
More than 150 of the great Dane's best-loved fairy tales.
Blixen, Karen *Seven Gothic Tales*
Blixen's darkly powerful masterpiece.
Frayn, Michael *Copenhagen*
Extraordinary play based on the visit of the great German physicist Werner Heisenberg to his erstwhile mentor and friend Niels Bohr.
Høeg, Peter *Miss Smilla's Feeling for Snow*
Bestselling thriller set in Copenhagen and Greenland.
Simpson, Jacqueline (ed) *Danish Legends*
This collection comprises over 160 Danish folktales and legends.
Shakespeare, William *Hamlet*
The bard's Danish blockbuster – possibly the greatest play ever written.
Tremain, Rose *Music and Silence*
Beautifully written fictional account of the latter years of Christian IV.

WEBSITES

City of Copenhagen
www.kk.dk
The website of Københavns Kommune, the city authorities, with information on living and doing business in Copenhagen.
Copenhagen News
www.copenhagennews.com
Portal to news about Denmark appearing in the world's media.
Copenhagen Post
www.cphpost.dk
Weekly news in English from the Danish capital.
Copenhagenize
www.copenhagenize.com
Mikael Colville Andersen's blog on 'Bicycle Urbanism for Modern Cities'.
Danish Youth Hostels Association
www.danhostel.dk
Search for a hostel and book online.

Danish Metereological Information
www.dmi.dk
Daily and long-term weather reports.
Danish Tourist Board
www.visitdenmark.dk
This national tourist board website has extensive information on the Denmark.
Denmark Hotels
www.dkhotellist.com
An online guide to all the star-rated hotels in Denmark.
DSB (Danish State Railways)
www.dsb.dk
Journey planner for train journeys within Denmark (in English).
Hamlet Sommer
www.hamletsommer.dk
The website for the annual theatrical festival.
HUR
www.moviatrafik.dk
Comprehensive site on Copenhagen's efficient and excellent public transport system.
Metro
www.m.dk
The official website of Copenhagen's shiny new Underground system.
Malmö Tourist Board
www.malmo.se
Information on the sights, attractions, restaurants, festivals and accommodation in this charming city.
Øresund
www.oresundsregionen.org/en/visit
An online guide to the strait that divides Denmark and Sweden, and the land on either side.
Rejseplanen
www.rejseplanen.dk
Useful site for journey planning within the city and country.
Skåne
www.skanetur.se
The website of the Swedish province of Skåne (Scania), now easily accessible via the Øresund Bridge.
Ungdomsinformation
www.ufm.dk
Copenhagen City Council's site is full of helpful information for those planning a longer stay.
Visit Copenhagen
www.visitcopenhagen.dk
The regularly updated official website of the city's efficient tourist authority offers detailed information about the city's hotels, restaurants, cafés, bars, galleries, theatres, theme parks and museums, and many useful links.

Index

INDEX

INDEX

Maps

MAPS

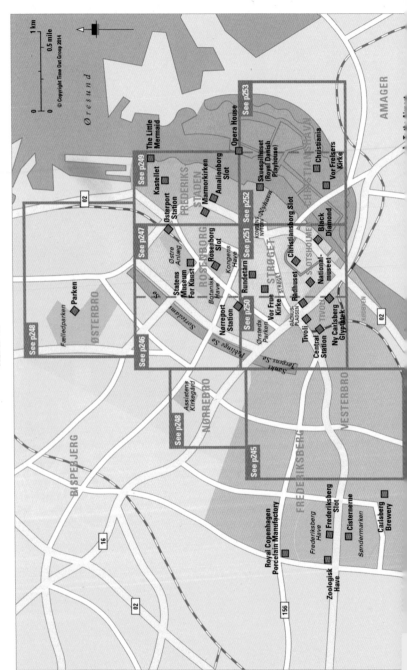

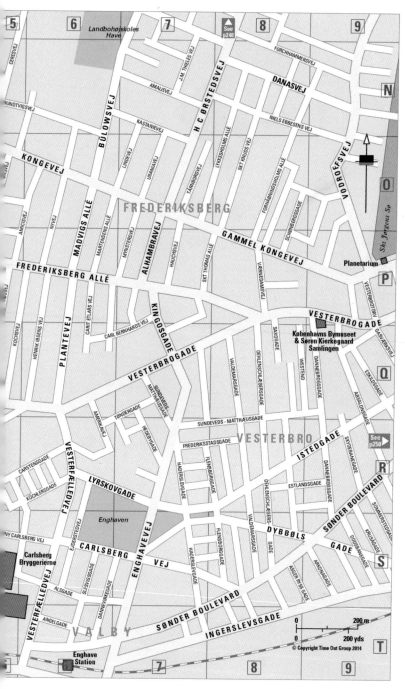

MAPS

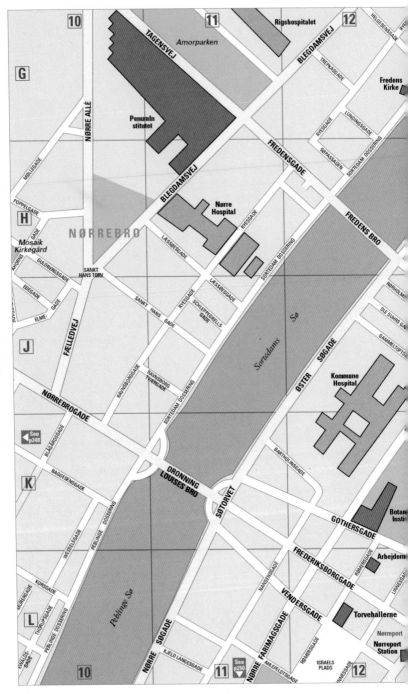

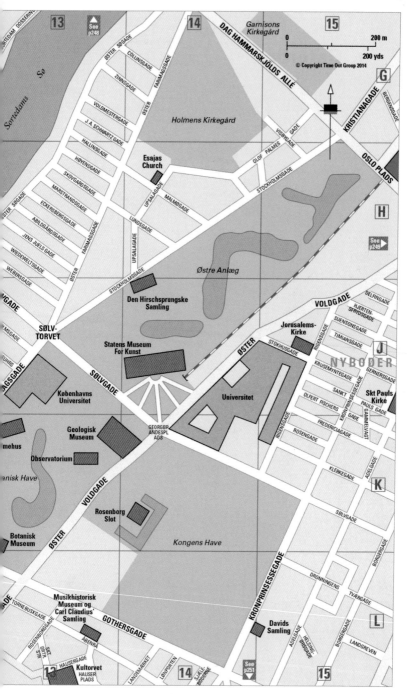

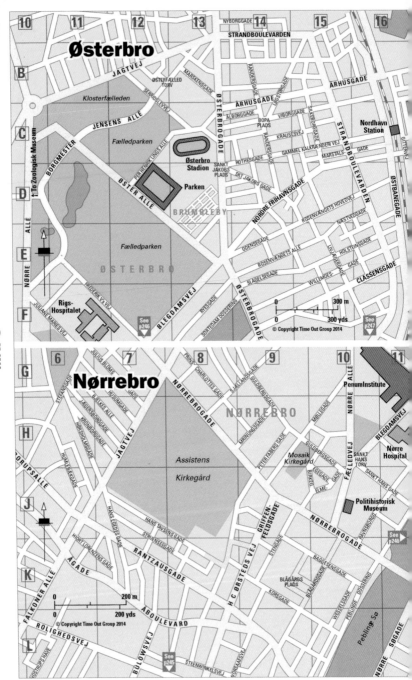

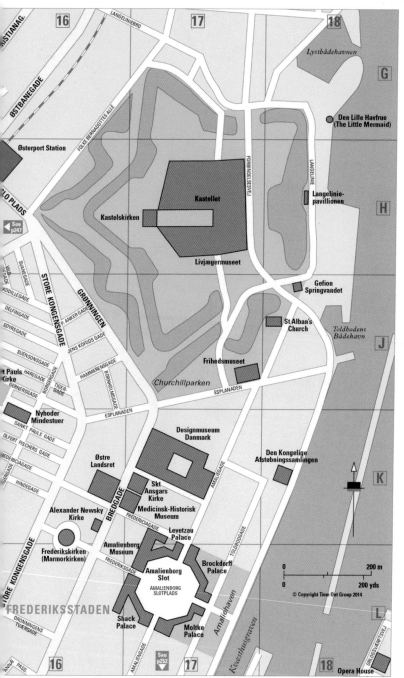

16

17

18

LANGELINIEBRO

Lystbådehavnen

G

ØSTBANEGADE

FOLKE BERNADOTTES ALLE

Den Lille Havfrue
(The Little Mermaid)

Østerport Station

FORBINDELSESVEJ

LANGELINIE

Langelinie-
pavillionen

H

Kastellet

Kastelskirken

See
p247

STJANEGADE

STORE KONGENSGADE

GRØNNINGEN

KODILLEGADE

DELFINGADE

SØVRSGADE

P. ANKER GADE

Livjægermuseet

Gefion
Springvandet

SUENSONSGADE

JENS KOFODS GADE

St Alban's
Church

*Toldbodens
Bådehavn*

J

t Pauls
Kirke

HAREGADE

BORGERGADE

TIGER-
GADE

HAMMERENSGADE

B:RNHOLMSGADE

Frihedsmuseet

GERNERSGADE

ESPLANADEN

Churchillparken

ESPLANADEN

Nyboder
Mindestuer

SANKT PAULS GADE

Designmuseum
Danmark

OLFERT FISCHERS GADE

Østre
Landsret

AMALIEGADE

Den Kongelige
Afstøbningssamlingen

K

:REDERICIAGADE

HINDEGADE

BREDGADE

Skt
Ansgars
Kirke

Medicinsk-Historisk
Museum

FREDERICIAGADE

Alexander Newsky
Kirke

Levetzau
Palace

0   200 m

0   200 yds

© Copyright Time Out Group 2014

TORE KONGENSGADE

Frederikskirken
(Marmorkirken)

FREDERIKSGADE

Amalienborg
Museum

TOLDBODGADE

Amalienborg
Slot

AMALIENBORG
SLOTPLADS

Brockdorff
Palace

L

FREDERIKSSTADEN

DRONNINGENS
TVÆRGADE

Shack
Palace

Moltke
Palace

Amaliehaven

Kvæsthusgraven

ANNE PASS

16

See
p252

17

18

Opera House

ORLOGSVÆRFTSVEJ

MAPS

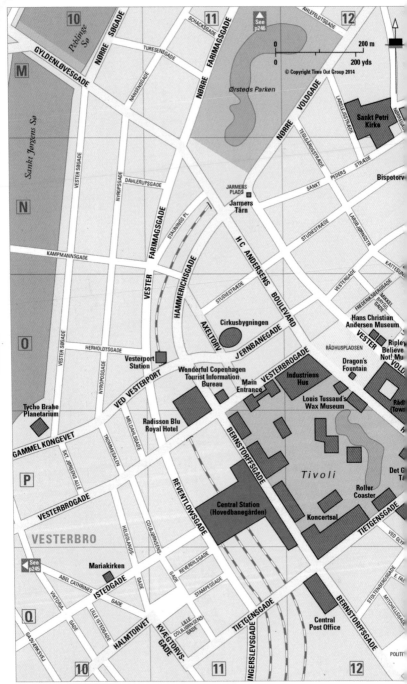

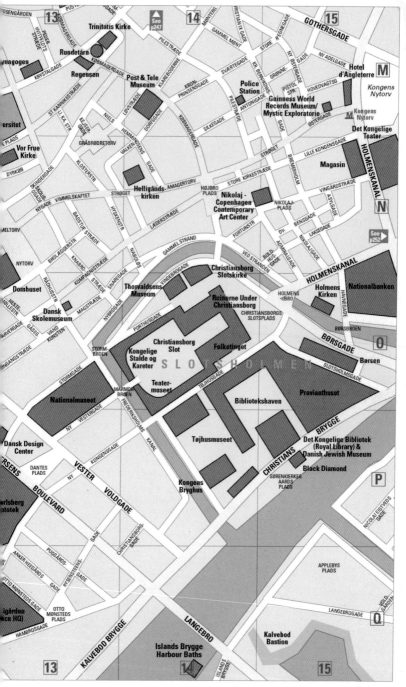

See p247

Trinitatis Kirke

Rundetårn

ynagogen

Regensen

Post & Tele Museum

Police Station

Guinness World Records Museum/ Mystic Exploratorie

Hotel d'Angleterre

Kongens Nytorv

Kongens Nytorv

Det Kongelige Teater

ersitet

E PLADS

Vor Frue Kirke

Magasin

GRÅBRØDRETORV

Helligånds-kirken

Nikolaj - Copenhagen Contemporary Art Center

MELTORV

See p252

NYTORV

Christiansborg Slotskirke

Domhuset

Thorvaldsens Museum

Ruinerne Under Christiansborg

Holmens Kirken

Nationalbanken

Dansk Skolemuseum

CHRISTIANSBORGS SLOTSPLADS

HOLMENS BRO

Christiansborg Slot

Folketinget

Kongelige Stalde og Kareter

S L O T S H O L M E N

Børsen

Teater-museet

Nationalmuseet

Biblotekshaven

Provianthuset

BRYGGE

Dansk Design Center

DANTES PLADS

Tøjhusmuseet

Det Kongelige Bibliotek (Royal Library) & Danish Jewish Museum

ERSENS

VESTER VOLDGADE

Black Diamond

rlsberg otek

BOULEVARD

Kongens Bryghus

CHRISTIANS

SØRENKIERKE AARDS PLADS

igården ice HQ)

OTTO MØNSTEDS PLADS

APPLEBYS PLADS

LANGEBROGADE

HAMBROGADE

KALVEBOD BRYGGE

LANGEBRO

Kalvebod Bastion

Islands Brygge Harbour Baths

MAPS

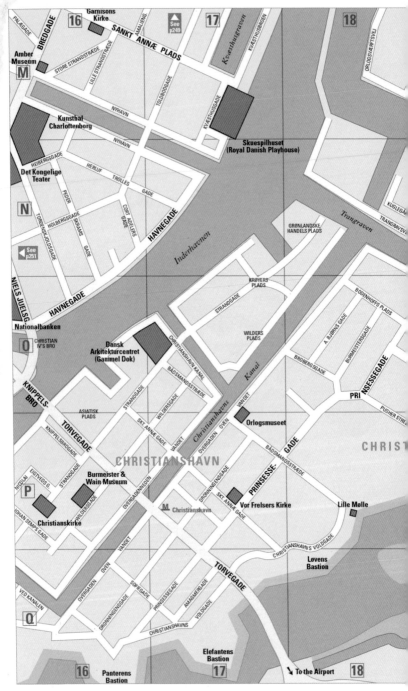

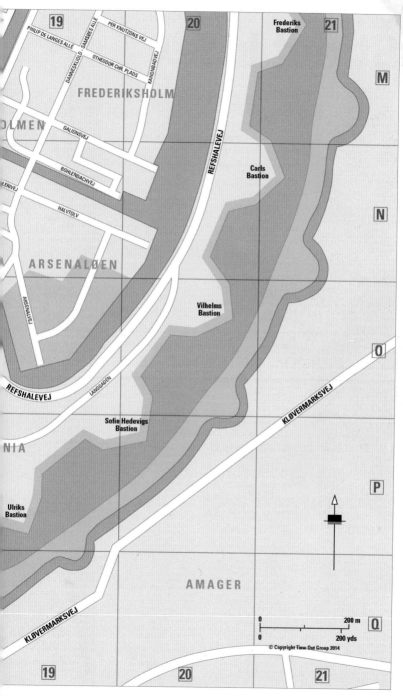

PHILIP DE LANGES ALLE
PER KNUTZONS VEJ
DANNESKJOLD
SAMSØES ALLE
OTHEODOR CHR. PLADS
KANONBÅDVEJ

FREDERIKSHOLM

OLMEN
GALIONSVEJ

BOHLENDACHVEJ

ERIVEJ

HALVTOLV

Carls Bastion

N

ARSENALØEN

ARSENALVEJ

Vilhelms Bastion

O

REFSHALEVEJ

REFSHALEVEJ

LANGGADEN

KLØVERMARKSVEJ

Sofie Hedevigs Bastion

NIA

Ulriks Bastion

P

AMAGER

0   200 m
0   200 yds
© Copyright Time Out Group 2014

KLØVERMARKSVEJ

Q

Street Index

Local Trains & Metro

Gilleleje Øst
Stæremosen
Søborg
Firhøj
Dronningmølle
Kildekrog
Hornelby Sand
Hornbæk
Saunte
Skibstrup

Gilleleje
Fjellenstrup
Pårup
Græsted
Græsted
Syd

Ålsgårde
Hellebæk
Højstrup
Marienlyst

Grønnehave
Helsingør
Snekkersten
Espergærde
Humlebæk
Nivå
Kokkedal
Rungsted Kyst
Vedbæk
Skodsborg

Helsingborg C

Tisvildeleje
Godhavn
Holløse
Vejby
Ørby
Helsinge
Duemose

Saltrup
Mårum

Grønholt
Kratbjerg
Fredensborg
Langerød
Kvistgård
Mørdrup

Hundested Havn
Hundested
Vibehus
Østerbjerg
Dyssekilde
Melby
Hanehoved
Frederiksværk
Lille Kregme
Kregme
Ølsted
Grimstrup

Kagerup
Gribsø
Slotspavillonen

Hillerød
Allerød
Birkerød
Holte
Vrum

Klampenborg
Ordrup
Charlottenlund

Skævinge
Corløse
Brødeskov

Narrum
Ravnholm
Ørholm
Brede
Fuglevad
Lyngby Local
Jærgersborg
Lyngby
Sorgenfri
Virum

Gentofte
Bernstorffs
vej

Hellerup

Frederikssund
Ølstykke
Egedal
Stenløse
Veksø
Kildedal
Ballerup
Malmparken
Skovlunde
Herlev
Husum
Islev
Jyllingevej
Vanløse
Flintholm

Farum
Værløse
Hareskov
Skovbrynet
Bagsværd
Stengården
Buddinge
Kildebakke
Vangede
Dyssegård
Emdrup
Ryparken

Svanemøllen
Nordhavn
Østerport
Nørreport

Kongens Nytorv
Christianshavn
Amagerbro
Lergravsparken

Bispebjerg
Nørrebro
Fuglebakken
Grøndal

Lindevang
Fasanvej
Frederiksberg
Forum

KB Hallen
Ålholm

Peter
Bangs
Vej
Langgade

Flintholm
Vanløse

Dybbølsbro
Enghave
Valby

Vesterport
København H
Islands Brygge

Øresund

DR Byen
UNIVERSITETET

Amager Strand

Bella Center

Sundby
Femøren
Kastrup
Lufthavnen

Ørestad
Vestamager

Tårnby

København Lufthavn
Kastrup

Hvalsø
Lejre

Roskilde
Trekroner
Hedehusene
Høje Taastrup
Taastrup
Albertslund
Glostrup
Brøndbyøster
Rødovre
Danshøj

Viby Sjælland

Borup

Gadstrup

Havdrup

Lille Skensved

Sydhavn
Sjælør
Ny Elleberg
Åmarken
Friheden
Avedøre
Brøndby Strand
Vallensbæk
Ishøj
Hundige
Greve
Karlslunde
Solrød Strand

Herfølge
Tureby

Jersie
Ølby
Køge

Egøje
Vallø
Grubberholm
Himlingøje
Hårlev
Varpelev

Lille-Linde

Metro

S-tog
S-train

Regionaltog
Regional trains
Lokalbaner
Local railways